LANGUAGE AND STYLE
OF
THE VEDIC *ṚṢIS*

SUNY Series in Hindu Studies,
Wendy Doniger, Editor

LANGUAGE AND STYLE OF THE VEDIC *ṚṢIS*

by

Tatyana J. Elizarenkova

Edited with an Introduction by
Wendy Doniger

State University of New York Press

Published by
State University of New York Press, Albany

Printed in the United States of America

For information, address the State University of New York Press,
State University Plaza, Albany, NY 12246

Library of Congress Cataloging-in-Publication Data

Elizarenkova, Tatyana J.
Language and style of the Vedic Ṛṣis / by Tatyana J. Elizarenkova; edited with an introduction byWendy Doniger.
p. cm. — (SUNY series in Hindu studies)
Includes bibliographical references and index.
ISBN 0-7914-1667-4 (alk. paper). — ISBN 0-7914-1668-2 (pbk : alk. paper)
1. Vedic language—Semantics. 2. Vedas. Rgveda—Language, style. 3. Rishis—India—History. I. Doniger, Wendy. II. Title. III. Series.
PK335.E45 1993
491'.2—dc20 92-40318
CIP

10 9 8 7 6 5 4 3 2 1

Contents

Foreword

by Wendy Doniger

This is an extraordinary book, which could have been written by no one but Tatyana Elizarenkova. It is extraordinary because it combines two disciplines that no one else would dream of combining, or be able to combine: the modern, trendy, obscure discipline of semiotics, and the ancient, dusty, arcane discipline of Vedic philology. It is even more extraordinary because it combines them in such away that they become mutually illuminating, that the obscurity of the one is not compounded by the arcanity of the other but, on the contrary, is clarified by it.

Tatyana Elizarenkova is perhaps the greatest living scholar of the *RigVeda*, and certainly the greatest linguist of the *RigVeda*. Her 1972 translation into Russian of selected hymns from the *RigVeda* is a benchmark in Vedic scholarship, but it is only a part of her larger translation of the entire *RigVeda* into Russian, of which several volumes are already published and the remaining volumes are now delayed by the crisis in Russian economic life. (Indeed, the present work, though composed originally in Russian, may also prove victim to that economic crisis, and it is not at all unlikely that this English translation may precede the Russian original, or perhaps that it will remain the only available version of the work.) Together with her husband, V. N. Toporov, Elizarenkova published in English a linguistic analysis of *The Pali Language* in 1976; in 1967 Toporov, together with their colleague V. V. Ivanov, published a linguistic analysis of *The Sanskrit Language*, also in English. She is also an expert on Hindi, and is published widely on its grammar. So much for the "the ancient, dusty, arcane" side of Elizarenkova.

The "the modern, trendy, obscure" side is also inextricably linked with the work of Toporov, for together they are driving forces in what is known as the Moscow Tartu school of semiotics. This school has profoundly influenced French structuralism, as have Russian scholars from the start, beginning with Vladimir Propp's *Morphology of the Russian Folktale*, which sparked the structural study of folklore. Yet the relationship between Vedic philology and structuralism is even more complex because Saussure's work, which is generally regarded as the founding work of French structuralism, draws heavily upon Vedic philology for its examples. In a very real sense, the present work of Elizarenkova is the first complete response to both the content and theory of Saussure's work.

The great contribution that Elizarenkova makes in this book is to our understanding of ambiguity, of the ways that grammatical ambiguity interact with poetic ambiguity. It is also a brilliant study in how to read the *RigVeda* (or, more broadly, how to read any ancient poetic text). We learn how to be sensitive to word order, and how to fill in what the poet has left out. This work also explains why certain words were selectively left out, in terms of ancient ritual riddle contests. The richness and solidity of the work grows out of the author's deep knowledge of the entire *RigVeda*, her ability to elucidate everything she shows us, and her instinctive knowledge of the ancient text, what is common and what is rare. The degree to which Elizarenkova has internalized the *RigVeda* reminds me of the story told of the printer who set F. Max Müller's first edition of this Sanskrit text. He made a number of corrections in the text, and he was always right; this surprised Professor Müller, who knew that the printer knew not a word of Sanskrit. He asked him how he did it, and the printer said that, setting the type, his arm got used to swinging in certain patterns between letters that frequently went together, and when he tried to set two letters that did not belong together, it felt wrong in his shoulders. Elizarenkova has a feeling in her shoulders about the patterns of the *RigVeda.*

If you are going to translate Sanskrit, there are advantages and disadvantages to being a native speaker of Russian. Russian is very much like Sanskrit in many ways: it uses compounds and passive constructions as Sanskrit does, and forms abstract nouns from verbs in the same way ("speaking-ness"). This has a historical cause: both Sanskrit and Russian are *sot* languages; that is, they have no "n" in the word for a hundred (unlike other Indo-European languages such as English, French, and Italian). It is therefore easier to render Sanskrit into Russian than into English, but the bill is presented when you try to get the Russian translation into English, for that is when you find that you have now got to solve many of the problems that an English translator would have solved long ago (word order, compounds, passive voice). In editing the manuscript, I've left some of it in the Sanskrit/Russian word-order—mostly in the poetry, less in the academic prose. I hope that the reader will find this charmingly quaint rather than simply annoying.

It is a great pleasure for me to have played a part in bringing this work to the attention of American Indologists. Elizarenkova has been my friend for many years. She was with me in Moscow when I learned that I was carrying my child, and she was with me in Moscow when I learned of my father's death. She was with me in New York when, after *glasnost*, she was allowed to leave Russia for the first time in many decades; I took her to the Statue of Liberty and Wall Street and Bloomingdales and we had tea in the Palm Room at the Plaza. It was a wonderful time.

These are hard times for Russian Indology in the grand style, which was once the leader in the field; the first great Sanskrit dictionary (and still the best available) is the St. Petersburg Dictionary. But then, these are hard times for American Indology too. In these shifting times, books like this will soon become extinct, like the language of the hymns themselves. Before that time comes, however, I am very glad that this book is here.

1
Introduction

This book is concerned with the investigation of causal interconnections between a linguistic system and the style of a text representing that language. The language is Old Indian in its most archaic, Vedic variety. The text is the *Ṛg Veda*, a collection of hymns to Aryan deities, which probably originated during the last centuries of the IInd and the first centuries of the Ist milleniums BC, and represents the very beginning of the Old Indian literary tradition.

It is well-known that the history of the Old Indian language–if it may be so termed–appears to be a history of styles succeeding one another, as opposed to a strict evolution of the language. More than thirty years ago Louis Renou wrote about this phenomenon in the foreword to his *Histoire de la Langue Sanskrite*,[1] and this thesis was brilliantly defended in the body of the book iself [121.2].

Thus the correlation between language and style appears to be central to the historical development of the Old Indian language. In a study of the *Ṛg Veda* text, which stands at the beginning of this development, the problem of such a correlation acquires special dimensions, because scholars customarily look for reflections of an earlier, undocumented stage of development in the current language. Interest in reconstruction has taken precedence over the study of the language system *per se*, its specific modes of functioning, and its analysis as the first documented stage in a long chain of further diachronic evolution.

The unique importance of the *Ṛg Veda* appears to be that, on the one hand, this enormously long text (1028 hymns with an average length of 10 stanzas per hymn) may be the last representative of the Indo-European tradition, but on the other hand, the first document of an original Indian culture. As far as our study of the interaction of style and language is concerned, the former approach tends to dominate.

The comparative and historical approach to the study of the RigVedic poetic language has a long and honorable tradition behind it. It was first sketched back in the 1850s by one of the most distinguished Indo-European scholars of that time, Adalbert Kuhn, who, having compared Ancient Greek and RigVedic data, succeeded in reconstructing not an isolated word, but a whole phrase, in which he recognized a Proto-Indo-European (PIE) poetic formula–"undying fame" in Old Indian: *śrávas . . . ákṣitam, ákṣiti śrávaḥ* and in Ancient Greek: *Kléos áphthiton* [99.467].

The existence of Common Indo-European poetic formulas presupposes the previous existence of a Common Indo-European language, a notion that was clearly defined only considerably later by J. Wackernagel in his influential article "*Indogermanische Dichtersprache*" [149.186-204],[2] where he succinctly described the main characteristics of that language from the point of view of morphology, metrics, syntax, and phraseology. A Common Indo-European poetic language could now be reconstructed on the basis of the comparison of a whole series of attested ancient poetic traditions from almost every area of the Indo-European world, including Celtic, Old Norse, Slavic, and Avestan traditions, among others. From these comparisons one can then speak of even narrower, more localized poetic traditions, such as the Indo-Iranian one, which can be reconstructed comparing the *Ṛg Veda* and Avestan data.[3]

During the last decennia, historical and comparative research of the Common Indo-European poetic tradition has been actively pursued. As a result of these studies, or rather, as an approximate summary of a certain stage of research, Rüdiger Schmitt published a monograph in which the Old Indian data figures prominently [136]. The number of securely-established Common Indo-European formulas and phrases has been steadily growing, work is in progress on themes and genres of Common Indo-European poetry (heroic, sacral, charms and incantations), and the Common Indo-European background of some metrical forms is also under investigation. Most importantly, the figure of the ancient poet and the nature of his creative act is now vigorously under discussion.

Modern research on the Common Indo-European poetic language is distinguished by its tendency to redefine the basic methods of investigation and to look for fresh approaches. Thus Wolfgang Meid [109] pays special attention to the chronological problems of Common Indo-European and its different stages. The similarities in the Greek and the Aryan data are regarded as common innovations originating in the postulated Eastern PIE and reflecting a regional poetic tradition. Only the reconstruction of formulas–as distinct from texts–is considered to be feasible: the former belong to *langue* whereas the latter belong to *parole*. Meid puts forward several principles for reconstructing the Indo-European poet's functions; he defines the RigVedic brahmin as a "transmitter of knowledge" (*veda*) who is charged with formulating "truth" in the language of his own time [109.12].

Enrico Campanile in his study of the Indo-European poetic culture

[62.32-33] also stresses the role of the Indo-European poet as the custodian and transmitter of the basic cultural and social needs of his society. In the initial stages of the Old Indian culture the poetic function was not yet separated from the priestly one–this separation occurred at a later time–and poetic art was still the focus of every kind of verbal activity.

Modern comparative linguistics, using the results of linguistic reconstruction, tries to transcend the confines of language proper and apply itself to cultural and historical fields, including reflections of PIE civilization. This resulted in Emil Benveniste's fundamental reconstruction of fragments of PIE religion, law, social customs, etc. [58]; and his methods have stimulated research in the more specialized field of Indo-European poetics. There have been attempts to analyze Old Indian data from the *Ṛg Veda* hymns to establish the degree to which they reflect the basic principles of Indo-European poetics and to define the goals of poetic art as well as the poet's functions [14.36-88; 145.189-251].

A new approach to PIE poetic language owes its appearance to the recently published papers of Ferdinand de Saussure concerning the RigVedic and other ancient Indo-European poetic traditions (including ancient Greek, Latin and ancient Germanic).[4] De Saussure suggests that ancient poetic texts belonging to those traditions were based on the principles of anagrams: in certain verses the words are arranged around the name of the deity being praised, which occupies the key metrical position. These words can indicate the name both in their complete form and by means of the syllables that constitute them. The RigVedic hymns, which illustrate this principle, testify to a very archaic procedure of grammatical and poetic analysis.[5] Most importantly, de Saussure pointed out the deliberate and intentional character in the construction of these texts, where formal phonetical and grammatical word-analysis reveals the text's poetic function.

In order to have a clear view of the problems that appear most relevant to modern studies in PIE poetic language, it will be useful to review, if only briefly, some general theories that have influenced the study of various aspects (including linguistic) of archaic cultures. New approaches to the study of oral literature and poetic language must also be discussed.

First to be mentioned is the hypothesis of Marcel Mauss [107], according to which the socioeconomic life of a certain type of archaic society is based on the circular exchange of gifts. The comparative ethno-sociological investigation of some contemporary societies of an archaic type (the North-American Indians, the so-called primitive tribes of Polynesia and Melanesia) led Mauss to conclude that the principle of the modern AmerIndian potlatch can be considered fundamental to any archaic society at a certain stage of its evolution. The potlatch is commonly defined as a feast set up by tribal chieftains in connection with various important events of social life involving gifts and reciprocal gifts on an ever-increasing scale, wherein all the participants are gradually drawn into the cycle of gift-exchange. Such an exchange concerns various rivalling social groups. The goal of the potlatch is social, not material: it enhances the social standing of the giver (although there is an extreme variant: annihilation of riches as proof of social superiority). The relationship between worshipper and deity follows the same lines: a sacrifice is expected to be reciprocated with a greater boon. Mauss found traces of this pattern in the ancient PIE culture; the Indian tradition of the Epic and Classical periods illustrates them in the *Mahābhārata* and the *Śāstras*.

Benveniste developed the linguistic aspect of Mauss's hypothesis, adducing data from ancient Indo-European languages [57.315-326]. Analyzing the semantics of the PIE root *dō-* (meaning "give" in most languages, but "take" in Hittite), he compares it with the Indo-Iranian verb *ā-dā* and concludes that *dō-* originally meant neither "give" nor "take," but was semantically ambivalent. The PIE root **nem-* had a similar meaning: compare Gothic *niman*, "take" but Greek *nemō*, both "apportion" (a share) and "receive" (a share). Such ambivalence is characteristic of a certain lexical stratum (both verbs and nouns) in various Indo-European languages; this fact makes probable the existence of a circular exchange custom in Indo-European prehistory, similar to the North American potlatch.

A novel approach to the study of oral folk traditions was initiated by Milman Parry and Albert Lord [103] who analyzed lexical repetitions in Homer and in the Serbo-Croation epics. They came to the conclusion that the basic unit of the epic language is the formula–a word or a word-group that is regularly used to represent a certain notion and that occupies a fixed position in the metrical scheme. The metrical conditioning of formulas produ a certain degree of predictability of epic diction. Their methods have been successfully applied to the Old Indian epics in Pavel A. Grintser's fundamental work [5].

Finally, the study of PIE poetics has been directly influenced by Roman Jakobson's work on general linguistics and poetic language. He argues, after Edward Sapir, that the primary essence and aim of the language consists in being a means of communication. The communicative purpose of the language gives rise to two of its principal dichotomies: the oppositions of markedness/unmarkedness and variation/invariance [51.306-318]. Language is a semiotic system whose signs are reciprocally transferrable (Charles Peirce); this property is very important for the communication process, since the possibility of code-switching is opposed to the linguistic multivocity that originates in homonymy and ellipsis.

About Peirce's division of signs into three classes: indices (contiguity relations between signifier and signified), icons (relations deriving from some common actual traits), and symbols (relations based on imputed contiguity), Jakobson notes: "Iconicity plays a vast and necessary, though evidently subordinate, part in the different levels of linguistic structure"[51.323].

Jakobson considers poetic language to be one of the varieties of the act of verbal communication in which the addresser sends a message to the addressee [50.193-230]. The difference between messages lies in a different hierarchical order of functions; the predominant function is referential (or denotative or cognitive). "The set (*Einstellung*) toward the message as such, the focus on the message for its own sake, is the poetic function of language" [50.202]. The most important characteristic of the poetic function is the projection of the principle of equivalence from the axis of selection onto the axis of combinaton [50.204].

Novel ideas and fresh approaches in neighboring areas of knowledge could not fail to make an impact on the historical and comparative study of PIE poetic language. Scholars cannot be satisfied with the notion of a "sum-total of formulas"–this has already been mentioned–but they try to study poetic language in its connection with the society where it originated and whose instrument it was. As Calvert Watkins has observed: "On the diachronic as well as the synchronic plane, we require a holistic model of language as a social fact, of language and culture, language and society, language and pragmatics" [151.105]. The task of reconstructing PIE poetry is unrealistic; scholars can only hope to reconstruct a few themes particular to that poetry, and some of the devices the poets used when elaborating on those themes in traditional poetry [153.271]. Among these devices, the leading role is played by formulas, and the task of their reconstruction has made great progress lately [152].[6] Data have been drawn from a greater variety of sources–in particular, the much wider use of Celtic and Hittite findings, especially from the studies of Watkins[7] and Campanile. Watkins rightly stresses that the study of PIE poetic language should be simultaneously synchronic and diachronic, both historically comparative and analytically descriptive [155.4]. This language is to be considered as a grammar of sorts with both a phonological component (the domain of metrics and phonetic figures) and a morphological component (the domain of grammatical figures). On a higher level it has a syntactic component (formulaics) and a semantic component (thematics). There is also a pragmatic component (the domain of poet-performer/audience interaction), which dominates the entire grammar [153.270]. Such are the ideas, methods of investigation, and tasks of the comparative and historical study of PIE poetic language at the present time.

Jan Gonda completed the groundwork for the stylistic study of the *Ṛg Veda*. For the last forty years he has been busy defining key problems of Vedic poetic style, having amassed and classified an enormous amount of data in a series of monographs. Gonda is fully justified in stressing the principle of stylistic repetitions as being central to this document of oral tradition [87]. He treats these repetitions as a special creative device of the Vedic *Ṛṣis*. Sounds and their combinations are repeated in certain positions of the metrical scheme; the same is true of individual words and balanced syntactic structures; in other words, this principle is consistently carried out on all linguistic levels. But Gonda observes that a mere enumeration of the types of repetitions cannot provide a key to the understanding of the hymns. These repetitions and various parallel structures should not be considered purely stylistic ornaments. The language of Vedic mantras abounds in formulas and is highly conventionalized. Its poetry is rather imitative, since the *Ṛṣis* were developing the traditions of oral folk literature [82.155-156].

Epithets of gods, enumerated in praise hymns and sometimes in long string formations, are treated from a functional point of view by Gonda. They are frequently used not for the mere description of deities, but rather, for inducing desirable qualities in them [79]. Constant epithets tend to function as theophoric proper names, but the latter are endowed in the *Ṛg Veda* with particular magic connotations [81]. Gonda has shown that the RigVedic style combines two opposite tendencies: on the one hand, repetition and redundancy manifests itself in the juxtaposition of synonyms or words of similar formal structure; on the other hand, extreme brevity is expressed by the regular omission of words and phrases which can be usually supplied by context (or ellipsis, although brachilogy may result in a logical shift) [78]. Phrases containing comparisons are frequently elliptical; such phrases are quite typical of Vedic poetic style [85].

Although of undoubtedly high value, Gonda's studies remain to a certain degree fragmentary because they are concerned with several unconnected–though very important–stylistic problems. There seems to be no supporting uniform theory that encompasses the range of stylistic features and with which those features may be consistently approached. Gonda also deals with certain parts of mythology (or rather, of a model of the universe seen by the authors of the text) that found direct expression in RigVedic language and style–in particular, the relationship between "gods" and "powers" in the *Ṛg Veda* [86], dyads [76], and triads [88]. Later, this book discusses Gonda's theories concerning the Vedic poet-*Ṛṣi* and his particular creative role.

Our understanding of RigVedic style has been greatly advanced by Louis Renou's work, and especially by his translations of and commentaries on hymnic cycles in "Etudes védiques et paniniénnes" [118]. Notwithstanding his conciseness, Renou's work opened up new vistas for further stylistic studies.

The cultic character of the *Ṛg Veda* collection makes it necessary that the ritual connected with a given text should be taken into consideration in a detailed study of its style and language. But the problem of the relationship between hymn and ritual remains quite obscure and cannot be discussed in detail here [9.37f.]. To put it bluntly: at the time of the composition of the *Ṛg Veda*, there was probably no single system of sacrificial rites. Different priestly families may have adhered to ritual variants distinct in particular details, and many hymns might have been recited as part of different rituals. Most probably, some of the hymns had no ritual application whatsoever and should be considered religious poetry in its purest form. In most cases it is quite impossible to separate ritual hymns from nonritual hymns, and this fact may be the basis of Renou's statement that the *Ṛg Veda* is outside of Vedic religion; i.e. unlike the other Vedas, it is not a manual for religious practice. A prayer that is not clearly connected with ritual can easily slip into magic [129.273]. One should certainly keep in mind the fact that the highly symbolic character and suggestive style of Vedic language does not help us to understand whether the poet's message is to be related to ritual or myth. Finally, the authors' aversion to a linear narration of events, their anticipatory breakthroughs and circular backtrackings, make it almost impossible to reconstruct an actual sequence of ritual actions.

The problem of a particular hymn's ritual relationship must not be neglected when discussing the *Ṛg Veda* collection as a whole. Much content and style in the *Ṛg Veda* can be explained if we apply to it Victor Turner's ideas: the special role of liminal rituals and the two alternating patterns in human relations–the usual pattern and the one that is valid only for the liminal period [46.170].

According to Franciscus Bernardus Jacobus Kuiper's hypothesis [22.47-100], based on Alfred Hillebrandt's suggestions, the RigVedic Aryans conceived of time as a cyclical process. At the end of every year the cosmos returned to its point of departure, an undifferentiated state of chaos, to be reborn. The aim of the New Year festival was to gain victory over chaos and to recreate the organized cosmos. The most archaic kernel of the RigVedic collection was connected with that New Year festival. These hymns were only one part of the New Year ritual and were included in poetic verbal contests. Other events also took place on that occasion: sacrificial rituals, generous ritual gift-giving, chariot-races, etc. This interpretation of the RigVedic collection is based on an understanding of the *Uṣas*-hymns as praises to the rebirth of the primordial light, of the triumph over darkness that gives hope for the new year. In this connection the Goddess is asked for riches, vital strength, male progeny, and prosperity. During such critical periods, when the forces of darkness and light are in confrontation, ritual should help the forces of light, and the importance of priest and poet in the Aryan society increases inordinately (this is the second pattern in Turner's terms [45.170]). According to Turner's notions of that archaic time, the society's survival was dependent on ritual activities.

Quite pertinent to the study of Vedic style and language is the idea of the universality of ritual as a force that gathers and refines all human means of understanding the world [42.7-60]. Ritual developed into a kind of "pre-art" that was originally syncretic and only later became differentiated into various independent branches. There can be no doubt of the existence of some kind of connection between the verbal text of the *Ṛg Veda*–at least of its most ancient strata–and Old Indian ritual, notwithstanding the rather opaque character of that connection. Such opacity mostly concerns the possibility of reconstructing the ritual on the basis of the preserved text. In some cases, particular features of language and style can be most adequately interpreted if we postulate a ritual connection.

This short survey of the present state of the art–the study of Indo-European poetic language and *Ṛg Veda* style, general aspects of the theory of poetic language and the theory of ritual–is offered to clarify the direction of our study. This work was conceived as a synchronic description of the poetic language of the *Ṛg Veda* as a uniform synchronic cross-section. In this regard the present work is basically different from comparative and historical studies in the domain of Indo-European poetic language which incorporate abundant Vedic data. The aim of comparative studies is reconstruction, and the Old Indian facts are thus used diachronicly. There can be no doubt that ignoring the results of the genetic approach can only detract from synchronic description and analysis. Some authors now require that the method of research should be both comparative-diachronic and descriptive-analytic (compare Watkins [151]). Modifying this requirement somewhat as it applies to a descriptive study, one may say that the method should be synchronic, but *diachrony should be contained in synchrony*. For instance, the description of Vedic poetic language should also deal with the problem of "the language of gods" *vs.* "the language of men" as it appears in the present text, although this problem has actually a Common Indo-European background. Such is this work's perspective on the correlation between synchony and diachrony.

Since the aim of this study is a synchronic description of the language of an ancient *poetic* text, one of the main tasks is to define the ways and means by which the linguistic poetic function made use of the given

RigVedic language system. A pragmatic approach to the language of an ancient document is fully justified for an analysis of the *Ṛg Veda*. In modern linguistics, pragmatics is defined as "a science investigating language in its relation to those who use it" [36.419]. It studies speech acts and the contexts wherein they are realized.

In this study the main structural unit of the *Ṛg Veda*, the hymn, or rather the praise-hymn (constituting an overwhelming majority of the collection), is functionally approached as an act of communication between the addresser-worshipper and the addressee-deity. With the help of a hymn, the believer sends a message to the deity. Such an act of communication is normally one-sided, since the worshipper calls upon the deity and speaks to him, but the deity hearkens to him in silence: the gods' direct speech is extremely rare in the *Ṛg Veda*. In communication acts of this kind, an exceptionally important role is played by an orientation toward the addressee, which finds its formal (grammatical) expression in nominal vocatives and verbal imperatives. This is "poetry of the second person," in Jacobson's words [50.203], because the addressee is completely dependent on the addresser.

Finally, the communicative purpose of the Vedic praise-hymn stresses the importance of its formal side. In order to be acceptable to the gods the hymn should be skillfully made, and the idea of skill denotes, in the first place, the formal construction of a piece of poetry. In this way the poetic function, the self-orientation of language, is highly important for the study of this text.

As shown in a previous paper [69.255-268], the RigVedic praise-hymn may be described as a standard model composed of two parts: explicative (descriptions) and appellative (addresses and invocations). The first part is built upon a hierarchy of oppositions covering distinctive features of various levels, such as the names of actions (characteristic and regularly repeated), epithets (constant actions), attributes (i.e., objects and qualities normally connected with a given deity), and external ties (immanent–such as family connections–or those related to story plot). Units of different levels can be connected by transformational relations: thus epithets, attributes, and ties can often represent implied actions, and may sometimes manifest themselves in the diachrony.[8]

Such a model is characterized by a constant switch of levels and code-change. The appellative part of the hymn normally–though not obligatorily–follows its explicative part. These two parts are usually in mutual balance. Sometimes, however, either of them may virtually disappear. The latter instance mostly applies to purely mythological descriptions or standard requests.

Even though the pragmatic approach to the language and style of the *Ṛg Veda* is not controversial, there are always grave obstacles in the path of the student dealing with a text from a long-gone civilization. Nothing is left of that time except the hymns of the *Ṛg Veda*, the unique remaining source about the people whose medium of communication was poetic language. But the study of the speech-act contexts and their concretized demarcation is often impeded or made will-nigh impossible by the intentional obscurity of the hymns. Their contents refer simultaneously to several levels: mythological, cosmological, and ritual. The information obtained from more recent Old Indian texts quite often turns out to be of dubious value because the *Rig Veda* stands at the very source of the Indian tradition and is self-contained. Thus, explaining *Ṛg Veda* obscurities by extrapolating from later tradition can dangerously distort the real picture.

The functional approach to the language of the *Ṛg Veda* presupposes a basic knowledge of the cultural milieu of the text. Although our study is a linguistic one, it requires some advance knowledge of the Vedic Aryans' model of the universe. A model of the universe should be interpreted as "a reduced and simplified reflection of the sum-total of all notions about the surrounding world that exist inside a given tradition and are regarded in their system-and-operation aspects" [27.167f.]. The *Ṛg Veda* presents one variant of the mytho-poetic model of the universe, the essence of which consists of representing nature not through a reflection of primary data but through code-switching, effected by sign systems [27.161f.]. The basic means of interpreting the universe is the myth.

The Vedic model of the universe is cosmos-oriented: it is both a measure and a part of everything. The life of an Aryan is related to the structures of space and time through the law of universal circulation (*ṛtá*) on the level of synchrony. Its diachronical aspect implies a cyclical replacement of chaos by the cosmos, and vice versa, and this is reflected in the annual ritual cycle. Synchrony and diachrony are inseparably linked together: it is a salient feature of a mytho-poetic model of the universe.

The dynamics of cosmology finds its reflection in the very etymology of the word *ṛtá-*, a past passive participle of the verb *ṛ-/ar-*: "to move, be moving." *Ṛtá* denotes the cycle that orders both the universe and society. It is in obeisance to the law of *ṛtá-* that the sun rises and sets. In Vedic mythology the various aspects of the sun are represented by several different deities: thus *Sū́rya* is the main sun-god (compare *svár-/sū́r-* "sun, light, heaven"); *Savitár* the Inciter (verb *sū-* "to impel, incite"); *Mitrá* the god of friendship and contract as well as of sun and light (as opposed to darkness); *Pūṣán* the god of solar energy, who gives prosperity to people, cattle and pastures;[9] *Uṣás* the goddess of the dawn (verb *vas-/uṣ-* "to light up"; *Agní-*

the god of fire (in all of its manifestations). Moreover, the common name for "god" is also related to light and day: *devá-* is from the root *div-/dyu-* "to shine" (cf. *dyaúḥ* "sky; day;" *dívā* "by day"). The daily solar cycle is treated as two suns, the diurnal and the nocturnal (in cosmological riddles). *Uṣas* and her sister Night change places regularly. At regular intervals it rains (*Parjanya*) and thunderstorms take place (*Indra* with the *Maruts*). The god *Soma* rises from the ground as sacrifice and returns again as rain.

Cyclical cosmic phenomena are reproduced by the cyclical performance of ritual. The mytho-poetic mind sees regular rituals (annual, monthly, and daily all within the lunar cycle) as upholding order in the universe, recreating the cosmos and preventing its disintegration at the end of each cycle. In this way the isomorphism of the micro- and the macrocosmos is manifest. Ritual permeates and controls all activities of Aryan man in all domains of life. Even ritual names in the *Ṛg Veda* are symbolic– *kárman-* "action, deed;" compare the later term *kriyā- id.*, i.e. action in general, par excellence. Ritual serves the main spheres of human life: magico-juridical (to guarantee justice, law, and order), military (to ensure protection and victory), material and biological (to provide wealth, male progeny, and the safety of the tribe).

These two isomorphic worlds are represented by two classes of active figures: the gods (*devá-* or *amṛ́ta-*) and the mortals (*mártya-*). This clear-cut binary opposition is to a certain extent disturbed by a rather inconsistent opposition which can be explained only diachronically: *devā́ḥ* "gods of the organized cosmos"–*ásurāḥ* "gods of the primordial world," on the one hand, and by a fragmentary opposition: *devā́ḥ–pitáraḥ* "gods" or "spirits of dead ancestors" (literally "fathers"), with their chief *Yama*, the king of the dead, on the other. Gods and humans took part in a constant exchange and circulation of gifts which acquired a specific socio-cultural aspect. Those who did not believe in Aryan gods are not considered human beings: they are described as *dā́sa-/dásyu-*, words denoting both aboriginal enemies and demons. Believers made sacrifices and composed hymns and songs to the gods, the gods in turn bestowed upon the believers solicited gifts: wealth, military victories, glory, abundance, and male progeny.

In such a model there is no hell and no paradise. The region of the gods lies in the North or North-East. *Yama*'s region of death lies in the South, if spatial reference-points are to be used. Terms of the most ancient space-orientation were always ambiguous; in most cases their semantics reflect undifferentiated spatial and temporal meanings, for example: *pára-* "distant," "high," "early"–*ávara-* "near," "low," "late;" or *pū́rva-* "frontal," "eastern," "early"–*ápara-* "back," "western," "late," etc.

The basic mode of orientation is the circle. Essential for spatial orientation is the opposition between center and periphery. For the Aryans the basic values in all the isomorphic spheres are connected with the idea of the center, with the correlated notion of the navel of the universe–*bhúvanasya nā́bhi-*, the navel of the earth–*pṛthivyā́ nā́bhi-*, and the navel of the sacrifice–*ṛtásya nā́bhi-* (in some contexts equivalent to *védi-* the sacrificial altar). The Vedic Aryans' ideas about time as a sequence of cycles has already been mentioned.

On the socio-ethical level, life is similarly organized by *ṛtá* (law). What conforms to *ṛtá* is good: the Aryan gods and the sacrifices made to them, as well as all Aryan prosperity bestowed by the gods. Evil is everything that contradicts law: the absence of the Aryan gods, or a lack of sacrifices. The terrestrial world is modelled after the opposition between "living" (literally "moving")–*jágat-* and "non-living" (literally "standing")–*sthātár-*. Inside the *jágat*-class man has no particular distinction among other living creatures, and the opposition is expressed by means of other marks, such as "biped"–*dvipád- vs.* "quadruped"–*cátuṣpad-*.

The king in Aryan society is an earthly reflection of *Indra*. The royal figure is primarily connected with the notion of military might, victory and glory. Reversing the connection, the result is that if there is no victory, the king should be replaced [134.106]. However, Gods are usually called kings at the peak of their might; thus King *Indra* slayed *Vṛtra* and King *Agní* overcame darkness. But the power of both magic and law is an attribute of the priests.

In the Vedic model of the universe, diachrony manifests itself through the cosmogonic myths that play a crucial part in the text. All principal myths of the *Ṛg Veda* can be read as fragments of cosmogonic tales. Certain characteristic divine actions can also be considered in the same way–for example, the three strides of *Viṣṇu* and the daily circuit of the universe by the *Aśvins*. The mytho-poetic mind treats cosmogonic schemes as both a precedent and a standard for further reproduction simply because they existed in "primordial" times [49.46 passim]. But the *Ṛg Veda* myths are not mere tales of ancient times (i.e., related to diachrony); travelling through generations of *Ṛṣis*, the composers and custodians of the hymns, they enter synchrony and in this way become destined for the future.

In the Vedic model of the universe, abstract forces are personified and play the role of demiurges along with the gods. The Word, or Sacred Speech, is personified as the goddess *Vāc*, who appears as the Creator of the universe. The most important number in this model is three. The universe is tripartite–although there still remains an archaic dual deity *Dyā́vā-Pṛthivī́* "Heaven-and-Earth". The cosmogonic feat of the great gods consists in creating a third intermediate element between heaven and earth. This intermediary could be aerial space, the world-tree, a pillar, or some other kind of support. The divisions of the cosmos itself could be multiplied by three, and the third, or highest heaven, is of the most special importance.

The most important color characteristics are the following: *śvetá-* "white" (also "light, shining"–verb. *śvit-* "to shine"), and *kṛṣṇa-* "black," as well as transformations of the pairs of opposites–"light"-"darkness," "day"-"night," "god"-"demon," "Aryan"-"*Dāsa*." Also important are *aruṣá-* and other adjectives for "red" together with all transformations of "fire." The colors also probably differed in their degree of intensity: "red" can be designated by more than ten synonyms, while the dark part of the spectrum is covered by a single term.

Finally, the Vedic model of the universe incorporates several characteristics of magic-mentality,[10] almost inseparable from religion at a certain stage of society's development. The difference between them could be briefly outlined as follows: while the religious outlook can be characterized by obedience to Divine Will, the magic mentality replaces the deity with abstract entities which can be manipulated with the help of magical techniques. The fundamental principle of any magic is total determinism without causal connections. The world structure is represented as a system of equivalences: everything can be caused by anything.[11]

The magic mentality finds its consequent expression in a whole system of a series of identifications that are characteristic of later Vedic texts–the *Brāhmaṇas* and the *Upaniṣads* [37.26f.]. This phenomenon is only incipient in the *Ṛg Veda* and lacks a systematic character [157.18f.]. In this respect the *Agni* hymn (2.1; 16 stanzas in all) is quite outstanding consisting mostly of equivalences of the following type:

tvám agne rā́jā váruṇo dhṛtávratas
tvám mitró bhavasi dasmá ī́ḍyaḥ
tvám aryamā́ sátpatir yásya sambhújam
tvám áṃśo vidáthe deva bhājayúḥ (4)

O Agni, thou art king *Varuṇa* (firm) keeper of the vows,
Thou art *Mitra* the wonder-working, the invoked.
Thou art *Aryaman*, the good ruler, whom I should like to resort to
Thou art *Aṃśa*, the god who bestows (generously) at sacrifice sharing[12]

However, these identifications cannot be perceived as magic equivalences, since an explanatory commentary is given at the end of the hymn:

tváṃ tā́n sáṃ ca práti cāsi majmánā
ágne sujāta prá ca deva ṛcyase
pṛkṣó yád átra mahinā́ ví te bhúvad
ánu dyā́vāpṛthivī́ ródasī ubhé

Thou art both similar to them and equal (to them) in greatness,
O Agni, beautifully born, you, O deity, also excel (them),
When thy might in (all its) greatness unfolds here
Along the heaven and the earth, along the both worlds!

Some scholars have suggested that the Vedic metaphorical phrases describing mystical correspondences between the divine world and the human world, and comprehensible only to the priests, play the role of identification with respect to a *tertium comparationis* [132.478-482]. This very general sketch of the Aryan model of the universe in the *Ṛg Veda* does not allow for an analysis of its internal contradictions, or for any consideration of fragments of several other accessory systems recognizable also in this document.

We should consider in some detail the Aryans' views of sacred knowledge. According to orthodox Indian classification, the *Ṛg Veda* (*ṛg-veda-*, the Veda of the hymns), belongs to the genre of the Vedas. Among them it is the most ancient and the most authoritative; the *Yajur Veda*, the *Sāma Veda*, and the *Atharva Veda* have borrowed on a grand scale from the *Ṛg Veda*. The same classification ascribes the Vedas to the *śruti*-tradition, in which the hymns are said to have been revealed by the gods to the mortal *Ṛṣis*. The *śruti*-tradition is contrasted with the *smṛti*-tradition, literally "memorizing," i.e., knowledge deriving from human authorities. Thus Old Indian texts are said to contain two kinds of knowledge: sacred and profane.

The orthodox Indian classification belongs to a much later period than the *Ṛg Veda* collection itself. The word-form *ṛg-veda* is not the standard usage adopted in this text because only its components are attested: *ṛ́c-* "hymn; verse," and *véda-* "knowledge." *Ṛ́c-* is a feminine root-noun from the verb *arc-* "to shine, glitter; to glorify in song" (compare masculine noun from the same root–*arká-* "a ray; brilliance; sun; laudatory song"). These etymological connections suggest that the notion of a hymn was associated with the idea of light and brilliance; in other words, it was a concept connected with vision. The noun *ṛ́c-* is quite well-documented in the *Ṛg Veda*, in both its singular and plural forms.

Véda- is a noun derived from the verb *vid-* "to know, to be aware of." It occurs in the *Ṛg Veda* only once, in a later stratum (8.19):

yáḥ samídhā yá ā́hutī
yó védena dadā́śa márto agnáye
yó námasā svadhvaráḥ (5)
tásyéd árvanto raṃhayanta āśávas
tásya dyumnítamaṃ yáśaḥ
ná tám áṃho devákṛtaṃ kútaś caná
ná mártyakṛtaṃ naśat (6)

(He) who with firewood, who with libation
Who, a mortal, with knowledge honors Agni,
Who with reverence, beautifully performing the rite, does it
His coursers race swiftly,
His is the most brilliant glory,
No anguish–either caused by a god
Or caused by a mortal–shall get him.

The context shows that *véda-* here denotes sacred knowledge; it is enumerated along with other ritual means of influencing the gods.

A word that occurs frequently in the *Ṛg Veda* is *dhī́-* (feminine), whose syncretic semantics reflects a whole set of ideas prevalent in that cultural milieu concerning the means used to understand the surrounding world and to influence the gods. It is a root-noun derived from the verb *dhī-* "to perceive, think, ponder, wish." The most probable original meaning was "to see," although the only authority for this is Grassmann [91.683-4]. In the *Ṛg Veda* it is quite reliably attested–without a prefix–in the following passage: *yā́vat táras tanvò yávad ójo / yā́van náraś cákṣasā dī́dhyānāḥ* (7.91.4) "As long as the body (has) the overcoming power, as long as (there is) might, / As long as men are able to *discern* with their gaze. . . ." Geldner's translation is: "mit dem Auge schauen" [74.2.262]; Renou's: "(sont) aptes-à-considerer du regard" [118.15.108]. Renou (*ibid.*) notes two other passages in the *Ṛg Veda* where this verb has the meaning "to look, gaze," where the prefixes, though making the direction more precise, do not alter its lexical meaning: *úd dyā́m ivét tṛṣṇájo nāthitā́só / dīdhayur dāśarājñé vṛtā́saḥ* (7.33.5): "Finding themselves in trouble, surrounded in the Ten-kings-battle, they were *looking* upwards, as (those who are) tormented by thirst (look up) at the sky (hoping for rain);" *tád ít sadhástham abhi cā́ru dīdhaya / gā́vo yác chā́san vahatúṃ ná dhenávaḥ* (10.32.4): "I was *gazing* at that pleasant place toward which milch cows should direct (their journey) like a wedding procession." In Old Iranian this original meaning is much more in evidence than in Old Indian [108.2.45]. But even in the *Ṛg Veda* the regular sense can be defined as "to examine through an inner gaze," or, in Renou's words: "voir par la pensée" [118.1.3].

This inner seeing is the meaning of the verbal root that serves as a starting point for Gonda's understanding of the nominal *dhī́-* ("vision," in his interpretation). In a special monograph devoted to this highly important notion of the spiritual world of the Vedic Aryans [90], Gonda developed his ideas in the following manner. According to Vedic notions, the gods, related to heavenly light, were omniscient, and knowledge was of a visual nature; thus, "to have seen" was "to know." The faculty of "vision" was the property of the *Ṛṣi*-poets who possessed that *dhī́-*. Gonda stresses that *dhī́-*

should be taken as an exceptional ability to see within one's mind various objects, connections and causes as they really are. It is an ability of suddenly recognizing the truth, the functions and influences of divine forces, and man's relationship to them [90.68-9]. The truth is hidden from humans and does not manifest itself; it is sacred. The *Ṛṣi*, with the help of *dhī́-*, can relate to the nonmanifest and thus, in his mind's eye, his view is divine, making him a participant in the sacral world. And thus the *Ṛṣi* becomes a person who by force of his *dhī́-* is able to penetrate the world of the gods.

In the conceptual system described by Gonda, the truth is suddenly revealed to a possessor of *dhī́-*: in other words, to him who is *dhī́ra-* "wise," i.e., "whose *dhī́-* is strong." This truth is a static picture, since what the *Ṛṣi* "sees" is situated outside of time, transcendental. It can equally refer to the present, the past or the future, as well as to numerous times at once. And this peculiarity of the *Ṛṣi*'s vision, as it will be shown below, is of immediate relevance to the language of the hymns.

The *Ṛṣi*'s ecstatic visions resemble a rapid succession of static pictures, and during the reading of the *Ṛg Veda*, a feeling of motion results from the speed of the sequence of the "stills," if such an analogy be allowed. There may be no strict, logical coherence between individual pictures. In the archaic mind such a sequence can be rather like a kaleidoscope. This manner of "seeing" hardly encourages a discursive account of events in their logical and causal linear sequence. The kind of account of mythological plots to which the modern man is accustomed is quite rare in the *Ṛg Veda*, at least in its older parts. In most cases myths are not told but only indicated. Often they are mentioned by means of stereotyped phrases, short and frequently formulaic. Many of those myths are not retold in extenso in the later Old Indian literature (the *Brāhmaṇas*, *Upaniṣads*, the Epics and the *Purāṇas*)–although it should be kept in mind that different versions do appear in different texts. The actual content of a myth, however, often remains obscure for us, even if it is referred to in the *Ṛg Veda* quite frequently.

More than once it has been suggested that plots familiar both to the *Ṛṣi* and his audience were in no need of further retelling, but this explanation seems insufficient because such references to plots or the formulaic listing of plots actually reflects the nature of the *Ṛṣi*'s vision. This form is entirely adequate to convey the rapid succession of pictures that appear as inner vision.

The process of mastering and transmitting sacred knowledge presupposes several stages. Its first stage appears in the hymns as a momentary intuitive breakthrough of Divine Truth. The deity reveals knowledge within the poet's heart (*mánas-*, *hṛ́d-*). In this way, the poet does not create truth–he receives it. After the poet "has seen" Truth, the next stage begins: presenting

Truth in verbal form as declaration. In Old Indian culture since the time of the *Ṛg Veda* the declaration of truth was considered to require an immense creative power that reached universal order and influenced the actions of the gods.

According to Gonda [89.ch.2], the Vedic *Ṛṣi* "transposes" the vision revealed to him into verbal form. This form is wholly dependent on tradition, or canon, which in the language of the hymns is called the creation of the ancient, or earlier, *Ṛṣis*. Following the canon the *Ṛṣi* puts his vision into words, thus transforming it into hymn, prayer, or some liturgical text. Being part of the ritual of divine worship, the hymn ascends as offering to the gods who had earlier conferred inspiration on the *Ṛṣi*. And so the circle is complete: an exchange between a deity and his worshipper in the assumed form of poetic art. The deity grants the poet access to mystery and inspiration, and he composes a prayer-hymn in order to support and praise the deity.

The main purpose of the hymn, according to Bernfried Schlerath [133.201-221], consists in the formulation of Truth (*ṛtá-*). Heinrich Lüders [104], whose ideas Schlerath developed, held that Truth was a certain static and absolute quantity occupying a definite place in the cosmos above the gods. A truthful hymn is one that conforms to the law of *ṛta-*, and in order to create such a hymn, a *Ṛṣi* had to use "true" words and phrases. So Schlerath concludes: "But the almost inevitable result of this is that the seemingly loosely connected elements–thought, word, and act–are linked together in a most intimate way" [133.220]. These elements certainly reflect a definite PIE concept, but Schlerath's findings are equally important for a purely synchronic approach. Such an interpretation models each stage of the truth-achieving, cognitive process; it represents the creation of a hymn as part of the general ritual worship of the gods. In other words, the making of a hymn becomes an integral part of the circle of exchange between deity and worshipper.

Both knowledge of the world and artistic creativity are inseparable from the problem of the subject of cognition and creation, i.e. the Vedic *Ṛṣi*, whose role has been attracting the attention of modern scholars of both the genetic and the synchronic aspects of Vedic culture.

The word *ṛ́ṣi-*, according to the *Great Petersburg Lexicon*, has the following meanings: "singer of sacred songs; poet; a saint of ancient times." It is usually derived from the verbal root *arṣ-*, *árṣati*, "to gush forth, flow swiftly; rush forth," which has an established Indo-European etymology.[13]

Various forms of the verb *arṣ-* occur more than 120 times in the *Ṛg Veda*, predominantly in Book 9 with only about 10 occurrences outside of that book. Thus this verb can be said to belong to Book 9; it describes the flow of the pressed *Soma* juice at various points of the rite requiring it:

through the strainer, in the vat, mixing with other substances, etc. In other books the verb *arṣ-* is only once used with reference to Soma (1.135.2); all other instances describe the flow of waters and rivers, usually in a cosmogonic context, or illustrate the perpetual law of universal rotation (the *ṛtá-*): 1.105.12; 2.25.4; 3.30.9; 4.18.6; 8.89.4. In three instances the verb *arṣ-* is applied to *ghṛtá-* "the ghee-fat." This word, as used in the *Ṛg Veda*, deserves to be considered in greater detail. It has been established that its referent is not just "ghee," an important substance used for ritual purposes in sacrificial offerings. The word has multilevel referents whose interplay and combination contribute to the message of several hymns, as in 4.58, whose subject is the deified ghee. We may quote two stanzas where *ghṛtá-* and *arṣ-* occur side by side:

etā́ arṣanti hṛ́dyāt samudrā́c
chatávrajā ripúṇā nā́vacakṣase
ghṛtásya dhā́rā abhí cākāśīmi
hiraṇyáyo vetáso mádhya āsām (5)
samyák sravanti saríto ná dhénā
antár hṛdā́ mánasā pūyámānāḥ
eté arṣanty ūrmáyo ghṛtásya
mṛgā́ iva kṣipaṇór ī́ṣamāṇāḥ (6)

These (streams of ghee) *flow* from the heart-ocean,
Surrounded by a hundred fences; they are not to be seen by a deceiver.
I inspect attentively the streams of *ghee*:
There is a golden rod in their midst
The torrents (of speech) flow together like rivulets,
Purified inside, both by heart and mind.
These waves of *ghee are running*
Like gazelles fleeing away from an arrow.

In the introduction to his translation of this hymn, Geldner stated that ghee was praised metaphorically as the actual sacrificial butter, as the *Soma* juice, and as poetic speech soaked in this ghee. But originally, according to him, the hymn was intended to accompany an ordinary *Soma* libation with an obligatory kindling of the sacrificial fire [74.1.488].

Renou, in his analysis of this hymn [118.1.3], noted that *ghṛtá-* was flowing in streams (and pouring into the "ocean," i.e., a *Soma*-vat), and that process was likened to the growth of poetic imagery. The level of poetic speech acquires more importance when compared to the levels of sacrificial ghee and the rite of *Soma* preparation. "The heart-ocean" is the source of poetic inspiration. "The fences" guard the poetic speech against ill-willed rivals, "the golden rod" denotes *Soma* in his role as the fertilizer of poetic thoughts and as a symbol of masculinity. "The heart" is the strainer through which poetic speech is filtered and purified: all these images are taken from the *Soma* ritual. In this connection some very interesting considerations were put forward by Gonda [90.69]: since ghee was thought to originate in the celestial ocean, this hymn combines three ideas: 1) the celestial origin of Sacred Speech, 2) the mediatory role of the gods, and 3) the heart as the place in which inspiration is revealed and from which Sacred Speech issues.

Another passage where the verb *arṣ-* appears together with *ghṛtá-* (as the direct object) is found in a hymn praising a generous patron:

tásmā ā́po ghṛtám arṣanti síndhavas
tásmā iyáṃ dákṣiṇā pinvate sádā (1.125.5)

For him waters (and) rivers *flow (with) ghee*,
For him this sacrificial reward always swells up.

The transitive *arṣ-* here (usually *abhí + arṣ-*) is similarly used in a ritual context.

All this seems to confirm the hypothesis that the semantics of the verb *arṣ-* in the *Ṛg Veda* is very closely connected with ritual in general, and more particularly with the *Soma* sacrifice. *Soma* passing through the sheep-wool strainer flowed into the wooden vessel; the priest tasted it, and the hallucinogenic liquid sharpened his intuition so that Truth was momentarily revealed in him. "Having seen" it and having given it the shape of a hymn, the priest-*Ṛṣi* filtered poetic speech through his heart and let it flow freely in order to enable it to reach the divine and heavenly spheres. This ritual orientation of the verb *arṣ-* could give rise to the nominal derivative *ṛ́ṣi-* with its complex semantics: a participant in a rite who drinks the sacrificial liquid and pours out praises in the form of a hymn.

This interpretation of the meanings of *arṣ-* can also find support in typological parallels from other Indo-European traditions. Benveniste has succeeded in showing [54.ch. 2 "The Libation"] that the verb *spéndō, spéndomai* in ancient Greek means "to sprinkle with a liquid in a rite intended to guarantee safety;" its noun derivative *spondḗ* denotes a libation accompanied by prayer. There are quite remarkable formal coincidences between words denoting praise and invocation on the one hand, and those denoting drinking, swallowing, etc. on the other, attested in several Indo-European languages. Thus, in Russian жрец means "a priest" and жрать means "to devour;" the correspondences of the latter mean "to drink" in some Slavic and Baltic languages [47.2.62-3] (Compare also Old Indian 1.*gṛ-*, *gṛṇā́ti*, *giráti* "to sing, praise"–2.*gṛ-*, *giráti*, *giláti*, *gṛṇā́ti* "to swallow"–*gur-*, *guráte* "to hail, laud;" each treated as different verbs on the synchronic level).[14]

An interesting parallel can be seen in Oleg N. Trubachev's ideas concerning the innovated terminology of priestly laudation in Proto-Slavic. He suggests that the verb **pěti*, **pojǫ* "to sing (praises)" is based on the more original **pojiti*, **pojǫ* "to water, give drink" respectful "to libate." He suggests that in sacrificial rites, the singing of praises was secondary and was originally preceded by a stage of silent ritual worship. He also adduced Old Indian evidence: a word pair in which the original *juhóti* "to pour" contrasts with the secondary *hávate* "to invoke" [44.319].

It should be kept in mind also that the verb *ar-/ṛ-* (from which *arṣ-* is derived with the help of the root-determinative *-s-*), "to set in motion, to begin moving, to rise, to excite, to be excited" (mainly transitive), frequently governs a direct object accusative of nouns with the meanings "voice," "speech," "hymn," "praise," "prayer;" for example, *íyarti vā́cam aritéva nā́vam* (2.42.1). "It *pushes out* (its) voice as a steerer (pushes) the boat" ("it" here denoting an ominous bird); *stómām̐ iyarmy abhríyeva vā́taḥ* (1.116.1) "I *set in motion* praises as the wind (sets in motion) clouds;" *ṛtā́d iyarmi te dhíyam manoyújam* (8.13.26) "Out (of the womb) of Truth I *send* to thee a prayer harnessed by thought," where, as Grassmann correctly noted, "out [of the womb] of Truth" means "from the heart" [91.283],[15] etc.

All these suggestions concerning the etymology of *ṛ́ṣi-* may corroborate the hypothesis that in the period of the *Ṛg Veda* the *Ṛṣi* participated in the ritual of divine worship and recited hymns that he composed in accordance with an ancient tradition, hymns that were performed in conjunction with sacrificial libations. In this way a *Ṛṣi* combined the functions of the poet, the reciter and the priest.

As a component of the overall ideal picture the Vedic Aryans held about cosmic law, Truth (*ṛtá-*) and the visionary faculty (*dhī́-*), the *Ṛṣi* assumed the role of the mediator between gods and mortals, since he was able to express in words intelligible to mortals the Divine Truth (*ṛtá-*) he had previously "seen." But his part was not confined to that particular function. At certain decisive turning points in the life of the society the poet-*Ṛṣi* was thought to have the function of a demiurge, a cosmic creator who assists the cosmos: his victory in the singers' verbal contest is a decisive contribution to the overcoming of the forces of chaos [22]. It is no coincidence that the goddess *Vāc* (the personification of Sacred Speech) is identified on the mythological level with the basic principle of the cosmic existence that prevails over the gods. And, as was to become usual in later Old Indian philosophy, *Vāc* combines in herself both subject and object, being at once speech (Vedic text) and poet (creator of the text) [14.64].

This dual nature of the *Ṛṣi* is expressed on the mythological level by the semi-divine status of the ancestors of the *Ṛṣis*. Here it should be noted that the families of the *Ṛṣis* kept separate and passed from generation to generation whole sets of hymns or even entire *maṇḍalas*–hymnic cycles. The oldest *maṇḍalas* (2-7) have been labelled "family maṇḍalas" by European scholars. For example, the *Aṅgirases* were considered to be demigods. On the one hand, they were divine singers who figured prominently in the myth of *Vala*, and on the other hand, they were believed to be the forefathers of a family of poets whose members were the authors of many hymns, according to the native commentary (*Anukramaṇī*). In Book 10 there are two examples of a composite "Seven *Ṛṣis*" (*saptarṣí-*), a kind of mystical unit identifiable with the seven stars of Ursa Major. In other passages of the *Ṛg Veda* the same unit is expressed by a syntactical combination of two separate words. These "Seven *Ṛṣis*" are identified typically with the poets' remote ancestors; for instance, *asmā́kam átra pitáras tá āsan saptá ṛ́ṣayo . . .* (4.42.8) "these our fathers were there, the seven *Ṛṣis* . . ." (where "fathers" may be translated as the dead ancestors). Generally speaking, the notion of the "ancient *Ṛṣis*" is to a great extent identical with that of the *pitáras*. In the *Ṛg Veda* many ancient *Ṛṣis* appear in the myths along with the gods, such as the *Bhṛgus* who were the first to generate fire, the *Ṛṣi Atri* who found the Sun hidden by the demon *Svarbhānu*, and many others.

The idea of continuity in a long chain of generations is highly relevant to the notion of the Vedic poet, since his intuitive ability "to see" was believed to be genetically inherited from his ancestors. By contrast, the *Ṛṣis* handed their divine knowledge over to successive generations: *mahó rujāmi bandhútā vácobhiḥ / tán mā pitúr gótamād ánv iyāya* (4.4.11): "I can smite mightily with words because of (my) kindred; / This has come to me from my father *Gotama*." See also:

uvā́ca me váruṇo médhirāya
tríḥ saptá nā́mā́ghnyā bibharti /
vidvā́n padásya gúhyā ná vocad
yugā́ya vípra uparā́ya śíkṣan // (7.87.4)

Varuṇa declared to me, the wise one: /
Thrice seven names does the cow carry. /
The knower of the sign (of names), let him pronounce (them as) hidden,
(If this) inspired one wishes to help the coming generation.

Here "the cow" is a metaphor for poetic speech. The inspired *Ṛṣi* must guard the mysteries of this metaphorical speech (i.e., the thrice seven names) and then transmit them to the future generation of poets.

For the Vedic Aryans the *Ṛṣi* was the connecting link between generations, the keeper and transmitter of sacred knowledge. In poetry his role could be described by the opposition of "former" (*pū́rva-*, *pūrvyá-*, *pratná-*) and "present" (*nū́tana-*) *Ṛṣis*, songs, praises, etc. The left member of the pair is marked. The temporal position of the right member can be denoted by the adverbs *nú, nūnám* "now," "at present" and its inclusion in the "ego-generation" marked by the case-endings of the first person singular pronoun. Or its temporal position can be overtly unmarked and defined solely by context. This opposition was exceptionally important, since the "former *Ṛṣis*" (ancestors) and their compositions represented an elusive ideal and standard which the "present" *Ṛṣis* could only strive to emulate. This opposition is already present in the *Agni* hymn which introduces the whole collection, and in which it is declared that "*Agni* is worthy of the invocations of the *Ṛṣis* / Both of the *former* and the *present* (ones)"–*agníḥ pū́rvebhir ŕ̥ṣibhir / ī́ḍyo nū́tanair utá* (1.1.2). The opposition can manifest in various ways:

yé cid dhí tvā́m ŕ̥ṣayaḥ pū́rva ūtáye
juhūré 'vase mahi
sā́ na stómām̐ abhí gr̥ṇīhi rā́dhasā-
úṣaḥ śukréṇa śocíṣā (1.48.14)

"Even those *former Ṛṣis* that invoked thee for support, Great One, / Accept our praises (now) favorably with the wish of rewarding us, O *Uṣas*, with brilliant brightness!"

tám̐ va índram̐ catínam asya śākaír
ihá nūnám̐ vājayánto huvema /
yáthā cit pū́rve jaritā́ra āsúr
ánedyā anavadyā́ áriṣṭāḥ (6.19.4)

"This *Indra* (who is) hiding (?) with his helpers, / We desire to call (him) here for you, (we who are) striving for the reward, / Just as (this) used to happen to the *former* singers, / The irreproachable, sinless, invulnerable (ones)."

In such phrases the *Ṛg Veda* hymns express the traditional character of the *Ṛṣis*' creative activities. The hymns of the "former" poets are canonical, and the "present" ones then only imitate them. It is mentioned more than once that the author of a given hymn is trying to laud the chosen deity in the style of the fathers–the ancient poets, for example: *aṅgirasvát* (1.31.17 passim) "after the fashion of the *Aṅgirases*," *bhr̥guvát* (8.43.13) "in *Bhr̥gu*'s style," and so forth.

If we take seriously the current opinion that the *Ṛṣis* did not make up new plots but confined themselves to transmitting their heritage, while at the same time using traditional formulas to embroider those plots, we must confront the problem of those new elements the authors were allowed to introduce into their works. In other words, in what relation did the requirements of the canon stand towards the freedom of the poets' art? This intriguing question can be touched upon here only in a most general manner with reference to its effects on Vedic language and style.

The idea of "a new song" composed by a *Ṛṣi* for a deity occurs in the *Ṛg Veda* in several passages.[16] In the hymn to the All-Gods the poet says: *stuṣé jánaṃ suvratáṃ návyasībhir gīrbhír . . .* (6.49.1) "I praise the justly ruling (divine) tribe with *new songs*;" or in the *Agni* hymn: *prá távyasīṃ návyasīṃ dhītím agnáye / vācó matíṃ sáhasaḥ sūnáve bhare* (1.143.1) "I bring to *Agni* a stronger *newer poem*, a thought (turned into) speech, to the son of strength."

Taking into consideration all the limitations imposed by traditional art upon individual creation, it would be interesting to know the *Ṛṣis*' own ideas about "a new song." The relevant evidence can be detected in the hymns. A few rather characteristic pronouncements are quoted below. Thus, in the *Indra* hymn (8.6) the *Ṛṣi* of the *Kāṇva* family declares:

ahám íd dhí pitúṣ pári
medhā́m ṛtásya jagrábha
aháṃ sū́rya ivājani (10)
ahám pratnéna mánmanā
gíraḥ śumbhāmi kaṇvavát
yénéndraḥ śúṣmam íd dadhé (11)
yé tvā́m indra ná tuṣṭuvúr
ŕ̥ṣayo yé ca tuṣṭuvúḥ
máméd vardhasva súṣṭutaḥ (12)

"Tis from my father I have taken over the wisdom of truth:
I have been reborn like the sun.
I decorate songs in the *Kāṇva*-style aided by a *former* work,
thanks to which *Indra* assumed (his) bravery.
Whichever *Ṛṣis* have not praised thee, whichever have, O *Indra*,
be strengthened only through my (song), O (truly) finely praised (one)!"

Geldner, in his commentary to verse 11, stressed the ambiguity of its phrasing: either the new hymn was based on an ancient composition, or the author merely alluded to the archaic poetic style of the *Kāṇva* family [72.2.295].

One should take note of the verb *śumbhāmi*, "I decorate:" the presumable meaning is that the new element introduced by the poet in his hymn is actually a formal improvement (compare Geldner's translation: "Ich putze"). This meaning is not immediately in harmony with our understanding of the poet's use of his traditional heritage. The *Ṛṣi* is creating a new refined form, though the content may remain quite old. He is choosing words that fit the truth, and is arranging them in such a way that the form can be semanticized. This is, the form serves the hymn's communicative function, which consists in influencing the deity praised (verse 12). In brief, these three stanzas appear as a model for the composition of a new song by the Vedic *Ṛṣis*.

There is another passage in the *Ṛg Veda* (duly noted by Geldner in his commentary) where the poet uses much clearer language in describing how the traditional material is worked into a new composition. In the *Indra* hymn 8.95 ascribed to *Tiraścī* of the *Aṅgirases* family, verse 4 declares: *śrudhī́ hávaṃ tiraścyā́ / índra yás tvā saparyáti*–"Listen, O *Indra*, to the call of *Tiraścī* who worships thee!" After that, verse 5 contains the following description:

índra yás te návīyasīṃ
gíram mandrā́m ájījanat
cikitvínmanasaṃ dhíyam
pratnā́m ṛtásya pipyúṣīm

"O *Indra*, [he] has for thee given birth to a *newer* inspiring song, an *ancient* work[17] out of a keen heart soaked in truth." This description reflects all the stages of a creative process. The ancient work, "soaked in truth" and having passed through the "keen" (attentive, seeing) heart (*mánas-*) of the *Ṛṣi*, becomes a "newer inspiring song" (the adjective *mandrá-* "pleasant, pleasing," but also "melodious" or "inspiring"–an epithet describing the form).

Scholars have always stressed the fact that in the *Ṛg Veda* the act of poetic composition is described in terms of handicraft. Thus Renou [118:1.16] observed that the creation of a poem is considered to be "work" (*ápas-*), and the poet is an artisan (*apás-*). The verbs used to denote this activity include those with a wide semantic range: *kar-* "to make, create," *jan-* "to give birth to," *dhā-* "to set, fix," but quite often such verbs have a very specialized meaning: *takṣ-* "to cut, trim (wood)," *vā-/u-* "to weave," *tan-* "to draw (a thread, string)." The comparison of poets to carpenters or weavers is quite typical in the *Ṛg Veda*, for example, *asmā́ íd u stómaṃ sáṃ hinomi / ráthaṃ ná tásteva tátsināya* (1.61.4): "It is for him I *put together* a praise-poem as a carpenter (constructs) a chariot for him who gives a reward;" *etáṃ te stómaṃ tuvijāta vípro / ráthaṃ ná dhī́raḥ svápā atakṣam* (5.2.11): "I, the inspired one, have *fashioned* this praise for thee, O born by strength, as a skilled (master constructs) a chariot." In the dictionary sub voce *takṣ-*, Grassmann gives the following basic meanings of the verb: "to fashion skillfully (out of wood), to carve, trim (a chariot, a sacrificial post, a column's capital, a throne)." Stress made upon the aspect of skillful work, fine shaping. The external look of the chariot, a sun-symbol, was extremely important; it is often described as "golden" (*hiraṇyáya*), "bright," "shining" (*citrá-*). Metaphorically, the prayer is often called "a chariot." Compare also Campanile's belief that the poet compares his art to carpentry because both are following traditional inherited standards and, for both, innovations as well as personal contributions are permitted only on a very limited scale [62.36].

Weaving in the *Ṛg Veda* is both a cosmogonic and a sacrificial symbol. Words belonging to this semantic field quite regularly have referents on different levels. For instance, the word *mayū́kha-* denoting wooden pegs used for fixing and stretching the cloth can be used in cosmogonic context: for example, the *Viṣṇu* hymn *vy àstabhnā ródasī viṣṇav eté / dādhártha pṛthivī́m abhíto mayū́khaiḥ* (7.99.3): "Thou has fixed separately, O *Viṣṇu*, these two worlds. / Thou hast fastened the earth *with pegs* on all sides."

The terminology of weaving is normally used in descriptions of sacrifices. For example, the well-known hymn about the establishment of sacrifice by the ancient father-*Ṛṣis* contains the following stanza:

yó yajñó viśvátas tántubhis tatá
ékaśataṃ devakarmébhir ā́yataḥ
imé vayanti pitáro yá āyayúḥ
prá vayā́pa vayéty āsate taté (10.130.1)

"The sacrifice that is drawn through with its threads on all sides / is offered with a hundred and one acts, serving the gods. / These fathers are weaving (it), (these) who have arrived. They sit by the spread out (sacrifice, saying): 'Weave forward! Weave backward!'"

The same verbs denote the process of hymn-creation: *asmā́ íd u gnā́ś cid devápatnīr / índrāyārkám ahihátya ūvuḥ* (1.61.8). "For him the wives themselves, the divine spouses, / For *Indra* they have *woven* a song about the serpent-slaying:" *ubhā́ u nūnáṃ tád íd arthayethe / ví tanvāthe dhíyo vástrāpáseva* (10.106.1). "You both [the *Aśvins*] are now striving for only such an aim: / You *stretch* out poetic thoughts, as a master (stretches) cloth." In these quotations the gods are the actors in a mythological projection of real life situations. But *Ṛṣis* are also directly referred to in an analogous context in the "Knowledge"-hymn wherein hack poets are described:

imé yé nā́rvā́ñ ná parā́ś cáranti
ná brāhmaṇā́so ná sutékarāsaḥ
tá eté vā́cam abhipádya pāpáyā
sirī́s tántraṃ tanvate áprajajñayaḥ (10.71.9)

"Those who move neither forward nor backward, / (Who) are neither (genuine) *brāhmans* nor (real) *Soma*-pressers, / Those who are deficient in Speech, / They *weave* on a woof (a useless) rag, not even understanding (it)."

In this way one can speak of the highly symbolic character of the weaving-terminology in the *Ṛg Veda*. The fact that it is correlated with three isomorphic levels makes it possible for the poets to manipulate the code-switching. The *Ṛg Veda* possesses a rich vocabulary that encodes the key notions of a certain model of the universe, the very opposite of a limited and peripheral "workshop" terminology. This vocabulary was probably selected because it has to do with the processes of shaping and treating various forms, and all of this was similar to the main tasks of the poet, who would "weave" his hymnic designs on the prepared warp of an old poem, or base his work upon the high standards of a "former" *Ṛṣi*.

The poets' standing in the Aryan social structure also calls for a brief discussion. It is well-known that they belonged to the class (*varṇa*) of the *Brāhmans*, and their trade was hereditary. The *Ṛg Veda* hymns were composed, transmitted, and preserved in oral form in the singers' (priestly) families; sometimes their names are mentioned in the texts. But in a systematic way they are registered in the general "list" (*anukramaṇī*) that was compiled in the times of the later Brahmanical tradition. This list of authors, was strongly influenced by mythology, in its inclusion of divine names. Several women also appear therein, but generally speaking, it was a male occupation.

We have no trustworthy evidence about the poets' lives or about relationships among the singers' families. The legend about the alleged enmity between *Viśvāmitra* and *Vasiṣṭha* is attested only in late sources: the *Ṛg Veda* does contain some vague allusions that could possibly be interpreted in that vein, but there is no certainty. It is known that the *Ṛṣis* depended on rich patrons, usually kings: the *yajamānas* who would reward them with cows, horses, gold, etc. The gods were asked to grant a boon to the patron and to the poet himself. There are some hymns (or parts of them) in the *Ṛg Veda* containing "gift-praises" (*dānastuti*), sometimes marked by gross exaggerations. Nevertheless, from time to time, the poet might voice his dissatisfaction with the gifts, in either plain language or in allusion. The *Ṛṣi* valued his position vis-à-vis his patron and was in constant competition with his rivals: the hymns abound in bitter attacks against competitions in poetic art.

In considering the social status of the poets it is appropriate to discuss the nature of the Vedic *Ṛṣi*'s art. His role as a keeper and transmitter of sacred knowledge, who is guided by the canon of ancestral songs, tends to incline scholars towards a hypothesis of the collective nature of that art. The problem of individual authorship was not relevant either for the Vedic period, or most probably for Old Indian culture as a whole.[18] Already in the late nineteenth century Hermann Oldenberg established the following fact:

when the family name of a singer is used in the hymn in the singular (and not, as in some *maṇḍalas*, exclusively in the plural) it normally refers not to the ancestor but to one of his descendants [115.199-247]. This can only mean that a hymn belongs to a whole family and not to its mythical progenitor, about whom there is practically no evidence.

So much for diachrony. Turning to the level of synchrony, we may say that the principle of collective creativity is represented by a "corporation" of *Ṛṣis* who were trained for verbal contests. In the *Ṛg Veda* this corporation is called *sakhyá-* literally "sodality." Valuable information is provided by hymn 10.71. Setting aside speculations concerning the nature of speech ("the wise ones created Speech with (their) thought in stanza 2 *et al.*), as well as the classification of the sodality members according to their ability and training (stanza 4, 5, and 7), let us consider what is said about their collective art:

yás tityā́ja sacivídaṃ sákhāyaṃ
ná tásya vācy ápi bhāgó asti
yád īṃ śṛṇóty álakaṃ śṛṇoti
nahí pravéda sukṛtásya pánthām (6)

"He who abandoned (in distress) his friend of like mind, / He has no claims on Speech! Whatever he listens to, he hears in vain: / For he has not recognized the path of good action!;"

sárve nandanti yaśásā́gatena
sabhāsāhéna sákhyā sákhāyaḥ
kilbiṣaspṛ́t pituṣáṇir hy èṣām
áraṃ hitó bhávati vā́jināya (10)

"All (his) friends rejoice in the friend who has returned with the fame of a winner in the contest. / For he is saving them from sin and obtaining food for them. He has been duly released into the contest." These quotations show that both the defeat of a member and his victory in the contest (entailing substantial rewards) were shared equally by the rest of the sodality. A breach of these corporative principles resulted in grave consequences for the offender.

A few words about the kind of contests for which the sodalities were training their members. The most convincing theory has been put forward by Kuiper in his article "The Ancient Aryan Verbal Contest," [22] which has been discussed above. Verbal contests were part of the annual rites of regeneration at the time of the winter solstice, when the confrontation of Chaos and Cosmos took place. Poets entered the competitions as representatives of their patrons. Verbal contests along with chariot races and military contentions (as well as die-casting, in later times) were held with the aim of "winning the sun" and establishing order in the universe. The goddess *Uṣas* presided over the distribution of generous gifts during these contests.

This sketch of the religious and social status of the Vedic *Ṛṣis* is based mainly on research done by Western scholars. It should be noted that interest in this range of problems has been growing lately among Indian scholars as well. The realization of the special role of the *Ṛṣis* in the archaic Aryan society of the ṚgVedic period has stimulated research in this area: much work has been published both in English and in modern Indian languages (Hindi, Marathi, Gujarati).[19] Although this topic has generated a stream of publications, both of a scientific and of a more popular character, their main lines of investigation are beyond the scope of the present monograph; our interest is primarily linguistic. Nevertheless, we cannot avoid mentioning a remarkable phenomenon: an uninterrupted chain of tradition and continuity, though altered and variable to a certain degree, between modern India and the world of the *Ṛg Veda* Aryan–especially in those cases when the author of a work on the Vedic poets happens to be both a well-known Sanskritist and a descendant of a Vedic *Ṛṣi*, such as Dandekar, who traces his origin from the *Ṛṣi Vasiṣṭha* [63.312-350].

2
Vocabulary

Some of the essential features of the model of the universe seen by the seers of the hymns find their fullest and clearest reflection in the vocabulary of the *Ṛg Veda*. On the one hand, this circumstance grants the scholar quite a few advantages, as it places at his disposal a general theory which permits him, using a single non-contradictory method, to interpret the historical and cultural situation as well as disparate linguistic facts. But on the other hand, the dangers of a vicious circle seem apparent. First, we construct a model of the universe on the the basis of the *Ṛg Veda* hymns, and then we interpret the vocabulary of the *Ṛg Veda* with the help of this very model. This danger must never be overlooked. In addition, there can never be any certainty that many, and sometimes quite essential fragments of this model, have been construed in adequate agreement with the perception of the Vedic *Ṛṣis* themselves. This uncertainty has to be applied to any interpretation of certain parts of the Vedic vocabulary.

The vocabulary of the *Ṛg Veda* is characterized by both polysemy and synonymy [8. ch. "Vocabulary"]. Using these very characteristics, the poets quite consciously introduce puns, a play on words, thus creating an intentionally obscure, allusive and suggestive style. However, before we discuss the stylistic use of lexical polysemy in the *Ṛg Veda*, we should consider the definition of this phenomenon. Polysemy, as such, presupposes the discrete character of meanings tied to a word. The *Ṛg Veda* lexicon, as represented in classical Western dictionaries [91; 59], contains an amazing number of polysemantic words. It is remarkable that the highest number of meanings—sometimes more than ten—is ascribed to words that encode the key notions of the model of the universe (for example, words that denote members of basic oppositions), as well as proper names that are widely used as symbols in Vedic poetry. But a modern Vedic scholar cannot be certain that, in Vedic times, quite different types of semantic syncretism were not prevalent. What we perceive as different meanings of the same word in the hymns might have appeared to the *Ṛṣi* as a single meaning in different contexts.

Central to the *Ṛg Veda* world-model was the notion rendered by the word *ṛtá-*. Grassmann gives the following meanings for its use as a noun:

"divine order," "eternal truth;" "justice, right;" "sanctity;" "truth;" "a pious deed;" "sacrifice." It seems most probable that all the "separate meanings" are really context-bound variants of a single syncretic invariant meaning which, in this particular case could be conventionalized as "cosmic law." On the speculative level it can manifest itself as "eternal truth," but on the ritual level as "sacrifice." Similarly, the various adjectival meanings of the word—"appropriate;" "good," "sacred;" "truthful, pious"—could be rather easily reduced to a single invariant: "conforming to the law of *ṛtá-*.'

We should evidently assume the existence of a single meaning with widely differing contextual variants in the case of the hardly translatable noun *dhā́man-*. Its semantic area is defined in the dictionaries as "a seat, place, residence, habitation;" "home, a favourite spot (especially, of *Agni* and *Soma*);" "retinue, a company (of gods);" "law, norm" [80]. Leaving aside for the moment the problem of the semantic evolution of these variants, it seems possible to suggest that for the *Ṛṣi* the meaning of *dhā́man-*(from the verb root *dhā-* "to set, put, place,arrange") manifest itself on the level of locality as "a place," on the level of speculation as "law, order," and on the level of social relations as "a retinue, escort."

The invariant semantics of *krátu*—*dakṣa-*, could be rendered by the opposition "spiritual power," "power of action," both of which have a multitude of meanings in our dictionaries. In the *Ṛṣi*'s mind, *krátu-* in different contexts may have corresponded to our notions of "ability, skill," "reason(ing), understanding;" "intuition, inspiration, aspiration;" and "sacrificial drink (*Soma* as a source of inspiration)." Nevertheless, the word preserves the unicity of its basic semantics. So, too, *dákṣa-* denotes the "ability to act," "skill;" "force, "(ill)will," all of which are perceived as various manifestations of a single property. In some contexts the opposition between the two members can be neutralized, and either of them may denote an undifferentiated mental-and-physical force at the same time, although other meanings of the neutralized member can also occur.

Principles of semantic syncretism, very different from those of modern scholars, tend to manifest themselves in a definite lexical stratum, namely, in the one dealing with various emotional and intellectual phenomena. The words denoting these phenomena are the same as those that denote the corresponding—for the Vedic mind—internal organ. This semantic syncretism is correctly rendered in Otto Böhtlingk's *Wörterbuch* where, for example, the word *mánas-* is defined both as "inner emotion," "spirit," "mind," "reason," "thought," and as "internal body-part," "heart." On the other hand, *hṛ́d-* or *hṛ́daya-* in the *Rig Veda* can mean not only "heart (as part of body)," but also "the focal point of various emotions" (as joy, fear, inspiration, etc.), and *hṛ́d-* in the strictly anatomical sense often has the wider meaning of "internal organs in general." Some contexts play on the opposition *mánas-*: *hŕd-*, but in others the opposition is neutralized, for example: *samyák sravanti saríto ná dhénā / antár hṛdā́ mánasā pūyámānāḥ* (4.58.6) "Together flow the rivers (of speech), like rivulets, purified within by the *heart (and) mind* (or: "by feeling and thought"), but: *yá índrāya vacoyújā / tatakṣúr mánasā hárī* (1.20.2) "(Those) who have fashioned by *thought* a pair of bay horses for *Indra*, (a pair) harnessed by word . . . "[20] and: *hṛdā́ yat taṣṭā́n mántrāň áśaṃsan* (1.67.4) " . . . when they uttered the sacred words hewn by the *heart*," where both *mánasā* and *hṛdā́* are used in similar phrases, and the lexical differences between them are quite obscure.[21]

A typical example of semantic syncretism in verbal roots is represented by verbs of visual perception, where the meaning "to see" is usually combined with the meaning "to appear, to seem." The difference in semantics is often indicated neither by inflexion (active/middle) nor by the stem-class. For example, *ví + khyā-*: *uccā́ vy àkhyad yuvatíḥ punarbhū́r* . . . (1.123.2) "High up *shone* a young woman, appearing again," and *ví nā́kam akhyat savitā́ váreṇyo* . . . (5.81.2) "the magnificent Savitar *glanced* at the sky-vault;" *cakṣ-*: *yéna cáṣṭe váruṇo mitró aryamā́* (8.19.16) ". . . (that splendor) in which *appear Varuṇa, Mitra, Aryaman*" and *tvā́ṃ caṣṭe muṣṭihā́* (6.26.2) "At thee *is looking* the fist-fighter;" *cit-*: *ákavārī cetati vājínīvatī* (7.96.3) "Rich in reward, she *manifests* (herself as) generous," and *tád índro ártham cetati* (1.10.2) "Here *Indra notices* the intention to sacrifice." But the verb *dṛś-* realizes the semantic opposition through the formal contrast of active *vs.* middle endings, for instance: *kó dadarśa prathamáṃ jā́yamānam* (1.164.4) "Who *saw* the one being born first . . . ?," and: *hótā mandró viśā́m dámūnās / tirás támo dadṛśe rāmyā́ṇām* (7.9.2) "The joyful *hotar*, the house (-ruler) of tribes / *Is seen* through the darkness of nights."

The intransitive meaning "to seem, appear" of the verb *dhī-* is conveyed by the active inflexion, while the transitive "to look, think, contemplate" ("to see with inner sight") is usually combined with middle endings, for example: *ákṣetravid yáthā mugdhó / bhúvanāny adīdhayuḥ* (5.40.5) " . . . (then all) beings *looked like* a (man gone) astray, not recognizing the place," and: *máhi mahé tavási dīdhye* (5.33.1) "Great (praise) for the great strong (one) I *contemplate*."[22]

The polysemy becomes even more complex in those cases in which the separate meanings of a word acquire a symbolic character. The metaphorical transfer of meanings occurs so frequently that the border-line between polysemy and homonymy almost disappears. However, even these cases may be accounted for by the imagery of thought, and we should recognize only one meaning as basic. For instance, when the *Ṛṣi* uses the word *gó-* (masculine) "a bull," (feminine) "a cow" to denote constellations ("a herd of cattle"), dawns ("reddish cows"), earth ("giver of food"), and rainclouds (i.e., they give rain as cows give milk), then the problem of polysemy appears to be a moot point.The same applies to the semantics of *ádri* = "a rock, a mountain" as well as "a sling-stone," "a *Soma*-pressing stone" and finally, "a thunder-cloud" (as in the myth of *Vala*).

Often in the *Ṛg Veda* a word meaning has denotation on different levels, some of which belong to the visible world or to myth (the demarcation-line between the two sometimes being almost evanescent), while others are related to ritual. For example,[23] *gharmá-* can simultaneously denote "solar heat" and "a pot on fire," or "hot milk" for the *Aśvins*; *páyas-* "(cow)milk," "rain," "the *Soma*-juice;" *mádhu-* "honey; mead," "sweetness," "milk," "sacrificial ghee," "the *Soma*-juice;" *vana-* "forest," "tree," "wood," "a wooden *Soma* vessel," "water" (particularly, the streams of water mixing with *Soma* in a vat); *samudrá-* "confluence," "terrestrial sea," "celestial sea," "the *Soma*-juices in a big vessel;" *sā́nu-* "mountain-top," "the back (of an animal or a demon)," "the surface of a *Soma*-strainer made of sheep-wool," etc.

Such a play on the denotations of words is a recurring feature of the *Ṛg Veda* hymns. The problem of reference in this poetic text sometimes acquires rather special dimensions. For some textual fragments the reference of the fragment as a whole can become decisive, while in other cases what is important is the reference of a clause. In turn, the reference of some individual words depends on the clause, or putting it differently, there is a one-to-one correlation between the meanings of a word and the ritual or some other level of reference. For instance, verse 9.26.5:

táṃ sā́nāv ádhi jāmáyo
háriṃ hinvanty ádribhiḥ /
haryatám bhū́ricakṣasam //

"The sisters urge on with stones this bay stallion on the mountain-top, the beloved one who gazes at the numerous (ones)." This is the symbolic level, and behind it the ritual level can be discerned: "The (priest's) fingers urge on the flow of the *Soma* juice with the help of the pressing stones on the surface of the strainer," etc. Since we are aware of the fact that this is a *Soma pavamāna* ("Purified *Soma*") hymn of Book 9, i.e., a hymn accompanying the *Soma*-preparation rites, we know the reference of the hymn and can, accordingly, select the appropriate ritual meanings in order to produce a correct interpretation of the text: *sā́nu-* "the surface of the strainer," *jāmáyaḥ* "sisters' denote the priest's fingers (compare the other meanings of the word: "brothers and sisters," "blood relatives," "members of a family");

hári- (literally "yellowish," "golden") denotes *Soma* because of its color; *ádri-* "a pressing stone." It would be interesting to note how the meanings change when these words are used in a mythological context, such as: *ví jayúṣā yayathuḥ sā́nv ádrer* . . . (1.117.16) "You two have driven along the *mountain-top* in (your) victorious (*chariot*)" (about the *Aśvins* driving across the sky.) Another mythological verse contains a play on the various denotations of the word *hári-*:

dyā́m índro háridhāyasam
pṛthivī́ṃ hárivarpasam
ádhārayad dharítor bhū́ri bhójanaṃ
yáyor antár hárиś cárat (3.44.3)

"*Indra* supported the sky that feeds the golden (one), and the earth that glows like gold, the plentiful nourishment (of these) two golden (ones), between which the golden (god) wanders."

In the first line, *hári-* as part of the compound is correlated with *Soma* or with the Sun, and in the second line with the earth. In the third line "the two golden ones" (*harít-*) denote Heaven-and-Earth; and in the fourth line, *hári-* is the Sun (according to Geldner) or *Indra* (according to *Sāyaṇa*—since the hymn is addressed to this god). In this way the various denotations of the word *hári-* are used in a pun within the bounds of a single mythological level. In another stanza that has been cited above (9.26.5), the formal indicator of the type of reference is found in the second line, as the phrases *háriṃ hi-* and *ádribhir hi-* are part of the *Soma pavamāna* phraseology and quite unambiguous in this sense.

The suggestive style of the hymns is often characterized by the double reference of a single word or phrase; there is a conscious tendency to achieve a simultaneous correlation with two levels, ritual and mythological, that may be seen, for instance, in 1.149.4 (a hymn to *Agni*):

abhí dvijánmā trī́ rocanā́ni
víśvā rájāṃsi śuśucānó asthāt
hótā yájiṣṭho apā́ṃ sadhásthe

"The twice-born one rose over the three bright spaces, / Blazing over all the voids, / The *hotar*-priest who is the best sacrificer at the confluence of waters." The phrase *apā́ṃ sadhásthe* "at the confluence of the waters" may refer both to the celestial sphere (where the three bright spaces belong), and to the ritual domain, since according to *Sāyaṇa*, the fire-altar used to be sprinkled with water. Another example of a double reference occurs in verse 9.64.17 (a *Soma*-hymn):

Marmṛjānā́sa āyávo
vṛ́thā samudrám índavaḥ
ágmann ṛtásya yónim ā́

"The powerfully clarified, full of vitality, / *Soma*-juices willingly went to the sea, / into the womb of the law." Both phrases (*samudrám* "into the sea" and *ṛtásya yónim ā́* "into the womb of the law") refer to the ritual sphere; in that context they denote a big vat where the clarified *Soma*-juices are mixed with several additives (water, milk, etc.). At the same time they can also have mythological connotations: they may denote the heavenly ocean of the mystic abode of the gods in heaven. Numerous other examples of this kind can be found elsewhere.

Another important feature of the vocabulary of the *Ṛg Veda* is the symbolic use of words with a very concrete basic meaning, particularly a small group of words denoting body-parts. Some of these words are more frequently used in their symbolic meaning (at the ritual and cosmic levels) while their basic, literal meanings are overshadowed. Obviously, no question of polysemy arises, since this is a clear metaphorical transfer of a single basic meaning onto different, but isomorphic levels. On a purely linguistic level, such words frequently make up fixed phrasal unities when joined with other words; the latter can belong to a single reference level as, for example, *devā́nāṃ cákṣus* "the gods' eye;" "the sun," or they may refer to several levels, as *amṛ́tasya nā́bhiḥ* "the navel of immortality" refers to (1) an altar, (2) the heavenly center, and (3) *Soma* or another sacrificial drink. The group of words for body-parts consists of the following nouns:

Ákṣi-, *akṣí-* "*eye:*"

1) (primary meaning) . . . *ā́kṣī́ ṛjrā́śve aśvināv adhattaṃ / jyótir andhā́ya cakrathur vicákṣe* (1.117.17) " . . . to *Ṛjrāśva*, O *Aśvins*, you have granted *eyes*. / You have done (it) so that the blind (man) has been the light;"

2) (secondary meanings) *ádhi śríyaṃ ní dadhuś cā́rum asmin / divó yád akṣī́ amṛ́tā ákṛṇvan* (1.72.10) "The immortals bestowed magic beauty upon him, / When they were creating the (two) *eyes* of heaven" ("him" refers to *Agni*, and "the two eyes of heaven" to the sun and moon).

Ū́dhar- "*udder:*"

1) (primary meaning) *ádhvaryavaḥ páyasódhar yáthā góḥ / sómebhir īm pṛṇatā bhojám índram* (2.14.10) "O you *adhvaryu*-priests! As the cow's *udder* (swells) with milk, / Fill the generous *Indra* with *Soma*-spurts!;"

2) (secondary meanings) *dunánty ū́dhar divyā́ni dhū́tayo / bhū́mim pinvanti páyasā párijrayaḥ* (1.64.5) "The Shakers milk the heavenly

udder. / The ones who rush around make the earth swell with milk" (to the *Maruts*, "the heavenly udder" is a rain-cloud, and "milk" is "rain"); *duhāná ū́dhar divyám mádhu priyám / pratnáṃ sadhástham ā́sadat* (9.107.5) "Having allowed them to milk the lovely mead from the heavenly *udder*, / (*Soma*) used to sit upon (his) primordial spot" (*Soma's* heavenly udder" was a celestial source from which flowed the mead-*Soma*, and following which he descended to the earth); *sunvánti sómaṃ rathirā́so ádrayo / . . . / duhánty ū́dhar upasécanāya kám / . . .* (10.76.7) "The hasty pressing stones press *Soma*; / . . . / They milk the *udder* to pour out a little (milk *viz. Soma*)" ("the udder" is the the the Soma-plant from which the juice is pressed); *tā́ tū́ te satyā́ tuvinṛmṇa víśvā / prá dhenávaḥ sisrate vṛ́ṣṇa ū́dhnaḥ* (4.22.6) "All these thy (feats) are true, O (god) of powerful virility: / The milch-cows are running out of the bull's *udder*" (a Vedic paradx: rain-streams flow out of the udder of Heaven or *Parjanya* "udder").

Gárbha- "womb," "entrails," "embryo,"
"fruit," "a newborn child," "offspring:"

1) (primary meaning) *gárbhe nú sánn ánv eṣām avedam / ahám devā́nāṃ jánimāni víśvā* (4.27.1) "Still being in the (mother's) *womb*, I knew / All the generations of these gods;" *yáthā vā́taḥ puṣkaríṇīṃ / samiṅgáyati sarvátaḥ / evá te gárbha ejatu / . . .* (5.78.7) "As the wind stirs up a lotus pond on all sides, / so let thy *embryo* stir!."

2) (secondary meanings) *ásūdayat sukṛ́te gárbham ádriḥ* (3.31.7) "The rock made (its) *fruit* ripe for the benefactor" (i.e., the *Vala*-rock opened up and gave out to *Indra* all it contained: milch cows, light, etc., just like a mother's womb when the time came); *asmā́ ukthā́ya párvatasya gárbho / mahī́nāṃ janúṣe pūrvyā́ya* (5.45.3) "Before this hymn the mountain's *entrails* (were agape) / For the first birth of the great (dawns)" (the *Vala*-myth); *yám ā́po ádrayo vánā / gárbham ṛtásya píprati . . .* (6.48.5) "Who the waters, the stones, the trees / feed as the *offspring* of the cosmic law . . . " (*Agni*); *tám íd gárbham prathamáṃ dadhra ā́po / yátra devā́ḥ samā́gachanta víśve* (10.82.6) "It was he whom the waters received as the first *embryo*, / In whom all the gods came together." Finally, in cosmogonic speculations, an important role was assigned to *hiraṇyagarbhá-* "the golden germ:" *hiraṇyagarbháḥ sám avartatā́gre / bhū́tásya jātáḥ pátir éka āsīt* (10.121.1) "In the beginning he arose as the golden *germ*. / After being born he was the one lord of (all) creation."

Cákṣus- "eye," "sight:"

1) (primary meaning) *ví me kárṇā patayato ví cákṣur / vídāṃ jyótir hṛ́daya ā́hitaṃ yát / ví me mánaś carati dūrā́ādhīḥ / . . .* (6.9.6) "My ears fly up, my

eye flies up, / (Flies) up this light that has been put into the heart, / (Soars) up my mind rushing into the distance. / . . . "(a self-description of a poet inspired by *Agni-Vaiśvānara*);
2) (secondary meaning) *úd u jyótir amṛ́taṃ viśvájanyaṃ / viśvā́naraḥ savitā́ devó aśret / krátvā devā́nām ajaniṣṭa cákṣur / . . .* (7.76.1) "The god *Savitar*, belonging to all people, sent / Upwards the immortal light, destined for all the tribes. / The gods' *eye* was born on the (gods') behest" ("the gods' eye" is the sun).

Tvác- "skin, hide:"

1) (primary meaning) *tvám makhásya dódhātaḥ / śíró 'va tvacó bharaḥ* (10.171.2) "Thou hast severed the head of the furious *Makha* from the *skin*" (about *Indra*); *mánave śā́sad avratā́n / tvácaṃ kṛṣṇā́m arandhayat* (1.130.8) "Punishing the vowless (people) for the sake of *Manu*, / He subjected to him the black *skin*" (i.e., *Indra* subjected the aboriginal tribes of the *Dāsas/ Dasyus* to the Aryans); *gavyáyī tvág bhavati nirṇíg avyáyī* (9.70.7) "The *hide* may be the cow's, the festive garb—the sheep's" (about ritual tools for *Soma*-pressing);
2) (secondary meanings) *ójiṣṭhaṃ te madhyató méda údbhṛtam / prá te vayáṃ dadāmahe / ścótanti te vaso stokā́ ádhi tvací / . . .* (3.21.5) "The strongest fat, extracted for thee from the middle, we offer (it) to thee, O *Vasu*, the drops flow for thee down onto the *hide*" (*Agni*'s hide is the flame);

yád īm ṛtásya páyasā píyāno
náyann ṛtásya pathíbhī rájiṣṭhaiḥ
aryamā́ mitró váruṇaḥ párijmā
tvácam pṛñcanty úparasya yónau (1.79.3)

"But when (*Agni*), swollen with the moisture of the cosmic law, / (Moves along) the straightest paths of the law, conducting (this moisture), / (Then) *Aryaman, Mitra, Varuṇa* who is (everywhere) around, / soak the *hide* in the womb of the nether (space)" (where "the hide" is the surface of the earth);

ayáṃ cakrám iṣaṇat sū́ryasya
ny étaśaṃ rīramat sasṛmāṇám
ā́ kṛṣṇá īṃ juhurāṇó jigharti
tvacó budhné rájaso asyá yónau (4.17.14)

"He set in motion the sun's wheel. / He stopped *Etaśa* who had run forth. / Angered, he hurls him upon the bottom / Of the *skin* / into the lap of the dark space" / ("He" is *Indra*; Etaśa is the solar horse; and the black bottom of the skin denotes the darkness of the night);

Nā́bhi- "navel:"

1) (primary meaning) *nā́bhyā āsīd antárikṣam / śīrṣṇó dyaúḥ sám avartata* (10.90.14) "From his *navel* came the aerial space, / From his head the sky evolved" (about the cosmic giant *Puruṣa*, whose different parts became elements of the universe);
2) (secondary meaning)

saṃgáchamāne yuvatī́ sámante
svásarā jāmī́ pitrór upásthe
abhijíghrantī bhúvanasya nā́bhiṃ
dyā́vā rákṣatam pṛthivī no ábhvāt (1.185.5)

"The two youthful sisters, blood relatives, joining in the parents' womb, sharing a common boundary, kissing the *navel* of the created world . . . O Sky and Earth, guard us from Terror!" ("the two youthful sisters" are the Sky and Earth, and "the navel of the created world" is "the center of the universe"); *ātmanván nábho duhyate ghṛtám páya / ṛtásya nā́bhir amṛ́taṃ ví jāyate* (9.74.4) "From the living cloud ghee and milk are milked. / The *navel* of the law, the ambrosia is born" (a description of the *Soma*-pressing ritual in which the critical moment, "the navel of the Law," is the appearance of the juice necessary for "the drink of immortality"; *úd u ṣṭutáḥ samídhā yahvó adyaud / várṣman divó ádhi nā́bhā pṛthivyā́ḥ* (3.5.9) "And the glorified youth (*Agni*) blazed up thanks to the fire-wood on the top of heaven, on the *navel* of the earth" ("top of heaven" is the sun in the sky, and "navel of the earth" is the offering fire on the sacrificial ground).

Pṛṣṭhá- "the back:"

1) *iśudhíḥ sáñkāḥ pṛ́tanāś ca sárvāḥ / pṛṣṭhé nínaddho jayati prásūtaḥ* (6.75.5) "The quiver strapped on a *back* wins the skirmishes and all the battles when it is set to work;" *kvà vó 'śvāḥ kvā̀bhī́śavaḥ / . . . / pṛṣṭhé sádo nasór yámaḥ* (5.61.2) "Where are your horses? Where (the) reins? . . . (Where is) the saddle on the (horses's) *back*? (Where is) the bit in the nostrils?;"
2) *átyo ná pṛṣṭhám pruṣitásya rocate* (1.58.2) "His *back* shines like a stallion's (back) when he is washed (with ghee)" (about the sacrificial fire; *Agni* whose constant epithet is *ghṛtápṛṣṭha-* "ghee-backed").

abhí kṣípaḥ sám agmata
marjáyantīr iṣás pátim
pṛṣṭhā́ gṛbhṇata vājínaḥ (9.14.7)

"The fingers have joined, / Polishing the lord of sacrificial delight; / They grab the backs of the race-horse" (about *Soma*, depicted as a race-horse whose back is polished by the priest's fingers); *ví tvád ā́po ná párvatasya pṛṣṭhā́d / ukthébhir indrānayanta yajñaíḥ* (6.24.6) "From thee, O *Indra*, they conduct (their procession) with (their) hymns and rites, like waters (streaming down) from the mountain ridge;" *nā́kasya pṛṣṭhé ádhi tiṣṭhati śṛtó* (1.125.5) "He rests, supported by the sky's *vault*" (literally "back"); *eté pṛṣṭhā́ní ródasor viprayánto vy ā́nacuḥ* (9.22.5) "These (*Soma*-juices), spreading around, reached the *backs* of the two worlds" (i.e., the sky and earth).

Mūrdhán- "head:"

1) (primary meaning) yás ta idhmáṃ jabhárat siṣvidānó / mūrdhā́naṃ vā tatápate tvāyā́ / bhúvas tásya svátavām̐ pāyúr agne / (4.2.6) "He who brings thee firewood, sweating profusely, / Or (he) who sets (his) *head* on fire because of (his) love for thee, / Be thou a self-powered protector for him, O Agni!"

2) (secondary meanings) *yā́ni sthā́nāny aśvinā dadhā́the / . . . / ní párvatasya mūrdháni sádantā- / íṣaṃ jánāya dāśúṣe vahantā* (7.70.3) "(Those) places which you have taken up, O *Aśvins*, / . . . / Sitting upon the mountain-top, . . . / (From there ride) to the people honoring (you), bring the sacrificial delight!" ("the mountain-top" is literally, the mountain's head"); *agnír mūrdhā́ diváḥ kakút / pátiḥ pṛthivyā́ ayám* (8.44.16) "*Agni* is the *head*, the peak; / He is the lord of the earth;" *mūrdhā́ bhuvó bhavati náktam agnís* (10.88.6) "At night *Agni* is (always) the *head* of the world;" *mūrdhán yajñásya sám anaktu devā́n* (2.3.2) "As *head* of the sacrifice he shall unite the gods" (he is *Agni*); *yáj jātavedo bhúvanasya mūrdhánn / átiṣṭho agne sahá rocanéna* (10.88.5) "Since thou, O *Jāta-Vedas*, hast taken the stand with (thy) light as *head* of the universe . . . '; *eṣá nṛ́bhir ví nīyate / divó mūrdhā́ vṛ́ṣā sutáḥ / sómo váneṣu viśvavít* (9.27.3) "This (juice) is passed by men (through the strainer), / The sky's *head*, the pressed(-out) bull, / *Soma*, in the wooden (vessels), (he is) the omniscient (one)."

Yóni- "womb," "lap:"

1) (primary meaning)

yás te gárbham ámīvā
durṇā́mā yónim āśáye
agníṣ ṭám bráhmaṇā sahá
níṣ kravyā́dam anīnaśat (10.162.2)

"That mangy one with an evil name, who lay down upon thy embryo, upon (thy) *womb*, / *Agni* will drive away that flesh-eater with an incantation!" (a charm against evil creatures that harm an embryo);

2) (secondary meanings) *yóniṣ ṭa indra niṣáde akāri* (1.104.1) "O *Indra*, a *lap* has been prepared for thee to sit down upon" (the "lap" is the sacrificial straw mat); *ghṛtám asya yónir . . .* (2.3.11) "Ghee is his *womb/lap*" (about *Agni* on whom ghee is poured); *sī́da hotaḥ svá u loké cikitvā́n / sādáyā yajñáṃ sukṛtásya yónau* (3.29.8) "Sit down, O *hotar*, skilled one, upon (thy) place! / Set the sacrifice on the *lap* of the good deed!" (about *Agni*); *ṛtásya yónau sukṛtásya loké / 'riṣṭāṃ tvā sahá pátyā dadhāmi* (10. 85.24) "In the *lap* of the law, in the world of the good deed / I set thee unharmed with (thy) husband" (benediction for the bride in the wedding hymn); . . . / *yónāv ṛtásya sīdatam / pātáṃ sómam ṛtāvṛdhā* (3.62.18) " . . . sit (both of you) on the *lap* of the law. / Drink *Soma*, O (you) law-confirmers!" (an invocation of *Mitra* and *Varuṇa*; "the lap of the law" is the place of offering).

This use of a series of words denoting human body-parts as metaphors for elements of the universe cannot be accidental in the *Ṛg Veda*. The key to its understanding should be sought in the model of the universe as seen by the *Ṛg Veda* Aryans. The archaic idea that the universe originated from the body of the gigantic primordial man who was sacrificed by the gods is clearly reflected in the *Puruṣa*-hymn 10.90. In this hymn a system of equivalences between the microcosm and the macrocosm is established. It has already been noted [40.215-28] that *Puruṣa* is characterized particularly by the opposition of totality and segmentation which enables the process of universe-generation to begin. The plot motivates the movement from one member of the opposition to the other, and in its turn, can reflect a certain ritual. This type of correspondence between parts of the body and cosmic elements had a long future in the Old Indian tradition, and its variants are also attested in other archaic cultures.[24] In the *Ṛg Veda*, this system of equivalences becomes operational because the two series of elements are interchangeable. Hence the idea of semantic transfer, or metaphor, in the use of a vocabulary of human body-parts.

The text of the *Puruṣa*-hymn belongs to the semiotic sphere wherein the head is the sign for the sky, the eye is the sign for the sun, etc. Thus we see an interplay of paradigmatic equivalences which are transferred into syntamatics, i.e., into the text. A single denotation is connected with two notions which are quite different, from the modern point of view. Such a situation is remarkable on two counts. First, it could be based on the the existing awareness of the identity of these two series, since the macrocosm and the microcosm are, generally speaking, isomorphic. Thus they could possibly have different names, but they are essentially manifestations of a single "arch-name." For theVedic model of the universe, identity is the conceptual framework wherein everything takes its due place. This is the collective heritage which is revitalized again and again by the poet-*Ṛṣi* in his creative activity. Second, the *Ṛṣi*'s generalizing and classifying work creates "a body code" of the cosmos. The evolution of this code can be illustrated as follows: "head" becomes "head of the sky." The *Ṛg Veda* reflects the second stage, that is, the explanatory collocations, much more consistently. Immediate identifications of the terms of the two series are rather infrequent, though examples do show some survivals. The further elaboration of these metaphorical phrases by the poets, being a purely literary device, results in an ever-growing erosion of the original identity.

An extreme case of polysemy in the *Ṛg Veda* is represented by the lexical group in which broadly opposed meanings within the semantics of a single word are combined. Here polysemy borders on antonymy, or even enantiosemy, an obvious paradox. This phenomenon is attested in the *Ṛg Veda*, and this semantic type can be met with both in noun (substantives and adjectives, primary and composite terms) and in verbs.

The key to the interpretation of this phenomenon was found by Renou in his fundamental "L'ambiguité du vocabulaire du Ṛgveda" [117.161-235]. He was the first to draw attention to the circumstance that *Rig Veda* lexicon can be divided into two zones: the "auspicious" in which the gods are included and the humans under their protection, and the less differentiated "inauspicious" layer, denoting forces that are inimical to gods and poets. One and the same word can have both a "positive" and a "negative" meaning on its particular "zone" context.

This concerns, in the first place, a rather numerous class of verbal roots. In a few cases the semantic difference is not connected with any corresponding morphological difference, for example, *ruṣ-*, *róṣati* "to undo" and "to perish;" *yu-*, *yóṣati* "to separate" and "to be separated;" *pī́-*, *pī́yati* "to insult"and "to be despised." However, in most cases semantic differences are reflected in grammatical opositions: "primary verb" *vs.* "causative," "passive" *vs.* "active." Sometimes the opposition in meaning corresponds (wholly or in part) to the difference in stem-classes. For instance, the verb *ar-* has the stem *ṛchá-* and the aorist *ā́rat* when an attacking enemy or a devasting sickness is involved, but forms other stems when describing favorable or neutral actions. Individual forms of a verb that has generally "auspicious" connotations may be used in a "negative" sense, and vice versa. The same ambivalence is characteristic of a certain number of nouns. Primarily it concerns epithets that can describe both gods and their opponents as, for example, *aprati-*, meaning both "irresistible" and "showing no resistance," adjectives of spatial orientation used with various prefixes that modify their meaning.

Renou also noted the ambivalence of certain proper names, mostly belonging to the mythological cycle of *Indra*, such as *Kútsa-*, who figures both as *Indra*'s favorite charioteer and his enemy. Some ethnonyms from the same cycle also share this semantic ambiguity, as do some theonyms.[25] Sometimes this phenomenon manifests itself in the transfer of the enemies' attributes to the gods and their worshippers, while sometimes quite the opposite is true. Such reversibility of actions and formulas of the two zones, attested for the *Ṛg Veda*, is a peculiar trait of the magical outlook in general. Renou summed up his research with the flowing remark: In the end, these features of Vedic sytle together with the conditions of the sacral milieu appear to be the decisive factors in the orientation that was acquired by its vocabulary" [117.235].

The importance of Renou's work can certainly be judged by these overt conclusions concerning the ambivalent semantics of a certain part of the Vedic lexicon. But equally important are some indirect results of his description that can be defined in the following way. In the language of the *Ṛg Veda* the stylistic level ranks as the highest in the linguistic hierarchy. Grammatical oppositions are not necessarily universal: a given formal opposition does not always correspond to a semantic one. In the same way, a single derivational pattern in word-formation can be interpreted differently on the semantic level. These conclusions can be of importance for the further stylistic and functional study of *Ṛg Veda* vocabulary.

The "auspicious" domain in the *Ṛg Veda* is vast and considerably elaborated. On the other hand, the "inauspicious" level is comparatively undifferentiated; this act may be due to proscriptive considerations. As noted above, Renou established the presence of a layer of ambivalent vocabulary with changeable meaning dependent on its "zone." Using this method, we should be able to go further and discover within the "auspicious" zone a certain group of lexical units which undergo a semantic shift if included either within the domain of the deity of within that of the worshipper. This particular archaic lexical stratum contains the semantic reflexes of the Vedic model of the universe (see "Introduction," above). The idea of an exchange between the deity and the worshipper is lexically expressed by a "conversive" meaning[26] attested for a whole group of "auspicious" words. This meaning acquires a different logical emphasis in different contexts. In the *Ṛg Veda*, its directionality can vary, depending on the word's association with a god or his worshipper [70.129-136]. In this way, the "auspicious" zone itself can be seen as bipartite. It should be stressed that the ambivalent vocabulary of "auspicious" *vs.* "inauspicious" does not take part in the bifurcation of the "auspicious" zone. These two lexical subsystems can be viewed as two nonintersecting sub-multitudes. Moreover, the conversive meaning of the "auspicious" is attested in various morphological and derivational classes: verbs, substantives and adjectives, primary words and compounds. Before describing the distribution of conversive meaning among forms derived from a common verbal-root, a small group of verbs should be discussed. Their meanings cannot be labelled "conversive," but they can be combined with different object-classes, and consequently, they may encode quite different actions. The meanings of such verbs depend on the reference-class of their subjects—either deity or worshipper. Some examples:

jan- "to give birth to, to generate:"
subject (1): gods; objects: the universe, the sun, the dawns, etc.;
subject (2): worshippers; objects: sacrifice, prayer, song, etc.;

1) *yá imé dyā́vapṛthivī́ jajā́na* (4.56.3) "Who *gave birth* to Heaven and Earth" (about a god—compare 1.160.4); *índro nṛ́bhir ajanad dī́dyānaḥ / sākáṃ sū́ryam uṣásaṃ gātúm agním* (3.31.15) "*Indra*, together with (his) men (-the *Maruts*), shining, *gave birth* / At the same time to the sun, the dawn, the (unobstructed) way, and fire;"
2) *ásmai te pratihāryate / jā́tavedo vícarṣaṇe / ágne jánāmi suṣṭutím* (8.43.2) "For thee, (who is) so joyfully waiting, / O Jātavedas, the far-moving, / O *Agni*, I *generate* this laudation;" *vaiśvānarā́ya dhiṣáṇām ṛtāvṛ́dhe / ghṛtáṃ ná pūtám agnáye janāmasi* (3.2.1) "For Vaiśvānara, the law-enhancer, we generate a poetic offering, clarified like ghee."

If the subject of the verb *jan-* has a deity as its referent, the verb is in the second person (addressed to the deity), or in the third person of a past tense (for a description of his feats), since the universe "was generated" in the past. But if the referent happens to be the worshipper, the verb is usually in the first person singular of the present. In this way the verbal grammatical categories indirectly differentiate the various referent-classes of the subject. In the contexts of the first group the verb *jan-* is functionally synonymous with other verbs encoding the cosmogonic act. In the contexts of the second group this verb is synonymous with verbs with the meaning "to sacrifice," "to donate," etc.

Tan- "to draw, to pull" (*ā́* + *tan-* "to stretch, to extend;" "to pierce"):
Among the numerous meanings attributable to this verb in the "deity-worshipper" interrelationship, the following object-opposition may be proposed:[27]

subject (1): gods; objects: cosmic elements wherein light is extended (*ā́* + *tan-*);
subject (2): worshippers; objects: sacrifice, prayer, etc.;

1) *ā́ dyā́ṃ tanoṣi raśmíbhir*
ā́ntárikṣam urú priyám
úṣaḥ śukréṇa ṣocíṣā (4.52.7)

"Thou *piercest* the sky (with thy) rays, / The wide glorious aerial space, / O *Uṣas*, (with thy) pure blaze;"

2) *víśvā matī́r ā́ tatane tvāyā́- / ádhā ma īndra śṛṇavo hávemā́* (7.29.3) "All the prayers I have *extended* to thee with love. / So listen to these calls of mine, O *Indra*!"

Bhar- "to carry" (*ā́* + *bhar-* "to bring"):
subject (1): gods; objects: wealth, gifts, power, glory, etc.;
subject (2): worshippers; objects: sacrifice, prayer, etc.;

1) *tám íd va índraṃ suhávaṃ huvema / . . . / yó mā́vate jaritré gádhyaṃ cin / makṣū́ vā́jam bharati* . . . (4.16.16) "We wish to call for your sake this easily-invoked *Indra* / . . . / who *brings* swiftly to a poet like me / The spoils that are to be seized(?) . . . ;"

sá na stávāna ā́ bhara
gātatréṇa návīyasā
rayíṃ vīrávatīm íṣam (1.12.11)

"Glorified with a new song, *bring* us wealth and support (consisting in) sons!;"

2) *asmā́ íd u tyám upamáṃ svarṣā́m / bhárāmy āñgūṣám āsyèna* (1.61.3) "It is to him I *bring* (with my) mouth / This highest, sun-winning, praise;" *bharéndrāya sómaṃ* (2.21.1) "*Bring Soma* to *Indra*!" (addressed to the priest).

Cud- "to sharpen," "to inspire," "to urge, to stimulate:"
subject (1): gods; objects: worshippers encouraged to battle, sacrifice, prayer; chariots, prayers, gifts;
subject (2): worshippers; objects: gods urged to donate gifts;

1) *asmā́n samaryé pavamāna codaya* (9.85.2) "*Sharpen* us for the fight, O *Pavamāna*!;" *tváṃ hí śū́raḥ sánitā / codáyo mánuṣo rátham* (1.175.2) "But thou art a hero (and) procurer. / *Urge* on the man's chariot!;"

2) *táṃ=tam íd rā́dhase mahá / índraṃ codāmi pītáye* (8.68.7) "Only him, *Indra*, I *inspire* for the great donation, for drinking."

The relations are somwehat obscured when the worshipper addresses the mediating gods, *Agni* and *Soma*, asking them to urge other gods to be liberal in gift-giving, for example: *tvám̐ no devátātaye rāyó dā́nāya codaya* (10.141.6) "*Encourage* the gods to endow us with wealth!" (to *Agni*); *yé te mádā . . . tébhir índram̐ codaya dā́tave maghám* (9.75.5) "Those thine intoxicating juices . . . *stimulate Indra* (with) them to donate a generous gift!."

Budh- "to awake(n)," "to notice," "to endow:"

subject (1): gods; objects: worshippers awakened for gift-receiving; invocations, sacrifices,etc.;
subject (2): worshippers; objects: gods awakened for gift-giving;

1) *juṣéthām̐ yajñám bódhatam̐ hávasya me* (2.36.6) "You both, enjoy the sacrifice! Take *notice* of my invocation! (to *Mitra* and *Varuṇa*);"

mahé no adyá bodhaya-
úṣo rāyé divítmatī
yáthā cinno ábodhayaḥ
satyáśravasi vāyyé
sújāte áśvasūnṛte (5.79.1)

"Awaken us today for great wealth, / O Uṣas, full of radiance, / Just as thou wokest us / At *Satyaśravas Vayya*'s (place), O noble one, generously donating horses!;"

2) *bódhāmasi tvā haryaśva yajñaír / bódhā na stómam ándhaso mádeṣu* (7.21.1) "We *awaken* thee, O (master) of dun horses, with sacrifices. / Heed our praise in (thy) intoxication with the *Soma*-juice!;"[28] *ghṛtaír bodhayatā́tithim* (8.44.1) ("With streams of ghee *awaken* the guest!") (*Agni*).

The primary stem *bódha-* and the causative *bodháya-* are used indifferently with both subject-classes.

The third person singular aorist passive *ábodhi*, with a passive or intransitive meaning, occurs exclusively with the subject of a god who either has been aroused by his worshippers or has awakened himself in order to enrich and support them. As a rule, this meaning is implicitly contained in a wider context; but quite explicit is, for example, 5.1.1-2: *ábodhy agníḥ samídhā jánānām* (1) "Agni is *awakened* by the people's firewood;" *ábodhi hótā yajáthāya devā́n* (2) "The *hotar* (*Agni*) has awakened to honor the gods."

Śru- "to hear:"

subject (1): gods; objects: worshippers, invocations, prayers, etc.;
subject (2): worshippers; objects: gods with positive qualities; various goods;

1) . . . *indra . . . śrudhí naḥ* (1.133.6) "O *Indra*, hear us!;" *ádhā ma indra śr̥ṇavo hávemā́* (7.29.3) "So, O *Indra, hear* these calls of mine!;"
2) *evā́ hí tvā́m r̥tuthā́ yātáyantam / maghā́ víprebhyo dádataṃ śr̥ṇómi* (5.32.12) "And I also *hear* that thou rewardest in time, / Making generous presents to the inspired ones;" *bhadráṃ kárṇebhiḥ śr̥ṇuyāma devā / bhadrám paśyemākṣábhir yajatrāḥ* (1.89.8) "The beautiful (thing), let us hear (it) with (our) ears, O gods! The beautiful (thing), let us see (it) with (our) eyes, O you, worthy of sacrifice!."

If the referent of its object is a deity, the verb *śru-* regularly appears with a double accusative, and the predicative accusative always denotes a positive quality, such as *revánt* (8.2.11), "wealthy;" *bhiṣáktama-* (2.33.4) "best-healing;" *sátpati-pā́ñcajanya-* (5.32.11) "the good lord of five tribes;" *śiśayá-* (10.42.3) "generous;" *svavŕ̥j-* (10.38.5) "possessing his own might." These epithets, included in the predicate group, have a suggestive, or evocative, function.[29] The deity was supposed to display towards the worshipper those divine positive qualities that he had heard so much about.

In summing up we could say that the first three verbs represent various aspects of the same "deep" action of serving the deity when the subject is a worshipper. The specific forms of such service—making a sacrifice or a laudatory song, extending it to the deity, or offering it—are dependent upon the proper lexical meaning of each of these verbs. In this way verbs with different meanings can become synonymous in the context of the exchange between god and his worshipper. The latter three verbs seem to have a symmetrical predicate as regards their class of subjects and objects. Putting it differently, if x is the subject-class, then y (at least, in part) is in the object-class, and vice versa, (where x = gods, any y = worshippers). None of these verbs has conversive meanings, but there are differences in syntactical constructions, determined by the respective subject-class. The list of such verbs is obviously far from complete. Sometimes the same verb has forms that differ in the choice of direct object and syntactical constructions, and on the other hand, there are forms with conversive meanings.

Here we shall discuss some of those verbs whose meanings appear to be conversive when their subjects are either gods or their worshippers. It ought to be mentioned at this point that quite often conversive meanings only partly represent the total semantic range of a given verb.

Kan-, kā- (*ā́ + kan-*) "to rejoice," "to be satisfied"—
"to seek," "to strive to cause joy:"

1) *ā́ yāhi kr̥ṇávāma te / índra bráhmāṇi várdhanā / yébhiḥ śaviṣṭha cākáno/* . . . (8.62.4) "Come! We want to compose for thee, / O *Indra*, invigorating prayers, / Through which, O Mightiest (one), thou shalt be *joyful*! . . . ;"

2) *tásmin sumnā́ni yájamāna ā́ cake* (3.3.3) "The sacrificer seeks to obtain favors fromhim" (*Agni*).

dāś- "to make a donation" ← "to honor" → "to serve (a god):"

1) *só apratī́ni mánave purū́ṇi- / índro dāśad dāśúṣe hánti vṛtrám* (2.19.4) "For the sake of man he (kills) numerous (enemies), who know not (their) equals; / *Indra honors* the one who *honors* (him); he slays Vṛtra;" *yásmai tvám̥ sudraviṇo dádāśo / 'nāgāstvám adite sarvátātā / . . . té syāma* (1.94.15) "O possessor of excellent wealth, to whom thou presentest as a gift / The full measure of sinlessness, O *Aditi* . . . we should like to be (similar) to those people!;" The verb *dāś*- in this meaning is normally used with a direct-object accusative (without mentioning the indirect object), or with an indirect-object dative.

2) *yó vām̥ yajñaíḥ śaśamānó ha dā́śati / . . . úpā́ha tám̥ gáchatho vīthó adhvarám* (1.151.7) "(He) who, exerting himself, *serves* you two with sacrifices, / . . . / Him you visit (and) taste (his) offering" (to *Mitra-Varuṇa*); this meaning of the verb *dāś*- requires a direct-object accusative and an indirect-object instrumental.

The meaning "to honor" belongs to both areas. When the subject is a deity, the "honoring" of the worshipper is expressed by *Indra*'s slaying of his foes and granting the worshipper those physical and spiritual advantages that he asks of the god. The subject-worshipper honors the god by means of sacrifices and hymns offered to him. In other words, this particular meaning of the verb *dāś*- could be included in the first group of non-conversives.

dhā- "to put, set, fix, arrange," "to create:"

Various forms of this verb are quite numerous and have a wide currency in the *Rig Veda*, but the conversive meaning is attested on the periphery of its paradigm, namely, in the desiderative stem: "to wish to create" (goods for the worshipper)—"to seek to establish oneself" (in the god's favors);

1) *té devā́saḥ sváravas tasthivā́m̥saḥ / prajā́vad asmé didhiṣantu rátnam* (3.8.6) "These erected divine posts, / Let them *strive to create* for us a treasure, consisting of progeny . . . ;"

2) *índreṇa mitrám̥ didhiṣema gīrbhír* (8.96.6) "We *should like to obtain* friendship with *Indra* by means of (our) songs!."

Pan- "to cause admiration"—"to show admiration:"

1) *nūnám̥ só asya mahimā́ paniṣṭa* (8.45.2) "Now this greatness of his *arouses admiration*" (a hymn to *Savitar*);

2) *índram̥ namasyā́ jaritúḥ pananta* (10.104.7) "The singer's praises *declare (his) admiration* for *Indra*."

Bādh- "to banish" (the enemy, the dark forces), "to widen" (the limits of the universe)—"to attack," "to besiege" (a god):

1) *pávamāna bā́dhase soma śátrūn* (9.94.5) "O *Soma Pavamāna*, thou *drivest* the foes *off*;" *śáṃsa mitrásya váruṇasya dhā́ma / śúṣmo ródasī badbadhe mahitvā́* (7.61.4) "I wish to praise *Mitra*'s (and) *Varuṇa*'s custom. / Their fury will *separate* Heaven and Earth (through its) might;"
2) *asmā́ íd u práya iva prá yaṃsi / bhárāmy āṅgūṣám bā́dhe suvṛktí* (1.61.2) "This I hand to him as a refreshment, / I bring praise in order to assail (him) with happy words" (a hymn to *Indra*).

Bhaj- "to endow, to apportion" (*ā́ + bhaj-*, *ví + bhaj-*)—"to taste," "to achieve," "to obtain:"
1) *sá tváṃ na indra sū́rye só apsv / ánāgāstvá ā́ bhaja jīvaśaṃsé* (1.104.6) "Thou, O *Indra*, *endow* us with a portion of the sun, of the waters, / of innocence, of the speech of those (who are) alive!;" *ábhūd deváḥ savitā́ vándyo nú na / . . . / ví yó rátnā bhájati mānavébhyaḥ* (4.54.1) "Now god *Savitar* has appeared before us, (the one) worthy of praise, . . . who *apportions* treasures to men . . . ;"
2) *bhakṣīmáhi prajā́m íṣam* (7.96.6) "We would like to *obtain* offspring (and) reinforcement."

The second type of meaning is regular for stems in the middle voice, while the first type is more characteristic of those in the active voice.

Van- "to like, prefer," "to accept readily;" "to donate" — "to obtain," "to win," "to gain profit:"

1) *áṣvinā púrudaṃsasā*
nárā ṣávīrayā dhiyā́
dhíṣṇyā vánataṃ gíraḥ (1.3.2)

"O Aśvins, rich in wonders, / O you two heroes, with (great) attention / Accept (our) songs favorably, O reverential (ones)!;" *ghraṃsáṃ rákṣantam pári viśváto gáyam / asmā́kam śárma vanavat svā́vasuḥ* (5.44.7) "Let him *grant* us a swelling, protecting us on all sides from (his) heat, / A shelter (for us), he who possesses every boon" (he is the god *Sūrya*);
2) *kó vām adyá purūṇā́m / ā́ vavne mártyānām* (5.74.7) "Who—of all the mortals—has *won* you today for himself?;" *ṛtáṃ yemāná ṛtám íd vanoti* (4.23.10) "He who adheres to the law, *obtains* from the law."

Sap- "to accept reverence"—"to honor, revere," "to serve:"
1) *té sīṣapanta jóṣam ā́ yájatrāḥ* (7.43.4) "Let these (gods), worthy of sacrifices, accept the honors with pleasure;"

2) *índraṃ vo nárah sakhyā́ya sepur / mahó yántaḥ sumatáye cakānā́ḥ* (6.29.1) "The heroes *revere Indra* for you for the sake of (his) friendship, / (They) who come, desiring favors of the great (god)."

Sādh- "to bring to the goal," "to fulfil"—
"to achieve the goal," "to be fulfilled:"

1) *tā́ na stipā́ tanūpā́*
váruṇa jaritṝ́ṇā́m
mítra sādháyataṃ dhíyaḥ (7.66.3)

"These two defenders of our kin (and) of ourselves, / (These) singers, O *Varuṇa* / O *Mitra*, *help* (our) prayers *to achieve the goal*!;"
2) *sā́dhantām ugra no dhíyaḥ* (6.53.4) "Let our prayers be *fulfilled*, O Terrible One!."

Sūd- "to initiate (the worshipper)," "to make (him) worthy"—"to make (the sacrifice) tasty, delicious," "to spice," "to prepare," "to make well:"

1) *ná sá jīyate maruto ná hanyate*
ná sredhati ná vyathate ná riṣyati
nā́sya rā́ya úpa dasyanti nótáya
ṝ́ṣiṃ vā yáṃ rā́jānaṃ vā súṣūdatha (5.54.7)

"He is not oppressed, O Maruts, he is not killed, / He does not come to grief, he is not unsteady, he is not harmed, / Neither his wealth nor his provisions run out, / (He) whom you *initiate*, be he a *Ṛṣi* or be he a king!;" *yā́n rāyé mártān súṣūdo agne / té syāma maghávāno vayáṃ ca* (1.73.8) "Let us become—(together with our) generous (patrons)—those of the mortals whom thou, O *Agni*, *makest worthy* of wealth!;"

2) *yát te sādé máhasā śū́kṛtasya*
pā́rṣṇyā vā káśayā vā tutóda
srucéva tā́ havíṣo adhvaréṣu
sárvā tā́ te bráhmaṇā sūdayāmi (1.162.17)

"If, during a ride when thou snortest hard, / Thou hast been struck with heel or whip, / Then—as a ghee-ladle in the sacrifices (expiates errors), / All this I shall *make well* with prayer" (addressed to the sacrificial horse); *táṃ tvā ayám pito / vácobhir gā́vo ná havyā́ suṣūdima* (1.187.11) "O Food, we have made thee tasty (by means of) speeches, as cows (make) the oblations."

Although the semantics of this verb remains rather vague, and its meanings cannot be considered conversive, they still differ clearly when the subject of the verb is the god or the worshipper. This fact is also reflected in the corresponding syntactical constructions. Worthy of note is the case of *Agni* the *Hotar* priest, in which the deity takes on the functions of the worshipper: then the meaning of the verb and the syntactical construction belong to the second type, for example: *agnír havíḥ śamitā́ sūdayāti* (3.4.10) "*Agni* the meat-carver shall *make* the sacrifice *delicious*!."

Svad- "to taste, eat with pleasure"—"to prepare:"

1) *svádasva havyā́ sám íṣo didhīhi* (3.54.22) "Taste the oblations with delight! Light up the sacrificial provisions!" (to *Agni*);
2) *svádāmi gharmám* (1.119.2) "I am *preparing* a hot-milk drink."

As in the case of the preceding etymologically related verb, the subject here, whose referent is the divine mediator (*Agni*), is regularly equated with the worshipper.

Hi- "to make (the worshipper) hurry" (to obtain a boon), "to inspire (worshippers)," "to send (riches, etc.)"—"to incite (the mediating gods in sacrifices)," "to stimulate (gods to make gifts)," "to be assiduous (in rites)," "to set in motion."

1) *sá no mahā́m̐ animānó*
dhūmáketuḥ puruṣcandráḥ
dhiyé vā́jāta hinvatu (1.27.11)

"He, the great, the boundless one, / The smoke-ensign, the all-bright one / Let him *incite* us to inspiration (and) reward!"

yáṃ tváṃ vipra medhásātā
ágne hinóṣi dhánāya
sá távotī́ góṣu gántā (8.71.5)

"(He) whom thou, O inspired *Agni*, *drivest* to the reward, so that he should gain wisdom, / With thy help he shall come (to possess) the cows;" *tvé tán naḥ suvédam usríyaṃ vásu / yáṃ tváṃ hinóṣi mártyam* (8.4.16) "It is easy to obtain wealth (consisting of) cows from thee for that mortal (among) us whom thou *inspirest*;"
2) *kavíṃ ketúṃ dhāsím bhānúm ádrer / hinvánti śáṃ rājyáṃ ródasyoḥ* (7.6.2) "The poet, the ensign, the source, the ray, (the offspring) of the rock, / They *incite* him, the happiness and kingdom of the two worlds" (they are the priests; he is *Agni*);

táṃ duróṣam abhī́ nárah
sómaṃ viśvā́cyā dhiyā́
yajñáṃ hinvanty ádribhiḥ (9.101.3)

"The heroes (priests) *set in motion* this hard-to-ignite (?) *Soma* / With power-thought, directed everywhere, / (This) sacrifice (they drive) with pressing-stones;" *éte śámībhiḥ suśámī abhūvan / yé hinviré tanvàḥ sóma uktaíḥ* (10.28.12) "Those (men) distinguished themselves by (their) sacrificial devotion (and) generous donation / Who *were zealous* in (their) hymns at the *Soma*-(pressing)." Some forms of the verb *hi-* appear to have conversive meanings, while other forms differ in their direct-object referents. This seems to depend on whether the verb's subject refers to the deity or the worshipper.

In the *Ṛg Veda* nouns have "auspicious" conversive meanings with reference to a deity or worshipper much more frequently than verbs do, and this fact can be explained by the particularities of the Old Indian system of derivations. It is still standard doctrine, taken over from the Indian grammarians, that the verb-root is basic to both inflexion and derivation, since the number of noun-roots is rather limited. In theory any verbal root can acquire nominal functions; it is irrelevant that for some roots such nouns are not attested. In the *Ṛg Veda* the root-nouns are much more numerous than in any other Old Indian text; after the *Ṛg Veda* they gradually fell into disuse. If a verbal root has conversive meanings, they are also inherent in the corresponding root-noun. The nominal derivational affixes, with the exception of some types of participles, are indifferent to active/middle distinctions, a feature which afforded ample opportunity for the development of conversive meanings in primary derivatives, depending on their reference to deity or worshipper. Compounds have even greater opportunities in this respect, since their structure itself admits of different grammatical interpretations, and in the end, too much is simply determined by context. Compounds are indifferent to some important oppositions that are usually grammaticalized in the verbal system, and this indifference is often made use of when these compounds are involved in the "auspicious" zone of the relationship between deity and worshipper. Compound words make up about half of all nouns with conversive meanings.

Of all the primary nouns, the root-nouns only rarely have a conversive meaning that reflects the "circular" gift-exchange between deity and worshipper. This is attested only in the following nouns:

íṣ- (feminine) "strength," "freshness;" "well-being," "prosperity"—
"an invigorating sacrificial drink," "delight in sacrifice:"

1) *tā́m agne asmé íṣam érayasva*
vaiśvānara dyumátīṃ jātavedaḥ
yáyā rā́dhaḥ pínvasi viśvavāra
pṛthú śrávo dāśúṣe mártyāya (7.5.8)

"This *well-being*, O *Agni*, obtain (it) for us, / O *Vaiśvānara*, this glistening (prosperity), O Jātaveda, / Desirable for all (of us), (by means of) which thou makest swell (thy) power to bestow, / The wide fame for the mortal who honors (thee)!;"
2) *sáṃ vām kármaṇā sám iṣā́ hinomi- / índrāviṣṇū ápasas pāré asya* (6.69.1) "With rite (and) *invigorating drink* I incite both of you, / O *Indra* and *Viṣṇu*, at the end of this (sacrificial) effort."

Dhī́- (feminine) "attention," "understanding," "intention" (divine)—"(poetic) speech," "prayer" (uttered by the worshipper):

1) *áśvinā púrudaṃsasā*
nárā śávīrayā dhiyā́
dhíṣṇyā vánataṃ gíraḥ (1.3.2)

"O Aśvins, rich in wonders, / O you two heroes, with strained *attention*, / Accept favorably (our) voices, O reverential (ones)!;"

2) *evā́ no agne amŕ̥teṣu pūrvya*
dhī́ṣ pīpāya bṛháddiveṣu mā́nuṣā
dúhānā dhenúr vṛjáneṣu kāráve
tmánā śatínam pururū́pam iṣáṇi (2.2.9)

"Thus, O primordial *Agni*, human *poetic speech* has swollen up (with milk) for us among the immortal inhabitants of the high heaven, (speech) has become a milch-cow for the singer, among the sacrificing communities, so that it might by itself create a hundred-fold multiform reward."

But the bulk of noun stems with conversive meaning is derived from verbal roots with the help of various suffixes, both primary (including the stem-forming vowels) and secondary. Most numerous is the group of adjectives with secondary suffixes, where the most widely used suffix is *-yu-* (whose function may be considered only rarely primary). This suffix can be combined with nominal (and even pronominal) stems of various structure and has a range of meanings even wider than that of the conversives. Next in productivity is the suffix *ya-/-ia-*, also quite vague semantically, as it merely indicates some relation with the meaning of the primary stem. As such, it permits functionally different interpretations of the act "to give"/"to take"—depending upon whether the subject is the deity or the worshipper.

These nominal stems are as follows:

áma- (masculine) "impetuosity," "fury" (of a deity)—"scare, panic," "terror" (of mortal men):

1) *ṛ́kṣo ná vo marutaḥ śímīvāñ ámo / dudhró gaúr iva bhīmayúḥ* (5.56.3) "Your *onslaught*, O Maruts, (is as) mighty as a bear, / As terrible as an obstinate bull;"

> *yó devó devátamo jā́yamāno*
> *mahó vā́jebhir mahádbhiś ca śúṣmaiḥ*
> *dádhāno vájram bāhvór uśántaṃ*
> *dyā́m ámena rejayat prá bhū́ma* (4.22.3)

"The god who, being born as the most divine one, / Great in prizes and in mighty explosions of rage, / In his *fury* shakes Heaven (and) Earth, / When he takes into hands the thunderbolt (that) desires (it);"
2) *séneva sṛṣṭā́maṃ dadhāty / ástur ná didyút tveṣápratīkā* (1.66.7) "Like an army set loose, he inspires *terror*, / Like a bowman's lightning ("arrow") with a dreadful appearance" (about *Agni*); *tvám ádha prathamáṃ jā́ya-mánó / 'víśvā adhithā indra kṛṣṭī́ḥ* (4.17.7) "Being born, first of all, at that time, thou / castest all these peoples into *terror*, O *Indra*!" This noun, *áma-* stands out as not quite typical, since the subject of the act in both situations is a deity, not a worshipper, nor is any worshipper's attribute mentioned in the second situation. The lexical meaning of the noun *áma-* is, as it were, differently evaluated, depending on its relation to the divine or the human sphere. In the second instance, we have a surface phrase *ámaṃ dhā-* or *áme dhā-* "to cast into terror."

bhāgá- (masculine) "lot," "fate," "destiny," "prize"
(bestowed by the deity on the worshipper)—"the god's share in sacrifice:"

1) *yám indra dadhiṣé tvám*
áśvaṃ gā́m bhāgám ávyayam
yájamāne sunvatí dákṣiṇāvati
tásmin táṃ dhehi mā́ paṇaú (8.97.2)

"The horse (and) bull thou hast, O *Indra*, destined as the unchangeable *prize* / For the sacrificer, for the *Soma*-presser, for him who generously meets the sacrificial costs, / Give that (horse and bull) to him, not to a miser!;" *yaśásam bhāgáṃ kṛṇutaṃ no aśvinā / sómaṃ ná cā́rum maghávatsu nas kṛtam* (10.39.2) "Create a glorious *destiny* for us, O Aṣvins, / Make us delightful—like *Soma*—for the generous givers!;"
2) *práti vīhi prásthitaṃ somyám mádhu / píbā́gnīdhrāt táva bhāgásya tṛpṇuhi* (2.36.4) "Accept joyfully the offered sweetness of *Soma*! / Drink from the agnīdh (priest's) cup, be sated with thy *share*!."

vratá- (neuter) "(god's) behest," "divine law"—"(worshipper's) vow:"

1) *ánu pū́rvāṇy okyā̀*
sāmrājyásya saścima
mitrásya vratā́ váruṇasya dīrghaśrút (8.25.17)

"We have always followed the ancient customary (behests) of the emperor, / the long-heard *behests* of *Mitra* and *Varuṇa*;" *ánu vratáṃ savitúr móky ā́gāt* (2.38.3) "Night has come, obeying *Savitar*'s law;"
2) *yó agnī́ṣómā havíṣā saparyā́d / devadrī́cā mánasā yó ghṛténa / tásya vratáṃ rakṣatam* . . . (1.93.8) "He who honors *Agni* and *Soma* with a libation, / With thought directed to the gods, with ghee, / Protect that (man's) *vow* . . . !."

várdhana- (neuter) "enhancement," "prosperity"—
"means of enhancing" (sacrifice, prayer):

1) *yó bhójanaṃ ca dáyase ca várdhanam / ārdrā́d ā́ śúṣkam mádhumad dudohitha* (2.13.6) "(Thou) who apportions food and *prosperity*, / From the moist (one) thou hast milked the dry (and) sweet (thing)" (to *Indra*);
2) *yásya bráhma várdhanaṃ yásya sómo / yásyedaṃ rā́dhaḥ sá janāsaíndraḥ* (2.12.14) "(He) for whom prayer (is) a *means of enhancing*, for whom *Soma* (is destined), / For whom this gift is made, he O people, (is) *Indra*!."

دهی - دهیان

dhītí- (feminine) "attention," "intention"
(of a deity toward his worshipper)—"poetic vision," "prayer:"

1) *yát te dhītíṃ āvṛṇīmáhé / 'dha smā nas triváṛūthaḥ śivó bhava* (6.15.9) "Since we choose thy *attention* (and) benevolence, / Be merciful to us, (granting) triple protection!;"

2) *sá no dhītī́ váriṣṭhayā*
śréṣṭhayā ca sumatyā́
ágne rāyó didīhi naḥ
suvṛktíbhir vareṇya (5.25.3)

"For our exceptional *vision* and for the best well-turned prayer, / O *Agni*, light up for us the riches, for beautiful speeches, O Chosen (one)!."

práśasti- (feminine) "fame," "gift of honor," etc.—
"praise," "glorification," "respect:"

1) *práśastiṃ naḥ kṛṇuta rudriyāso* (5.57.7) "Create fame[30] for us, O sons of *Rudra*!;"

mahī́r asya práṇītayaḥ
pūrvī́r utá práśastayaḥ
nā́sya kṣīyanta ūtáyaḥ (6.45.3)

"Grand is his rule, / And numerous (are) the *gifts (in his) honor*, / His supports are inexhaustible" (about *Indra*);
2) *ayám vām yajñó akṛta práśastim* (1.181.1) "This sacrifice has created *respect* for you."

rātí- (feminine) "gift," "(gods') favor"—"gift,"
"sacrifice," "offering" (made by a worshipper):

1) *devā́nām rātír abhí no ní vartatām* (1.89.2) "The gods' *gift* shall turn toward us!;"
2) *iyám ta indra girvaṇo / rātíḥ kṣarati sunvatáḥ* (8.13.4) "This presser's *offering* is flowing for thee, O *Indra*, who delights in songs of praise!" ("the offering" is the *Soma*-juice).

ávas- (neuter) "help," "favor"—"support" (through sacrifice):

1) *divásprthivyór ávasā madema* (5.49.5) "Let us rejoice in the *help* of Heaven-and-Earth!;" *ávo dhāta vidhaté rátnam adyá* (6.65.3) "Bestow today *favor* (and) treasure upon the one who honors (you)!" (addressed to the dawns);
2) *pūrvī́bhir hí dadāśimá / śarádbhir maruto vayám / ávobhiś carṣaṇīnā́m /* (1.86.6) "We honored you, O Maruts, during many autumns / Thanks to the peoples' *support*." The second meaning is attested in the *Rig Veda* in several isolated cases only, and the idea of *ávas-* is associated almost exclusively with the divine sphere.

práyas- (neuter) "reward," "joy"—"sacrificial delight:"

1) *tvám . . . agne . . . / yás tātṛṣāṇá ubháyāya jánmane / máyaḥ kṛṇoṣi práya ā́ ca sūráye* (1.31.7) "Thou, O *Agni*, . . . demanding (the same thing), createst consolation and *reward* for the protector (of the sacrifice);"
2) *ápād dhotrā́d utá potrā́d amatta- / utá neṣṭrā́d ajuṣata práyo hitám* (2.37.4) "He drank from the hotar's cup, and grew inebriated from the potar's cup, / and he enjoyed the *sacrificial delight* from the neṣṭar's cup" (about the deity *Draviṇodas*).

rā́dhas- (neuter) "gift," "generosity," "reward"—
"sacrificial donation," "offering:"

1) *ní no rayím subhójasam yuvasva / ní vīrám gávyam áśvyam ca rā́dhaḥ* (7.92.3) "Bestow fine-tasting wealth upon us, / Be(stow) a son (upon us) and a *reward* (consisting) of cows and horses!;" *ā́ tvā śakyām upamám rā́dho ánnaiḥ* (10.29.3) "I would like to incite thee to utmost generosity (by means of sacrificial) foods!;"
2) *brā́hmaṇād indra rā́dhasaḥ / píbā sómam ṛtū́ñr ánu* (1.15.5) "O Indra,

from the brahman's *offering* / Drink *Soma* at the proper time!."

ṛtā́van- "he who fixes the law," "supporting (the law)"—
"he who conforms to the law," "pious:"

1) *dhārā́yanta ādityā́so jágat sthā́*
devā́ víśvasya bhúvanasya gopā́ḥ
dīrghā́dhiyo rákṣamāṇā asuryàm
ṛtā́vānaś cáyamānā ṛṇā́ni (2.27.4)

"The *Aditya*s support (everything) moving and motionless. / (They are) the gods, the herders of the universe, / With far-reaching mind, protecting the *Asura*s' world, / *Supporting the Law*, punishing the offence;"
2) *prá vām sá mitrāvaruṇāv ṛtā́vā / vípro mánmāni dīrghaśrúd iyarti* (7.61.2) "To both of you, O *Mitra-Varuṇa*, this *pious* / Poet addresses (his) compositions, (he) the far-heard (one)."

námasvant- "accepting worship"—"offering worship:"
1) *námasvantā dhṛtadakṣā́dhi gárte / mitrā́sāthe varuṇéḷāsv antáḥ* (5.62.5) "*Accepting worship*, O you (both) acting firmly, you sit / Upon the throne, O *Mitra*, O *Varuṇa*, in the midst of libations;"
2) *sá sukrátur ṛtacíd astu hótā / yá āditya śávasā vāṃ námasvān / āvavártad ávase vāṃ havíṣmān* . . . (7.85.4) "He shall be a very wise hotar, knowing the Law, / Who, O Ādityas, *offering worship* (and) libations, / Will be able to convert you two to assist (us) through (his) power . . . " (about *Mitra-Varuṇa*).

sūnṛ́tāvant- "beneficial"—"sacrificing liberally;"
1) . . . *revád asmé vy ùcha sūnṛtāvati* (1.92.14) "Make the wealth shine for us, O beneficial (one)!" (to Uṣas);
2) *yuvā́ṃ citrā́ṃ dadathur bhójanaṃ narā / códethāṃ sūnṛ́tāvate* (7.74.2) "You have given fine food, O you two heroes. / Hurry (hither) for the sake of the generous (sacrificer)."[31]

dāśvā́ṃs- "merciful"—"respectful:"

ómāsaś carṣaṇīdhṛto
víśve devāsa ā́ gata
dāśvā́ṃso dāśúṣaḥ sutám (1.3.7)

"O helpers, protectors of the people, / O All-Gods, come (hither), / Merciful to the pressed (*Soma*) of the person who respects (you)."[32]

ukthía- "praiseworthy"—"containing praises:"
1) *pávasva soma kratuvín na ukthyó / 'vyo vā́re pári dhā́va mádhu priyám* (9.86.48) "Clarify thyself, O *Soma*, seeking the mind's power for us, O *Praiseworthy* (one); / Run in circles upon the sheep-wool strainer, (thus becoming) the delicious mead!;'
2) *gā́ya gāyatrám ukthyàm* (1.38.14) "Sing the song that contains (only) praise" (address to a priest).

It should be mentioned that in the case of a god-priest, like *Brahmaṇaspati* the god of the prayer, the word *ukthyà* has to be interpreted in the second way:

prá nūnám bráhmaṇas pátir
mántraṃ vadaty ukthyàm
yásminn índro váruṇo mitró aryamā́
devā́ ókāṃsi cakriré (1.40.5)

"Right now *Brahmaṇaspati* / is reciting a verse, *containing praise*, / In which *Indra, Varuṇa, Mitra, Aryaman*, / —The gods—take delight."

dhíṣṇya-[33] "arousing inspiration"—"winning over (the god's) favor:"
1) *tád aśvinā śṛṇutam dhiṣṇyā yuvám* (1.89.4) "hear this, O *Aśvins*, you who *arouse inspiration*!;"
2) *káś chándasāṃ yógam ā́veda dhī́raḥ / kó dhíṣṇyām práti vā́cam papāda* (10.114.9) "Which sage knows the yoking in of the meters? / Which (of them) has possessed the speech that *wins over* (the god's favor?."

namasía- "worthy of worship"—"worshipful," "adoring:"
1) *ayám mitró namasyàḥ suśévo / rā́jā sukṣatró ajaniṣṭa vedhā́ḥ* (3.59.4) "This *Mitra*, *worthy of adoration*, very benevolent, / Was born as a king (with) kind authority, an establisher (of rites);"
2) *tā́ gṛṇīhi namasyèbhiḥ śūṣaíḥ / sumnébhir índrāváruṇā cakānā́* (6.68.3) "Glorify both of them in songs *full of adoration*, / *Indra* and *Varuṇa*, (whose) favors are desirable."

somyá- "worthy of *Soma*," "fond of *Soma*," "*Soma*-lover"—
"busy in *Soma*-pressing," "preparing the *Soma*-juice:"

1) *índraḥ sá dā́mane kṛtá*
ójiṣṭhaḥ sá máde hitáḥ
dyumnī́ ślokī́ sá somyáḥ (8.93.8)

"This *Indra* is ready to give (the gifts); / The Mightiest One is prepared to be intoxicated; / He, the splendid, loud, *Soma-worthy* one;"

yás te ánu svadhā́m ásat
suté ní yacha tanvàm
sá tvā mamattu somyám (3.51.11)

"Pause by the pressed (*Soma*) / that will be to thy taste! Let it intoxicate thee, O *Soma-lover*!" (to *Indra*);
2) *ichánti tvā somyā́saḥ sákhāyaḥ / sunvánti somām̐ dádhati práyām̐si* (3.30.1) "The friends, busy over *Soma*,[34] are looking for thee. / They press *Soma*. They prepare the sacrificial delights" (to *Indra*, about the priests).

yajñíya- "worthy of sacrifice," "honorable," "divine"—
"offering sacrifices," "honoring," "pious:"
1) *yájāmahai yajñíyān hánta devā́n* (10.53.2) "Let us now honor the gods, (the ones) worthy of honor!;"
2) *práti vām̐ rátham̐ nṛ́patī jarádhyai / havíṣmatā mánasā yajñíyena* (7.67.1) "I would like to arouse your chariot, O you two lords of men, / By means of *pious* thought, sacrifice-entailing" (to the Aśvins).

Noun stems of various structure, actually attested or securely reconstructible for the *Ṛg Veda*, serve as the bases for denominative verbs, some of which are characterized by conversive meanings. Their typical suffix, -*yá*-, is in itself indifferent both to (in)transitivity and diathesis. Among the meanings held by Renou to be typical of these verbs, he cites in particular, "to be like (somebody/something)" and "to cause (one) to be like" [120.304]. This semantic opposition is consistently played upon in the circular exchange between the deity and the worshipper. Very occasionally conversivity could be implicit in the semantics of the primary noun. This group includes the following verbs:

uruṣy- "to seek space" (of *Agni* on behalf of himself)—
"to create space," "to save" (of the god on behalf of the worshipper):
1) *ayám agnír uruṣyaty / amṛ́tād iva jánmanaḥ* (10.176.4) "This *Agni seeks space* for himself / Both from *being born* and from immortality" (he strives to break away both from the men and the gods—a well-known motif in the *Ṛg Veda*);

2) *yó asmai havyaír ghṛtávadbhir*
ávidhat prá tám prācā́ nayati bráhmaṇas pátiḥ
uruṣyátīm ám̐haso rákṣatī riṣò
'm̐hóś cid asmā urucákrir ádbhutaḥ (2.26.4)

"(He) who celebrated him with ghee-offerings, / Him *Brahmaṇaspati* leads forward. / He saves him from straits, protects (him) from injury. / The amazing god *creates a wide space* even from narrowness for him."

The correlation of meanings in this verb does not fit the semantic opposition between the god and the worshipper as the subject of action: in this case the deity appears regularly as the subject. However, the meaning changes according to whether the deity's action is performed for its own ends or for the worshipper's sake.

duvasy- "to reward," "to bestow a gift"—"to honor" (the god):

1) *anehásaḥ stúbha índro duvasyati* (3.51.3) "*Indra rewards* for faultless melodies;" *yuvám pedáve puruvā́ram aśvinā duvasyathaḥ* (1.119.10) "You *bestow* on Pedu the much-desired (horse), O *Aśvins*;"

2) *sūktaír devaṃ savitā́raṃ duvasya* (5.49.2) "*Honor* the god *Savitar* with hymns!"

The relationship of the constructions is identical with that of the verb *dāś-* (see above).

panasy- "to cause (the worshipper's) admiration"—
"to be appreciated," "to be acknowledged" (by the god):

1) *sanā́t sá yudhmá ójasā panasyate* (1.55.2) "Since ancient times this fighter (*Indra*) *arouses admiration* (by his) strength;"

2) *ākaré vásor jaritā́ panasyate* (3.51.3) "He who showers the goods *appreciates* the singer" (about *Indra*).

vājay- "to bring reward"—"to strive for reward:"

1) *ā́d dákṣiṇā yujyate vājayántī* (5.1.3) "Then the *rewarding* Dakṣinā is yoked;"

2) *devásy savitúr vayáṃ*
vājayántaḥ púraṃdhyā
bhágasya rātím īmahe (3.62.11)

"(Counting on) the god *Savitar* for inspiration we, *striving for the reward*, pray for *Bhaga*'s gift."

sumnāy- "to be benevolent, merciful"—"to ask for favors:"

1) *sumnāyánn íd víśo asmā́kam ā́ cara* (1.11.43) "Come to our settlements, (thou) full of benevolence" (to *Rudra*);

2) *máruto yád dha vo diváḥ*
sumnāyánto hávāmahe
ā́ tū́ na úpa gantana (8.7.11)

"O *Maruts*, do come to us, when we, *asking for (your) favors*, invoke you down from the sky!."

The next step in derivation consists in the formation of *u-* stem adjectives from various denominative verb stems; some denominative stems are actually attested only withinthis class of adjectives. It contains a group of adjectives with conversive meanings within the "auspicious" zone, meanings that depend on the opposition "god"—"worshipper." These *u-* stems are rather heterogeneous, morphologically speaking. In the case of *yájyu-*, the primary suffix *-yu-* combined with the root *yaj-* allows us to include this adjective on purely formal grounds. But a formal analysis of these stems is not as revealing as a description of the influence of the functional aspect upon their semantics.

Although Renou conventionally labels the *u-* stems as "participles" based on secondary verb stems [120.155] because they function as verbal adjectives, they do not reflect such purely verbal categories and meanings as tense, voice, transitivity, etc. This freedom from purely verbal verbal categories provides a wide range of possible context-bound semantic interpretations of these adjectives. A list of these *u-* stem verbs follows:

udanyú- "carrying water"—"thirsting for water:"

1) *prá vo marutas taviṣā́ udanyávo / vayovṛ́dho aśvayújaḥ párijrayaḥ* (5.54.2) "O Maruts! Let your brave, *water-carrying* (chariots) (rush) forth, / the strength-increasing, horse-yoked, circulating (ones)!;"

2) *iyáṃ vo asmát práti haryate matís / tṛṣṇáje ná divá útsā udanyáve* (5.57.1) "This prayer of ours is pleasing to you, / Like heavenly wells to the thirsty one who seeks water."

panasyú- "exciting admiration"—"expressing admiration:"

1) *índrāya sā́ma gāyata*
víprāya bṛhaté bṛhát
dharmakṛ́te vipaścíte panasyáve (8.98.1)

"For *Indra* sing the melody, / The lofty one—for (him), the lofty, the inspired (one), / For the Law-creator, the perspicacious, *admiration-exciting* (one);"

2) *prá vo dhíyo mandrayúvo vipanyúvaḥ / panasyúvaḥ saṃvásaneṣv akramuḥ* (9.86.17) "Forward your prayers have moved, harmonious, laudatory, / *Admiring*, at the time of sacrificial feasts."

yájyu- "accepting reverence," "worthy of reverence,"
"revered"—"reverent," "revering" (the gods):"

1) *sá na índrāya yájyave*
váruṇāya marúdbhyaḥ
varivovít pári srava (9.61.12)

"Flow around (here), at our (place), for *Indra, the revered one*, for *Varuṇa* (and) the *Maruts*, finding a wide outlet!" (to *Soma*);
2) *bhū́rīṇi hí tvé dadhiré ánīkā- / ágne devásya yájyavo jánāsaḥ* (3.19.4) "A multitude of faces, O *Agni*, have put into thee the god-*revering* peoples."

vājayú- "obtaining the prize"—"striving for the prize:"

1) *tvā́ṃ na indra vājayús*
tvā́ṃ gavyúḥ śatakrato
tvā́ṃ hiraṇyayúr vaso (7.31.3)

"O Indra, thou art for us a *prize-obtainer*, / Thou art a cattleobtainer, O a hundred-times sagacious, / Thou art a gold-obtainer, O Vasu!;"
2) *úpem asṛikṣi vājayúr vacasyā́ṃ* (2.35.1) "*Striving for the prize*, I have poured out (my) eloquence."

vipanyú- "admirable," "fond of being admired"—"admirer:"

1) *ā́ no gantam mayobhúvā-*
áśvinā śambhúvā yuvám
yó vām vipanyū dhītíbhir
gīrbhír vatsó ávīvṛdhat (8.8.19)

"Come to us as joy-bearers, O Aśvins, as two luck-bearers, / (Come) to Vatsa who has inspired you with prayers / (and) praise-songs, O you two, *fond of being admired;*"
2) *vayáṃ hí vāṃ hávāmahe / vipanyávo víprāso vā́jasātaye* (8.87.6) "We, the *admiring* poets, call on you in order to win the prize" (to the *Aśvins*).

sumnāyú- "merciful"—"asking for mercy:"
1) *ā́ vāṃ rátham avamásyām vyùṣṭau / sumnāyávo vṛ́ṣaṇo vartayantu* (7.71.3) "In the earliest morning the *merciful* brave (horses) shall bring your chariot" (about the *Aśvins*' horses);
2) *táṃ tvā vayáṃ sudhyò návyam agne / sumnāyáva īmahe devayántaḥ* (6.1.7) "To thee (as such), O *Agni*, we, the pious ones, appeal again, *asking for mercy*, devoted to the gods."

About half of the nouns with conversive meanings are made up of compound words, and their semantics is much more context-conditioned than that of non-compounds. A list of these compound nouns follows:

ádabdha- "undeceivable"—"devoted" ("not-deceiving"):
1) *vidvā́ñ ádabdho ví mumoktu pā́śān* (1.24.13) "May the Knower (i.e. *Varuṇa*), the *undeceivable* one, loosen the nooses!;"

2) *satyáṃ tád indrāvaruṇā kṛśásya vām*
mádhva ūrmíṃ duhate saptá vā́ṇīḥ
tā́bhir dāśvā́ṃsam avataṃ śubhas patī
yó vām ádabdho abhí pā́ti cíttibhiḥ (8.59.3)

"True it is, O *Indra* and *Varuṇa*: *Kṛśa*'s seven voices flow to you with a wave of mead. / O lords of beauty, support the worshipper by means of them (the voices), / who, in (his) prayers, shows respect to you with *undeceiving devotion*."

anamīvá- "not bringing diseases"—"free of disease:"

1) *anamīvó rudra jā́su no bhava* (7.46.2) "O *Rudra*, be thou not a disease-bringer to our descendants!;"
2) *anamīvā́saḥ . . . vayám mitrásya sumataú syāma* (3.59.3) "*Free of disease* . . . we should wish to be at *Mitra*'s mercy."

anehás- "incomparable"—"free of sin:"

1) *śivé no dyā́vāpṛthivī́ anehásā* (6.75.10) "(Let the) *incomparable* Sky-and-Earth (be) merciful to us!;"
2) *vayám mitrásyā́vasi / syā́ma saprásthastame / anehásas tvótayaḥ . . .* (5.65.5) "Let us be in *Mitra*'s greatest favors, *free of sin*, aided by thee . . . !."

áśvamiṣṭi- "(one) obtaining horses"—"seeking horses:"

1) *ayā́ te agne vidhema-*
ū́rjo napād áśvamiṣṭe
enā́ sūkténa sujāta (2.6.2)

"Through this (song), O *Agni*, we want to honor thee, / O off-spring of vigor, horse-obtainer, / With this hymn, O fine-born (one);"
2) *úd vāvṛṣasva maghavan gáviṣṭaya / úd indrā́śvamiṣṭaye* (8.61.7) "Pour (thyself) out, O generous one, for the cow-seeker, / O Indra, for the horse-seeker!"

ukthásuṣma- "maturing on praise-songs"—"emitting praise:"

1) . . . *ukthásuṣmān vṛṣabharā́n svápnasas / tā́n ādityā́m̐ ánu madā svastáye* (10.63.3) " . . . For the sake of luck greet these Adityas, who mature on praise-songs,bearing an ox-burden, and rewarding well!;"
2) *samudrám̐ na síndhava ukthásuṣmā / uruvyácasaṃ gīra ā́ viśanti* (6.36.3) "Like rivers (into) the sea, the songs that emit praise penetrate into the boundless Indra."

uruśáṃsa- "wide-ruling"—"with a far-reaching voice:"

1) *áheḷamāno varuṇehá bodhy / úruśaṃsa mā́ na ā́yuḥ prá moṣīḥ* (1.24.11) "O *Varuṇa*, stay here without anger! / O *wide-ruling* (one), do not steal the term of our life!;"

2) *asmábhyaṃ tád divó adbhyáḥ pṛthivyā́s*
tváyā dattáṃ kā́myaṃ rā́dha ā́ gāt
śáṃ yát stotṛ́bhya āpáye bhavāty
uruśáṃsāya savitar jaritré (2.38.11)

"Let us obtain the desired bounty given by thee, from the sky, from the waters and from the earth, / bringing happiness to the eulogizers, to the friend, the singer *with a far-reaching voice*, O Savitar!."

kṛtábrahman- "he to whom a prayer is made"—"he who made a prayer:"
1) *tū́rvann ójīyān tavásas távīyān / kṛtábrahméndro vṛddhámahāḥ / rā́jābhavan mádhunaḥ somyásya* . . . (6.20.3) "Winning (in the capacity of) the mightier one, stronger than the strong one, / Mightily grown as *a prayer was made to him*, / *Indra* became the king of *Soma*'s mead . . . ;"
2) *kṛtábrahmā śūśuvad rātáhavya ít* (2.25.1) "Only he, *who has made a prayer* (and) offered a sacrifice, will become stronger."

yatásruc- "to whom the offering ladle is extended"—
"he who extends the offering ladle:"

1) *yé vṛkṇā́so ádhi kṣámi*
nímitāso yatásrucaḥ
té no vyantu vā́ryaṃ
devatrā́ kṣetrasā́dhasaḥ (3.8.7)

"(Those) that, cut down, (are) on the ground, / That (are) dug in, *to whom the offering ladles are extended*, / Let them reward (us) with the desirable gift, / (They) that mark the gods' fields!" (about the deified sacrificial poles);
2) *híraṇyavarṇān kakuhā́n yatásruco / brahmaṇyántaḥ śáṃsyaṃ rā́dha īmahe* (2.34.11) "(To these gods) of a golden hue, the outstanding ones, we pray with sacred words; ladles extended, for a favor (that is) worthy of celebration" (to the *Maruts*).

rātáhavya- "he to whom libations are offered"—
"he who performs a libation:"
1) *índrāviṣṇū havíṣā vāvṛdhānā́- / ágrādvānā námasā rátahavyā / ghṛ́tāsutī dráviṇaṃ dhattam asmé* . . . (6.69.6) "O *Indra-Viṣṇu*, growing on libation, / (You), the first-tasters, *to whom the sacrificial drink is offered* with reverence, / Whose drink (is) ghee,—bring us wealth!;"

2) *yó rātáhavyo 'vṛkā́ya dhā́yase / kīréś cin mántram mánasā vanóṣi tám* (1.31.13) "(He) *who has performed a libation* to obtain safety, / That verse (of his)—though he be weak—thou shalt love (it) in (thy) mind" (to *Agni*).

sunīthá- "good leader," "leading excellently"—
"he who has good leaders," "well-guided:"

1) *ādityā́ rudrā́ vásavaḥ sunīthā́*
dyā́vākṣā́mā pṛthivī́ antárikṣam
sajóṣaso yajñám avantu devā́
ūrdhvám̐ kṛṇvantv adhvarásya ketúm (3.8.8)

"The *Ādityas*, the *Rudras*, *Vasu*, *the good leaders*, / Heaven-(and)-Earth, The Land, the aerial space, / The unanimous deities shall help (our) sacrifice. / Let them erect the sacrificial standard!;"

2) *sunīthó ghā sá mártyo*
yám marúto yám aryamā́
mitráḥ pā́nty adrúhaḥ (8.46.4)

"That mortal *has good leaders* / Whom the *Maruts, Aryaman, / Mitra*, the blameless (ones), protect."

sumatí- "(divine) favor"—"(worshippers') prayer:"
1) *devā́nām bhadrā́ sumatír ṛjūyatā́m̐ / devā́nām̐ rātír abhí no ní vartatām* (1.89.2) "*The beautiful favor* of the gods (is) for those who follow the straight path: / The gods' gift shall turn towards us!;"
2) *áchā gíraḥ sumatím̐ gantam asmayū́* (1.151.7) "(O you), devoted to us, come to our songs, to (our) *prayer*!."

sumánas- "benevolent" (towards the worshipper)—
"joyful in spirit" (with respect to the gods):

1) *ebhír no arkaír*
bhávā no arvā́ñ
svàr ṇa jyótiḥ
ágne víśvebhiḥ sumánā ánīkaiḥ (4.10.3)

"Thanks to these songs of ours / Turn (thyself) towards us, / Like the sun's light, / *Benevolent* in all (thy) faces!" (to *Agni*);
2) *krī́ḷantas tvā sumánasaḥ sapema- / abhí dyumnā́ tasthivā́m̐so jánānām* (4.4.9) "*Joyful in spirit*, playful, / eclipsing (other) people's splendor, we wish to care for thee.

suyajñá- "receiving excellent sacrifices"—
"(one) establishing a fine sacrifice:"

1) *índraḥ suyajñá uṣásaḥ svàr janat* (2.21.4) "*Indra, the receiver of excellent sacrifices*, gave birth to the dawns (and) to the sky;"
2) *táva práṇītī táva śūra śármann / ā́ vivāsanti kaváyaḥ suyajñā́ḥ* (3.51.7) "Under thy guidance, under thy protection, O hero, / The *excellently sacrificing* poets are striving to win" (to *Indra*).

If *Agni* appears as a priest, officiating at sacrifices, then the epithet *suyajñá-* has the worshipper's connotation, which is evidence for the purely functional semantics of this lexical group. For example:

samidhyámānaḥ prathamā́nu dhármā
sám aktúbhir ajyate viśvárāraḥ
śocíṣkeśo ghṛtánirṇik pāvakáḥ
suyajñó agnír yajáthāya devā́n (3.17.1)

"Being inflamed in accordance with the primeval ordinances, / He anoints himself with ointments, (he), desirable to everyone, / with flaming hair, ghee-garbed, the purifying (one), *Agni, the excellent sacrificer,*—in order to make a sacrifice for the gods."

surā́dhas- "rich in gifts," "generous"—"generously endowed:"

1) *abhí prá vaḥ surā́dhasam*
índram arca yáthā vidé
gó jaritṛ́bhyo maghávā purūvásuḥ
sahásreṇeva śíkṣati (8.49.1)

"I wish to direct (a song) for your sake to the *richly-donating* / *Indra*, as he is known, / (To this one) who, like a protector possessing various goods, / is ready to support the singers, even with a thousand (cows);"

2) *váruṇaḥ prāvitā́ bhuvan*
mitró víśvābhir ūtíbhiḥ
káratāṃ naḥ surā́dhasaḥ (1.23.6)

"Let *Varuṇa* become a supporter (to us), / (And) *Mitra* with all (of his) reinforcements! / Let them make us *generously endowed*!"

suvā́c- "worthy of fine speech"—"eloquent:"

1) *pṛkṣáprayajo draviṇaḥ suvā́caḥ / suketáva uṣáso revád ūṣuḥ* (3.7.10) "The dawns, endowing (us) with powers of satiation, (the dawns), *worthy of beautiful speech*, riches (incarnated), (the dawns) with beautiful brightness lit up the wealth;"
2) *daívyā hotārā prathamā́ suvā́cā / mímānā yajñám mánuṣo yájadhyai*

(10.110.7) "The two divine hotars should be honored, the first, the *eloquent* ones, measuring out the man's sacrifice."

svabhiṣṭí- / suabhiṣṭí- "superior," "helping"—
"favored," "having benefited from:"

1) *abhī́m avanvan svabhiṣṭím ūtáyo* . . . (1.51.2) "The reinforcements have subdued him, *the superior one*" (him is *Indra*);
2) *ásāma yáthā suṣakhā́ya ena / svabhiṣṭáyo narā́ṃ ná śáṃsaiḥ* (1.173.9) "Let us acquire good friends thanks to him, (let us become) the *favored* ones, as (is) usual in the glorification of heroes!;"

svávas-/suávas- "helping excellently"—"obtaining excellent help:"

1) *híraṇyahasto ásuraḥ sunītháḥ / sumṛḷīkáḥ svávā̐n yātv arvā́ṅ* (1.35.10) "The golden-handed Asura, the good leader, / Extremely merciful, *the excellent helper*, let him come here!;"
2) *sá ít sudā́nuḥ svávā̐n ṛtā́vā- / índra yó vāṃ varuṇa dā́śati tmán* (6.68.5) "Only that only one *obtains* beautiful gifts (and) *excellent help*, (and is) the righteous one, / O *Indra* and *Varuṇa*, who himself honors both of you."

stómavāhas- "attracted by praise"—"bringing praise:"

1) *gántéyānti sávanā háribhyām / babhrír vájram papíḥ sómaṃ dadír gā́ḥ /* . . . *stómavāhāḥ* (6.23.4) "The frequenter of *Soma*-pressings, with (his) pair of bay (horses), / The vajra-bearer, the habitual *Soma*-drinker (and) cow-giver, / . . . (has been) *attracted by praise*" (about *Indra*);
2) *ávīvṛdhanta gótamā / índra tvé stómavāhasaḥ* (4.32.12) "Have been inspired by thee, O *Indra*, the men of *Gotama*'s clan bringing praises."

hitáprayas- "the one, for whom the sacrificial meal is prepared"—
"the one, who prepared the sacrificial meal:"

1) *utá tyā́ me raúdrāv arcimántā*
nā́satyāv indra gūrtáye yájadhyai
manuṣvád vṛktábarhiṣe rárāṇā
mandū́ hitáprayasā vikṣú yájyū (10.61.15)

"And also these two *Rudras*—the glittering *Nāsatyas*, O *Indra*—I have to honor (them) in order to succeed. / They grant gifts to him who has spread the sacrificial straw-mat, like *Manu*, / To the joyous ones *for whom the sacrificial meal has been prepared*, who are revered among the tribes;"

2) *vayáṃ vo vṛktábarhiṣo*
hitáprayasa ānuṣák
sutásomāso varuṇa havāmahe
manuṣvád iddhā́gnayaḥ (8.27.7)

"We invoke you, O *Varuṇa*, we who have successively spread the sacrificial straw, *prepared the meal*, pressed the *Soma*, (and then) built the fire, like *Manu*."

The complete list of compounds with conversive meanings contains only a single substantive (*sumatí-*); all the rest are adjectives. As a result, the *tatpuruṣa* and *dvandva* classes of compounds are not represented. The greater part of them are *bahuvrīhis* (15), and the rest—*karmadhārayas* (4). The latter category contains three words with the negative prefix *a-/an-*, whose presence in the substantival or adjectival stem stimulates the appearance of conversive meanings. The most numerous type of compounds is made up of words with the adjectival prefix *su-* "good," "excellent," "kind" (eight in all: one *karmadhāraya* and seven *bahuvrīhi*). When this prefix is joined to a substantive, the result is as a rule, a compound adjective with conversive meanings. But the antonymous adjectival prefix *dus-/dur-/duḥ-* "bad," "evil," "mis-," "ill-," which is also quite productive in the *Ṛg Veda*, naturally lacks derivatives with conversive meanings, since its semantics belongs in the "inauspicious" zone where no semantic bifurcation takes place. This is a further illustration of the decisive role of semantics and style in the language of the *Ṛg Veda*; of lesser importance was the purely derivational, or as will be shown below, the grammatical aspect.

In conclusion, it should be noted that the presence of conversive meanings of the "auspicious" words—depending on the "god-or-worshipper" application—is attested in various and relatively numerous lexical classes. They include primary verb-stems, nouns with primary and secondary suffixes, denominative verbs, and various compounds. In short, this phenomenon can be detected in almost every type of derivation, and thus cannot be accidental; it should rather be considered an important feature of the *Ṛg Veda* language. All of this re-opens the "language of gods" vs. "language of men" discussion relative to this Old Indian text and several other ancient Indo-European poetic traditions, as detailed below.

Synonymy has always been an outstanding feature of Old Indian vocabulary throughout its course of evolution, which is quite natural for a language with an abundant literary tradition. The core of lexical synonymy is the principle of rendering different features of a single denotate (signatum). Sometimes the semantic motivations of such words are quite obvious, synchronically speaking, while in other cases the facts of other Indo-European languages shed relevant light. In several instances—and we see the beginning of this already in the *Ṛg Veda*—the source of synonyms lies in substratum languages, whose importance in that regard grows with time. Thus, in the *Ṛg Veda* "man/male/human" was conveyed by derivatives of the Indo-European roots *man-* "to think:" *mánu-*, *mánuṣa-*, *mánus-*, *mānavá-*, *mā́nuṣa-*; *jan-* "to give birth / to be born:" *jána-*; and *mar-* "to die:" *márta-*, *mártya-*. But then there are words for "man" whose semantics can be elucidated only at the Indo-Iranian level, or even deeper, at the PIE level: *āyú-*, *nár-*, *nára-*, *nárya-*; *vīrá-* . Finally, we find words for "man" of obscure etymology: *púṃs-*; *pūrú-*, *pū́ruṣa-*, *púruṣa-*, which could be considered a borrowing from some other language.

This example is quite typical of the Old Indian language as a whole, but the *Ṛg Veda*, a document of archaic cult poetry, is distinguished by certain specific traits in the formation and use of synonyms. Generally speaking, one can observe a certain opposition between lexical and functional, or contextual synonymy, wherein the latter is clearly predominant. Putting it differently, words relating to different denotates and thus having different lexical meanings, can function as synonyms in certain phrases or, in broader terms, in certain contexts.

In the *Ṛg Veda*, functional synonyms are usually those lexical groups that reflect important concepts; through this peculiarity of their usage the Aryan model of the universe can be clearly discerned. An example of this can be seen in the semantic field, so essential for the Vedic *Ṛṣi*, constituted by the verbs "to know," "to be aware of," "to recognize," "to think," all of which are central to his mental activities and, in a way, regulate all other kinds of activity, since his knowledge is sacral by nature. There are two close synonyms, verbs whose basic lexical meaning is "to know:" *jñā-* and *vid-*, *vétti*. *The Great Petersburg Dictionary* defines the primary meaning of *jñā-* as "kennen, wissen, bekannt-, vertraut sein, Kenntniss haben von, erkennen, in Erfahrung bringen, forschen nach, inne werden, merken, kennen lerner, erfahren," and that of *vid-* as: "Etwas oder Jmd kennen lernen, erkennen; wissen, begreifen, sich auf etwas verstehen, Etwas oder Jmd erkennen, wissen von Jmd, ein Bewusstsein von Etwas haben, eine richtige Vorstellung haben von." The semantic range of *man-* "to think" is given as "meinen, glauben, sich einbilden, sich vorstellen, vermuten, dafürhalten," etc. (*ibidem*).

As is generally known, "visual knowledge" was quite important for the Vedic *Ṛṣi*, since he was a visionary to whose inner eye supreme verities were revealed: "comprehension" signified "seeing." We have seen that only after a god had shown his chosen adept the mysteries of the universe could the latter become a *Ṛṣi* (compare hymn 7.88 telling how *Varuṇa* made the poet *Vasiṣṭha* a *Ṛṣi*). Thinking was also seen, to a large extent, as a process of inner vision. At the level of language this concept was made manifest by the use of verbs of visual perception (withor without adverbs or prefixes) that were used as synonyms for "to know," "to recognize," "to ponder," as in the following:

īkṣ- "to look," "to see;" "to have inner sight;" "to perceive;"[35]
áva + *īkṣ-* "to notice," "to discern," "to recognize:"
áva yát své sadhásthe / devā́nāṃ durmatī́r ī́kṣe / rā́jann ápa dvíṣaḥ sedha . . . (8.79.9) "When I *perceive* the gods' unfriendliness in my house, O king, drive away the signs of enmity . . . !."
cakṣ- "to appear;" "to see, look, notice;" "to declare," "to speak;" "to consider;" *práti* + *cakṣ-* "to notice, perceive;" *ví* + *cakṣ-* "to recognize, make out:"

práti cakṣva ví cakṣva-
índraś ca soma jāgṛtam
rákṣobhyo vadhám asyatam
aśániṃ yātumádbhyaḥ (7.104.25)

"Observe! Recognize![37] / O *Indra* and *Soma*, be vigilant! / Hurl the deadly weapon at the rakṣases, / (And) the javelin—at the sorcerers!;" *tád ín náktaṃ tád dívā máhyam āhus / tád ayáṃ kéto hṛdá ā́ ví caṣṭe* (1.24.12) "They (repeatedly) say this to me by night, and that by day; / this *makes apparent* (to me) the insight in (my) heart."[38]
ci- "to look," "to see," "to perceive;"
ní + *ci-* "to note," "to discern," "to understand:"

ádhā hí kā́vyā yuvám
dákṣasya pūrbhír adbhutā
ní ketúnā jánānāṃ
cikéthe pūtadakṣasā (5.66.4)

"But you two, O admirable ones, through the mind's fortresses *understand* poetic insights, thanks to the illumination of the peoples, for you purify the mind!" (to *Mitra-Varuṇa*); *ví* + *ci-* "to discern:" *cíttim ácittiṃ cinavad ví vidvā́n / pṛṣṭhéva vītā́ vṛjinā́ ca mártān* (4.2.11) "Let him knowingly *discern* people's reason and unreason, just as straight and curved (horses') backs (can be discerned)!;" *etác caná tvo ví ciketad eṣāṃ / satyó mántraḥ kaviṣastá ṛ́ghāvān* (1.152.2) "Not everybody will *understand* this. True (is) the amazing utterance pronounced by the poets."
cit- "to see," "to perceive,""to notice;" "to intend," "to seek;" "to ponder," "to decide;" "to comprehend," "to know;" "to appear," "to manifest (oneself):"
dvā́daśa pradháyaṣ cakrám ékaṃ / trī́ṇi nábhyāni ká u tác ciketa (1.164.48) "Twelve fellies, one wheel, / Three naves—indeed, who can *understand* this?" (a cosmic riddle); *mūrā́ amūra ná vayáṃ cikitvo / mahitvám agne tvám aṅgá vitse* (10.4.4) "We the foolish ones, (can) not (comprehend thy) greatness. Only thou, O wise (and) knowing *Agni*, canst *imagine* (it);" *ihá*

bravītu yá u tác cíketat (1.35.6) "Let him who has *recognized* this proclaim it here!."

dhī- "to look;" "to observe;" "to appear;" "to ponder, meditate:" *tè 'vindan mánasā dī́dhyānā / yáju ṣkannám prathamáṃ devayā́nam* (10.181.3) "*Meditating* in mind,[39] they found / The sacrificial formula rushing, first along the divine path;" *ánu + dhī-* "id:" *ṛtáṃ śáṃsanta ṛtám ít tá āhur / ánu vratáṃ vratapā́ dī́dhyānāḥ* (3.4.7) "Glorifying the law, the law they do proclaim, / Like vow-keepers *meditating* upon the vow;" *abhí + dhī-* "to contemplate, plan, conceive:" *abhí táṣṭeva dīdhayā manīṣā́m / átyo ná vājī́ sudhúro jíhānaḥ* (3.38.1) "Like a carpenter (designing a chariot), I *conceived* a poem, / Like a racer, winning prizes, well-trained, running up!;" *ā́ + dhī-* "to recollect," "to think over:" *eté dyumnébhir víśvam ā́tiranta . . . ā́ yé me asyá dīdhayann ṛtásya* (7.7.6) "Those (people) surpassed everything (by their) splendor, . . . (those) who remember (gratefully) this rite of mine."[40]

paś- / darś- "to look," "to see," "to recognize," "to conceive through inner sight;" *paś-*:

pataṃgám aktám ásurasya māyáyā
hṛdā́ paśyanti mánasā vipaścítaḥ
samudré antáḥ kaváyo ví cakṣate
márīcīnām padám ichanti vedhásaḥ (10.177.1)

"The bird anointed with the magic of the Asura, / The sagacious ones *comprehend* (it) in heart and mind. / The poets discern (it) inside the ocean. / The sages seek the trace of the sunrays;"

ví + paś- "to see the constituent parts," "to discern," "to perceive:"

cákṣur no dhehi cákṣuṣe
cákṣur vikhyaí tanū́bhyaḥ
sáṃ cedáṃ ví ca paśyema (10.158.4)

"Give sight to our eye, / (This) sight to ourselves, in order to see! / We desire to encompass and to *discern* this (universe) (by means of) sight; *darś-*: *dhrā́jir ékasya dadṛśe ná rūpám* (1.164.44) "The onrush of one is *perceived*, not (his) form."

Thus, it appears that under certain conditions all verbs of visual perception may function as synonyms of various verbs of cognition. In the first place, they denote the knowledge of objects that have form and color, i.e., visual knowledge ("to look" → "to have seen" → "to discern" → "to comprehend"). However, they may also have a wider application, being used with such abstract notions as "a god's greatness," "law," "prayer," etc., and in that case they are synonymous with the verb *man-*, denoting the highest, most abstract form of knowledge, as different from *jñā-* "to find out" (compare *jan-* "to generate") and *vid-* "to know" (compare *vid-* "to find"). The peculiarity of the *Ṛg Veda* seems to be this particularly wide application of the "vision" verbs in the area properly belonging to the "knowledge" verbs, an application that appears to be based on the role of visual knowledge in the *Ṛṣi*'s view of the world. But this particular type of synonymy finds numerous typological parallels in other languages.

A striking instance of the context-bound synonymity of words with radically different lexical meanings is Renou's exemplary analysis of the semantic field of the verbs for "giving" [123.471-80]. First, several verbs are lexically synonymous: *dā-* "to give," *rā-* "to donate," "to give," *dhā-* "to set," "to give." Secondly, in various contexts the meaning "to give" is assumed by other verbs, usually reflecting the outward form of the giving deity: *dī-* "to shine," *duh-* "to milk," *vas-* "to light up," *vṛṣ-* "to rain," *stan-* "to thunder," *áva* + *dhū-* "to shake off." The worshipper calls on the solar deities "to shine up" or "to light up" wealth, on *Indra*—"to thunder" it, on the *Maruts-* "to shake it off," etc. The proper lexical meaning of each of these verbs is to a certain extent "levelled out" and subordinated to the general context semantics, thus reducing them to synonymity. The important fact—from the linguistic point of view—is their appearance in identical syntactic structures: "Thunder out / rain down / light up [etc.] wealth" = "Give wealth!;" only these structures make them synonymous.

It should also be emphasized that the semantics of these verbs is conceptually significant. "Donating" is seen as a motive force of the circular exchange between deity and worshipper. From the worshipper's standpoint, the god's action is the marked one, and it is this aspect that presupposes the presence of functional synonyms of the verb "to give," and their absence from the verb "to take." Incidentally, the principal verbs of "giving" express the conversive meaning "to take," "to receive" by means of the same verbal root in the middle voice (sometimes, with an additional adverb/prefix). This reflects the PIE situation as reconstructed by Benveniste, whereby the same root could simultaneously mean "to give" and "to take" [54, Ch. 6 "Giving, Taking and Receiving"].

The worshipper's response to the deity's "giving" and "donating" consisted in "honoring" him. In the *Ṛg Veda* this meaning is attested in a considerable number of verbs. The core of the group is represented by several verbs whose principal lexical meaning is "to honor" (a god). This meaning makes them exact synonyms; the differences among them are normally due to differing sets of (secondary) meanings, i.e., the number of additional lexical meanings included in the whole semantic range of a verb. The basic syntactic structure is: accusative case of the honored deity's name;

instrumental case of the noun denoting the means of honoring; dative case of the aim of honoring). Not so frequent is the construction with the deity's name in the dative, although it is quite regular with some verbs. Here the means of honoring may appear in the instrumental, though sometimes it is expressed by the direct object in the accusative.

In the following examples, the sequence of each verbal construction reflects its frequency in the text. *dāś-* "to honor:" *yáḥ samídhā yá ā́hutī / yó védena dadā́śa márto agnáye* . . . (8.19.5) "Which mortal *showed respect* for *Agni* (dative) with fire-wood (instrumental), which (mortal) with libation (instrumental), (and) which—with knowledge (instrumental) . . . ; *samídhā yó níśitī dā́śad áditiṃ / dhā́mabhir asya mártyaḥ* . . . (8.19.14) "Which mortal *honors Aditi* (accusative) with fire-wood (instrumental), with inflammation (instrumental), with its (various) shapes (instrumental) . . . " (its) = of the fire); *yó vāṃ dā́śad dhavíṣkṛtim* . . . (1.93.3) "Who *respectfully* offers the prepared libation (accusative) to both of you (accusative-dative-genitive) . . . ."

namasy- "to revere," "to worship:" *śúcim arkaír bṛhaspátim / adhvaréṣu namasyata* (3.62.5) "*Worship* the pure *Bṛhaspati* during the rites with praise-songs (instrumental)."

sap- "to worship," "to serve," "to respect:" *índraṃ vo nárah sakhyā́ya sepur* (6.29.1) "Heroes *worship Indra* (accusative) for you, for the sake of (his) friendship." The means of honoring are usually omitted in constructions with this verb.

sapary- "to honor:" *tisró yád agne śarádas tvā́m íc / chúciṃ ghṛténa śúcayaḥ saparyā́n* . . . (1.72.3) "The pure ones have been *honoring* thee (accusative), O *Agni*, the Pure One, by means of ghee (instrumental) during three autumns. . . ;" *mahó devā́ya tád ṛtám saparyata* (10.37.1) "*Dedicate* mightily this truthful (word) (accusative) to the god (dative)!."

All of these verbs are very close in their lexical meaning, but they differ somewhat in the type of the frequency of their syntactic structures. Common to all of them is the construction wherein the verb governs the accusative of the name of the honored deity, and the instrumental case of the noun denotes the means of honoring. The construction next in frequency has the dative of the divine name and the instrumental of the means of honoring both governed by the "honoring" verb. The same two constructions are typical of a number of other verbs which have different lexical meaning but acquire the semantics of various kinds of worship in the general context of honoring the deity (through sacrifice, libation, invocation, chanting, laudation, etc.). ṭhese verbs which can be considered quasi-synonymous, are as follows:

yaj- "to worship," "to sacrifice:" *devāvī́r devā́n havíṣā yajāsi* (3.29.8) "Inviting the gods, thou shalt *worship* the gods (accusative) with libation (instrumental), compare also: *sómasya nú tvā súṣutasya yakṣi* (3.53.2) "Now I will *sacrifice* to thee (accusative) the well-pressed *Soma* (genitive partitive);" *svādukṣádmā yó vasataú syonakṛ́j / jīvayājáṃ yájate sópamā́ diváḥ* (1.31.15) "(He) who offers a sweet dish, (who) prepares a soft bed in (his) dwelling, / (Who) sacrifices a live victim (accusative), he (goes) to the highest heaven;"

hu- "to make a libation," "to offer," "to honor:" *imā́ gíra ādityébhyo ghṛtásnūḥ / sanā́d rā́jabhyo juhvā̀ juhomi* (2.27.1) "These songs, floating in ghee, I libate (them) with (my) tongue for the *Ādityas*, kings from the ancient past, (= "I worship the *Āditya*s with songs"), compare also *yamā́ya ghṛtávad dhavír / juhóta . . .* (10.14.14) "To *Yama make a sacrificial libation* full of ghee!."

īḍ- "to ask," "to pray;" "to offer," "to invoke;" "to honor;" "to praise:" *yás te agne námasā ī́ṭṭa / ṛtáṃ sá pāty aruṣásya vṛ́ṣṇaḥ* (5.12.6) "(He) who *offers* thee (dative-genitive), O *Agni*, an oblation (accusative) with reverence, / He guards the law of the purple bull;"[41] *tvā́ṃ hí ṣmā carṣaṇáyo / yajñébhir gīrbhír ī́ḷate* (6.2.2) "It is thee (accusative) that people *invoke* (= worship) with oblations (and) praise-songs"—compare *ī́ḷe ca tvā yájamāno havírbhir / ī́ḷe sakhitváṃ sumatíṃ níkāmaḥ* (3.1.15) "And I *invoke* thee (accusative), sacrificing with libations; I invoke (thy) amity (accusative), benevolence (accusative), craving (for them)."

mah-"to gladden," "to rejoice;" causative "to glorify;" "to make great:" *sárasvatīm ín mahayā suvṛktíbhi / stómair vasiṣṭha ródasī* (7.96.1) "It is *Sarasvatī* (accusative) that I will glorify (= worship) with hymns (instrumental) / And with praises (instrumental), O *Vasiṣṭha*, (as well as) both worlds (accusative)!"—compare *ágne víśvebhir agníbhir / devébhir mahayā gíraḥ* (3.12.4) "O *Agni*, together with all the (other) *Agnis* / (And) with the gods, *make* (my) songs (accusative) *well-formed*."

vand- "to praise," "to glorify;" "to elevate (in prayers)," "to worship:" *girā́ vandasva marúto áha* (8.20.20) "Praise then the *Marut*s with laudatory speech" (= worship) —compare *vandā́rus te tanvàṃ vande agne* (1.147.2) "As thy *eulogizer* I *eulogize* myself, O *Agni*."

stu- "to laud," "to praise:" *éto nv índraṃ stávāma / śuddháṃ śuddhéna sā́mnā* (8.95.7) "Come here now! We shall *laud* (= worship) *Indra* the pure with a pure tune!" (a rare construction for this verb—with an instrumental). Compare the following typical construction:

stávā nú ta indra pūrvyā́ mahā́ny
utá stavāma nū́tanā kṛtā́ni
stā́vā vájram bāhvór uśántaṃ
stávā hárī sū́ryasya ketū́ (2.11.6)

"I will now *praise*, O *Indra*, thy previous great (deeds). / We also will *praise* (thy) present deeds. / I will *praise* the *vajra* in (thy) hands, (which is) desirous (of feats). I will *praise* the bay pair, the signs of the Sun."

arc- "to shine," "to flash;" "to sing," "to laud;" "to worship;" *abhí* + *arc-* "to eulogize:" . . . *árcantī́ndram marútaḥ sadhásthe* (5.29.6) "The *Maruts* began to *praise* (= to worship) *Indra* on the spot;" *abhí tyáṃ vīráṃ gírvaṇasam arca- / índram bráhmaṇā jaritar návena* (6.50.6) "*Sing* (= worship) that hero, the praise-loving one, / *Indra* (accusative), with a new prayer (instrumental) O singer (or: "O worshipper")!"—compare *árcā-mārkáṃ náre víśrutāya* (1.62.1) "We shall *sing* a song (accusative) for the famous hero (dative)" (*Indra*).

gā- "to sing;" "to eulogize;" *abhí* + *gā-* "to eulogize:" *gā́ye tvā námasā girā́* (8.46.17) "I *sing* (I worship) thee (accusative) with reverence (and) praise-song;"[42] *abhí vo vīrám ándhaso mádeṣu gāya / girā́ mahā́ vícetasam / índram* . . . (8.46.14) "Intoxicated by *Soma*, *eulogize* your hero, the perspicacious *Indra* (accusative), with a lofty song (instrumental)"—compare *tigmájambhāya táruṇāya rā́jate / práyo gāyasy agnáye* (8.19.22) "For the sharp-toothed, young, glittering / *Agni* (dative) thou art *singing* (the ear's) delight (accusative)."

gar-/gir- "to invoke," "to praise," "to proclaim:" *tā́ gṛṇīhi namasyèbhiḥ śūṣaíḥ / sumnébhir índraváruṇā cakānā́* (6.68.3) "*Sing* (praise) *Indra* and *Varuṇa* (accusative), (who) seek pleasure in favors, with hymns (instrumental) worthy of (their) worship!;" *sámiddham agníṃ samídhā girā́ gṛṇe* (6.15.7) "I *praise* (I worship) the ignited *Agni* (accusative) with fire-wood (instrumental), with speech (instrumental)."

Although the verbs of the group do not differ in their semantics as widely as do the verbs of "giving," the lexical differences among them are quite noticeable. When used in identical syntactic structures, in an overall ritual context, these verbs acquire a common meaning: "To worship (a deity) by various means."

In the study of Vedic language it is necessary to draw a line between synonymy as a linguistic phenomenon and the isofunctional use of signs that encode various units of other semiotic systems such as myth, ritual, etc. In his analysis of the semantic structure of the *Ṛg Veda*, in particular of one of its oldest fragments, cosmogony, viewed as a single text, Boris Oguibenine demonstrated that a number of attributes of the Vedic deities can be regarded as isofunctional and treated as variants of the elementary cosmogonic act [30].[43] Such attributes include the following actions: to establish, to fix a support (*ruh-* causative, etc.); to be an intermediary in creating space (*antár* + *car-*, etc.); to hold fast, keeping the distance between the two cosmic zones; to be the basis (*stabh-*, etc.); to fill the space (*prá-*, etc.); to be undivided, embracing the whole creation (*eka- bhū-*, etc.); to outgrow the universe (*pra* + *ric-*, etc.). The semantic invariant in this series may be defined as "to create an ordered universe, or Cosmos" as opposed to Chaos. This is a matter of the functions of signs in a certain fragment of a mythological system. But the verbs and phrases that encode the units of this system—the author calls them "attributes" of mythological characters—cannot be considered synonyms.

The isomorphism of the macro- and microcosmic levels can be manifested, for instance, in the identification of the units of different levels, such as myth and ritual. In linguistics, this phenomenon appears as the problem of double reference (see above).

The play with different signs that encode a single mythological character in different contexts cannot be viewed as related to linguistic synonymy, either. If, for example, in some cases the sun is called "a bird" (*pataṃgá-, suparṇá-*), and its course "the bird's foot print;" and elsewhere it appears as "a horse" (*étaśa-*), we still cannot regard the words "bird" and "horse" as synonymous in the *Ṛg Veda*. A further instance concerns *Soma*: in various contexts the *Soma*-juice, the basis of the drink of immortality, is variously called "mead" (*mádhu-*), "clarified butter—ghee" (*ghṛtá-*), "milk" (*páyas-*), "rain" (*vṛṣṭí-*), and so on. Since each of these words can refer to different denotates in the hymns, the intricacies of the nominations and references of this text in general should become quite evident. The same applies to synonymy, polysemy, and metaphorical usage in the narrow sense.

The wide use made of synonymy in the *Ṛg Veda*, wherein all the main word-classes are involved (verbs, nouns, and adjectives), has been given various interpretations. According to one hypothesis, this phenomenon can be reduced to the undifferentiated use of words that belong to a lofty and a low style, a confusion that could be the starting point for reconstructing a more archaic PIE opposition between the "languages of men and gods. This interpretation which is based on a comparison of other Indo-European poetic traditions, should be thoroughly checked in synchrony, i.e., "from the inside," judging the facts on purely internal grounds.

The problem of the two opposed languages (that is, "the language of gods" and "the language of men") as attested in some ancient Indo-European poetic traditions, was studied most thoroughly, both in a general way and with detailed investigation of concrete facts, by Hermann Güntert. First, he analysed the language of the *Avesta*; more precisely, he made a systematic study of the function of synonyms in this text [93.1-34]. As the author stresses on the very first pages, this function conformed to Zarathustra's dualistic outlook: when designating the same notion, the

Avesta can use various synonyms depending on the context, that is, when speaking about Ahura Mazda's followers or about his enemies, the *daēvas*. The sum total of the words that have positive figures, their attributes and actions as their referents, constitutes the Ahuric language, and the words describing demons the Daēvic language. The Daēvic words are characterized by negative emotional connotations or by a semantic component that deprives an action of its neutral meaning (for instance, "to run" as compared with "to go"). The Daēvic words may have rude or colloquial overtones, while the Ahuric words are, generally speaking, emotionally neutral; that is why the Ahuric vocabulary may sometimes be applied to the description of the daēvas, but the opposite does not occur. But the Ahuric words also include stylistically elevated literary devices of the kenning-type. In this way, to put it in modern terms, the marked members of a privative opposition are the Daēvic words (i.e., presence/absence of a distinctive feature). This phenomenon is rather widely attested in the *Avesta*, and such stylistic polarization concerns whole lexical classes (for example, body-parts, verbs of motion, etc.), though some strata are not involved in this opposition. The undoubted merit of the author's work consists in the study of the function of language in a given text, wherein he is able to show the ways in which "the model of the universe" of the authors of the text regulated the function of its vocabulary. "The split of the whole cosmos into two parts should also cut through the Avestan language," as Güntert put it, thinking about the basic tenets of Zarathustrianism [93.28].

The next stage in research concerning the "language of gods" and the "language of men" was the study of Greek and Old Norse material. In Güntert's classic "On the language of gods and spirits" [94] this opposition is traced in the Homeric epics and in the "Speeches of Alvis" (*Alvíssmál*) of the Elder Edda. His basic basic idea is that prehistoric man saw the name as containing the essence of its bearer; this entails a belief in the magic power of the word, the necessity to conceal one's name, the existence of hidden names known only to priests and witches, etc. The belief in the existence of a special "divine language" (or the language of spirits, good or bad) is also rooted in archaic conceptions of the power of words.

In the Homeric poems there are only six cases of a single denotate with double designates, but the attribution to "the language of gods or men" is explicitly stated in the text. In four cases the opposed pairs occur, while in two only the "divine" words are attested. Güntert noted that the "Geistersprache" vocabuarly seems to belong to the ordinary Greek of the time (within which it is not an *ad-hoc* formation), while the words of the "Göttersprache" are quite foreign to everyday speech and should be seen as poetic descriptive terms. This elevated style is characterized by two main categories: sacral archaisms and sacral metaphors.

The Old Norse material was represented by a fragment very similar to the Old Indian *brahmodya*, cosmologic riddles which constituted the basis of the sacred knowledge of the Brahman-priests. In the Edda the god Thor asks the dwarf Alvís—in order to expose and punish him—about the names of various cosmic elements in the language of men and in the languages of various mythic figures, such as the Ases, the Vans, the giants, the elves, and the dwarves. Alvis's answers are made up of strings of synonyms that could be explained—according to Güntert—by techniques of versification and alliteration. The Scandinavian author adhered to the archaic concept of a special "language of gods"' an innovative feature may be seen in the redistribution of this language among several classes of mythic beings. This tradition also contains sacral archaisms and metaphors.

In this connection, Güntert cites the views of the Old Indian grammarians who were themselves guardians of the sacred poetic speech.[44] He observes that the language of gods is represented by the Vedic hymns; an idea that shall require our attention further on. A new stage in the study of this problem is marked by introducing Old Irish linguistic data.[45] Using the Old Irish grammatical tradition—mainly *The Scholars' Primer* (Auraicept na n-Éces), a treatise on grammar and poets compiled in the eighth through tenth century AD—Calvert Watkins discovered three language-type oppositions: 1) ordinary – archaic (*gnáthbérla – senbérla*); 2) professional – poetic (*bérla na Féine*) – *bérla na filed*); 3) select, cultivated – secret, hidden (*bérla tóbaide – bérla fortchuide*) [154.1-17]. Watkins reduced these oppositions, mentioned by the Old Irish grammarians, to an original binary opposition between a neutral, semantically unmarked member and a marked member (one or more) with a distinctive feature. We should interpret in this way the opposition between the "language of gods"—and the "language of men" (i.e., between the neutral and the marked member) in all those ancient Indo-European traditions where this contrast can be attested. As for the Old Irish pattern, the right-hand members are the marked ones and represent the language of sacred poetry (archaic, poetic, secret).

The last of the Old Irish oppositions has been the object of Watkin's special attention, since in form (both members are passive past participles) they have a perfect counterpart in the Old Indian terms for different kinds of language: *saṃskṛta-* "perfect"—*prākṛta* "crude, raw." Such a parallel is also of interest in the interpretation of the Old Indian tradition.

Both Güntert and Watkins pay special attention to a passage from a late Vedic text (*Śatapatha-Brāhmaṇa* 10.4.6.1) that uses various synonyms for "horse" in a marked context: *háyo bhūtvā́ devā́n avahad vājī́ gandharvā́n árvā ásurān áśvo manuṣyā̀n* "As *háya* he carried the gods, as *vājín*—the

Gandharvas, as *árvan*—the Asuras, as *áśva*—men." According to Watkins, *áśva-* here is the unmarked member of the opposition, while the other synonyms are the marked ones and belong to an elevated poetic style [151.5].

No examples of a similar distribution of synonyms have been adduced from the *Ṛg Veda* by these scholars. Nor are the "language of gods" and "language of men" directly attested in the *Ṛg Veda*, as is the case with the Homeric poems. It is known from the hymns that *Vāc*, Sacred Speech, was deified and regarded as a mighty cosmogonic force (10.125), that its innermost part is secret, it is hidden from the people and only the Brahmans can attain it (1.164.45). Nevertheless, the notion of these two languages was known to the Old Indian tradition, and it can be met, for instance, in the *Mahābhārata*:

> *yasmāt kṣaram atīto 'ham akṣarād api c' ottamaḥ*
> *ato 'smi loke vede ca prathitaḥ puruṣ' ottamaḥ* (*Bhagavad Gītā*, 15.18)

"Since I have surpassed the transient and am higher than the intransient, thus I am known as the supreme person both in ordinary speech (*loke*) and in the *Veda* (*vede*)." Zaehner translated this passage as: "so am I extolled in Vedic as in common speech . . . " [58.368][46] which seems quite convincing. This interpretation is also corroborated by devices of sound symbolism. The center of the verse is taken up by sound play *kṣara* – *akṣara*, i.e., "transient" – "intransient," but the word *akṣara* also has the meanings of "word," "syllable," "the sacred syllable *oṃ*." The contrast between *loke* and *vede* is obviously archaic and reflects the Common Indo-European opposition between the "language of men" and the "language of gods." The fact that it appears in the *Mahābhārata*, while there is no trace of it in the *Ṛg Veda*, cannot be claimed as a sign of its lateness. There are plenty of cases in which definitely archaic phenomena, absent from or obscured in the *Ṛg Veda* because of its circumscribed cultic content, appear in later Vedic literature (for example, in the *Brāhmaṇas*) or in the epics.

As Güntert notes, referring to Liebich's study [102], the Old Indian grammarians (even such late ones as Kumārila) regarded the whole of the *Ṛg Veda* as the "language of gods." The contrast between poetic and common everyday speech is maintained in the Old Indian grammatical tradition. Pāṇini defines it as the opposition between *chandas* and *bhāṣā*, that is, "metrical Vedic language" and "colloquial speech" [47] (compare *bhāṣ-* "to speak"), and the rules that he prescribed for *bhāṣā* are constantly broken in *chandas*. Kātyāyana designates this opposition as *laukikavaidikeṣu* "in the colloquial speech and in the Vedic language," which is directly related to the *Bhagavad Gītā* passage quoted above.

The Buddhist tradition—and in very different literary genres, at that—

also preserves the notion of two quite distinct languages. There is a passage in the well-known Buddhist philosophical treatise *Tarkasaṃgraha*, written in Sanskrit: *vākyaṃ dvividhaṃ vaidikaṃ laukikaṃ ceti / vaidikam īśvaroktatvāt sarvam api pramāṇam / laukikaṃ tv-āptavākyaṃ pramāṇam / anyad apramāṇam* [140.53; 349][48] "There are two kinds of utterances: Vedic and colloquial. The Vedic one is completely true because of the divine nature of expression. But the colloquial one is true only in the case of its expression by an authority. The rest is untrue." Here have the same formal opposition of *vaidika—laukika* that occurs in Kātyāyana's phrase.

Finally, one of the *Pālī Jātaka*s mentions *Indra*'s two different names, one of which is current in the world of the gods, and the other among mortals.[49]

> *Yamāhu devesu Sujampatīti*
> *Maghavā ti nam āhu manussaloke . . .* [71.403-4]

"(Him) who is called *Sujampati* among the gods, they call *Maghavan* in the world of men." It is remarkable that in *Pālī* too the word *loka* refers to men and their speech while *Indra*'s name is a kenning in the "language of the gods."

This subject awaits further exploration, but even a first approach makes it evident that the Old Indian tradition as a whole has preserved a deep-rooted notion of the "languages of gods and men." At various stages this opposition was expressed in different ways, one of which is represented by *veda – loka*, or *vaidika – laukika.*

Thus, if we are not able to discover in the *Ṛg Veda* any manifest contrast between the "language of gods" and the "language of men," this fact cannot be accidental and should be carefully examined. The form that this opposition acquired in the *Avesta*, the nearest relation to the *Ṛg Veda* among other Indo-European texts (the Ahuric language *vs.* the Daēvic language), would not be possible in the hymns, because of the fundamental differences in the basic concepts. The *Ṛg Veda* has not clear-cut duality, that "split," in Güntert's previously quoted words, which divides the Avestan cosmos in two halves. The opposition between *deva*s-gods and *asura*s-demons (inverted as compared with the *Avesta*) is attested in this text, but the *asura*s are quite ambivalent as members of this opposition. This problem has produced an abundant literature, and most recently has been minutely and consistently analysed by Kuiper [100].[50] There are gods who are called *asura*s (the *Āditya*s, in the first place), and there is a story about some mythic figures going from the Father-*Asura* over to the gods (10.124), etc. Since the Vedic system of religious beliefs is radically different from that of the *Avesta* it would be a mistake to expect a similar differentiation of synonyms related to the opposition between the gods and the *asuras* along the Avestan lines.

There is another reason, a very important one as far as the *Ṛg Veda* is concerned. In this text the Asuric world of chaos and evil is basically tabooed: it is not described, but is passed over in silence. If the *Avesta* exposes and indicts the *daēvas*, in the *Ṛg Veda* we observe nothing of the kind. It is rather indicative that Gonda's book on epithets in the *Ṛg Veda* contains long lists of divine epithets, while those of the demons are almost absent [79.130]. The world of the gods and everything related to it, the world of their priests and poets, is described in rather abundant detail. Of course, it is true that the cult language is quite esoteric and as such does not yield clear and unambiguous information.

As has been mentioned above, inherent in the Vedic vocabulary is a constant play on polysemy that can pass over into autonymy, depending on the inclusion of a given word in the "auspicious" or the "inauspicious" zones—the so-called "ambivalent" stratum of the lexicon, in Renou's terms. The same applies to shifts in the lexical meaning of a word, the modulation of its conversive meanings within the "auspicious" zone in the case of its divine or human application. Only a small group is constituted by ambivalent words in the latter case. Much more numerous and structurally diversified are the words with conversive meanings.

Summing up, one may say that the function of synonyms in the *Ṛg Veda* is based on rules quite different from those of the *Avesta*. These rules, in their turn, have an extralinguistic foundation in the differences between the religious outlooks of these two texts. The procedure adopted by Leonard G. Hertzenberg in this connection [4.18ff.] does not seem quite justified. He regularly adduces Old Indian examples in order to illustrate the stylistic opposition between the Avestan Ahuric and Daēvic synonyms, but the Old Indian facts can serve only as evidence of a genetic relationship between the two languages; they do not shed any light on the Avestan distribution of the corresponding synonyms.

A few examples will suffice to show that any functional parallels in the distribution of synonyms between the *Ṛg Veda* and the *Avesta* are non-existent. Güntert already noted that Ahuric words, being neutral, could sometimes be applied to the *daēvas*, but the reverse was not possible. Daēvic words had no referents in the Ahuric sphere since they possessed clearly negative emotional connotations. In that case the correct method seems to require asking the question: can a given Avestan Daēvic word refer to "auspicious" notions of the *Ṛg Veda*? It could be useful to discuss in this light some of the Avestan oppositions treated by Hertzenberg.

"To go, walk"—Ahuric *čar-*; Daēvic *pat-*. In the *Ṛg Veda car-* has the meaning "to wander," and *pat-* "to fly" (as primary, basic meanings). The verb *pat-* encodes the principal act of the Aśvins who fly swiftly across the sky and rush precipitately in order to aid the adorator, for example, 8.1.6: *yád antárikṣe pátathaḥ purubhujā / yád vemé ródasī ánu* . . . "When you two *fly* through the air, O much-needed ones, / Or when (you *fly*) along these two worlds . . . ." The verb *pat-* also encodes the movements of *Sūrya, Vāta, Indra*, the *Marut*s, etc. In connection with the demons it is used very rarely as, for instance, in 7.104.18: *gṛbhāyáta rakṣásaḥ sám pinaṣṭana / váyo yé bhūtvī́ patáyanti naktábhir* . . . "Grab the *rakshasa*s, crush (them) / Who, having become birds, *fly* (about) in the nights!."

"An eye"—Ahuric *dōijra-*; Daēvic *aš-*. In the *Ṛg Veda*, the Daēvic *aš-* has an etymological cognate in the heteroclitic stem *ákṣi-/akṣí-, akṣán-*. It is usually applied to *Soma, Agni*, the *Aśvins*, and other gods, to the worshippers of the Aryan gods and to various deified objects, for example, 10.21.7: *tvā́ṃ yajñéṣv ṛtvíjaṃ / cā́rum agne ní ṣedire / ghṛtápratīkam mánuṣo . . . śukráṃ cétiṣṭham akṣábhir* . . . " "It is thee, O *Agni*, whom people seated as the dear priest at the offerings—the ghee-faced, the bright one, the keenest observer with *eyes* . . . ;" compare 1.72.10: " . . . *divó yád akṣī́ amṛ́tā ákṛṇvan*" . . . when they created the two immortal *eyes* of heaven" (i.e., the sun and the moon).

"A host, army"—Ahuric *spāsa-*; Daēvic *haēnā-*. The noun *sénā-*, corresponding to the Daēvic word, does not necessarily denote the "enemy troops" and serves as a general term in the *Ṛg Veda*. It is applied to *Dāsa*'s host (5.30.9), but also to *Agni*'s host (8.75.7), to that of the *Marut*s (1.186.9), of *Soma* (9.96.1), and some other deities. There also occur the compounds *indrasenā́* (feminine nomen proprium) (literally "*Indra*'s host"), *devasenā́* "a divine host" (10.103.8).

The number of examples can be easily increased, but even those mentioned make it evident that the rules governing the distribution of synonyms and their "social stratification" differ widely in the *Ṛg Veda* and in the *Avesta*.

After this short discussion of the Common Indo-European opposition between the "language of gods"—and the "language of men" as applied to the Vedic hymns, some conclusions are called for. The most probable interpretation seems to be the "internal" one, that is, the one suggested by the Old Indian tradition itself. According to the latter, the *Ṛg Veda* as a text, as a document *in toto*, is considered to be the "language of gods" as opposed to everyday colloquial speech. This position is reflected in the post-Ṛg Vedic Old Indian literature, and in grammatical and philosophical treatises of various schools.

Within the text of the hymns this opposition does not manifest itself.

Probably, it was just superfluous from the point of view of their communicative aims. The goal of the text was communication with the gods; it was produced and preserved in a self-contained priestly Brahmanical milieu, where the art of hymn composition was traditional. The poets adhered to the canonical poems of the "former *Ṛṣis*" that were thought to be of semi-divine origin, sacred knowledge (*veda*) was revelation or illumination, and the poets and priests were mediators between gods and men. Such a go-between ought to speak to the gods in their own language, and that language, in Vedic terms, had been revealed by the gods to the "former *Ṛṣis*" in ancient times. In the poet's view, the addressee of the communication act was a deity, not a man, and therefore there could be no question of the "language of men" in the hymns of the *Ṛg Veda* itself.

The language of the Vedic cult poetry displays all those features which, in Güntert's opinion, were typical of the Common Indo-European "language of gods." Sacral archaisms and sacral metaphors are the prime characteristics of its style. But the originality of the lexical function of this text is based on a consistent play of polysemy and on the interplay of conversive meanings within a single word. The choice of a particular meaning in a given context largely depends on the inclusion of the word in a particular mythological zone or social sphere.

Thus, if the "language of gods" has been preserved in the form of the Vedic hymns, the problem of the "language of men" of that period is much more complicated, since no evidence of such a language has come down to us. One has to be satisfied with surmises and hypotheses, based on the *Ṛg Veda* itself. We shall deal with the subject in a rather cursory way, as it is only of tangential importance for our discussion.

There are some grounds for the supposition that the spoken language during the period of the composition of the *Ṛg Veda* was of the Middle Indian type; this is a purely linguistic, not a chronological attribution. At least, that language was characterized by strong Middle Indian tendencies; still, both languages, one of the cult and the other of everyday life, shared the background of a common dialect.[51]

At present there can be no doubt that the language of the *Ṛg Veda* was receptive to various borrowings from the non-Indo-European substratum languages;* another source was the Indo-Aryan vernacular, where the origin of the so-called Prākritisms is usually sought. These Prākritisms in the language of the cult poetry (which we understand largely through the work of Paul Tedesco, Thomas Burrow and Manfred Mayrhofer), necessarily pose the problem of their origin. The solution requires several hypotheses concerning the linguistic situation in India at the turn of the second and first millennia BC, and particularly the relationship between the cultic and the spoken languages of the Aryans. Renou, in his "Introduction générale" to the Wackernagel-Debrunner grammar [148.63a] put forward his suggestions in very careful but somewhat contradictory terms. In his opinion, the *Ṛg Veda* represents the state of language before the tenth century BC [148.1]. It was an artificial language, different from the vernacular [148: 2]. The phonetic basis of the priests' spoken language was identical with that of the hymns. But outside of the priestly milieu a more popular language was in use which was distinguished by all the main features of an Early Middle Indian type of the *Pālī* variety; some of the forms, attested in the *Ṛg Veda*, seem to confirm this thesis[148.7]. There was no full-fledged *Prākrit* at the time, though some Middle Indian traits seem to have made their appearance [148.54-55 (note)].

A synchronic analysis of the *Ṛg Vedic* language makes it possible to pick out—at each level—some tendencies that greatly resemble those of Middle Indian. They are most noticeable in syntagmatics and even more prominent in phonetics. One can mention the tendency to keep the hiatus caused by the nonautomatic treatment of glide-clusters (*níak, yújia-, tanúā-*, etc.), the disyllabic scansion of long vowels in certain grammatical forms and lexemes (Genitive case plural: *-ām*—disyllabic, *dhūrṣú*—trisyllabic, etc.), the relaxation of external vocalic *sandhi* rules, the appearance of intrusive vowels in some consonant-clusters (*ind°ra-, smát/sumát*, etc.), the sporadic voicing of single intervocalic voiceless stops (*nāthitá-/nādhitá-*), and a number of other phonetic phenomena along the Middle Indian lines. In morphology there are several well-known flexions and affixes that are absent from Sanskrit but persist in Middle Indian. In addition, some syntagmatic peculiarities recall those of Middle Indian: they include a wider range of combinational distribution of some Vedic morphemes as compared with Sanskrit [7], and they use the injunctive in a wide range of temporal meanings that could be reflected in the augmentless preterites in all Middle Indian languages, where the personal paradigm in the past tenses was preserved exclusively in this type. Some syntactic peculiarities of the *Ṛg Veda* can be explained within the framework of the hypothesis that there was a common dialect background for both Vedic and Middle Indian languages. The syncope of endings (compare the group-flexion in some *Prākrits*) of the cases when the bare stem or the stem with a lengthened final vowel assumes the role of various caseforms, is an example which supports this hypothesis.

The presence of such Middle Indian tendencies, manifested to various degrees at various levels of the *Ṛg Veda* language, allows us to hypothesize that the "language of men" at that time was represented by a kind of *Prākrit* (in the broadest sense of the term). It is probable that the oldest name for the sacral language used by the Vedic Aryans was *vāc-* [38.178]. In this way, the original opposition ("language of gods" *vs.* "language of men") is represented by *vāc-* —*prākṛta-* in the Old Indian tradition. With the passage of time, as the language of the hymns and the goddess *Vāc*, Sacred Speech personified, became relics of the distant past, the left-hand member of the opposition was replaced by *saṃskṛta-*, isomorphous with the right-hand member.

This is the most general sketch of the development of the tradition of the "language of gods" *vs.* the "language of men" in ancient India, the origin of which is to be sought in the "divine language" of the Vedic hymns.

Generally speaking, the lexical level reflects the "model of the universe" of a speakers' community in a most obvious and immediate manner. In the study of such an archaic cult document as the *Ṛg Veda*, in the study of the function of its vocabulary, it is necessary to reckon with the peculiarities of the Vedic mythological system, as well as with the intimate intertwining of religious and magical strands of thought, which constituted the originality of Vedic man.

As is well known, the mythological system of the *Ṛg Veda* is rather heterogeneous. The central place is held by a pantheon in which the individual gods are more or less anthropomorphic. But this part has close ties with other fragments of another kind of mythological patterning, wherein the gods are zoomorphic, or in which some cosmic or landscape elements are deified, or abstract ideas, "notions," are personified.[52] There are no clear-cut distinctions between these heterogeneous modes of mythological patterning.

It is widely held that the so-called "abstract deities," i.e., the personified abstract notions or agents, represent a later mode of patterning [see , for example, 106.115]. Undoubtedly, there are some grounds for this assertion, since a number of "abstract deities" make their first appearance in the last and latest Book Ten. But some personified abstract "notions" have have been attested since the oldest "family" *maṇḍala*s: moreover, the general situation is considerably obscured by the general Vedic tendency to give a magic interpretation to various abstract notions such as "force," "energy," "might," "deception," "enmity," and many others. Consequently, in the text these notions sometimes acquire an existence of their own, half-independent of those figures that are usually regarded as the bearers of these qualities [84.30].

Although the *Ṛg Veda* is a document of the higher hieratic cult as distinct from the *Atharva Veda*, a collection of magic charms, some Atharvanic motifs are altogether apparent in the hymns. Not only have some charms and incantations found their way into the *Ṛg Veda*, but the affinity runs deeper: they share the common belief in the power of the word that can influence real life, they connect the name and the nature of the object so named, etc.

The problem of the personified and impersonal nature of deified forces and objects in the *Ṛg Veda* was first raised by Gonda in his discussion of the god *Agni*'s definition as "the son of strength" [86]. He observed that here the shift from "an impersonal potency" to "a divine person" is made so easily as to be hardly noticeable [86.6]. In the Vedic poet's mind "a divine being *is* a power-substance, *has* it, and *is to realize it*" [86.35]. Powers that belong to various areas of nature can assume concrete forms and can enter the gods and even mortals [86.66]. In this connection Gonda discusses several passages of the *Ṛg Veda* that involve the translation of several words for "power" (*sáhas, ójas, távas,* etc.) proposed by Geldner and their (im)personal treatment in the Böhtlingk-Roth and Grassmann Dictionaries. Although Gonda correctly stressed the purely mythological aspect of the problem, he also drew attention to its linguistic consequences: the ambiquity of some nouns with the suffixes *-as, -ti, -man* in the *Ṛg Veda*, where in some contexts they can be interpreted as abstracts, denoting impersonal forces and agent nouns, as substantives, and as adjectives, corresponding to definite mythic figures. Linguistic ambiguity, in this case, is a consequence of the corresponding part of the outlook of the "model of the universe."

The linguistic manifestation of the mythological relationship between gods and powers should be seen in a still wider framework. Vedic language reflects this relationship in the semantics of a number of nominal stems (radical, *-ti, -as, -man*), and in the peculiarities of their gender system.

The root-stems are much more widely represented in the *Ṛg Veda* then in any later text, both as independent words—although their paradigms are usually defective—and as final members of compounds. This archaic stem-class combines the grammemes of all the three genders. Since the neuter is extremely rare, only the masculine and the feminine will concern us here.

These stems function as substantives as well as adjectives. Since the inflexion is not gender-differentiated, the gender can be determined only with the help of an adjective or participle in agreement. Sometimes the gender determination is apparent from the context, in cases where the root-noun refers to a male or a female. For example, *rā́j-* (m.) "king," (f.) "queen" (with prefix-derivatives): *dvayā́m̐ agne rathíno viṃśatíṃ gā́ / vadhū́mato maghávā máhyaṃ samrā́ṭ / abhyāvartī́ cāyamānó dadāti / . . .* (6.27.8) "O *Agni*, (horse-)pairs with chariots, twenty bulls / with cows the generous great king grants me / *Abhyāvartin*, *Cāyamāna*'s son" / (where the masculine gender of *samrā́ṭ* is deduced from the concord); *utá gnā́ vyantu devápatnīr / indrāṇy àgnā̀yy aśvínī rā́ṭ* (5.46.8) "And the divine wives shall also come willingly, the gods' spouses, *Indrāṇī*, *Agnāyī* (and) *Aśvinī* the queen" (where the gender of *rā́ṭ* is determined by its reference to a goddess).

An archaic distribution of gender grammemes can be observed with relation to the semantics of the root-stems. Those with the abstract meaning of action nouns are feminine, but when functioning as agent nouns they are usually masculine substantives, or adjectives. Renou remarked that the agent noun meaning in this case can often be regarded as rather superficial: The proper meaning of *srídh-, mṛ́dh-, ríṣ-, spṛ́dh-, dvíṣ-* is more like "enmity" (with additional overtones) than "enemy," although—when required— they can then shift to the masculine" [120.146].

It seems that this semantic rule of gender-grammeme distribution of the root-stems served as the basis for the authors of the classic dictionaries (that is, the *Great Petersburg Dictionary*, and in particular, Grassmann's) in their ascription of gender to Vedic root-nouns, notwithstanding the fact that there are a number of contexts wherein the gender cannot be determined either syntactically (i.e., by means of concord), or with reference to a particular denotate. The very semantics of a stem (abstract or concrete) is often quite vague; and this vagueness would be common, since it is a reflection of the features of the "model of the universe" we have been discussing. We shall illustrate this indeterminacy of the root-stems with a few examples.

gír- (adjective) "celebrating," "praising;" (masculine) "singer," "eulogizer;" (feminine) "(praise-)song," "eulogy:"

párītó vāyáve sutáṃ
gíra índrāya matsarám
ávyo vā́reṣu siñcata (9.63.10)

"From here make libation-rounds for *Vāyu*, for *Indra*, of the pressed intoxicating (*Soma*), *O eulogies* (or: *O eulogizers*), onto the sheep strainer!" The lexical meaning of *gíraḥ* can be either abstract or concrete (there is no indication of gender in this phrase). From the point of view of grammar, at the beginning of the line *gíraḥ* is either vocative plural or accusative plural. Hence the possibiity of different interpretations; thus, Geldner translates: "Ergiesset von da dem Vāyu den ausgepressten (*Soma*), die Lobreden, für *Indra* den berauschenden (*Soma*) auf die, Schafhaare," referring in his commentary to Sāyaṇa and to Ludwig, who understood *gíraḥ* as "Sänger" [74.3.47]. Renou's version is: "Tout autour (en partant) d'ici, versez pour *Vāyu* (le soma) pressé (émettez) les chants, (versez le soma) enivrant / pour *Indra*, dans (le tamis en) piols de brebis" [118.8.36]. In his commentary he cites Oldenberg and Neisser who, for various reasons, decline to interpret *gír-* as "singer," and he himself suggests an alternative: "arrosez (le *soma*, objet de la) Louange" [118.8.94].

This example can serve as an illustration not so much of some kind of lack of differentiation in the "model of the universe" as reflected in language, but rather of the difficulties of interpretation caused by a nondiagnostic context, which is frequent in the *Ṛg Veda*. The designations of various evil forces vacillate between personified and impersonal ones in the hymns, and the linguistic conditions facilitate the ambiguity in nondiagnostic contexts.

drúh- (adjective) "harmful;" (masculine, feminine) "the harmful one;"[53] (feminine) "harm," "injury," "evil."

tvā́ yujā́ ní khidat sū́ryasyéndraś
cakrám̐ sáhasā sadyā́ indo
ádhi ṣnúnā bṛhatā́ vártamānam
mahó druhó ápa viśvā́yu dhāyi (4.28.2)

"With thee as (his) ally *Indra* squeezed the wheel (of the Sun)—mightily, at once, O Drop, / —(which) rolled along the high ridge (of the sky). / Taken away is the whole term of life of (that) great (masculine) *Harmful one*;" here *drúh-* refers to Śuṣṇa the demon: the following stanza tells of the slaughter of the Dasyus by *Indra* and their burning by *Agni*; *drúhaṃ jíghāṃsan dhvarásam aníndrāṃ / tétikte tigmā́ tujáse ánīkā* . . . (4.23.7) "Desiring to crush the *harmfulness*, the pernicious one, not acknowledging Indra (feminine), / He whets the sharp arrow-points for the attack, . . . :" in this case *drúh-* appears rather as a female personification of evil, not an abstract idea; *sá ṛṇacíd ṛṇayā́ bráhmaṇas pátir / druhó hantā́ mahá ṛtásya dhartári* (2.23.7) "This *Brahmaṇaspati* is a collector of debts, a crime-avenger, / A crusher of evil in upholding the great (universal) Law," where the abstract meaning of *drúh-* results from the opposition with *ṛtá-*; but its gender is ambiguous as the context is nondiagnostic.

dvíṣ- (feminine) "hate," "enmity;" personified: "hate," "foe" (gender ambiguous):

té asmábhyaṃ śárma yaṃsann
amṛ́tā mártyebhyaḥ
bā́dhamānā ápa dvíṣaḥ (1.90.3)

"Let them give us protection, / The immortals to the mortal ones, / Driving away enmities (accusative plural, or: "the enemies?");" both Geldner and Renou translate *dvíṣaḥ* as an abstract noun;

táṃ tvā vayáṃ havāmahe
śṛṇvántaṃ jātávedasam
ágne ghnántam ápa dvíṣaḥ (8.43.23)

"Such as (thou art) we invoke thee / The attentive *Jātavedas*, / O *Agni*, destroying *enemies*" (or: "enmities"); Geldner's choice: "die Feinde," and Renou's "les inimitiés" [118.13.72].

Both contexts are nondiagnostic and contain analogous constructions. The choice between an abstract and a concrete meaning of the noun *dvíṣ-* remains difficult.

pari-bā́dh- (feminine) "a torturer, tormentor:"
bhindhí víśvā ápa dvíṣaḥ / páribādho jahī mṛ́dhaḥ (8.45.40) "Smash all the *haters* (feminine)! Kill the *tormentors*, (all those) *despising* (us)!;" this is an interesting example since all the three accusatives belong to the root-stems under discussion. The first is modified by an adjective in the feminine. Their semantics may be defined as the semi-personified treatment of an abstract notion.

níd- (feminine) "mockery," "invective," "scorn;" "a mocker," "a contemptor:" although the majority of passages is nondiagnostic from the formal point of view, a clear correlation between the feminine and the abstract meaning can be detected. Nevertheless, a few rare cases remain obscure, for example; *yuvám̐ sū́ryaṃ vividáthur yuvám̐ svàr / víśvā támāṃsy ahataṃ nidáś ca* (6.72.1) "You two have found the sun (and also) the sky; you have crushed all (kinds of) darkness (plural) and the *mockers*." Geldner translated *nidáś ca* as "und die Schmäher," referring to the commentary of Sāyaṇa, who thought that the *asura*s were meant; but an abstract meaning is quite conceivable here.

bhid- (adjective) "a breaker, destroyer;" (feminine) "splitting;" "a split," "a breach:" *bhinát púro ná bhído ádevīr . . .* (1.174.8) "Break, like fortresses, the ungodly (feminine) *breaches* (?)!" (or: "the godless breakers" (?) Geldner has: "Brich die gottlosen Einbrüche (?) wie ihre Burgen;" Renou: "Brise comme des citadelles les brisures ennemies") [118.17.51]. In Grassmann's dictionary this *bhíd-* is regarded as an agent noun; "Spalter, Verwunder, Zerstörer," and in the *Great Petersburg Dictionary* it is translated as "Wand."

bhúj- (feminine) "tasting," "enjoyment, delight;" concrete: "one who tastes:" the usual one is the abstract meaning, for example: *sá tvám̐ na indra sū́rye só apsv / ànāgāstvá ā́ bhaja jīvaśaṃsé / mā́ntarām bhújam ā́ rīriṣo naḥ . . .* (1.104.6) "Thou, O *Indra*, do apportion us a share in the sun, in the waters, / In blamelessness in the speech of the living! / Do not harm our inner *delight*! . . . "

The following passage is more obscure: *agním īḷe bhujā́ṃ yáviṣṭhaṃ / śāsā́ mitrám̐ durdhárītum* (10.20.2) "I invoke *Agni* as the youngest of the (sacrifice) *tasters*, / As a friend that can hardly be restrained with a command;" an abstract meaning of *bhujā́m* cannot be excluded outright ("as the youngest of [all] delights"); moreover, *mitrám̐* can also be interpreted in the same sense ("as friendship . . . that cannot be stopped"). Geldner translates: "den Jüngsten der (Opfer)geniesser," compare his comments ad loc.

mṛdh- (feminine) "fighting," "battle;" "an enemy:" most occurrences are in the plural: *paścā́ mṛ́dho ápa bhavantu víśvās* (10.67.11) "Let all (feminine) the *enemies* be (left) far behind!" (or: "battles?"—but this idea would be foreign to a Vedic Aryan); Geldner has the abstract "Alle Unbilden," but his version does not contain the idea of enmity.

ríp- (feminine) "deceit," "a trick;" "a deceiver:" all the dictionaries label it feminine; nevertheless, several passages seem to offer a personified understanding of this abstract notion, for example: *yá índro hárivān ná dabhanti tám̐ rípo* (7.32.12) "Him who is *Indra*, the owner of the bay (horses), the *deceivers* will not harm."

ríṣ- (feminine) "harm" or "a wrecker" (Böhtlingk-Roth, Grassmann): all the contexts are nondiagnostic; the noun occurs mostly in the ablative with verbs meaning "to protect," "to guard;" the passages are rather uniform and admit of both meanings, and there is no formal indication of gender, for example;

yó no maruto vṛkátāti mártyo
ripúr dadhé vasavo rákṣatā riṣáḥ
vartáyata tápuṣā cakríyābhí tám
áva rudrā aśáso hantana vádhaḥ (2.34.9)

"That wily mortal, O *Maruts*, who placed us among wolves,—O *Vasus*, protect us from *harm*! (or: "from *the harmful one*") / Run him over with a red-hot wheel! O Rudras, (knock) the deadly weapon out of the accursed (enemy's hand)! Kill (him)!" Geldner's version: "so schützet uns vor Schaden," Renou's: "gardeznous du dommage [1u'il peut nouscauser]!" [115.10.26]. According to Sāyaṇa, a *rakshas* is meant here.

In addition, *ríṣ-* occurs twice in an identical formula in the dative with the verb *dhā-* and a meaning close to that of an infinitive: *mā́ no 'hir budhnyò riṣé dhād* . . . (5.41.16; 7.34.17) "Let the Serpent of the Depths not give us up to harm!"

spṛ́dh- (feminine) "fight(ing);" "an enemy, adversary:" *ā́bhi spṛ́dho mithatī́r áriṣaṇyann / amítrasya vyathayā manyúm indra* (6.25.2) "Reliable because of these (supports), stir the fighting (feminine) *enemies* (and) the foe's fury, O Indra!."

srídh- (feminine) "one who errs, blunders;" "a renegade" (Böhtlingk-Roth):

punānáḥ soma dhā́rayā-
índo víṣvā ápa srídhaḥ
jahí rákṣām̐si sukrato (9.63.28)

"Purifying thyself in the stream, O Soma, / (Drive) away all (feminine) the *renegades*, O drop! / Slay the rakṣases, O fine-spirited one!;" in this context *srídhaḥ* should be interpreted as a personified abstract notion because of the *rakṣas*-word in the next clause. However, Geldner suggests: "ver(bann) alle Fehlschläge;" and Renou has: "re(foulant) toutes nocivités" [118.8.37].

The above examples show that for the most part this class of root-stems denotes various abstract forces inimical to the Aryan and also perceived by him as personified incarnations of all kinds of enemies.

Another class of nominal stems with analogous functions in the *Ṛg Veda* consists of verbal stems with the suffix *-ti*; as Debrunner pointed out, these derivatives have an abstract meaning [65.622], and their original gender was feminine[65.642], for example: *bhaj-* "to apportion, to allot"—*bhaktí-* (feminine) "allotment," *san-* "to seize, to grab"—*sātí-* (feminine) "seizure," "booty, loot."

According to Benveniste, in the stems with the *-ti-* suffix the corresponding notion is regarded as something actually achieved, real and objective [55.93]. But in the *Ṛg Veda* there is a tendency, remarked on by some scholars, to personify the abstract notions denoted by the stems in *-ti-*, so that they often function as agent nouns; they either keep their feminine gender or are tranferred to the masculine [65.636]. Still, there is a number of contexts wherein the degree of personification of the stems in *-ti-* cannot be established for certain. Some examples:

The root *man-* "to think," "to imagine."
matí- (feminine) "thought," "opinion;" concrete—
"the thinking one," "the understanding one:"

túviśuṣma túvikrato
śácīvo víśvayā mate
ā́ paprātha mahitvanā́ (8.68.2)

"O (lord) of powerful fury, of powerful mind, / Might, all-comprehending one, (literally "O *thought* about everything") / Thou hast filled (the world) with (thy) greatness!."

ánumati- (feminine) "agreement," "approval;" proper noun of a goddess: *jyók paśyema sū́ryam uccárantam / ánumate mṛḷáyā naḥ svastí* (10.59.6) "May we see the sun for a long time (to come)! / O Anumati-*Harmony*! Be kind to us for the sake of (our) happiness!"

sómasya rā́jño váruṇasya dhármaṇi
bṛ́haspáter ánumatyā u śármaṇi
távāhám adyá maghavann úpastutau
dhā́tar vídhātaḥ kaláśā̃ abhakṣayam (10.167.3)

"Following the statutes of *Soma* the King (and) *Varuṇa*, / Under the protection of *Bṛhaspati* and *Anumati*, / Today, O generous one, while praising thee, O creater (and) establisher, I have drunk from the goblets."

This personified abstract notion is represented here as a goddess, and as such it is used along with other theonyms.

prámati- (feminine) "care," "protection;" "a protector:"

Since this noun usually appears in apposition, its lexical meaning remains ambiguous, for example: *tvā́m ánu prámatim ā́ jaganma* (4.16.18) "To thee have we come, to (thy) *protection*" (or: "to the *protector*"); *yajñó mánuḥ prámatir naḥ pitā́ hí kam* (10.100.5) "Sacrifice (is) *Manu*, for it is our *protection* (or: "*protector*") and father;" Geldner: "denn es ist unsere Vorsehung und Vater."

durmatí- (feminine) "hostility," "envy;" "an evil-wisher," "envier:" *vṛ́ṣā śúṣmeṇa bādhate ví durmatī́r / ādédiśānaḥ śaryahéva śurúdhaḥ* (9.70.5) "The bull in fury pursues the *envious people* (feminine), / Like an archer, aiming at (his) prey;" Geldner and Renou [118.9.20] offer the same interpretation.

abhímāti-, (feminine) "pursuit," "attack;" "pursuer," "attacker:" *agne sáhasva pṛ́tanā abhímātīr ápāsya* (3.24.1) "O *Agni*, win the battles, drive away the *pursuers* (feminine); Geldner: "treibe die Nachsteller fort;" Renou: "repousse les pensées agressives" [118.12.65].

úpamāti- (feminine) "appeal for help;"
"one who can be approached for help," "friendly:"

ā́ no agne vayovṛ́dhaṃ
rayím pāvaka śámsyam
rā́svā ca na upamāte puruspṛ́haṃ
súnītī sváyaśastaram (8.60.11)

"Bring us, O *Agni*, the strength-increasing wealth, O purifying one, which is praiseworthy, and give us, O *friendly one*, the much-desired (wealth), that is self-shinging under (thy) beautiful guidance!."

The root *man-* is most productive in the *Ṛg Veda* both in number and in the variety of such *-ti-* stem derivatives.

bhū- "to be," "to become."

Its *-ti-* derivatives with various prefixes function as abstract nouns (feminine) and as adjectives, i.e., the agent noun of the quality-bearer is treated as an adjective.

abhíbhūti- (feminine) "superiority;" adjective "superior," "extremely powerful:" *utá smāsya panayanti jánā / jūtíṃ kṛṣṭipró abhíbhūtim aśóḥ* (4.38.9) "And more: people praise his / Swiftness, the superiority of a speedy (horse), filling the lands"—with abstract meaning; *távéd idám abhítaś cekite vásu / átaḥ saṃgŕ̥bhyābhibhūta ā́ bhara* (1.53.3) "For it is thy wealth that is so eye-catching on all sides! / Taking of it, bring (something) here, O *superior* one!" (or: "O *superiority* / incarnate / ")—both interpretations are admissible; *tásmin mimāthām abhíbhūty ójaḥ* (4.41.4) "Upon it you two shall measure (your) *superior* (neuter) power!"—an adjective.

prábhūti- (feminine) "power," "possession," "might;" "ruler;" "powerful:" *ágne rāyo nŕ̥tamasya prábhūtau / bhūyā́ma te suṣṭutáyaś ca vásvaḥ* (3.18.3) (literally: "O Agni, let us be fine extollers of thy goods, *possessing* the bravest wealth!"—with an abstract meaning; *asmā́ ū ṣú prábhūtaye / váruṇaya marúdbhyó / 'rcā vidúṣṭarebhyaḥ . . .* (8.41.1) "I want to sing beautiful praise to this *lord Varuṇa* (or: "to *Varuṇa* the power") (and) to the *Maruts*, the wisest ones . . . "—meaning unclear. Geldner in his translation treats *prábhūtaye* as an infinitive "das es ihm genüge" (which is unconvincing), but adds in the commentary that an adjectival meaning is also possible. Renou translates: "A ce (dieu) Varuna le dominateur" [118.5.72], and specifies in his commentary: "prábhūti 'domination (incarnée)" [118.7.28].

víbhūti- "all-embracing," "mighty," "strong:" only the adjectival meaning is attested in the *Ṛg Veda*: *mahā́m ánūnaṃ tavásaṃ víbhūtim / matsarā́so jarhr̥ṣanta prasā́ham* (6.17.4) "The great, the perfect, the strong, the *all-embracing* one (*Indra*) / Let the inebriating drinks arouse (him), the victorious one." It occurs in later texts as an abstract noun.

In all other cases verbal roots have only a couple of derivatives in *-ti-*; they refer to abstract notions with various degrees of personification. On the formal side they are represented by uncompounded words with and without prefixes, as well as by compounds.

Compound words are a problem apart. Stems in *-ti-*, appearing as the final elements of compounds, can acquire adjectival meanings, but since the compound as a whole belongs to the *bahuvrīhi*-class, this position cannot be regarded as diagnostic. The same applies to the so-called "pseudo-compounds" with an initial *a-*, *su-* or *dus-*. Nevertheless, the following list of stems in *-ti-* with personified abstract meanings contains a number of compounds, since their *-ti-*stem semantics admits of different interpretations.

as- "to be."

abhíṣṭi- (feminine) "help," "assistance," "support:"

ā́ yám pr̥ṇánti diví sádmabarhiṣaḥ
samudráṃ ná subhvàḥ svā́ abhíṣṭayaḥ
táṃ vr̥trahátye ánu tasthur ūtáyaḥ
śúṣmā índram avātā́ áhrutapsavaḥ (1.52.4)

"(He) whom (those) seated on the sacrificial straw(-mat) in heaven fill / as rivers (fill) the ocean,—(his) own beneficent *assistances*, / (his) *supports* at *Vṛtra*'s slaying, followed behind him / Behind *Indra*,—they the invincible, the unbent ones;" in this passage the two abstract feminines *abhíṣṭayaḥ* "assistances" and *ūtáyaḥ* "supports" are portrayed as separate entities that act quite independently of *Indra*, so that they seem to be to a certain degree personified.

av- "to help,"
ūtí- (feminine) "to help," "support;" "a helper." Vide supra.
iṣ- "to move," "to send," "to impel," "to encourage."
iṣṭí- (feminine) "search," "desire," "demand;" "an object of desire:"

ádabdhebhis táva gopā́bhir iṣṭe / 'smā́kam pāhi triṣadhastha sūrī́n (6.8.7) "Through thy protectors, suffering no deceit, O *desirable one*, / Protect our patrons, O (thou) dwelling in three abodes!;" following Renou, we see a vocative case in *iṣṭe* (and not a syncopated instrumental case plural based on *iṣṭébhir*, as Geldner believed). Renou translates: "ô (dieu, objet de notre) recherche" [118.13.42].

kar-/kir- "to remember," "to praise,"

sukīrtí- (feminine) "fine praise," "good fame," "beautifully extolled:" *sukīrtím bhikṣe váruṇasya bhū́reḥ* (2.28.1) "I beg good fame of the abundant *Varuna*;" *préṣṭhaṃ vo átithiṃ gṛṇīṣe 'gníṃ . . . ásad yáthā no váruṇaḥ sukīrtír* (1.186.3) "I shall sing your dearest guest—*Agni* . . . so that he should be *Varuṇa* for us, the *beautifully extolled* one. . . ."

cítti- (feminine) "comprehension," "reason," "thought"—both abstract and personified: *cíttim ácittiṃ cinavad ví vidvā́n* (4.2.11) "May he—as a wise man—distinguish between *comprehension* and *incomprehension*,"—the abstract meaning is quite evident;

ví yó vīrútsu ródhan mahitvā́-
utá prajā́ utá prasū́ṣv antáḥ
cíttir apā́ṃ dáme viṣvā́yuḥ
sádmeva dhī́rāḥ sammā́ya cakruḥ (1.67.9-10)

"(The one) who grows in plants thanks to his greatness, / And in the progeny and within (those who) have conceived / (The one who is) the *reason* of the waters, (who stays) at home for all (his) time,— / Having measured (it), as experts (measure) a dwelling, they built (a hearth for *Agni*)"—the meaning remains unclear, but some kind of personification seems likely. Geldner translated; "der Geist der Wasser," but Renou: "(lui qui est) la pensée-active des eaux" [118.12.15]. Grassmann suggested for *cítti-* in this passage the meaning "der Verständige, Einsichtige."

tar-/tir-/tur-"to cross (over)."

prátūrti- (feminine) "a breakthrough," "a rush forward;" "a precipitating one:" *tvám índra prátūrtiṣv / abhí víśvā asi spŕdhaḥ* (8.99.5) "O *Indra*, thou art superior to all opponents in (thy) *rushes forward*;" *imā́ asya prátūrtayaḥ / padáṃ juṣanta yád diví* (8.13.29) "These (tribes) of his, *rushing forward* (feminine), / Chose the spot which is in heaven;" the word "tribes" (*víṣaḥ* feminine) is supplied from the preceding verse, but Geldner prefers another translation: "diese seine Kampf-truppen," that is, the *Maruts'* troops that are the subject of the verse; in his commentary he suggests an alternative interpretation: the word can be an adjective referring to the noun *víśaḥ* from stanza 28;

suprátūrti- (adjective) "easily rushing forward:"

sákhāyas tvā vavṛmahe
deváṃ mártāsa ūtáye
apā́ṃ nápātaṃ subhágaṃ sudī́ditiṃ
suprátūrtim anehásam (3.9.1)

"We, (thy) friends, have chosen thee, / The god, (we) the mortals, for (our) aid, / The offspring (masculine) of the waters, the happy, the charmingly bright (one), / The (god) easily *rushing forward*, the innocuous one;" the stem *suprátūrti-* appears in the *Ṛg Veda* only as an adjective. The same applies to *sudī́diti-* (root *dī-* "to shine, glisten").

dā- "to bind:"

áditi- (feminine) "unboundness," "guiltlessness, innocence," "endlessness," nomen proprium proper noun of a goddess; adjective "limitless," "endless:" *ā́ sarvátātim áditiṃ vṛṇīmahe* (10.100.1-11) "We beg for ourselves perfect bliss (and) *innocence*." Geldner has: "Wir erbitten Vollkommenheit von der *Aditi*," but in the commentary he concedes that *áditi-* can be an abstract here. Both Neisser [111.21] and Renou see here anabstract notion, compare "Nous demandonspar-choix l'integrité (des biens, en sorte qu'il n'y ait) point d'attache (avec le mal)" [118.5.63]; *ádite mítra váruṇotá mṛḷa / yád vo vayáṃ cakṛmā́ kác cid ā́gaḥ* (2.27.14) "O *Aditi, Mitra*, as well as *Varuṇa*, pardon (us), / If we have committed any sin against you!;" *yásmai tváṃ sudraviṇo dádāśo / 'nāgāstvám adite sarvátātā / . . . prajā́vatā rā́dhasā té syāma* (1.94.15) "O lord of beautiful riches, to whom thou grantest / Guiltlessness in full measure, O *boundless one*, / . . . A gift (that) brings progeny,—we would like to be (like) those (ones);" here *áditi-* is an attribute of *Agni* (in other passages it can be applied to *Savitar*, *Soma*, the *Maruts* and some other gods). But this interpretation has been contested: Geldner sees here the name of the goddess, supplying in his translation: "Wen du auch, reich an Gut, (Wie) *Aditi* Schuldlosigkeit in vollem Masse gewähren wirst . . . ," but in the commentary he admits that the adjective is also conceivable. Renou translates: "ô (*Agni* agissant ainsi a l'instar d') *Aditi*," and comments: "It seems likely that *adite* is used here instead of *aditir iva*, in other words, it is a vocative of assimilation" [118.12.25,96]. Both Grassmann and Neisser saw here an adjective.

dī- "to glitter," "to glare."

sudītí- (feminine) "beautiful brilliance;" "glittering beautifully:" *sudītī́ sūno sahaso didīhi* (7.1.21) "Glitter with a beautiful glitter, O son of power!;" *táṃ citráyāmaṃ hárikeśam īmahe / sudītíṃ agníṃ suvitā́ya návyase* (3.2.13) "To this bright-pathed, golden-haired, *beautifully shining Agni* do we turn for a new success."

sudī́diti- the same, see above.
dhī- "to think," "to ponder."
dhītí- (feminine) "a thought," "meditation," "a prayer:"

gúhā satī́r úpa tmánā
prá yác chócanta dhītáyaḥ
káṇvā ṛtásya dhā́rayā (8.6.8)

"When secret *thoughts* begin to blaze by themselves, / The Kaṇvas (blaze) with a stream of Truth;" the notion rendered by *dhītáyaḥ* is half-personified here and is seen as separate from the poets who normally send them up to the gods.

nī- "to lead."
sunītí-, súnīti- (feminine) "good leadership," "excellent guidance;" "one who guides excellently," "a god leader:"

yá ā́nayat parāvátaḥ
súnītī turváśaṃ yádum
índraḥ sá no yúvā sákhā (6.45.1)

"(He) Who has led here from afar Turvaśa and Yadu with (his) *good guidance*, he is *Indra*, our young friend;" *índra . . . bháva súnītir utá vāmánītiḥ* (6.47.7) "O *Indra* . . . be (for us) a *good leader* and (even) an excellent leader!" Some other compounds with *-nīti-* as the last element (compare *vāmánīti-*) function in the same way.

yuj- "to yoke."

sváyukti- adjective "one who yokes oneself in:" *yuvám bhujyúm bhurámāṇaṃ víbhir gātám / sváyuktibhir* . . . (1.119.4) "To Bhujyu who was floundering (in the sea) you went on (the backs) of *self-yoked* birds." This stem is exclusively adjectival in the *Ṛg Veda*.

rā- "to give," "to donate."

rātí- (feminine) "a gift," "a boon;" "a giver," "a well-wisher:" *sásantu tyā́ árātayo / bódhantu śūra rātáyaḥ* (1.29.4) "Let those ill-wishers sleep! Let the *well-wishers* keep awake, O hero!;" the personified meaning of this word is sparsely attested.

árāti- (feminine) "ill-will," "enmity," "trouble;" "an ill-wisher;" "an enemy," "a demon:" *eṣá syá sómo matíbhiḥ punānó / 'tyo ná vājī́ táratī́d árātīḥ* (9.96.15) "This very *Soma*, purified by prayers, / outruns the *enemies* like a victorious racer;" Geldner understands it in a more concrete manner: "entgeht . . . den Feinden," while Renou renders it as an abstract notion: "traverse les inimitiés" [118.9.45].

The former application is much more common in the *Ṛg Veda* (compare the reverse with *rātí-*) so that *árāti-* can become a name for a class of evil spirits that personify the qualities of niggardliness and ill-will. For example: *átrā púraṃdhir ajahād árātīr / máde sómasya mūrā́ ámūraḥ* (4.26.7) "Then Puraṃdhi left the *Arātis* (accusative plural feminine) behind, / The wise one, *Soma*-drunk, (left) the unwise." Here Puraṃdhi is an unclear mythic figure that personifies abundance. In this context both names must evidently stand in opposition, conforming to their semantics.

varj- "to turn," "to derive," "to extract," etc.

suvṛktí- (feminine) "a laudatory speech;" "one who is beautifully praised:" *vísṛṣṭadhenā bharate suvṛktír / iyám índraṃ jóhuvatī manīṣā́* (7.24.2) "Like a released stream this *speech of praise* is rising, / (This) prayer, loudly invoking *Indra*;" *puró vo mandrā́ṃ divyā́ṃ suvṛktím / prayatí yajñé agním adhvaré dadhidhvam* (6.10.1) "The cheerful, heavenly, *beautifully-praised Agni*—set (him) in front of you at the time of the sacrificial rite."

śaṃs- "to declare solemnly," "to extol."
áśasti- (feminine) "a curse," "hate;" "an imprecator," "a hater:"

yáṃ yuváṃ dāśvàdhvarāya devā
rayíṃ dhatthó vásumantam purukṣúm
asmé sá indrāvaruṇāv ápi ṣyāt
prá yó bhanákti vanúṣām áśastīḥ (6.68.6)

"The wealth, O gods, consisting of goods, abundant in cattle, which you two (usually) grant to him who performs the honoring rite, / O *Indra*-and-*Varuṇa*, let it be exclusively ours, (the wealth) that destroys the *curses* of the envious ones!" The rest of the contexts are nondiagnostic and admit of both abstract and concrete interpretations. For example: *sá paúṃsyebhir abhibhū́r áśastīr* (1.100.10) "He suppresses the *cursers* (feminine) (or: the *curses*) through (his) virile powers." Geldner's translation is intentionally ambiguous: "Er bringt mit seinen Manneskräften die Lästerzungen schweigen." Renou's rendering: "Lui, (il) domine les (gens) aux mauvaises paroles, grâce à ses actes-mâles" [118.17.34]. But the corresponding nominal root-stem has an adjectival meaning in the *Ṛg Veda*—*aśas-* "cursing," "hating."

About two thirds of the stems in *-ti* that have a concrete or personified meaning are derivatives formed with the help of adverbial prefixes, adjectival prefixes (*su-, dur-*) or the privative *a-*. We therefore observe among them a rather high percentage of "pseudo-compounds" of the *karmadhāraya* and *bahuvrīhi* type. The appearance of the *-ti*-stems as final elements of compounds consisting of two equally-semantized nominal stems, such as *áśvam-iṣṭi-* "desirous of a horse," *havyá-dāti-* "accepting/bringing offerings," etc., supports the adjectival meaning of these stems.

There are some obscurities in the gender distribution of stems in *-as*, which are obviously connected with the peculiarities of the Vedic "model of the universe." According to a well-known rule, *-as-* stems with the accent on the root-vowel and with an abstract meaning (most often action nouns) belong to the neuter; oxytonic stems are agent nouns [3.113-4]. But actually very few oxytonic stems in *-as* are attested in the *Ṛg Veda*, and there are only isolated cases of minimal pairs where the difference in meaning is related to the position of the accent, as in *ápas-* "work;" *apás-* "active."

What concerns us here is not the degree of retention of the original relationship between the position of the accent and the *-as*-stems semantics,[54] but rather, the manner in which some stems of this class relate to their denotates. The problem was first raised and discussed by Gondain connection with *Agni*'s epithet *sūnúḥ sáhasaḥ* "son of power" [86]. He was quite justified in questioning the opinion held by such authorities as Grassmann, Roth, and Geldner, that the noun *sáhas-* (neuter) "power, strength" could also be used as an adjective "strong." Gonda believes that they interpreted the word as an adjective in phrases where it is actually used in apposition: this problem has already been discussed here in connection with the stems in *-ti*. The same can be said about another word for "strength"—*ójas-* (neuter). In contexts such as *yūyáṃ devāḥ prámatir yūyám ójo* (2.29.2) "You, O gods, are encouragement, you are strength," abstract notions are clearly personified.

One can also note a similar semi-personified, or rather concrete perception of abstract notions expressed by the nouns *dvéṣas-* (neuter) "hate," "hostility;" "a hate," "an enemy," and *dákṣas-* (neuter) "strength," "skill;" "strong," "skilful." Probably the most instructive example can be seen in the minimal pair *rákṣas-* (neuter): *rakṣás-* adjective. The semantics of the second member of the opposition is quite unambiguous: *rakṣás-* means "harmful," "the harmful one." But since the word *rákṣas-* is it is not exclusively used to render the abstract idea of "harm, damage," but can also be personified, and in that case it becomes synonymous with *rakṣás-*.

Word-composition gives support to the adjectival meaning of this stem-class as well (compare supra). For example: *cétas-* (neuter) "brilliance," "wisdom," but the derivatives are adjectives: *prácetas-* "wise," "attentive," *vícetas-* "brilliant," "sagacious," *súcetas-* "benevolent," *suprácetas-* "very wise."

Such a "personal" treatment of an abstract idea can be met with in some other stem-classes, too. Compare the stem *dāmán-*, noted by Gonda, with an accent that was originally typical of agent nouns; its basic meaning was the abstract "generosity," "liberal giving," and the narrower, "personified" meaning was "giver" (6.44.2).

In another paper Gonda suggested that *bráhman* "was the name for a fundamental upholding force which was thought of as immovable, solid, and supporting" [84.32]. The bibliography of the term *bráhman* has become quite extensive by this time. The semantics of this word concerns us here only as far as it touches upon the problem of the interrelationship of stylistic, grammatical, and semantic factors. Although the *Ṛg Veda* offers a formally marked opposition of two stems (the position of the accent): *bráhman-* (neuter) "a prayer," "a sacred word," "a magic charm," "inspiration" *vs.* *brahmán-* (masculine) "an implorer," "an incantator," also the name of a class of priests—the semantic interpretation of the neuter stems remains far from certain. In several passages *bráhman-* is regarded as an independent force, which the gods receive from the poets who sing their praises, or which can be obtained by drinking *Soma*, with which help heroic deeds are accomplished. For example, *ádhākṝṇoḥ prathamáṃ vīryàm mahád / yád asyā́gre bráhmaṇā śúṣmam aírayaḥ* (2.17.3) "Then thou hast performed the first great feat: / (That one) when, in the beginning, thou hast aroused (thy) fury by means of his *sacred word*" (to *Indra*), where "his" refers to the "poet-singer;" *úd gā́ ājad ábhinad bráhmaṇā valám* (2.24.3) "He drove out the cows, he split Vala by means of *an incantation*" (to *Brahmaṇaspati*). It is also a kind of substance which the initiated can—by means of their wisdom—"set in motion" for their own ends (this is a clearly magical concept), for example, . . . *prathamajā́ bráhmaṇo víśvam íd viduḥ / dyumnávad bráhma kuśikā́sa érira* . . . (3.29.15) " . . . the first-born ones know everything of the *sacred speech.* / The people of the *Kuśika*-clan set in motion the brilliant sacred speech." This view of an autonomous abstract *bráhman-* in the *Ṛg Veda* is confirmed in the subsequent development of its meaning: through the stage of a semi-personified notion it evolved into the proper name of the supreme deity of Hinduism.

A special case of gender manifestation is represented by the noun *vṛtrá-* in the *Ṛg Veda* (based on the verb *var-* "to obstruct," "to stop," "to envelop"), which is masculine in the singular and neuter in the plural (compare Böhtlingk, Grassmann), with the respective meanings of "an enemy (masculine);" the proper name of the dragon slain by *Indra* (masculine); and "obstruction," "barrier" (neuter). Its semantic invariant is "force of resistance," and in various Vedic contexts this invariant is represented as personified to various degree. There are some clear passages wherein the character of the denotate can be regarded as certain, for example, *vṛtréṇa yád áhinā bíbhrad ā́yudhā / samásthithā yudháye śáṃsam āvíde* (10.113.3) "When, bearing (thy) arms, thou camest against the dragon *Vṛtra* in order to fight (him), in order to gain glory, . . . " (a hymn to *Indra*): here *vṛtrá-* is obviously the proper name of *Indra*'s adversary. But there are other passages where *vṛtra-* can be either a proper name or a common noun. For example, consider Renou's translations of the first stanza in 3.37: *vā́rtrahatyāya śávase / . . . / índra tvā vartayāmasi* "Pour la force apte à briser les résistances . . . / ô *Indra*, nous t'orientons vers ici;" then stanza 5: *índraṃ vṛtrā́ya hántave . . . úpa bruve* "Je m'adresse à *Indra* . . . pour qu'il tue *Vṛtra* . . . ," as well as in stanza 6: . . . *tvā́m īmahe . . . índra vṝtrā́ya hántave* . . . " . . . nous t'implorons, . . . ô *Indra*, pour tuer *Vṛtra*" [118.17.80]. Geldner's versions are: stanza 1: "zur Übermacht, die die Feinde erschlägt," stanza 5: "das er den *Vṛtra* (Feind) erschlage," stanza 6: "den *Vṛtra* (Feind) zu erschlagen." The worshipper can be seen as asking *Indra* for the repetition of his fundamental cosmogonic exploit—the killing of the dragon *Vṛtra*—and thus the establishing of order in the universe—or this may be just a case of killing a (personal) enemy.

The semantic peculiarities of this noun are related to certain anomalies in the expression of its gender and number. The dictionaries refer to *vṛtrá-* in the singular as masculine, and as neuter in the plural. But the neuter singular also occurs in a collective sense, for example,

> *píbā sómam abhí yám ugra tárda*
> *urváṃ gávyam máhi gṛṇāná indra*
> *ví yó dhṛṣṇo vádhiṣo vajrahasta*
> *víśvā vṛtrám amitríyā śávobhiḥ* (6.17.1)

"Drink *Soma*, O terrible one, thanks to which (*Soma*) thou shalt bore through the cow-pen, O *Indra*, mightily praised one, / (Thou), O daring one, with the thundering cudgel in hand, who with (thine own) powers shalt smash all *hostile* (accusative plural neuter) *obstacles* (accusative singular)!" (or: "thou shalt kill any insidious *enemy*"). There is also the difficulty that the second line uses the wording of the *Vala* myth, but in the third and fourth lines the vocabulary is that of the dragon-slaying (*Vṛtra*) myth, and this is duly noted by Geldner in his commentary.[55]

The neuter plural of *vṛtrá-* does not in itself correspond to an abstract meaning. Many passages suggest a very concrete sense as in, for example, *agnír vṛtrā́ṇi jaṅghanad / draviṇasyúr vipanyáyā* (6.16.34) "May *Agni* utterly destroy the *enemies* (accusative plural neuter), / Seeking (their) wealth, with (great) success!"

Thus there are grounds to believe that some anomalies in gender distribution within a certain group of abstract nouns in the *Ṛg Veda* reflect peculiarities in the reference of these nouns, peculiarities which, in their turn, seem to be conditioned by specific traits of this "model of the universe."

This tendency to a partial or complete personification of some abstract nouns has resulted in their transformation into proper names in the *Ṛg Veda*. The correlation between a proper name and an appellative noun in this text is rather complex, and its proper interpretation requires a brief outline of the mythopoetic locus of the proper name in the *Ṛg Veda*.

The views of the *Ṛṣis* with regard to name were perfectly "realistic:" they considered the name (*nā́man-* neuter) to be a reflection of the essence of its bearer; if a thing or a person has different names, each of them corresponds to a definite quality that the name-bearer possesses.[56] Moreover, the *Ṛṣis* regard the proper name as the very essence of the denotate; the two aspects were inseparable. Only something with a name could be said to exist, and until there is a name, there cannot exist a corresponding object or person. This status of the name—in theVedic model of the universe—results in the sacralization of every operation concerning it. It may be said that the name as such was sacred during the Vedic period. In nonritual spheres this property probably appears considerably later.

One of the fundamental operations with names, as it appears in the text, was precisely "naming:" *nā́ma dhā-* literally "to put/set a name," "to fix a name." In the broad context of the *Ṛg Veda* this operation acquires cosmogonic value since "fixing a name" meant "creating an object.[57] For instance, *dádhāti putró varam páram pitúr / nā́ma tṛtī́yam ádhi rocané diváḥ* (1.155.3) "The son *fixes* (his) father's (name) here and yonder, / The third *name* (he sets) in the bright part of the sky." The passage deals with the three strides of *Viṣṇu*—the son whose father was the Sky. *Viṣṇu*, in making his strides, created the universe, and fixing names to cosmic elements in this context is equivalent to his strides.[58]

Renou has remarked on the intimate semantic ties between *nā́man-* and the noun *dhā́man-*, derived from the root *dhā-*. He says, "In fact, both terms complement one another; in this case, *nā́man-* represents the global and abstract aspect of the same notion whose multiple and accidental side is represented by *dhā́man-*" [115.1.21]. Later on the role of *dhā́man-* was taken by *rūpa-*; this development was reflected in the concept rendered by the compound *nāmarūpá-* "name-and-form."

The phrase *nā́ma + dhā-* has another meaning in the *Ṛg Veda* besides that of "naming," viz. "to strengthen," for the Vedic *Ṛṣis* believed that naming was equivalent to endowing someone with a certain substance. In this connection, the following can be cited:

bhū́ri nā́ma vándamāno dadhāti
pitā́ vaso yádi táj joṣáyase
kuvíd devásya sáhasā cakānáḥ
sumnám agnír vanate vāvṛdhānáḥ (5.3.10)

"The father, gives (thee) many names, glorifying (thee), O *Vasu*, if thou enjoyest it. / Will not *Agni*—invigorated (and) happy in (his) strength—gain (for us) the god's favor?" *Agni*'s father in this case is the sacrificing priest, for he has given birth to the god and invigorates him by giving him names.

In the middle voice, then, *nā́ma + dhā-* means "to acquire a name" and "to be strengthened, invigorated," for example, *dádhāno nā́ma mahó vácobhir / vápur dṛśáye venyó vy ā́vaḥ* (6.44.8) "*Acquiring*—thanks to the (poets') speeches—a great *name* (for himself), / The beautiful one displayed (his) splendor for contemplation (about *Soma*).

The phrase *nā́ma bhar-* "to bear/carry a name" means "to possess (or control) the qualities of the name-bearer," for example, *bíbharti cā́rv índrasya nā́ma / yéna víśvāni vṛtrā́ jaghā́na* (9.109.14) "He *carries the* dear *name* of *Indra*, / With whose help he destroyed all (his) enemies" (about *Soma*); or

paró yát tvám paramá ājániṣṭhāḥ
parāváti śrútyaṃ nā́ma bíbhrat
átaś cid índrād abhayanta devā́
víśvā apó ajayad dāsápatnīḥ (5.30.5)

"When, higher (than all), thou were born as the highest one, / *Carrying* into the distance (thy) *name*, worthy of fame, / The gods at once started fearing *Indra*. / He conquered all the waters ruled by the *Dāsa*."

In this way a figure of mythology can bear its own proper name and the name of some other person, and the latter's functions are transferred to the former. It has been observed by several scholars that a proper name in the *Ṛg Veda* can be regarded as a myth or a plot encoded in a certain way.

It should be stressed that the verb *bhar-* (as well as *dhā-*) is frequently used in descriptions of the cosmogonic activities of the Vedic gods. Thus the oftcited passage in 1.185.1 tells of Heaven and Earth: *víśvaṃtmánā bibhṛto yád dha nā́ma* "The two themselves *bear* whatever (has) a *name*." "They bear," that is, they comprise, thus creating the organised universe, since "whatever (has) a name" denotes all objects and elements contained in the cosmos. It is no accident that the same verb *bhar* is the predicate where the subject is *Vāc*, the proper name of the Sacred Speech: . . . *ahám mitrā́váruṇobhā́ bibharmy / ahám indrāgnī́ ahám aśvínobhā́ //1// ahám sómam āhanásam bibharmy / ahám tvā́ṣṭāram utá pūṣáṇam bhágam / . . .* (10.125.1c-d, 2a-b) "I *carry* both *Mitra* and *Varuṇa*, both *Indra* and *Agni*, and both of the *Aśvins*. / I carry the raging *Soma*, I (carry) *Tvaṣṭar, Pūṣan* and *Bhaga*."

To utter or invoke the name of a deity: *nā́ma hū-*, *nā́ma vac-* meant for the Vedic *Ṛṣis* a communion with the inner essence of the deity [118.4.79,118]. The very utterance of someone's name had to induce the name-owner to act according to the name's nature. This magical attitude toward the name resulted, in particular, in the frequent use of divine names as appeals; on the linguistic side it is rendered by vocatives, which capriciously the flow of the Vedic poet's narration, thus creating a very special correlation between the descriptive and the appellative functions of language (more on this below). The proclamation of a divine name in the *Ṛg Veda* should probably be seen as a variant of the more general magic procedure of the "Declaration of Truth," to which Old Indian culture attributed wide-ranging creative properties.

Usually, the name of a deity is proclaimed aloud and in public, but there is also another way: a mental rendition of the name, the concentration of the poet's mental effort around it; as has been observed by Renou, the latter device is encoded by the phrase *nā́ma man-*, literally "to think a name." One is reminded—in this connection—of the mental sacrifice that was alleged to be as efficacious as a real one in the opinion of the Vedic Aryans.

Finally, the phrase *nā́ma grabh-* "to seize a name" is common in Vedic charms, where it denotes the full domination of the "name-seizer" over the person whose name "has been captured," for example, *navānā́ṃ navatīnā́m / viṣásya rópuṣīṇām / sárvāsām agrabhaṃ nā́ma / . . .* (1.191.13) "Of the ninety nine / destroyers (feminine) of poison, / Of all (of them) I have *seized* (their) *name*."

This short list of the principal predicates whose object is *nā́man-* gives a very general idea of the role of this word in the Vedic "model of the universe." In the *Ṛṣi*'s mind, a name always touched upon a mystery; the energy nucleus of the name was its intrinsic "naming" force which was at the same time a creative force. The sacred act of name-proclaiming was like tearing down a veil covering the inner essence of the name, and "to know the name" was equal to gaining access to the mystery.

Among attributive constructions expressed by concord the phrase *gúhyaṃ nā́ma* "a secret name" frequently occurs; it points to the true nature of the denotate that can be made manifest by means of some kind of magic procedure that is tantamount to acquisition of knowledge. These ideas are aptly illustrated by the two initial stanzas of 4.58 (a hymn in praise of ghee):

samudrā́d ūrmír mádhumāñ úd ārad
úpāṃśúnā sám amṛtatvám ānaṭ
ghṛtásya nā́ma gúhyaṃ yád ásti
jihvā́ devā́nām amṛ́tasya nā́bhiḥ (1)

vayáṃ nā́ma prá bravāmā ghṛtásya-
asmín yajñé dhārayāmā námobhiḥ
úpa brahmā́ śṛṇavac chasyámānaṃ
cátuḥśṛṅgo 'vamīd gaurá etát (2)

"The mead-wave arose out of the ocean. / (Mixed) with *Soma*, it acquired the qualities of the *amṛta*, / That is the secret *name* of ghee: / Tongue of the gods, navel of immortality //. (2) We will proclaim the *name* of ghee-fat. / In this sacrifice we will make (it) stay (here) by bowing. / Let the brahman hear (it), when it is being pronounced. / The four-horned gaur-ox has emitted it."

The ghee-fat is seen here in a mystic way: not only is it the clarified butter being poured into the fire, but it is also identified with *Soma* (the navel of immortality) and with poetic speech (—the tongue of the gods). The latter two definitions are interrelated, for *Soma* is known to stimulate poetic inspiration. At the same time, *Soma* is a gaur-ox, since both the juice and the animal are of brown-yellowish color. And thus the knowledge of the fat's "secret names"—which is the privilege of the brahman-priest—really means the understanding of its true, though hidden, nature.

The concept of "secret names" conforms with the general Vedic teaching that true supreme knowledge is concealed from the human mind; what is accessible to mortals is only its lesser part. Speculations of this sort are reflected, for instance, in the riddle-hymn 1.164.45:

catvā́ri vā́k párimitā padā́ni
tā́ni vidur brāhmaṇā́ yé manīṣíṇaḥ
gúhā trī́ṇi níhitā néṅgayanti
turī́yaṃ vācó manuṣyā̀ vadanti

"Speech is measured into four parts. / The Brahmans who are wise know them. / Three (quarters), which are secretly put away, they do not activate. / The fourth (quarter) of speech (is what) men speak."

Words, too, can be secret (1.72.6; 10.53.10), and the phrase *gúhyāni padā́*, "secret words," is almost synonymous with *gúhyā nā́māni*, secret names." Secret words are also filled with creative force, for example, *vidvā́ṃsaḥ padā́ gúhyāni kartana / yéna devā́so amṛtatvám ānaśuḥ* (10.53.10) "Use secret words as experts (do), / by which means the gods have achieved immortality."

After these general remarks about the *Ṛṣis*'s views concerning proper names, let us determine their range of application in the *Ṛg Veda*. Admittedly, this is a highly complex problem, since one is not able to draw a clear line between a common and a proper noun in the usage of this text [29.220]. In Gardiner's widely-accepted opinion, the weaker the semantic motivation of a noun, the more properties of a proper name it possesses. Such names—mainly theonyms—are extremely rare in the *Ṛg Veda*: *índra-, marút-, váruṇa-*. But generally speaking, such a lack of motivation from a modern scholar's standpoint should not be identified with the *Ṛṣi*'s standpoint, for whom quite different etymological links were important. The rest of the proper names in the *Ṛg Veda* are actually common nouns, more or less widely used in the former function. There are not absolute formal or semantic criteria for distinguishing them, so that grave problems of interpretation arise in numerous cases.

The *Ṛṣis* used to play with proper names in their hymns. In theory, two processes of name-playing should be possible: 1) transforming common nouns into proper names, and 2) transforming proper names into nouns. The former possibility is most frequently used, as it is the most appropriate one for theVedic "model of the universe" with its inherent tendency for the complete, or at least partial personification of various abstract powers and ideas. The poet quite often "indulges in brinkmanship:" the degree of personified or abstract perception constantly vacillates and shifts, and it becomes impossible to determine with certainty if a deity's name is intended, or just an abstract notion. Such an ambiguous position of a name would always be connected with a *hic et nunc* situation, as in the following stanza dealing with the *Maruts*:

ā́pathayo vípathayó-
'ntaspathā ánupathāḥ
etébhir máhyaṃ nā́mabhir
yajñáṃ viṣṭārá ohate (5.52.10)

"(Those) "walking toward the path," "walking off the path," / "Walking in the middle of the path," "walking along the path"— / Under these names they grant me the sacrifice, after scattering widely around."

The poet would test the names for most various properties. They could be quite accidental, as in the instance quoted above, or they could function as conventional epithets and appear in many contexts as regular proper names. This process developed along the following lines: an attribute or an apposition to a deity's proper name → theonym. Such epithets/proper names cannot be regarded as mere verbal ornamentation; Gonda, after a thorough study of their role in the *Ṛg Veda* [79], correctly concluded that they have rather important functions: they usually appeal to a single characteristic trait of a deity that seems most important at the moment in order to provoke its manifestation. An epithet's motivation is not always conditioned by its actual context, and this circumstance rather confirms its transformation into a deity's proper name, like *jātávedas-* literally "the knower of (all) creatures," or *vaiśvānará-* "belonging to all men" (Grassmann, but according to Gonda—"related to him who is in complete possession of vital force"), when applied to *Agni*; *maghávan-* "generous" or *vṛtrahán-* "*Vṛtra*'s slayer" in the case of *Indra*, etc. Nevertheless, boundaries between appellative epithets and proper names are not always fixed, and a standing epithet that regularly replaces a deity's proper name can be sometimes applied to another god as, for instance, *Agni* (not *Indra*!) *vṛtrahán-* in 1.59.6; 6.16.14.

Vedic style is fond of chains of theonyms: lists, epithets of a particular god, and especially appeals to him in the vocative, as in:

yám trā́yadhva idám-idaṃ
dévāso yáṃ ca náyatha
tásmā agne váruṇa mítrā́ryaman
márutaḥ śárma yachata (7.59.1)

"(Him) whom you protect, O gods, whom you guide hither and thither, / To him, O *Agni, Varuṇa, Mitra, Aryaman,* (and) *Maruts*, grant (your) protection!;"

úṣo vā́jena vājini prácetā
stómaṃ juṣasva gṛṇato maghoni
purāṇī́ devi yuvatíḥ púraṃdhir
ánu vratám carasi viśvavāre (3.61.1)

"O *Uṣas*, O rewarding with reward, O understanding one, / Enjoy the poet's praise-song, O generous one! / O goddess, ancient (and yet ever) young like *Puraṃdhi*, / Thou followest the (divine) vow, O possessor of all goods!."

When modern scholars translate and interpret the hymns, the choice between a common noun and a proper name frequently becomes all-important, since it determines the key to understanding a passage or a hymn, or perhaps the whole collection. A dual interpretation is typical of such important words as *īḷā-* (feminine) "a libation" and proper name of a goddess: *nírṛti-* (feminine) "destruction," "abyss," and proper name of a goddess; *párvata-*

"knotty," "protruding," "a hill," "a mountain," and a (personified) proper name, as well as many others.

Previously, there was a lively debate concerning the names of the *Āditya*-gods (the sons of the goddess *Aditi*—"Nonboundedness"). Except for *Váruṇa-*, all of them function both as proper names and common nouns: *mitrá-* (masculine) "a friend" and a theonym; (neuter) "friendship," "friendly contract;" *aryamán-* (masculine) "a companion," "a match-maker," "a best-man;" god's name; *bhága-* (masculine) "a giver, bestower;" "a lucky lot," "luck, happiness;" god's name; *áṃśa-* (masculine) "a portion, share," and a theonym; *dákṣa-* "skilful," "skill," "ability;" a god's name. The etymology of *váruṇa-* has not been established with certainty.[59] Although the *Ādityas* are traditionally classified as celestial gods, more than thirty years ago Paul Thieme proposed to regard them as personified abstract notions, so that in every Vedic passage *váruṇa-* should be rendered as "True Speech" (on the basis of his tentative etymology), *mitrá-* as "Agreement, Contract," *aryamán-* as "Hospitality," and so forth [141]. His extreme position has not found acceptance among scholars, but the possibility of presenting the problem in this way is in itself important.

The play with proper names in *Ṛg Veda* is often connected with the problem of reference. When a number of theonyms can also function as common nouns, denoting concrete objects or cosmic elements (such as *agní-* (masculine) "fire" and theonym; *sū́rya-* (masculine) "sun" and theonym; *sóma-* (masculine) "a certain plant [possibly "fly-agaric"?] and theonym), there is always room for ambiguity. And this ambiguity is fully exploited by the authors— although we should never exclude the possibility of semantic syncretism in those cases where we just see different meanings. When these mythological figures act as deities they show few anthropomorphic traits. We know for certain that *Agni* has a wife, *Agnayī*, that *Sūrya* is *Uṡas*'s lover and has a daughter, that *Soma* was the bridegroom of *Savitar*'s daughter, and that their marriage-feast serves as a model for humans; but all such traits and motifs pass almost unnoticed among the descriptions of natural phenomena: the flames of the sacrificial fire, the rays of the blazing sun, the juice of the plant, the source of the divine drink of immortality. Hence the high degree of ambiguity in their treatment, which is yet another peculiarity of the style of the *Ṛg Veda*. This linguistic problem is just one particular move in the *Ṛṣi*'s play, based on the context's reference to more than a single level.

3
Metrics and Phonetics

Sound-play, which is a general characteristic of poetry, reached remarkable heights of sophistication in the *Ṛg Veda*; it conforms to the rules of poetic creative activity, but it is also endowed with definite communicative functions. Phonetic features are usually classified as prosodic and inherent. Both classes of features can be used in the *Ṛg Veda* to convey additional information in the communication act between worshipper and deity, and they will be treated separately. As a preliminary, we shall touch on some general mythological notions of the Vedic *Ṛṣis* that are directly concerned with language.

The *Ṛg Veda* is a poetic text, and its language is metrically organized in a certain way, so that it differs, for instance, from colloquial speech. This special regulated character of the archaic language of the hymns, its close ties with divine worship–and verbal worship was seen as an essential part of ritual, as important as (or even more important than) sacrifice–the solemn manner of recitation, and the musical part of the delivery of the hymn, taken as a whole, rendered the language truly divine in the *Ṛṣis'* mind.

Sacred Speech is personified as the goddess *Vāc* (*vā́c-* (feminine) from the verb *vac-* "to speak"). As W. Norman Brown put it, *Vāc*, being a very vague personification, whose feminine gender alone is clear, nevertheless occupies a very prominent position in the priests' world-view and competes with the male deities *Prajāpati*, *Viśvakarman*, *Puruṣa* and *Bṛhaspati/ Brahmaṇaspati*, as well as with the neuter Brahman [61]. One self-laudatory hymn in the *Ṛg Veda* (10.125) is wholly dedicated to her. She is described by the verbs "to move" (*car-*) in the company of the gods, "to carry" (*bhar-*) the gods, "to give birth to" (*jan-*), "to extend" (*ví* + *sthā-*), "to embrace, envelop" (*ā́* + *rabh-*) all existing creatures. All of these verbs are predicates encoding an essential cosmogonic act [30.20-47]. In this way *Vāc* plays the role of a demiurge, the personified manifestation of a certain cosmogonic power. The specific form of her creative activity is rendered by the verb "to speak" (*vad-*). Her essential nature is manifested through her being forever identical with herself, despite the countless multitude of her temporary forms; compare: *tā́m mā devā́ vy àdadhuḥ purutrā́ / bhū́risthātrām bhū́ry āveśáyantīm* (10.125.3) "Me–such as I am–the gods distributed in many places, / (Me), possessing many dwellings, (and) entering many (forms)."

The interrelations of *Vāc* with other deities can be termed "quasi-symmetrical." On the one hand, she gave birth to the father of all beings at the top of the sky (10.125.7), and everybody lives through her (stanza 4), but, on the other hand, the gods distribute her in various places; that is, they seem to wield power over her. Such changes in the relationship between parents and children are well attested in the *Ṛg Veda*: *Puruṣa* and *Virāj* (10.90.5), *Aditi* and *Dakṣa* (10.72.4).

At the same time, *Vāc* is represented as a self-sustaining force, possessed of the highest authority in the universe, and the ruler of everything that sustains gods and men: compare 1.164.39:

ṛcó akṣáre paramé vyòman
yásmin devā́ ádhi víśve niṣedúḥ
yás tán ná véda kím ṛcā́ kariṣyati
yá ít tád vidús tá imé sám āsate

"(One) who does not know that syllable of the hymn in highest heaven, where all the gods sit, what shall he do with the hymn? Just those who know it sit (together) here."

This passage, incidentally, indicates *Vāc*'s function as mediator between gods and men. She holds power over the secret syllable that keeps together the universe, and she may grant her knowledge to the mortals, priests; see for example 10.125.5:

ahám evá svayám idáṃ vadāmi
júṣṭaṃ devébhir utá mā́nuṣebhiḥ
yáṃ kāmáye táṃ-tam ugráṃ kṛṇomi
tám brahmā́ṇaṃ tám ṛ́ṣiṃ táṃ sumedhā́m

"I, by myself, say what / gives joy to gods and men. / Whom I love, him I make powerful, / Him (I make) a Brahman, him–a *Ṛṣi*, him–a wise man." According to the interpretation of W. Norman Brown, *Vāc* created the matter of the universe and the means for its organization; she also taught *Agni* the use of the syllable (*akṣara*), so that he would be able to transmit it to gods and men. The priests' task was to secure for humans the transmission of supreme knowledge that would enable them to keep renewing the cosmic origins.

Sacred Speech appears to men veiled in a mystery that is almost impenetrable. It is revealed only to the initiated few, and the average person cannot even imagine the limits of its power. It is openly declared by the

Ṛṣi Dīrghatamas in the Riddle-Hymn:

catvā́ri vā́k párimitā padā́ni
tā́ni vidur brāhmaṇā́ yé manīṣíṇaḥ
gúhā trī́ṇi níhitā néṅgayanti
turī́yaṃ vācó manuṣyā̀ vadanti (1.164.45)

"Speech is measured into four parts. / The Brahmans who are wise know them. / Three (quarters), which are secretly put away, they do not activate. / The fourth (quarter) of speech (is what) men speak." This description emphasizes the cosmogonic nature of *Vāc*; another cosmogonic force–the giant *Puruṣa*–is described in very similar terms: *pā́do 'sya víśvā bhūtā́ni / tripā́d asyāmṛ́taṃ diví* (10.90.3) "A quarter of him (is) all creatures. / Three quarters (are what is) immortal in heaven."

Those priests who had the knowledge of that concealed part of the nature of *Vāc* and were able to understand her pronouncements became masters of supreme knowledge, preeminent among their colleagues:

utá tvaḥ páśyan ná dadarśa vā́cam
utá tvaḥ śṛṇván ná śṛṇoty enām
utó tvasmai tanvàṃ ví sasre
jāyéva pátya uśatī́ suvā́sāḥ (10.71.4)

"One, looking, does not see Speech; / (Another) one, listening, does not hear her. / But to some (other) one she gives (her) body, / As a passionate wife, beautifully attired, (gives herself) to (her) husband."

The role of the priest-poets consisted in revealing this secret that remained concealed (the correlation *parokṣa-pratyakṣa* would have a great future in different spheres of Old Indian culture).

And when it is said in the "Knowledge-Hymn" that the *Ṛṣis* have generated Sacred Speech, the context seems to stress this particular role:

bṛ́haspate prathamáṃ vācó ágraṃ
yát praírata nāmadhéyaṃ dádhānāḥ
yád eṣāṃ śréṣṭhaṃ yád aripráṃ ā́sīt
preṇā́ tád eṣāṃ níhitaṃ gúhāvíḥ (10.71.1)

"O *Bṛhaspati*, the first beginning of Speech (was born), / When they set themselves in motion, giving names (to things). / Whatever they had of the best of the immaculate, / Whatever was hidden in them, was revealed through love" (where "they" are the original priests).

The mediating function of Speech is closely linked with that of *Agni*, the god of sacrificial fire. It is frequently mentioned in the hymns, for example, in 1.173.3:

nákṣad dhótā pári sádma mitā́ yán
bhárad gárbham ā́ śarádaḥ pṛthivyā́ḥ
krándad áśvo náyamāno ruvád gaúr
antár dūtó ná ródasī carad vā́k

"Let the hotar appear, circling the raised (sacrificial) seats! / Let him bring the autumnal fruit of the earth! / Let the horse, when led (to the altar), neigh! Let the cow low! / Let Speech like a messenger wander between the two worlds!" Sāyaṇa informs us that this hotar denotes *Agni*, the fire carried around the sacrificial ground; at the same time he is the neighing horse, while Speech is the lowing cow.

Such is their relationship in mythological synchrony. But in diachrony, in Brown's reconstruction (see above), the goddess *Vāc* taught *Agni* to use the *akṣara* syllable. At the same time, another divine mediator between gods and men, *Soma*, also has close ties with *Vāc*: in the hymns, only *Agni* and *Soma* are called *padavī́ḥ kavīnā́m* "leaders of poets"[60] (*Agni* in 3.5.1, and *Soma* in 9.96.9 and 18); and it is known that *Soma* was the source of the poets' inspiration. It should also be noted that these two gods are more ritual-oriented than the rest.

It has been frequently emphasized that the functions of priest and poet are closely related [133]: both serve as mediators between the divine and the human worlds; one has the sacrifice as his tool and the other–the word. Both recreate the original act of the demiurge, organizing the Cosmos out of the elements of Chaos [14.43]. But the principal tool of *Vāc* is not even a word–it is a syllable. And though the word *akṣára-* (a verbal noun from the root *kṣar-* "to flow, to stream," literally "unspreading (around)" "nontransient") means both "a word" and "a syllable," in cosmogonic contexts its prosodic connotation obviously prevails, for example:

gaurī́r mimāya salilā́ni tákṣaty
ékapadī dvipádī sā́ cátuṣpadī
aṣṭā́padī návapadī babhūvúṣī
sahásrākṣarā paramé vyòman

tásyāḥ samudrā́ ádhi kṣaranti
téna jīvanti pradíśaś cátasraḥ
tátaḥ kṣaraty akṣarám
tád víśvam úpa jīvati (1.164.41-42)

"The buffalo-cow lowed, fashioning floods of water, / Having become one-footed, two-footed, four-footed, / Eight-footed, nine-footed, with a thousand syllables in the highest heaven. // From her flow forth the seas, / (And) on it live the four quarters (of the world). / From her flows (what is) nontransient. / On it everything exists." Here the (buffalo-) cow symbolizes Sacred Speech, and the floods of water are the primordial entity out of which the universe was created. Then several puns follow: *padá-* "a (verse-) foot," *akṣára-* "a syllable" and "nontransient." Thus, verse-feet of various numbers of syllables are intended here, and the "supreme syllable," the cosmic creator, is recognized as the "nontransient" element.

One of the names of a cow–the word richest in synonyms in the *Ṛg Veda*–was *ákṣarā-* (feminine);[61] Sāyaṇa glossed it with "speech" in some passages (for example, 8.15.9; 36.7), but with "cow" in others, such as 3.31.6.

Concluding these mythological speculations it can be said that in the *Ṛg Veda* metrical speech that consists of verses (*pādas*) is sacred, and verses are measured in syllables (*akṣaras*). This speech was regarded as the supreme cosmogonic force, linked to sacrifice and mediation between gods and men. At this point one has to ask whether the worshipper intended to convey information to the deity using the peculiarities of metrical speech. But such a discussion first calls for a brief sketch of Vedic versification.

The latter was based on syllabic principles: the main distinctive feature was the number of syllables in the verse-line (*pā́da-* masculine "foot," "leg," "a quarter" [= "the foot of a quadruped"]).[62] The *pādas* constitute the basis of Vedic metrics, and larger metric units are based on their combinations.

The quantitave features of syllables within a *pāda* were fixed only to a certain extent. Syllables could be long and short; their quantity was determined by the length of the syllabic vowel as well as by the number of the following consonants. The position of stress was irrelevant to prosody. The sequence of long and short syllables was fixed only for the last four or five syllables of the *pāda* (the so-called cadence), while the first and the last syllables of the *pāda* were prosodically irrelevant. On the whole, the verse-rhythm tended to be iambic.

Main types of *pāda*:

8-syllable *pāda* (°°°°⏑–⏑⏓);[63]
5-syllable *pāda* (⏓–⏑–⏓) (rare);
(these two types of short *pāda* lack the caesura);

11-syllable *pāda* with the caesura after the fourth or the fifth syllable:
1) °°°° || °°°–⏑–⏓, and
2) °°°°° || °°–⏑–⏓;

12-syllable *pāda* with the caesura after the fourth or the fifth syllable:
1) °°°° || °°°–⏑–⏑⏓, and
2) °°°°° || °°–⏑–⏑⏓;

Various *pādas* can combine to form verses of different metres. Combinations of the same *pādas* occur most frequently: three 8-syllable *pādas* make up the *Gāyatrī* metre, four 8-syllable *pādas*–the *Anuṣṭubh*, four 5-syllable *pādas*–the *Dvipāda Virāj*, four 11-syllable *pādas*–the *Triṣṭubh*, four 12-syllable *pādas*–the *Jagatī*, and so forth. Metres that combine different *pādas* are much less common: 8 + 8 + 12–the *Uṣṇih*, 12 + 8 + 8–the *Purauṣṇih*, 8 + 12 + 8–the *Kakubh*, 8 + 8 + 12 + 8–the *Bṛhatī*, 12 + 8 + 12 + 8–the *Satobṛhatī*, 8 + 8 + 8 + 8 + 8 + 12 + 8–the *Atiśakvari*, 12 + 12 + 8 + 8 + 8 + 12 + 8–the *Atyaṣṭi*, and some others (in the long metres the refrain occurs twice).

A metrical unit of higher rank is the stanza, in which verses of identical metres (most often in threes–*tṛca*) or of different metres (*pragāthā*) are combined in accordance with certain rules. The highest metrical unit is the hymn constituted by the combination of verses and stanzas. The end of the hymn is often marked by a verse based on a metre different from that used in the body of the poem: the body of the hymn in the *Jagatī*, the end in the *Triṣṭubh*; the body in the *Gāyatrī*, the end in the *Anuṣṭubh*. The *Gāyatrī* alone could not be used in the final verse of a different metre.

These basic principles of Vedic metrics should be regarded as the tendencies that are most frequently actually manifested in the text, as general rules that emerge against the background of numerous deviations and anomalies. Such deviations concern the number of syllables in the *pāda*, the sequence of long and short syllables in the cadence, and the place of the caesura within a *pāda*. The internal caesura is, on the whole, a weaker demarcator than the external one which marks the boundary between two *pādas*. All of these factors compound the uncertainty. Moreover, since the written version of the text as preserved up to the present does not conform to its original metrical form in great or many details, it has to be reconstructed according to rules many of which still remain rather uncertain.[64]

In this situation we are hardly in a position to discuss seriously the problem of the semiotic value of metrical irregularity in a given case. It seems unreasonable to abandon such attempts completely, but the degree of our confidence in the results thus obtained should be low.

Metres in the *Ṛg Veda* are connected with certain mythological images and views. The "Riddle-Hymn" contains an original theory on the correlation between metre and hymn:

yád gāyatré ádhi gāyatrám ā́hitaṃ
traíṣṭubhād vā traíṣṭubhaṃ nirátakṣata
yád vā jágaj jágaty ā́hitam padáṃ
yá it vidús té amṛtatvám ānaśuḥ (1.164.23)

"That the *Gāyatrī* (foot) is based on *Gāyatrī* (hymn), / Or that the *Triṣṭubh* (foot) is made from the *Triṣṭubh* (hymn), / Or that the *Jagat* (foot) is based on the *Jagat* (hymn)– / (Those) who know that have attained immortality."

From the standpoint of modern Western interpreters just the reverse must be true, and Geldner calls it a paradox in his commentary; at the same time he remarks that the deeper meaning of this statement remains to be explained. Perhaps the key to the secret lies in the next stanza, where everything seems to be turned back to normal, and the smaller unit becomes the measure of the larger one:

gāyatréṇa práti mimīte arkám
arkéṇa sā́ma traíṣṭubhena vākám
vākéna vākáṃ dvipádā cátuṣpadā-
akṣáreṇa mimate saptá vā́ṇīḥ (1.164.24)

"With the *Gāyatrī* (foot) he measures a song, / With the song–a chant, with the *Triṣṭubh* (foot)–a recited stanza, / With the stanza of two feet and four feet–a hymn. / With the syllable they measure the seven 'voices.'"

The issue seems to be the independent existence of the names of the metres and chants in the *Ṛg Veda* as "real" mythological characters, or at least semi-personified images. The hymn on the origin of sacrifice speaks about the metres:

agnér gāyatry àbhavat sayúgvā-
uṣṇíhayā savitā́ sám babhūva
anuṣṭúbhā sóma ukthaír máhasvān
bṛ́haspáter bṛhatī́ vā́cam āvat

virā́ṇ mitrā́váruṇayor abhiśrī́r
índrasya triṣṭúb ihá bhāgó áhnaḥ
víśvān devā́ñ jágaty ā́ viveśa
téna cākḷpra ṛ́ṣayo manuṣyā̀ḥ (10.130.4-5)

"The *Gāyatrī* became *Agni*'s girl (literally "yoked together with"); / *Savitar* joined with the *Uṣṇih*; / *Soma*, magnified with hymns, (joined) with the *Anuṣṭubh*; / The *Bṛhatī* supported *Bṛhaspati*'s speech. /

The *Virāj* (was) *Mitra*-and-*Varuṇa*'s advantage; / The *Triṣṭubh* (was) here part of *Indra*'s (sacrificial) day; / The *Jagatī* came to All-the-Gods. / (And) then the human *Ṛṣis* conformed to it."

All the names of the metres are feminine here, and the gods are all males. The "personal" treatment of metres in this context can hardly be doubted. Returning to 1.164.23-24, it should be kept in mind that Vedic mythology offers examples of symmetrical (and quasi-symmetrical) relations between genitors and their progeny (see above). This general model can be helpful in an attempt to describe the present variant: the hymns have generated the metres, while the metres measure (that is, create) the hymns.

The stanzas of 10.130. cited above, are full of mythological information. While they describe the establishment of sacrifice by the "first *Ṛṣis*" they also fix correspondences between certain metres and deities. It is no accident that the *Gāyatrī* takes precedence here: the hymns openly state their preference for this metre, though, in actual fact, the *Triṣṭubh* is used more frequently. See, for instance: *gāyatrásya samídhas tisrá āhus / táto mahnā́ prá ririce mahitvā́* (1.164.25) "They say there are three kindling-sticks in the *Gāyatrī* (stanza); / Therefore in power (and) might it has surpassed (all the other metres)." "Three" is a sacred number and represents totality;[65] but in this case the number may also refer to the three sacrificial fires.[66]

The correspondences between mythological characters and metres, fully elaborated later in the *Brāhmaṇas* and the *Upaniṣads*, are represented in the *Ṛg Veda* by rather contradictory statements. Thus, the funeral hymn 10.14.16 states: *triṣṭúb gāyatrī́ chándāṃsi / sárvā tā́ yamá ā́hitā* "The *Triṣṭubh*, the *Gāyatrī*, the metres– / All these are composed for *Yama*." Other passages call the *Triṣṭubh* the joy of *Indra* (8.69.1), of the *Maruts* (8.7.1), and of *Soma* (9.97.35), and the *Anuṣṭubh* is said to be pleasing for *Indra* (10.124.9).

These examples make apparent the absence from the *Ṛg Veda* of a unified system of correspondences between mythological figures and metres. Neither do the fragments quoted fully represent the actual conditions of the text: hymns in the *Triṣṭubh* are indeed quite typical for *Indra*, but this metre is the most common one in the collection, and the situation cannot be seen as diagnostic. This metre also predominates in the *Agni* hymns (it is used in about half of them), while the *Gāyatrī* hymns make up slightly more than a quarter of them. But such hymns, on the other hand, constitute about two-thirds of all hymns to *Soma-Pavamāna* of Book 9. No more confidence can be placed in other correspondences.

It would be interesting to explore the possibility of ascertaining some connections between a certain metre and a family of singers. Such a possibility is hinted at in 10.130.5d, where the verb *cākḷpre* "they conformed (to it)," is used (literally "they made themselves correspond to it"). Oldenberg believed that rare and artificially long metres (they may also be called stanzas) with a partial double repetition of the preceding verse–the *Atyaṣṭi* and the *Atiśakvarī*–were connected with a certain poet or a circle of poets. The individual metrical anomalies of Book 7, produced by the *Vasiṣṭha* family, are well known. According to Arnold, these hymns are frequently characterized by a late caesura in an 11- and 12-syllable verse; that is, the caesura occurs after the fifth–not the fourth–syllable; the middle of the verse-line tends to the scansion ˘ // ¯ ˘ ; and after the eighth syllable a secondary caesura occurs [53.179],[67] for instance: *sómaḥ śukró ná / vāyáva / ayāmi* (7.64.56). The rivals of the *Vasiṣṭhas*, the poets of the *Viśvāmitra* clan, author of Book 3, by contrast, more frequently used an early caesura. Strophic hymns belong mainly to Book 8. Nevertheless, no scholar has managed to elaborate a complete chronological stratification of the *Ṛg Veda* based on purely metrical features; neither has Arnold's classification gained widespread acceptance.

A hymn based on a single metre represents a normal case–the coda in a different metre is not considered here. The change of metres (strophic hymns excepted) is marked, as are hymns composed in different metres. But it cannot be established with certainty if such a change of metre within a hymn reflects some characteristics of its content, although in some cases there seems to be a link. Oldenberg has observed that different metres appear in hymns that lack a unified narrative plot. They may be a collection of disparate verses, as in the marriage hymn 10.85, or the funeral hymns 10.14 and 18; they can be verses accompanying various moments of the ritual, as in the hymns to the sacrificial pole 3.8 and to the patron-gods of the fields 4.57, and in a charm against a weapon 6.75. Or they may be remarks in dialogues, probably previously separated by now lost prose (*ākhyāna*): the conversation between *Agastya* and the *Maruts* (and *Indra*) in 1.170; between *Agastya* and *Lopāmudrā* (1.179); and between *Indra*, *Viṣṇu* and others, concerning the intended slaying of *Vṛtra* (8.100) [53.143].

The Indian orthodox tradition requires that the recitation of hymns composed in a certain metre should be assigned to quite definite rituals. In later Vedic texts the identification of metres with daily offerings is an intergral part of a whole system of identifications. Thus, the *Chāndogya Upaniṣad* 16.1 declares that the *Gāyatrī* accompanies the morning libation, the *Triṣṭubh* is used at noon, and the *Jagatī* at the third libation. Now, such general statements are absent from the *Ṛg Veda*–the chains of identification were still being elaborated at the time–and even if something of the kind did exist it was not generally and consistently adopted. One might suppose that every single hymn was connected to a ritual–which is obviously quite improbable–but then the Upaniṣadic prescriptions would contradict the Ṛg-Vedic facts: for example, the hymn to Night (the evening "grace"–10.127) is composed in the *Gāyatrī* metre, and the majority of the *Uṣas* (Dawn) hymns are in the *Triṣṭubh*.

It should be natural to come across the expressive and figurative use of metres in the language of hieratic poetry; and indeed, such cases have been commented upon. Geldner observed that the hymn to the *Aśvins* (1.120) belonged to a *Ṛṣi* unsatisfied with his fee, and the text is full of veiled but angry thrusts against misers, couched in bitter and ironic terms. According to the *Anukramaṇī*, its twelve stanzas are composed in nine different metres, mostly rare ones and with an irregular number of syllables.

We may also suppose that the metres that follow one another in the short hymn 3.21 (stanza 1 in the *Triṣṭubh*, and stanza 5 in *Virāḍrūpā Satobṛhati* [12 + 8 + 12 + 8]) accompany the fall of the drops of melting butter into the sacrificial fire, somehow reflecting the changing rhythm of those melting drops.

One can easily cite additional examples, but still there are many cases where the interchange of metres has no expressive value, and any objective criteria are hard to arrive at.

Paul Thieme has discussed a symbolic use of the verse-line in the *Ṛg Veda*, when the internal structure of the number and quantity of syllables and the position of the caesura is disturbed. These irregularities symbolize the events described in the hymn, and he called this phenomenon *Sprachmalerei* ("language-painting") [143.64-81]. A careful analysis of the verses with an irregular *pāda* structure confirms the probability of such a correlation, for example, *ádhi yád apā́ṃ snubhíś carāva* / *prá preñkhá īñkhayāvahai śubhé kám* / (7.88.3c-d) "When we two move along the crests of the waters, / We shall swing in the swing for brilliance." The metrical structure of these *Triṣṭubh pādas* is as follows:

⏑⏑⏑⏑⏑ | – ⏑ – ⏑ – ⏑
– – ⏑ – ⏑ | – ⏑ – ⏑ – –

The beginning of the third *pāda*, consisting of five short syllables with the caesura bisecting the word *apa/aṃ*, is most unusual. As Thieme says, these deviations symbolize the boat's movement: its ascent onto the wave crest (the sequence of five short syllables) and its abrupt fall afterwards (the caesura in the middle of the word). The fourth *pāda* may be regarded as a verse without a caesura (which breaks the rule), or the caesura may be seen within the word *īñkha/yāvahai*. Thieme believes that the metre of this *pāda* is peculiar in another respect: the constant swinging on the waves finds its correspondence in the symmetrical sequence of long and short syllables within the *pāda*, which is identical in both directions. This approach is also valid for verses 3.59.2d; 4.26.4a-b; 5.59.2a-b; 7.86.4d; 10.95.10a.

The verses analysed by Thieme were taken from the regular monologue hymns that represent the bulk of the *Ṛg Veda*. The dialogue hymns, in which the exchanges between speakers can become rather heated, are quite significant in this respect. Such is the famous dialogue in 10.10, for instance, between *Yama* and *Yamī*, in which *Yamī* unsuccessfully tried to persuade *Yama* to commit incest with her. Arnold's commentary on the metrics of this hymn of 14 stanzas suggests that verses 12a and 13a-b should be emended [143.318]. But when we turn to the contents of the hymn it becomes obvious that these two stanzas are the emotional turning point in the dialogue: *Yama* has resolutely rejected his sister, but she denounces him with equal vehemence. This episode is narrated in the following lines:

ná vā́ u te tanvā̀ tanvàṃ sám papṛcyām
pāpám āhur yáḥ svásāraṃ nigáchāt
anyéna mát pramúdaḥ kalpayasva
ná te bhrā́tā subhage vaṣṭy etát

bató batāsi yama naívá te[68]
máno hṛ́dayaṃ cāvidāma
anyā́ kíla tvā́ṃ kakṣyèva yuktám
pári ṣvajāte líbujeva vṛkṣám

"(*Yama*:) "Never will I join (my) body with thy body! / They call 'evil' (a man) who enters (his) sister. / Arrange they amorous pleasures with some other (man), not with me! / Thy brother, O lovely one, does not want this." (*Yamī*:) "Thou art miserable, O *Yama*! Neither thy mind nor thy heart have we been able to find! Some other (woman) will surely embrace thee, / As a girth (embraces) a harnessed (stallion), as a creeper (embraces) a tree!"

The metre is the *Triṣṭubh*. In the first *pāda* of stanza 12, the essential information, *Yama*'s refusal, appears for the first time, and the remaining *pādas* contain mere variations on the theme. It is here that the regular verse scheme is broken: first, there is a superfluous syllable; second, in the middle of the *pāda*, between the caesura after the fourth syllable and the cadence, the line contains exclusively long syllables; taken together, the whole is perceived as something heavy and slow:

⏑–⏑–,–––– | –⏑––.

In the first two *pādas* of stanza 13, the exact limits of the *pādas* are not clear, and the precision of the trochaic rhythm of the cadence is obscured (in 13b we have ⏑⏑–⏑ instead of –⏑–⏓). Arnold proposed to emend it in the following way: *bató bata / asi yama ná evā́ / táva mánaḥ /*. It seems more likely that metrical confusion should symbolize *Yamī*'s muddled emotions after hearing *Yama*'s outright rejection.

Another possible example can be found in an incantation against poisonous insects and the like, at the very end of Book 1. The whole hymn (1.191) is composed in the *Anuṣṭubh* metre, but the refrain, with slight variants in stanzas 10-13–the hymn is not quite uniform in structure–contains *pādas* of 6, 7, 10, and 8 syllables;[69] for instance, the refrain in stanza 10: *só cin nú ná marāti / nó vayám marāma- / āré asya yójanaṃ hariṣṭhā́ / mádhu tvā madhulā́ cakāra* / "Neither shall he die, / Nor will we die! / The driver of the bay (horses) has destroyed his essence. / The honey (-herb) has made honey of thee."

Oldenberg cites these verses as instances in which the metrical change is directly correlated with the content [113.160]. Indeed, this is an essential feature of incantations when the desired condition is depicted as actually reached;[70] the magical functions of the word are expressed precisely in the refrain. His interpretation is quite attractive, but we cannot exclude a different explanation. In tenor this ṚgVedic pseudo-hymn appears to be perfectly Atharvanic. Its metre, the *Anuṣṭubh*, is basic to the *Atharva Veda*, but rather peripheral to the *Ṛg Veda*. The *Atharva Veda* collection of charms is of a much more popular nature than the hymnic collection of the *Ṛg Veda*, and its metrical form is rather mixed, sometimes tending to prose (some parts of the *Atharva Veda* are wholly in prose). This general situation could help explain the metrical faults in 1.191.10-13.

The problem illustrated by this incantation should also concern–in a general way–the hymns of the *Ṛg Veda* proper if we take into consideration the numerous deviations from the standard metrical schemes attested here, deviations which are usually explained away for chronological or other reasons. Thieme was well aware of this when he raised, for the first time, the issue of the expressive function of metrics in the *Ṛg Veda*: "I certainly do not believe that I have found a universal recipe for the wholesale justification of every single hitch in the verse of the *Ṛg Veda*, or of what we believe to be a hitch. I believe it to be only one of the possibilities that should be considered if we dare not emend the text or arbitrarily modify the rules of pronunciation" [143.72].

The prosodic level is also represented by rhythmic hints at the word that denotes the key notion or idea of the hymn, usually the addressee of the hymn, the deity praised by the poet. Still, before we analyse this particular mode of prosodic marking, the more general functions of rhythmic units (*pādas*, stanzas, and hymns) should be briefly discussed. Rhythmic hints usually occur at quite definite positions of the metric scheme. In this respect the marked position in the *pāda* is its beginning; its end is only secondarily marked. The *pāda* beginning is the strongest position not only for rhythmic but also for phonetic hints at the name of the deity being praised. Within larger rhythmic units the beginning of the *pāda* can also function as the beginning of a verse or of a whole hymn, and that can be quite important.

The principle of repetitions is widely used in the *Ṛg Veda*, just as in any text intended for oral transmission: these repetitions appear as symmetrical and balanced syntactic structures, words, and sounds. Gonda analysed this phenomenon in a special monograph [87]. Here we would only like to stress the fact that repetitions are conditioned by metrical schemes. In that case, a rhythmic hint at a deity's name, in order to be perceived as such, should take up a position in its *pāda* symmetrical with the one filled in by this theonym in (the) adjacent *pāda*(s). In some hymns, each stanza begins with the name of the god being praised (or a pronoun that refers to him); several examples will be given below. The choice of a synonym can also be conditioned by the rhythmic particularities of a *pāda*. Such rhythmic hints at a theonym are most telling when the theonym is represented by a word of sufficient length, simple or compound, or even a word-group.

Hymns about the divine horse *Dadhikrā́-*, or *Dadhikrā́van-*, are very interesting in this respect. The etymology of the name is unclear: from the purely formal point of view, the first component seems to be a reduplicated formation; it bears a superficial identity with *dā́dhi-/dadhán-* "sour milk" (from *dhā-* "to suck") or with *dádhi-* "giver" (from *dhā-* "to put"), and to such finite forms of this verb as (second person singular present medial voice) *dadhiṣe*. It has been observed that hymns to this deity usually prefer *kar-/kir-* (*kṝ-*), among all the verbs meaning "to sing" or "to praise," [118.15.164]. Geldner interprets this as the echoing effect reflected in various forms of this verb when juxtaposed with the second component (*-krā*) of the horse's name [74.471, comm. ad 4.39.6a]. Another explanation cannot however be excluded: this verb has an intensive present with a reduplicated stem whose derivatives represent a kind of a rhythmic echo of the horse's name, for example, *dadhikrā́m . . . carkirāma* (4.39.1) "We are praising *Dadhikrā*, *dadhikrā́vna íd u nú carkirāma*" (4.40.1) "We want to praise this *Dadhikrā* right now." The probability of this hypothesis is strengthened by the frequent use of reduplicated perfect forms of the verb *dhā-* in the vicinity of the horse's name. Thus at the beginning of a *pāda* in the very first stanza of the first hymn in the *Dadhikrā* cycle we come across a rhythmic hint contained in the second person dual perfect active voice of the verb *dhā-*: / *kṣetrasā́ṃ dadathur . . .* (4.38.1c) "You two have given the land-conqueror . . . " (the "two" are presumably *Mitra* and *Varuṇa*). The horse's name itself is not explicitly mentioned in this stanza; but it appears in an identical phrase at the beginning of a *pāda* in the next stanza: / *dadhikrā́m u dadathur . . .* (4.38.26) "You two have also given *Dadhikrā*." In the next hymn the members of this collection are disjointed but each begins a pāda: / *dadikrā́vṇaḥ . . .* / *yám . . .* / *dadáthur . . .* (4.39.2) "(That) *Dadhikrāvan* whom you two have given . . . " or: / *dadhikrā́m . . .* / *dadáthur . . .* (4.39.5)

"You two have given *Dadhikrā*." Finally, the last hymn of the cycle (4.40) abounds in intensive reduplicated forms whose rhythm recalls both of the names of the divine horse. In that hymn all the words containing rhythmic hints are at the end of the *pāda*, while the name itself is mostly at the beginning of the *pāda*: *pāda* 1a has been cited above; 3d / *dadhikrā́vṇaḥ . . . táritrataḥ* / "*Dadhikrāvan* . . . (who) breaks forward;" 4c / *krátuṃ dadhikrā́ ánu saṃtávītvat* / "*Dadhikra*, on his own, powerfully gathering (his) spirit," where the initial is taken up by a phonetic hint at the theonym followed by the name itself; 4d / . . . *ánv āpánīphaṇat* / "galloping speedily."

Numerous examples of this kind occur in technically refined hymns to the god of prayer and sacrifice *Bṛ́haspáti/Bráhmaṇas páti* (the latter means literally "Lord of Prayer"). For instance, a series of hymns to this deity in Book 2 contains various examples of complex formal plays in which the sounds and the rhythmic hints at the deity's name are interwoven, and words, or word-groups, that underlie such associations usually take up marked positions in the *pāda*. Sometimes these associations are etymologically based (when the word *bráhman-* "prayer" is involved) but more often they find support in rhythmic similarity of form, or, sometimes, in rather basic phonetic likenesses. Some examples: 2.23.2d–*víśveṣām íj janitā́ bráhmaṇām asi* "Thou art the genitor of all prayers" (compare the *pāda*-end with *brahmaṇas pati-*); 4c *brahmadvíṣas tápano manyumī́r asi* "Incinerating (the enemies), thou art destroying the fury of an adversary of prayer," where the word *brahma-* begins the *pāda*, and the end contains a rhythmic hint at *brahmaṇas pati-*; *hárasvatī* / "She who cuts down" (compare *bṛhaspati-*); 16a . . . *druhás padé* / "in the foot-track of deceit" (compare vocative *bṛhaspate*); 2.24.7b *mahás patháḥ* (compare *bṛhaspati-*), etc.

The name of the divine couple *Mitrā́váruṇā* is also involved in such complex formal plays. In the hymns devoted to them, their names are sometimes mentioned far apart and sometimes coupled together in a compound name; sometimes their unity is conveyed by rhythmic hints, as in the following example:

ákravihastā sukṛ́te paraspā́
yáṃ trā́sāthe varuṇéḷāsv antáḥ
rā́jānā kṣatrám áhṛṇīyamānā
sahásrasthūṇam bibhṛthaḥ sahá dvaú (5.62.6)

"With hands not reddened with blood, protecting the pious one from afar, / Whom you two save, O *Varuṇa* (and *Mitra*), in the midst of sacrificial libations, / O (you) two kings, lacking in animosity, you bear power / Upon a thousand columns, both of you together."

The rhythmic hints at the composite *mitrā́váruṇā* are symmetrically positioned in this stanza: at the beginning of the first and the last *pāda*. In addition, the first *pāda* has a compound word whose first element contains a phonetic hint at *mitra-* and the last *pāda* has another compound whose *auslaut* hints at the name *váruṇa-*; at the same time, this is an indication of the sequence of elements of this compound theonym.

The pattern of distribution of rhythmic hints at a deity's name in the overall metrical scheme of a hymn is sometimes quite strict. For instance, in 7.5, which is addressed to *Agni* in his aspect of *Vaiśvānará-*, when this name appears it always begins the *pāda*, while the rhythmic (often also phonetic) hints occur only at the end of the *pāda*, for example, 5a . . . *vāvaśānā́* / – 5d / – *vaiśvānarám* . . . ; 8b / *vaíśvānara* . . . – 8c . . . *viśvavāra* / .

Rhyme as such is not a characteristic of Vedic poetic language. Actual rhymes may occur in some cases in the marked positions of the *pāda*, that is, initially or finally, but in reality they are rather a variety of repetition or rhythmic hints and thus cannot be regarded as independent constituents of the verse.

Much more extensive use is made of figurative "sound-picturing," that is playing with inherent features in order to transmit special information from the poet to the deity whom he is praising. In this field of sound (and sound-group) semantization overlaying the regular grammar and creating a particular "pictorial supra-text" the *Ṛṣis* have displayed their unrivalled craftsmanship.

Most typical for the *Ṛg Veda* are laudatory hymns whose aim is to provide a given deity with the utmost praise to obtain in return the requested gifts. This situation has to be regarded as a kind of communication act wherein the worshipper is the addresser, the deity is his addressee, and the message is contained in the hymn.[71] In order to put the hymn's communicative function into practice, its author, the *Ṛṣi* had to attract the deity's attention from the start, had to make himself heard, not some other person; he had to make the deity disregard the calls and offerings of the author's rivals and bestow the divine gifts exclusively on the hymn-maker. Sometimes this aim is expressed in the hymn on the main content level as, for example, in the short hymn 4.29 which is given here in full:

ā́ na stutá úpa vā́jebhir ūtī́
índra yāhí háribhir mandasānáḥ
tiráś cid aryáḥ sávanā purū́ṇy
āṅgūṣébhir gṛṇānáḥ satyárādhāḥ (1)

ā́ hí ṣmā yā́ti náryaś cikitvā́n
hūyámānaḥ sotṛ́bhir úpa yajñám

sváśvo yó ábhīrur mányamānaḥ
suṣvāṇébhir mádati sáṃ ha vīraíḥ (2)

śrāvā́yéd asya kárṇā vājayádhyai
júṣṭām ánu prá díśam mandayádhyai
udvāvṛṣāṇó rā́dhase túviṣmān
káran na índraḥ sutīrthā́bhayaṃ ca (3)

áchā yó gántā nā́dhamānam ūtī́
itthā́ vípraṃ hávamānaṃ gṛṇántam
úpa tmáni dádhāno dhury ā̀śū́n
sahásrāṇi śatā́ni vájrabāhuḥ (4)

tvótāso maghavann indra víprā
vayáṃ te syāma sūráyo gṛṇántaḥ
bhejānā́so bṛháddivasya rāyá
ākāyyàsya dāváne purukṣóḥ (5)

(1) "O praised one, come to us with (thy) rewards (and) supports. / O *Indra*, drunk (on *Soma*), on (your) bay horses / (Pass) by the many pressing of (my) rival, / O (thou) sung in praises, inspired by true generosity. /

(2) Because the brave (and) attentive one arrives / When the (*Soma*) pressers call him to the sacrifice, / The master of fine horses, (he) who (is) famed for fearlessness / Feasts in the company of (*Soma*)-pressing men.

(3) Make his ears hear the craving for booty, / (Direct him) to the part favorable to intoxication![72] / Incited to gift-giving, let mighty *Indra* / Establish for us secure water-crossings and absence of fright! /

(4) (He is the one) who comes with supports to the needy, / To the inspired one who invokes (him and) sings (him) because of that, / (*Indra*) with *vajra* in hand, (who) himself lashes to the pole / Swift horses–thousands, hundreds (of them). /

(5) Aided by thee, O generous *Indra*, / We, the inspired ones, the patrons of sacrifice (and) singers,– / We would like to obtain a share in the wealth of him who resides in high heaven, / In the desirable (place), rich in food, (destined) for donation! /."

We have attempted elsewhere to present a model of an "average hymn" aimed at praising a deity [69.255-268]. Such a model consists of two component parts: appellative (the worshipper's address to the deity) and explicative (the description of the deity). The latter contains several levels: a description of the deity's actions and his ties with other deities, and a list of his epithets and attributes. The deity's connections, epithets and attributes are regarded here as "reduced" actions of the god. One can observe a constant switching between the appellative and explicative parts, linked by relations of transformation. This switching can be exemplified by the just-cited *Indra*-hymn: "brave" (as applied to *Indra*) means (in the context "Help us in our fight against the enemies!") "Grant us victory!," "Make us fearless!" etc.; "attentive" can be transformed into "Take notice of our hymn and sacrifice!;" "with supports to the needy"–describing *Indra* implies an appeal: "Come to us, we are in need of thy help!" etc.

This act of communication can be called one-sided, since the information is transmitted by the worshipper while the deity merely listens. Direct speech of the gods toward the worshipper is extremely rare in the *Ṛg Veda*: for example, the *Maruts*' words addressed to the *Ṛṣi Śyāvāśva* (5.53.3-4), or *Savitar*'s injunction to the unlucky gambler (10.34.13). It is important to the worshipper that the deity should notice him and listen to his words. On the plane of language this importance is reflected in the particular role of the appellative function that is manifested in invocations (verbal imperatives) and appeals (nominal vocatives).

Here we should again remind ourselves of those notions of magic, peculiar to the Vedic *Ṛṣis*, concerning the word in general and theonyms in particular. Pronouncing the deity's name was seen as a kind of "Declaration of Truth" full of creative possibilities. To pronounce the deity's name was highly important in itself, since the speaker was able in this way to become privy to the deity's nature. Since Vedic poetics sets such importance on the mysterious, the hidden and the suggestive, the declaration of the divine addressee's name becomes a refined craft of sound-play, sound suggestions, anagrams, etc. And in this way, in the communication act represented by the delivery of a Vedic praise-hymn, the basic information transmitted on the figurative "iconic" level is correlated with the addressee, i.e. the deity that is the object of praise, and whose name is frequently incorporated into the sound-texture of the hymn.

The linguistic aspect of the problem was discussed for the first time in the posthumously published "Anagrammes" of de Saussure [138], in which he used the data of several ancient Indo-European poetic traditions, including the *Ṛg Veda*. He analysed the devices used to create a new text consisting of sounds and their combinations on the basis of the underlying content-text [139]. The meaning of such sound combinations is defined according to some content-feature. This secondary "figurative" text has its own norms that can be described on various levels–phonetic, morphological, or syntactic.

De Saussure was also the first to point out that the PIE poet, be he the Old Indian *kavi-* or the ancient Latin *vātēs*, was quite conscious of the external form of the words and was preoccupied with the analysis–but also with the synthesis!–of phonetic elements.[73] The "word-dissecting" operation was especially favored in the Celtic poetic tradition,[74] but in the Old Indian tradition, as attested in the *Ṛg Veda*, this particular device found much more limited application and was used mainly with the name of the deity addressed by the hymn.

The name of the lauded deity can be directly expressed in the hymn, and sometimes it appears as a distinct pattern, embroidered on the canvas, as it were, of the metrical scheme. It can also be indicated by sound-hints intertwined in the hymn's texture. That this is a fully conscious effort, and not an accident, is suggested by those cases in which instances of surface sound-play share a common etymological basis. Hymns to *Savitar* abound in puns involving various forms of the verb *sū-* "to vivify," "to set in motion," "to impel" as well as a variety of its nominal derivatives. Indeed, the very name of this god who personifies the Sun's life-giving force–*savitár*–is an agent noun from the verb *sū-*, "the impeller." In hymn 4.54 (to *Savitar*) the play with finite forms of *sū-* and its nominal derivatives can be traced throughout all the six stanzas: (1) *savitā* nominative singular; (2) *suvási* second person singular, *savitar* vocative singular; (3) *savitar* "id.," *suvatād* second singular imperative; (4) *savitúr* genitive case singular, *suváti* third person singular; (5) *suvasi* second person singular, *savitaḥ* vocative singular, *savā́ya* dative case singular of *savá-* "impulsion;" (6) *savitaḥ* vocative singular, *savā́so* nominative case plural of *savá-*, *āsuvánti* third person plural of *ā́ + sū-*.

The same play can be observed in the *Savitar*-hymn 6.71. where some additional complexities are introduced, namely, the occasional semantization of random sequences of sounds recalling the theonym *savitár-*. Stanza 1: the etymologically justifiable consonance between nominative case singular *savitā* and *sávanāya*, dative case singular of *sávana-* "setting in motion," "incentive;" and the pun involving the syllable *su-* (adjective prefix "good") in the words *sukrátuḥ* and *sudákṣo*, based upon the very common Vedic morphonological alternation between *u* and *av*. Stanza 2: the derivatives from the root *sū-*: *savitúḥ* genitive case singular and *sávīmani*, locative case singular of *sávīman-* "command," *prasavé*, locative case singular of *prasavá-* "setting in motion;" the play on the syllable *-su-* in the word *vásunaś*. Stanza 3: *savitaḥ* vocative singular and its nonetymological counterpart *suvitā́ya* "for lucky journey," "for luck." Stanza 4: from the root *sū-*: *savitā́* nominative case singular and *suváti* third singular present. Stanza 5: *savitā́* id. and the play on the prefix *su-* in the word *suprátīkā*. Stanza 6: derivatives from the root *su-*: *savitar* vocative and *sāvīḥ* third singular injunctive aorist.

Punning based on the root *sū-* in conjunction with the name *savitár-* can be traced throughout the whole of the *Ṛg Veda*. Etymologically based sound-hints at a theonym are also used in the hymns to *Uṣas*, the dawn goddess. The very name *uṣás-* derives from the root *vas-*, *ucháti* "to light up," "to shine." The verb denotes this goddess's typical action, when through her brilliance she delivers immeasurable riches to her adoring sacrificer.

At this stage a short digression is called for in order to comment upon the functions of Vedic verbs meaning "to shine," "to glitter," "to be brilliant," which form a group of synonyms that are quite important in a text whose mythological system pays so much attention to solar deities. In this group comprising more than fifteen verbs,[75] we can single out a few that are applied exclusively to gods and not to their worshippers nor to objects of the worshippers' world. For instance, the verb *rāj-* has as its subjects various theonyms–*Agni*, *Sūrya*, the *Maruts*, and others; the subject of the verb *dī-* is in most cases *Agni*, and only rarely does this verb occur with other theonymns (*Soma, Indra, Sūrya, Bṛhaspati*); the subject of the verb *vas-* is almost exclusively *Uṣas* (and only quite occasionally some deity of her entourage) or some other mythological figure endowed with her functions. This particular case can probably be interpreted on purely formal grounds: since the noun *uṣás-* is based on the verb-root *vas-*, *ucháti*, and the various forms of this verb represent sound-hints at the noun. The noun *uṣás-* itself is combined with different verbal predicates denoting "shining:" *arc-, bhā-, rāj-, ruc-,* beside *vas-*. But *vas*, because of its symbolic and figurative function, is best suited to represent *Uṣas-* as compared with the rest of the gods, for example, *uvā́soṣā́ uchā́c ca nú* (1.48.3) "*Uṣas* has (always) shone, and she will shine now," or: *távéd uṣó vyúṣi sū́ryasya ca* (7.81.2) "Thou, O *Uṣas*, lightest up, and the Sun."

In conjunction with the theonym *sóma-*, which is at the same time the ritual name of the substance from which the juice was pressed to produce the divine drink of immortality (*amṛ́ta-*), we constantly come across the verb *su-* "to press" and its various other nominal derivatives. Phrases of the type *ádhvaryavaḥ sunuténdrāya sómam* (10.30.15) "O you *Adhvaryus*, press the *Soma* for *Indra*!" are common in the *Rig Veda* and are repeated in multiple diverse variants, for example, *sunótā somapā́vne / sómam índrāya vajríṇe* (7.32.8) "Press the *Soma* for *Indra*, the *Soma*-drinker, the *vajra*-wielder!;" *ásāvi sómo* (9.82.1) "The *Soma* is pressed out;" *ayáṃ sóma indra túbhyaṃ sunve* (9.88.1) "This *Soma*, O *Indra*, is being pressed out for thee," etc.

As a proper name, *sóma-* can be replaced by some other nominal derivative of the root *su-*; that noun then becomes a synonym and a sound-hint at this name, and in this way participates in the same form-play. This function is most frequently fulfilled by *sutá-* (past participle of the root *su-*) "pressed (out)," also as a noun (masculine) "the pressed out *Soma*-juice." For example, *dūrā́d índram anayann ā́ suténa* (7.33.2a) "From afar have they brought *Indra* with *Soma*'s help" (Geldner has: "durch ihren *Soma*"). But note the adjectival use of *sutá-* further on in the same stanza: *pā́śadyumnasya vāyatásya sómāt / sutā́d índro vr̥ṇītā vásiṣṭhān* (7.33.2c-d) "*Indra* preferred the *Vasiṣṭhas* to *Soma* pressed at *Pāśadyumna Vāyata*'s (place)." Compare also *sutá-* in predicative use: *ayám vām mádhumattamaḥ / sutáḥ sóma r̥tāvr̥dhā* (1.47.1) "This sweetest *Soma* has been pressed for the two of you, O Law-increasers!"

The noun *sávana-* (neuter) (derived from the root *su-* with the help of the suffix *-ana-*) has two meanings: the noun of action "pressing, pressure" as well as the result of the action "the pressed out *Soma*-juice;" in this latter meaning the noun is synonymous with *sóma-* and *sutá-*, for example, *áthā sunudhvaṃ sávanam mádāya / pātá r̥bhavo mádhunaḥ somyásya* (4.35.4) "So press you the pressing (of *Soma*) for intoxication! Drink, O you *Ṛbhus*, the Somic sweetness!" Geldner translated *sávanam* as "die Trankspende," while Renou offered: "le (soma destiné au) pressurage," adding in the commentary: "*sávanam* (accusative case) interne, à valeur prégnante – *sunudhvaṃ sómaṃ sutám*." The noun *sávana-* is quite frequent in the *Rig Veda* and plays an active role in puns based on various derivatives of the root *su-*.

Another noun derived from this root is *savá-* (masculine) "pressure," "pressed out juice" which can also be synonymous with *Soma*, for example, *ādā́ya śyenó abharat sómaṃ / sahásraṃ savā́m̐ ayútaṃ ca sākám* (4.26.7) "The eagle brought the *Soma*, having taken (it): a thousand and ten thousand pressings at once."[76] Sāyaṇa glossed *savān* in this instance with *savānāṃ yajñānāṃ*. This word–unlike *sutá-* and *sávana-* –is rare in the *Rig Veda*.

All of these names of the ritual drink, etymologically connected with the root *su-*, are brought into play on the expressive level, thus broadening the range of sound-hint possibilities, since they represent different degrees of the morphonological alternations of the root-vowel or different phonetic variants of the same degree: *-u-/-uv-* – *-o-/-av-*. An example of this can be seen in the *Indra*-hymn 1.16 (in the *Gāyatrī* metre), inviting this god to the morning *Soma*-pressing. The *Soma* here is the main subject of the "message" delivered from the worshipper to his deity, and the *Sprachmalerei* is based on the various names of the ritual liquid, while *Indra* as addressee is also involved in the sound-play:[77]

ā́ tvā vahantu hárayo
vŕ̥ṣaṇaṃ <u>sóma</u>pītaye
índra tvā sū́racakṣasaḥ (1)

imā́ dhānā́ ghṛtasnúvo
hárī ihópa vakṣataḥ
índraṃ sukhátame ráthe (2)

índram prātár havāmaha
índram prayaty àdhvaré
índraṃ sómasya pītáye (3)

úpa naḥ sutám ā́ gahi
háribhir indra keśíbhiḥ
suté hí tvā hávāmahe (4)

sémáṃ na stómam ā́ gahy
úpedáṃ sávanaṃ sutám
gauró ná tṛṣitáḥ piba (5)

imé sómāsa índavaḥ
sutā́so ádhi barhíṣi
tā́m̐ indra sáhase piba (6)

ayáṃ te stómo agriyó
hṛdispṛ́g astu śáṃtamaḥ
áthā sómaṃ sutám piba (7)

víśvam ít sávanaṃ sutám
índro mádāya gachati
vṛtrahā́ sómapītaye (8)

sémáṃ naḥ kā́mam ā́ pṛṇa
góbhir áśvaiḥ śatakrato
stávāma tvā svādhyàḥ[78] (9)

(1) "Let the bay horses bring thee,
The bull, to *Soma*-drinking,
O *Indra*, (the horses) bright as the Sun!
(2) To these barley corns, soaked in ghee,
Let *Indra* bring hither
The bay pair in the swiftest chariot!
(3) *Indra* we invoke in the morning,
Indra–during the rite,
Indra–to *Soma*-drinking.

(4) Rush hither to our pressed (*Soma*),
O *Indra*, upon the long-maned bay (horses)–
Since we invite thee to the pressed (*Soma*)!
(5) Come to this praise of ours,
To this feast of the pressed (*Soma*)!
Drink (it) like a bull, tormented by thirst!
(6) These *Soma* juices, the squeezed out
Drops, (are) on the sacrificial straw.
Drink them, O *Indra*, for vigor!
(7) Let this excellent praise
Touch thy heart, the most beneficent one!
So drink the pressed *Soma*!
(8) To each feast of the pressed (*Soma*)
Indra comes for (his) intoxication,
Vṛtra's slayer (comes) to the *Soma* drinking.
(9) Fulfil this desire of ours
With cows, horses, O Mighty (one) like a hundred.
We will glorify thee with a beautiful prayer."

The basic communicative aim of this hymn lies in attracting the deity's attention to *Soma*. The hymn's contents can be rendered in this way: *Soma* has been pressed and prepared for thee, it is here–so drink and enjoy it, and in exchange for it fulfil our desires and bestow gifts on us. Each of the nine stanzas contains either some name for *Soma* or its sound-hint. All the three names of the liquid derived from the root *su-* are used here: *sóma-*, *sutá-*, and *sávana-*. The basic name, *sóma-*, occurs both as an independent word (stanzas 3, 6, 7) and as a member of the compound *sómapītaye* (stanzas 1, 8) "to *Soma* drinking." *Soma*-drinking, which is quite important on the communicative level, is overtly marked by a double rendering: both by a compound and by a syntactical combination, *sómasya pītáye* (stanza 3). The various names of *Soma* can be combined but their precise meanings are modified in different contexts: *sávanaṃ sutám* (stanzas 5, 8) "to the feast of the pressed (*Soma*)," *sómāsa . . . sutā́so* (stanza 6) "*Soma*'s juices," *sómaṃ sutám* (stanza 7) "the pressed *Soma*." Each of these words, in its turn, represents a name for the pressed juice, and in this way the same motif is being rehashed under different guises.

Each of the *Soma* names is underscored in the hymn by sound-hints. The form *sutá-* is echoed by *sū́ra°* (stanza 1), *sukha°-* (stanza 2), *°snúvo* (stanza 2), *suā́dhyàḥ* (stanza 9). The form *sóma-* is echoed by *sémáṃ* (stanzas 5, 9) (this sound chain is the result of the *sandhi sá* + *imáṃ* ("he (on) this") as well as by *stómam* (stanza 5), *stómo* (stanza 7), inflected forms of the noun *stóma-* "praise." Finally, *sávana-* is reflected in *stávāma* (stanza 9) "we will glorify."

The sound theme of the addressee of the hymn is pushed off into the background. In the first two stanzas the name *índra-* introduces the third *pāda*. In the third stanza this theme grows stronger, since the accusative case singular *índram* introduces each *pāda*, and the whole stanza is a zeugmatic repetition: the predicate *havāmahe* "we invoke" in the first *pāda* governs the symmetrical case series in the second and third *pādas*. After that there is a fall-off. In stanzas 4 and 6 vocative *indra* does not begin the *pāda*, though at the end of the first *pāda* in stanza 6 there is a sound-hint at the theonym in the noun *índavaḥ* "drops," and for the last time nominative case *índro* begins the *pāda* in stanza 8.

The degree to which the Vedic *Sprachmalerei* is "communication-bound" can be judged by the curious peculiarity of the Book 9 hymns to *Soma Pavamāna* (literally "*Soma* being purified"), in which the forefront is taken up by puns with various forms of the verb *pū-* "to purify, clarify" (*pávamāna-* present participle medial voice from this root) and its nominal derivatives, but not by the derivatives of *su-* "to press." The hymns in this *maṇḍala* are known to be liturgy-oriented [118.9.1ff.]: they accompany the process of turning *Soma* into the divine drink of immortality, and the focal point of the rite is the purification of the *Soma* juice.

All of these extra-linguistic facts are directly reflected on the expressive level. In Book 9 one cannot find hymns similar to 1.16, which plays so forcefully upon the theme *su-* while jamming other sound themes. Instead, Book 9 is pervaded by the *pū-* theme, whose every facet is thoroughly exploited. Both verbal and nominal derivatives of the root take up the strong position in the *pādas*, serving as a fulcrum in repetitions and as the focus of sound- and rhythmic hints. Thus, Book 9 is characterized by an etymologically based *Sprachmalerei*. For instance, out of the six stanzas of hymn 9.36 (*Gāyatrī*), five stanzas contain a *pāda* beginning with a word derived from the root *pū-*, and we can observe a consistent pattern in the positioning of marked words. In the first three stanzas the beginnings of the second *pādas* are: *pavítre* (stanza 1) "in the strainer," *pávasva* (stanza 2) "purify thyself," *pávamāna* (stanza 3) "O *Pavamāna*!" (= "O Self-purifying one!"). In stanzas 4 and 5 the marked word is moved to the beginning of the third *pāda*: *pávate* (stanza 4) "he purifies himself," *pávatām* (stanza 5) "let him purify," while the second *pāda* of this stanza ends with a sound-hint: *pā́rthivā*. Finally, the last stanza, 6, contains no forms based on the root *pū-*, but the stanza–and the hymn–ends with the word *pate* "O lord!" which can be felt to be a sound-hint in the context (compare *pavate*).

Moreover, some hymns of Book 9 play with participles that function as rhythmic hints at the name *pávamāna-* (present participle medial voice from *pū-, pávate*) or with another middle participle, *punāná-*, based on another present stem (*punāti*) from the same root *pū-*. An example is provided by the following stanzas from Book 9.109:

nŕ̥bhir yemānó / jajñānáḥ pūtáḥ
kṣárad víśvāni / mandráḥ svarvít (8)
índuḥ punānáḥ / prajā́m urāṇáḥ
kárad víśvāni / dráviṇāni naḥ (9)

(stanza 8) "Subdued by men; having (just) been born, purified, / Let (him) pour (us) all (the goods), (he) the happy-sounding (one), finding the Sun!

(stanza 9) "The self-purifying juice, choosing offspring for itself, / Let it create all riches for us!"

All of these middle participles in *-āná-*: *yemāná-, jajñāná-, urāṇá-* reiterate the rhythm of *punāná-* which determines the formal play throughout these stanzas. Long fragments of hymns in Book 9 (10.1-5; 13.1-3, 6; 14.4-5, etc.) are constructed along the same expressive lines.

Thus it can be said that in discussing the praises of *Soma* we are able to determine with a high degree of accuracy whether a hymn belongs to Book 9 or to some other Book if we base our analysis on the nature of the sound-play, that is, on sound-hints at the deity's name.

We have mainly discussed the etymologically-based *Sprachmalerei*. But the hymns no less frequently attest the transmission of expressive information through the semantization of random sound sequences. The word transmitted on the expressive level–usually a theonym or sometimes a "message" for the gods–is cut up by the poet into separate sound elements: individual sounds and their combinations, syllables, and morphemes. Since the basic principle is that of consonance, only this aspect of the morpheme is taken into account. Such sound sequences can be distributed over different words, and individual sounds in these combinations can be reshuffled out of the original sequence. Their similarity to the original pattern can grow or fade; in short, they are like sound-echoes or flashes appearing here and there.

De Saussure has shown–taking up the *Agni* hymns–the way in which a whole poem is built around a key word, a theonym, and the role of its sound-hints (though the theonym can remain unmentioned) as well as the part played by a figurative case-grammar. An *Agni*-hymn introduces the *Rig Veda* collection and this circumstance makes the "grammar of poetry" programmatic for this *Saṃhitā*.

The second hymn (1.2–*Gāyatrī*) is intended for *Vāyu*, *Indra*-and-*Vāyu*, and *Mitra*-and-*Varuṇa* (triadic stanzas). In the first triad each verse begins with the name *vā́yu-*, while at the very beginning of the hymn this theme is supported by the sound-play *vā́yav ā́ yāhi* "O *Vāyu*, come . . . . " The next triad also contains verses with initial theonyms, and it becomes obvious that their order of appearance is conditioned by sound-play: only the first name is subsequently taken up by sound-hints: stanza 4, *pāda a* / *índravāyū*, *pāda c* / *índavo*; stanza 5, *pāda a* / *vā́yav índraś ca*, *pāda c* / *tā́v ā́ yātam*. . . ; stanza 6, *pāda a* / *vā́yav índraś ca*. . . , *pāda b* / *ā́ yātam*. . . In the last triad the play becomes even more complex. Stanza 7: the gods are invoked separately, and the principle of sound-echo correlation is upheld: *pāda a* / *mitrám*. . . , *pāda b* / *várunaṃ ca*. . . , *pāda c* . . . *ghṛtā́cīm*. . . . *Ghṛtā́cīm* reflects the final syllable of *mitrá-* with a transposition of the sounds and prepares the sound-theme of the following stanza with its *ṛtá-*, the cosmic law of the rotating universe whose guardians were *Mitra* and *Varuṇa*. The link of *Mitra-Varuṇa* with the law is rendered in a symbolic way so that their name is surrounded in stanza 8, *pādas a-b*, by *ṛtá-* used independently or in a compound: *ṛténa mitrāvaruṇāv* / *ṛtāvṛdhāv ṛtaspṛśā* "O *Mitra-Varuṇa*, (you who) increase the Law through the Law, (you who) cherish the Law, . . . " *Pāda c* in this stanza begins with *krátum*, a sound-hint at the name of *mitrá-*. Only the final ninth stanza contains in *pāda b*–after the theonyms *mitrā́váruṇā* at the end of *pāda a*–a symmetrically positioned sound-hint at *váruṇa* in the word *urukṣáyā*.

In each stanza of this hymn the sound-hints are preceded by the explicitly pronounced theonym. This situation is prevalent in the hymnic collection although it cannot be seen as obligatory. Thus, the *Uṣas* hymn 7.77 (of six stanzas) contains the goddess' explicit name only in stanza 3, while the bulk of phonetic information on her name is found in stanza 1, especially in its first *pāda*:

úpo ruruce yuvatír ná yóṣā
víśvaṃ jīvám prasuvántī carā́yai
ábhūd agníḥ samídhe mā́nuṣāṇām
ákar jyótir bā́dhamānā támāṃsi (1)

"Approaching, she shone like a young wife, / Impelling every living being to move. / It is time for mortals to kindle *Agni*. / She has created light, driving off darkness."

The initial *pāda* emphasizes the *u*-sound key, although in normal conditions, this vowel is only fifth in the vocalic frequency table [8.88]. Since *u* represents the beginning of the goddess' name there can be no doubt as to the *Ṛṣi*'s intention. Then there are two sound-hints at the theonym: *yóṣā* and *mā́nuṣāṇām*; it should be stressed that the nominative case singular from the stem *uṣás-* is *uṣā́s* with its frequent *sandhi* form *uṣā́* (dropping the final *-s*).

But sound-hints at *Uṣas* appear even after she is explicitly mentioned in stanza 3: compare *dvéṣa* in stanza 4 *pāda c*, and *íṣam* in stanza 5 *pāda c*. Similarly, the *Uṣas* theme is treated at the beginning of hymn 6.65.1, also addressed to her: *eṣā́ syā́ no duhitā́ divojā́ḥ kṣitī́r uchántī mā́nuṣīr ajīgaḥ*. . . "This daughter, born by the sky, lighting up, has awakened the human tribes for us."

The *Ṛg Veda* employs on the expressive level certain clichés that seem to be fixed for this or that deity. For instance, the hymn to the *Aśvins* (4.45) opens with a description of the early morning and the appearance of the dawn, the time when these gods go out in their chariots, and these lines contain a typical example of the *Uṣas Sprachmalerei*:

> *eṣá syá bhānúr úd iyarti yujyáte*
> *ráthaḥ párijmā divó asyá sā́navi*
> *pṛkṣā́so asmin mithunā́ ádhi tráyo*
> *dṛ́tis turī́yo mádhuno ví rapśate* (1)
> *úd vām pṛkṣā́so mádhumanta īrate*
> *rátha áśvāsa uṣáso vyùṣṭiṣu* . . .

(1) "Now this ray is rising. The chariot, circling (everything) is being yoked at the top of this heaven. / Upon it (are) the three (who make up) a pair, bringing the nourishing force. / The fourth one, a (skin) bag, is bursting with honey."

(2) "Your chariots and horses, bringing the nourishing force, rich in honey, / Leave (here) when the dawn starts shining . . . ."

Quite typical for the clichés expressive of *Uṣas* in this fragment are the pronoun *eṣá* (implying *uṣā́*), the play on the vowel *u*, and the noun *vyùṣṭi* from the root *vas-* "to kindle, light." The adjective *pṛkṣá-* "bringing the nourishing force" does not properly belong to the sphere of *Uṣas* as it is an epithet of the *Aśvins*' horses (as well as of some other gods).

The hymn to the *Aśvins* (8.8) is introduced with the following invocation: *ā́ no víśvābhir ūtíbhir / áśvinā gáchataṃ yuvám* "Come to us with every support, O *Aśvins*!" where the beginning of the first *pāda* contains an anagram of the *Aśvins* name. Generally speaking, the very first *pāda* of the first stanza of a hymn quite often sets the key-note for the whole text on the expressive level. Thus the Indra hymn 3.45.1a-b: *ā́ mandraír indra háribhir / yāhí mayū́raromabhiḥ* "Come, O *Indra*, upon swift bay (horses) whose hair (is like) the peacock's (tail)!" And further on in this hymn we can observe the tendency to place words containing the syllable *ra* in metrically marked positions in the juncture of two *pādas* (and sometimes in other positions of the metrical scheme). Thus, for example: stanza 2 / *vṛtrakhādó* . . . / *purā́m* . . . /. . . *ráthasya* . . . *abhisvarā́* / *índro* . . .; stanza 3 / *gambhīrā́m̐* . . .

/ *krátum* . . . / *prá* . . . / *hradám̐* . . . ; stanza 4 . . . *rayím bhará* / . . . *pratijānaté* / . . . *índra sampā́raṇam*; stanza 5 . . . *indra svarā́ḷ* . . . / . . . *sváyaśastaraḥ* /.

This expressive principle in some cases seems to fix the lexical range typical of hymns to a certain deity. This fact is rather obvious in the case of the *Indra* hymns. Invocations to this god constantly employ such words as *vṛtrá-* proper name of a demon, *vájra-* "the thunder-cudgel," *rátha-* "chariot," *púr-* "fortress" (cases with endings containing a vowel: *púram, purā́, purā́m,* etc.), *puraṃdará-* "fortress-smasher," *śū́ra-* "hero," *vīrá-* "man," *ugrá-* "terrible," *turá-* "rapidly proceeding," *tárutra-* "saving," "victorious." Taken separately, almost all of these words occur in hymns to other gods, but in the *Indra* hymns they attract each other under the influence of his name and so take part in a kind of magic play.

Among the means of the expressive level one should mention the role of particles and adverbs-prefixes, that is, very short words that gravitate to the beginning of a sentence, which is usually identical with the beginning of a *pāda*. This position may often determine their role as a musical key to the whole hymn. In the *Agni* hymns this function can be fulfilled by the particle *aṅgá* "only," "namely;" in the *Indra* hymns, by the particle *íd* "even," "just," "indeed" (with its *sandhi* variant of *ín* before a following *n-*), the adverbs-prefixes *ní* "down," *prá* "forward;" and in the *Uṣas* or *Maruts* hymns, by the particle *u* "now," "here" and the adverb-prefix *úd* "up," etc. The deliberate aspect of this play is corroborated by some stanzas from the *Indra* hymn 2.11 where "figurative information" can become highly condensed as in, for instance, stanza 8:

ní párvataḥ sādy ápráyuchan
sám mātṛ́bhir vāvaśānó akrān
dūré pāré vā́ṇīm vardháyanta
índreṣitaṃ dhamánim paprathan ní (8)

"The mountain sat down, without dodging. / He roared, thundering in tune with the mothers. / Strengthening the sound to the farthest limits, / They spread the whistling raised by *Indra*." The adverb-prefix *ní* opens and closes this stanza, and the following one is introduced by *índro* (stanzas 16 and 17, *pādas a-b*):

bṛhánta ín nú yé to tarutra-
ukthébhir vā sumnám āvívāsān
stṛṇānā́so barhíḥ pastyā̀vat
tvóta íd indra vā́jam agman (16)
ugréṣv ín nú śūra mandasānás
tríkadrukeṣu pāhi sómam indra . . . (17)

(16) "High indeed are those, O savior, / Who seek (thy) favor either with hymns, / (Or) by spreading the housemaster's sacrificial straw. / Only through thy help, O *Indra*, have they come to the prize."

(17) "O hero, drunk here on the terrible (juices), / And drink *Soma* at the Trikadruka(-feasts), O *Indra*! . . . . "

The different *sandhi* forms of the particle *íd* take up symmetrical positions in the *pādas*: they always occupy the second place. The alternation of the two variants *íd*/*ín*, both reflecting the name *índra-*, cannot be considered accidental in this particular case.

One of the *Uṣas* hymns begins with the following phrase (7.76.1a): *úd u jyótir amṛ́tam viśvájanyam* "Upwards (shines) the immortal light destined for all people. . . . " The same formal means are also used for the sound symbols of the name *marút-*. Compare, for example, 8.7.17:

> *úd u svānébhir īrata*
> *úd ráthair úd u vāyúbhiḥ*
> *út stómaiḥ pṛ́śnimātaraḥ*

"They appear with (their) roar, / (They) ap(pear) with chariots, ap(pear) with winds, / (They) ap(pear) with praises, Pṛśni's sons." The symbolic character of such anaphoric repetitions is supported by the fact that in the same hymn the sound sequence *úd*/*út* is played upon within different words, compare for example, stanza 10, *pāda c*: *útsaṃ kávandham udríṇam* . . . "the well, the vat with water."[79]

In all the cases discussed above the name of the lauded deity has tended to occupy strong positions in the *pāda*, primarily at the beginning of the *pāda* but also at its end. In a number of hymns, each stanza begins with a theonym; this is a good illustration of the "expressive grammar" of cases (on this see below). Certainly, this tendency represents no obstacle to the use of a theonym in the praise-hymns in other metrical positions. But there is one deity, *Rudra*, who has three special hymns in the *Ṛg Veda* (1.114; 2.33 and 7.46) in which his proper name, *rudrá-*, never occurs at the beginning or the end of the *pāda*. His name is always hidden in its middle, and the marked metrical positions can be occupied only by its sound-hints. The possible reason for this is to be sought in the mythological ideas underlying this divine figure. *Rudra* was a terrible god, a killer of both men and beasts, whom they tried to propitiate but remained in constant terror of.[80] As far as we can judge, the *Ṛṣis* with their notions about the magic power of the word had no wish to mention his terrible name explicitly and preferred to invoke him more covertly. Thus, the *Rudra* hymn 2.33 (fifteen stanzas in the *Triṣṭubh* metre) contains fifteen instances of *rudrá-* (once in each stanza), with none of them at the beginning or end of the *pāda*. At the very beginning of the hymn (stanza 1, *pāda a*) he is called *pitar marutām* "Father of the Maruts," a phrase that contains a sound-hint at *rudrá-*. In *pāda d* of the same stanza he is explicitly named for the first time, though with extreme caution: *prá jāyemahi rudra prajā́bhiḥ* "We want to be reborn, O *Rudra*, in (our) children!" Here *Rudra*'s name is surrounded on both sides by the noun *prajā́-* "offspring" and its phonetic echo: this is the *Ṛṣis* magic device for appealing to the god's creative function. Later, the theonym may be marked by sound-hints but the name itself is always placed in an unmarked position in the metrical scheme, for example, stanza 4, *pāda a*: *mā́ tvā rudra cukrudhāmā námobhir* . . . "We do not want to make thee angry, O *Rudra*, either with worship . . . . " Still, the sound-hint at *rudrá-* can begin a *pāda*, as for instance in stanza 5, *pāda c*: / *ṛdūdāraḥ* . . . "kind-hearted" (compare the theonym's variant with svarabhakti in *rudoráḥ*); in *pāda d*: / *babhrúḥ* "brown" (the same in stanza 9, *pāda b*).

An extreme case of the expressive rendering of the lauded deity can be seen in those few hymns where the god remains unnamed, while his name is represented only by sound-hints. This is true of the famous hymn 10.125 to *Vāc*, the goddess of Sacred Speech. The addressee has become known from the *Anukramaṇī* commentary, wherein the praised deity is listed as *Vāc Āmbhṛṇī* (i.e., *Vāc*, daughter of *Ṛṣi Ambhṛṇa*); she is also listed as the author, since the hymn is outwardly one of self-praise. Although the goddess's name is not stated openly, the whole hymn–as several authors have pointed out [39.317-9; 145.75-7]–is built around the persistent repetition of the syllables *ā̆m*/*aṃ* and *vā̆* contained in the goddess's name. All of the stanzas in this self-praise hymn begin with the pronoun *ahám*, except for one stanza in the middle (stanza 4 of the total eight), which begins otherwise and contains a word, etymologically related to *Vāc*, namely, *uktám* "(something) said, pronounced," along with a highly alliterative conjuration(-invocation) to listen attentively. This cannot be accidental in this particular passage, it is the secret core of the hymn: *śrudhí śruta śraddhiváṃ te vadāmi* (4d) "Listen, O famous one, I am telling thee (things) worthy of faith!." These features of the hymn seem to confirm the hypothesis that this is not an ordinary poetic text but rather a kind of short handbook for its correct analysis [25.67].

It has been already observed by a number of authors that this hymn with its appeals to listen and comprehend the hidden mystery of audible Speech is quite unusual in many respects. The bulk of the *Ṛg Veda* contains explicit appeals to a deity: his name is loudly proclaimed and afterwards it may be echoed and glimpsed in various sound sequences interwoven in the hymn's expressive texture. An example of this is hymn 10.121, which the Western tradition usually calls the hymn to the "Unknown God," while the native

Anukramaṇī states that it is addressed to god *Ka* (literally "who?," "what?"). The formal grounds for such an attribution are found in the refrain introduced by an inflected form of this pronoun: *kásmai devā́ya havíṣā vidhema* "What god shall we honor with a libation?." The whole hymn–omitting a few deviations–is made up of stanzas represented by parallel syntactic structures: the first three verses consist of attributive clauses with the relative *yá-* "who," "which" as the head-word, and the main clause, that is the fourth verse (or refrain), is introduced by the pronoun *ká-*,[81] for example:

yéna dyaúr ugrā́ pṛthivī́ ca dṛḷhā́
yéna svà stabhitáṃ yéna nā́kaḥ
yó antárikṣe rájaso vimā́naḥ
kásmai devā́ya havíṣā vidhema (5)

"(He) by whom the huge sky and earth were fixed. / By whom the sun was set up, by whom–the heavenly vault, / Who measures out the space in the air,– / What god shall we honor with a libation?"

The use of the pronoun *ká-* in the marked position in the *pāda* and its prominence in the emphatic structure of the clause gave sufficient reasons to the author of the *Anukramaṇī* for treating this *ká-* as a theonym. The native exegete of the *Ṛg Veda* was also aided in this interpretation by his general idea of the norm: the god's name should be explicitly declared in the hymn and placed in metrically marked positions.

It is noteworthy that the riddle-hymns (like 1.164 and the hymns to the All-Gods) do not contain solutions represented by sound-hints on the expressive level; the hymns to the All-gods include stanzas where the intended deity is not named but has to be guesses from his typical features. The solution is expected to be given by the worshipper, whose knowledge is to be tested by such a hymn. However, the expressive level, containing additional information about the deity, is activated only when the hymn's communicative aim is to attract the god's attention.

A prominent feature of the expressive level of a praise-hymn is its polyphonic character. Different sound themes may interlace, but the theme of the lauded deity is the most frequent one. Sometimes this level also contains the "message"-theme in the communication act between the god and his worshipper. The typical praise-hymn most clearly displays this theme in its final part, although there are cases in which various parts of the hymn are constantly switched over, that is, the descriptive part with the enumeration of the god's feats and his praises, and the appellative part containing direct appeals to the deity with requests of gifts and various boons [110.255-68]. In hymn 4.32 to *Indra*, on the content-level requests are much more prominent than descriptions of heroic deeds of this god. The final part of this hymn of 24 stanzas, beginning with stanza 19, features the key-word *bhū́ri* "much," "plenty" (that is "shalt thou give to they worshipper"), which becomes the pivot of the sound-play, backed up in the three final stanzas by the word *babhrū́* "ruddy," an epithet of *Indra*'s horses. These stanzas (in the *Gāyatrī* metre) shall be quoted in full:

. . . *bhūridā́ asi vṛtrahan* (19)

bhū́ridā bhū́ri dehi no
mā́ dabhrám bhū́ry ā́ bhara
bhū́ri ghéd indra ditsasi (20)

bhūridā́ hy ási śrutáḥ
purutrā́ śūra vṛtrahan
ā́ no bhajasva rā́dhasi (21)

prá te babhrū́ vicakṣaṇa
śáṃsāmi goṣaṇo napāt
mā́bhyāṃ gā́ ánu śiśrathaḥ (22)

kanīnakéva vidradhé
náve drupadé arbhaké
babhrū́ yā́meṣu śobhete (23)

áram ma usráyāmṇé
'ram ánusrayāmṇe
babhrū́ yā́meṣv asrídhā (24)

(19) ". . . Plenty dost thou give, O slayer of *Vṛtra*!"

(20) "O giver of plenty, give us plenty! / Not a little, (but) plenty do bring us! / Indeed, thou wishest to give plenty, O *Indra*!"

(21) "Indeed, thou art famous for giving plenty / In many places, O heroic slayer of *Vṛtra*. / Give us a share in the boon!"

(22) "I glorify thy pair of ruddy (horses), / O (mighty) in insight, O descendant of the cow-winner. / Do not weaken the cows for this pair's sake!"

(23) "Like a pair of new wedding(?) figurines, small (ones), a wooden pedestal, / The ruddy pair drives out in splendor."

(24) "Ready for me in the early drive-out, / Ready (for me) in the late drive-out / Is the ruddy pair (never) going astray."

The "message" sound-theme starts in the last *pāda* of stanza 19 where it stands at the beginning of the *pāda*, the strong position, with an echo in *dabhrá-* (in a inverted order) and *bhará-* in the third *pāda.* Its climax is reached in stanza 20, where the theme is developed through the repetition of *bhū́ri* in metrically marked positions to an accompaniment of sound-hints. With stanza 21 this theme is gradually weakening: *bhūridā́*, commencing the first *pāda*, is taken up by its rhythmic hint *purutra* at the beginning of the second *pāda*, and then finds its feeble reflection in the initials *bh-* of *bhajasva* in the middle of the third *pāda.* Stanza 22 opens a transition to a new key-word, *babhrū́*: its second syllable is phonetically identical (with a minor transposition) with the initial of *bhū́ri*. The word *babhrū́* is "hidden" in the middle of the *pāda*; in addition, *bh* is supported by the first word of the third *pāda–mā́bhyām* (the *sandhi* result of *mā́* + *ābhyāṃ-*). In the very last two stanzas, *babhrū́* is symmetrically placed at the beginning of the third *pāda.* In stanza 23 at the end of the second and third *pādas*, the sounds of the key-word are reflected (in reverse) in *arbhaké* and almost fading away in *śobhete.*

In a short hymn to *Indra* (6.40: five stanzas of *Triṣṭubh*) two sound themes intertwine: the theme of the addressee of the communication and that of the "message." The former theme is less prominent. The hymn begins with the name of *índra*, oft-repeated afterwards (explicitly as well as in sporadic sound-hints), as, for instance, in stanza 2 at the juncture of the third and fourth *pādas*: . . . *ádrir* / *índuṃ* . . . . The "message" theme seems to be prevalent on the expressive level. The gist of the hymn consists in an invitation to *Indra* to take part in *Soma*-drinking. The appeal (*ā́ yāhi* "come!"–adverb-prefix *ā́* + root *yā-*) is explicit in stanzas 3 and 4. However, the first stanza, when the invitation is not yet expressed, already contains a play on the sound-chain *-ā̆yā̆-* and its echo *-ya-* in several words:

índra piba túbhyaṃ sutó mádāya-
áva sya hárī ví mucā sákhāyā
utá prá gāya gaṇá ā́ niṣádya
átha yajñā́ya gṛṇaté váyo dhāḥ (1)

"O *Indra*, drink! It has been pressed for thy intoxication. / Hold back (thy) horse-pair, unyoke the two companions / And join in the singing, sitting down amidst the crowd (of singers). / And give strength to the singer for sacrifice!"

This theme can be heard throughout the whole length of the hymn down to the very end, symbolizing the repeated invitation offered to the god: stanza 2 . . . *mádāya* . . . *pītáye* . . . , stanza 3 . . . *hárayo* . . . *tvāyatā́* . . . *suvitā́ya* . . . , stanza 4 . . . *uśatā́ yayātha* . . . *somapéyam* . . . *váyo* . . . . In the final stanza 5 the verb *ā́ yāhi* is omitted, in contrast with the preceding stanzas, but it can be restored from the context: the ellipsis of various sentence-parts, including verbal predicates, is rather frequent in the *Ṛg Veda* and can be considered a characteristic of its style.

A short hymn to *Indra* (3.44: five stanzas in the *Bṛhatī* metre) is also an invitation to this god to drink *Soma*, specially prepared for him. On the expressive level, the "message" theme is evidently dominant: it is possible to reduce it to the phrase: "Let it be pleasing!" (that is the *Soma* juice to *Indra*). The theme is formally expressed by means of the interplay of various derivatives of the verb *har-*, *háryati*[82] "to desire," "to please" and of the adjective *hári-* "bay," "golden" which is the constant epithet applied both to *Indra*'s horses and to the *Soma* juice. Here we give the whole text of the hymn with translation.

ayáṃ te astu haryatáḥ
sóma ā́ háribhiḥ sutáḥ
juṣāṇá indra háribhir na ā́ gahy
ā́ tiṣṭha háritaṃ rátham (1)

haryánn uṣásam arcayaḥ
***sū́ryam** haryánn arocayaḥ*
vidvā́ṃś cikitvā́n haryaśva vardhasa
índra víśvā abhí śríyaḥ (2)

dyā́m índro háridhāyasam
pṛthivī́ṃ hárivarpasam
*á**dhāraya**d dharítor **bhū́ri** bhójanaṃ*
yáyor antár háriś cárat (3)

jajñānó hárito vṛ́ṣā
víśvam ā́ bhāti rocanám
háryaśvo háritaṃ dhatta ā́yudham
ā́ vájram bāhvór hárim (4)

índro haryántam árjunaṃ
vájraṃ śukraír abhī́vṛtam
*ápāvṛṇod dháribhir **ádri**bhiḥ sutám*
úd gā́ háribhir ājata (5)

(1) "Mayest thou desire this / *Soma* pressed with golden (stones)! / O *Indra*, while enjoying (it), come to us upon (thy) golden horses! / Ascend the golden chariot!"

(2) "Desirous, thou hast lit the dawn, / Thou hast lit the sun, (being) desirous. / (Thou), the penetrating expert, O master of golden horses, thou growest, / O *Indra*, above all the treasures."

(3) "*Indra* has propped up the sky / That feeds the golden (one), (and) the earth with the golden image, / (He has propped up) the plentiful food of the both golden (ones), / Between whom the golden (god) wanders."

(4) "After he has been born the golden bull / Illuminates the whole brilliant space. / The master of golden horses takes in his hands / (His) weapon–the golden *vajra*."

(5) "The brilliant *vajra*, desirous (of booty), / Covered with bright ornaments), / *Indra* has found, (*Soma*) pressed with golden stones. / He has driven out the cows with the help of (his) golden (horses)."

The sound-sequence *harya-* that can be isolated in a number of words of the hymn is homonymous with the second singular imperative of the verb *har-*, i.e., "wish! desire!." Within the Vedic morphonological system *-ya-* often alternates with *-i-*, and this rule underscores the affinity between *harya-* and *hari-*. The resulting *sandhi* variant of *hari-* after *-d*, that is, *dhari-*, in stanza 3 *pāda c* is included in the sound-play with the preceding verb *adhārayat* (from *dhar-*). Finally, in the same *pāda* the word *bhū́ri* appears as a rhythmic- and sound-hint at *hári-*. In other verses the key-word is rhymed with various phonetically kindred words: stanza 2, *pādas a* and *b* begin with *haryánn . . . sū́ryam*, and then another *haryánn . . .* ; in stanza 5 *pāda c* there is a collocation *dháribhir ádribhiḥ*, and further on (*pāda d*): *háribhir*.

We have been discussing praise-hymns typical of the *Ṛg Veda*, whose communicative aim is to compel the deity to attend the worshipper's sacrifice, and to make the sacrifice desirable to him so that he will reward the sacrificer with rich gifts. This aim was expressed with the help of additional information on the expressive level. But this level could also contain symbolizations of more abstract "messages" that conveyed the basic concept of the speculative hymns of the *Ṛg Veda*. An interesting example of complex polyphonic sound symbolism can be seen in the famous cosmogonic hymn 10.129 (in the *Triṣṭubh* metre), whose text and translation are given here in full:

nā́sad āsīn nó sád āsīt tadā́nīṃ
nā́sīd rájo nó vyòmā paró yát
kím ā́varīvaḥ kúha kásya śármann
ámbhaḥ kím āsīd gáhanaṃ gabhīrám (1)

ná mṛtyúr āsīd amṛ́taṃ ná tárhi
ná rā́tryā áhnā āsīt praketáḥ
ā́nīd avātáṃ svadháyā tád ékaṃ
tásmād dhānyán ná paráḥ kíṃ canā́sa (2)

táma āsīt támasā gūḷhám ágre
'praketáṃ saliláṃ sárvam ā idám
tuchyénābhv ápihitaṃ yád ā́sīt
tápasas tán mahinā́jāyataíkam (3)

kā́mas tád ágre sám avartatā́dhi
mánaso rétaḥ prathamáṃ yád ā́sīt
sató bándhum ásati nír avindan
hṛdí pratī́ṣyā kaváyo manīṣā́ (4)

tiraścī́no vítato raśmír eṣām
adháḥ svid āsī́3d upári svid āsī3t
retodhā́ āsan mahimā́na āsan
svadhā́ avástāt práyatiḥ parástāt (5)

kó addhā́ veda ká ihá prá vocat
kúta ā́jatā kúta iyáṃ vísṛṣṭiḥ
arvā́g devā́ asyá visárjanena-
-áthā kó veda yáta ābabhū́va (6)

iyáṃ vísṛṣṭir yáta ābabhū́va
yádi vā dadhé yádi vā ná
yó asyā́dhyakṣaḥ paramé vyòman
só aṅgá veda yádi vā ná véda (7)

(1) "There was no nonreal nor was there anything real then. / There was neither the aerial space nor the sky above it. / What moved to and fro? Where? In whose protection? / What kind of water was there–a deep abyss?"

(2) "There was neither death nor immortality then. / There was no sign of day (nor) of night. / That one breathed without stirring the air, according to its own law, / And other than that (one) there was nothing."

(3) "Darkness was hidden by darkness in the beginning. / All this (was) an undistinguishable abyss. That vitally active (force) that was enclosed in the void, / That One was generated by the power of heat."

(4) "Desire came upon it in the beginning. / That was the first seed of thought. / The origin of the real in the non-real / The sages found through meditation, seeking in (their) heart."

(5) "Their cord was extended across. / Was there below? Was there above? / There were seed-placers. There were powers of extension. / (There was) impulse beneath. (And) satisfaction above."

(6) "Who really knows? Who will here proclaim (it)? / Whence was (it) produced, whence (is) this creation? / The gods (appeared) afterwards, with the creation of this (universe). / Who then knows whence it has arisen?"

(7) "Whence this creation has arisen: / Perhaps it formed itself, or perhaps it did not– / The one who oversees this (universe) in the highest heaven, / Only he knows or (perhaps) he does not know."

The apophatic form of the description of Chaos,[83] so distinctive of this hymn, is also significant for the *Ṛg Veda* as a mythological system that still lacked a unified cosmogonic theory. As far as its contents are concerned, behind all the theories on the origin of life alluded to here one can see the prevalent idea that the origin of existence is basically incomprehensible, that the gods appeared only subsequently to it, and that it remains unknown whether they are able to solve the mystery of existence. The hymn implies the archaic Indo-European question-and-answer structure of discourse,[84] in the version that became the favorite one in the *Ṛg Veda*, that is, questions without answers.

On the expressive level the contents of the hymn are reflected in several sound-themes interwoven in a complex pattern, each of them backed up here and there by splashes of sound associations. One of the basic themes expresses negation by the sound combinations *na*, *an-*, *a-* and kept up by the sound-hints *mā̆*, *am*. The hymn begins with the negation *ná* linked to the verb *āsīt* "(there) was not" and concludes with another negated verb-form *ná véda* "knows not." These are the limits within which one can observe sound variations of this theme manifest in various combinations of nasal consonants with the vowel *a*. In these seven stanzas the syllable *nā̆* occurs eighteen times, and nine of them are the independent negative particle. The syllable *mā̆*–its echo–occurs fourteen times but, unlike *na*, it appears only as part of various words, although there is also an independent word *mā́-* –a prohibitive particle used with verbs. This syllable is an echo reinforcing the background of negation, and the same function is fulfilled by the reversed sound sequences *a* + a nasal consonant (*n* or *m*).

A second sound-theme is determined by the verb *as-* "to be" (imperfect *āsīt*, present participle *sát-* "being, existing," *á-sat-* "non-being"), constantly repeated in different ways and scattered in the guise of the syllable *as* throughout many words of the hymn. As a nominal stem-marker, a flexion, or part of some noun-cases, it is also quite frequent in pronominal forms, such as *támasā*, *tápasas*, *asya*. Once in *pāda a* of stanza 5, this theme is performed in a different key in which the sibilant is not a dental but a palatal or a cerebral *tiraśćī́no vítato raśmír eṣām*. And the beginning of the hymn (stanza 1, *pāda a*) symbolizes the close connection between these two themes: *nā́sad āsīn nó sád āsīt tadā́nīm*.

The third sound-theme seems to be more independent. It is based on interrogative pronouns and adverbs with the initial consonant *k-*: *ká-* "who?," *kím* "what?," *kúha* "where?," "*kutás*" "whence?." Its echo-motifs also occur in sound-sequences contained in other words, twice at the *pāda*-beginning: *praketáṃ* (compare *ké* nominative case plural masculine from *ká-*) in *pāda b* of stanza 3, and *kā́mas* in *pāda a* of stanza 4, and once in the middle of *pāda d* of stanza 4–in *kaváyo*. This theme has a tense and uneven ring, with its rises and falls. The rises occur in stanzas 1 and 6 (plus a weak one in stanza 2). However, at the end of the hymn, shifting of the correlated pronominal series (*kó* "who?"–*yó* "who, that" (relative)–*só* "that") produces a synthesis of these three themes in *pāda d* of stanza 7: *só aṅgá veda yádi vā ná veda.*

Finally, there is yet another kind of hymn in which the information on the expressive level is mainly concerned with the "message:" these are the magic spell-hymns which are marginal in the *Ṛg Veda* (though they are dominant in the *Atharva Veda*) and are represented mostly in Book 10, especially in its final part. Since in the magic outlook a word and its denotate are held to be identical, the utterance of a word produces power over its denotate. Spells are characterized by magic plays with key-words that denote basic concepts; the play consists in word repetitions, their placement in strong positions of the metrical scheme, and their role as the focal points of sound symbolism. These words usually belong to the "message" sphere of the communication act, irrespective of the positive or negative character of that sphere, that is, whether one has to deal with white or black magic, for instance, charms for the return and multiplication of cattle or incantations against rivals. An example of it can be seen in hymn 10.173, a charm for the consolidation of royal power that is chanted during the royal consecration and accompanied by a *Soma* sacrifice. The *Anukramaṇī* classifies the hymn as a *rājñaḥ stutiḥ*, "praise of the king," although this text's structure and style run counter to such a definition. It cannot be a praise-hymn; it looks like a typical magic spell. Moreover, its metre, the *Anuṣṭubh*, is normally used for *Atharva Veda* charms. Here is the hymn's text with a translation:

ā́ tvāhārṣam antár edhi
dhruvás tiṣṭhā́vicācaliḥ
víśas tvā sárvā vāñchantu
mā́ tvád rāṣṭrám ádhi bhraśat (1)

ihaívaídhi mā́pa cyoṣṭhāḥ
párvata ivā́vicācaliḥ

índra ivehá dhruvás tiṣṭha-
ihá rāṣṭrám u dhāraya (2)

imám índro adīdharad
dhruvám̥ dhruvéṇa havíṣā
tásmai sómo ádhi bravat
tásmā u bráhmaṇas pátiḥ (3)

dhruvā́ dyaúr dhruvā́ pṛthivī́
dhruvā́saḥ párvatā imé
dhruvám̥ víśvam idám̥ jágad
dhruvó rājā viśā́m ayám (4)

dhruvám̥ te rā́jā váruṇo
dhruvám̥ devó bṛ́haspátiḥ
dhruvám̥ ta índraś cāgníś ca
rāṣṭrám̥ dhārayatām̥ dhruvám (5)

dhruvám̥ dhruvéṇa havíṣā-
abhí sómam mṛśāmasi
átho ta índraḥ kévalīr
víśo balihṛ́tas karat (6)

(1) "I have brought thee (here). Stay among (us)! / Stand firm (and) unwavering! / Let all the tribes desire thee! / Let not the kingship depart from thee!"

(2) "Stay right here, do not retreat, / Unwavering like a rock! Like *Indra*, stand firm here! Establish here (thy) kingship!"

(3) "*Indra* has established him / Firmly, with a firm sacrifice. / Of him let *Soma* approve, / Of him–*Brahmaṇaspati*.

(4) "Firm is the Sky (and) firm the earth, / Firm (are) these mountains, / Firm (is) all this world, / Firm (is) this king of (all) the tribes."

(5) "Firm (should) king *Varuṇa* (make) they (kingship), / Firm–god *Bṛhaspati*, / Firm (should) *Indra* and *Agni* (make) thy / Kingship–let them establish it firmly!"

(6) "With a firm sacrifice the firm / *Soma* we touch. / Thus let *Indra* make all the tribes / Bring tribute to thee alone."

The key word of this spell is *dhruvá-* "firm," "steadfast." In the six stanzas it occurs fifteen times. The reason for its repetition and its expected result was that the king's power should be firm. Gradually gaining strength, the key word in stanzas 4-5 becomes a pivot for anaphoric repetitions;

stanza 4 is wholly based upon this principle with a repetition of *dhruvá-* in the first *pāda* and after the caesura; in stanza 5 *pādas a-c* are anaphoric repetitions, while *pādas c-d* are chiasmic. At the same time in stanza 4 the word *dhruvá-* is, syntactically speaking, the chief component of rhythmically balanced structures. The case is always the nominative while gender and number are determined by agreement. But in stanza 5 the key word appears in the same form, *dhruvám̩*, in all the *pādas*, and agreement is explicit only in the last one; in the rest of them either agreement is implied or *dhruvám̩* ought to be interpreted as an adverb. In short, the magic use of the word in this context dominates over its grammatical use. The combination of *dhruvá-* with itself occurs twice within *pāda*-limits: *dhruvám̩ dhruvéṇa havíṣā* in stanza 3 *pāda b* and stanza 6 *pāda a*. Finally, the vertical and horizontal repetitions of *dhruvá-* within the metrical scheme are upheld by sound-hints: various forms of the verb *dhar-* "to hold" (*dhāraya* in *2d*, *adīdharad* in *3a*, *dhārayatām* in *5d*) and the sound *dh* contained in several words (*edhi*, *ádhi*).

The magic *Sprachmalerei* is rather "dense" in this spell, which is exemplary in this respect. According to the *Anukramaṇī*, the following spell (10.174) is also to be classified as a "praise-hymn," notwithstanding the fact that it has been taken over by the *Atharva Veda* almost completely (except for stanza 4) and is composed in the *Anuṣṭubh* metre. This charm is a request for the king's victory in battle, and its key word-combination is *abhí* + *vṛt-* "to win," "to prevail." The play consists in alternately joining the prefix and the root in a single noun-stem in a strong position in the *pāda* or disjoining them in such a way that the adverb-prefix is placed at the beginning of the *pāda* and the finite verb is at its end; thus the whole *pāda* becomes encircled by the key word. See, for example, stanza 1:

abhīvarténa havíṣā
yénéndro abhivāvṛté
ténāsmā́n brahmaṇas pate
'bhí rāṣṭrā́ya vartaya

"By means of a victory-bringing libation, / Through which *Indra* has won, / Let us gain victory, O *Brahmaṇaspati*, / For the sake of kingship!"

After that we can trace the following pattern in the appearance of expressive information: stanza 2 *abhivṛ́tya* . . . / *abhí* . . . *árātayaḥ* / *abhí* . . . / *abhí* . . . / ; stanza 3 *abhí* . . . / *abhí* . . . *avīvṛtat* / *abhí* . . . *bhūtā́ny* / *abhīvartó* . . . / ; stanza 4 . . . / *ábhavad* . . . / . . . / . . . / . . . *kílābhuvam* / ; stanza 5 . . . / *abhírāṣṭro* . . . / . . . *bhūtā́nām̩* / . . . /. The *abhí* repeated at the beginning of the *pāda-* may symbolize the combination *abhí* + *vṛt-*. But besides that, fragments of this sound-theme appear as echoes in the sound-hints: *árātayaḥ ~ vartaya*; *bhūtā́ny, ábhavad, abhuvam, bhūtānām ~ abhí*. In the two concluding stanzas expressive information fades away.

In discussing the formal structure of spells in the final parts of Book 10 one cannot avoid mentioning the very last hymn of the *Ṛg Veda*–10.191. The *Anukramaṇī* attributes the first stanza (of the four) to *Agni*, and the subject of the rest is alleged to be *saṃjñānam*, "concord." The connection with *Agni* is not accidental: a hymn to this god stands at the very beginning of the *Ṛg Veda* collection, and another should rightly come at its end, since *Agni* is the personification of the sacrificial fire. But from the formal point of view, this hymn is a magic spell in which the persistent repetition of key-words, supported by the semantization of related sound sequences in other words of the text, should achieve the desired result, that is, that all people who worship the Aryan gods should come together with shared thoughts. The metre is the *Anuṣṭubh* (typical of the *Atharva Veda* spells), except stanza 3 (*Triṣṭubh*). As Geldner has observed, every stanza of the hymn also occurs in the *Atharva Veda*, but without forming a single whole.[85] Here are the text and the translation:

sáṃ-sam íd yuvase vṛṣann
ágne víśvāny aryá ā́
iḷás padé sám idhyase
sá no vásūny ā́ bhara (1)

sáṃ gachadhvaṃ sáṃ vadadhvaṃ
sáṃ vo mánāṃsi jānatām
devā́ bhāgáṃ yáthā pū́rve
saṃjānānā́ upā́sate (2)

samānó mántraḥ sámitiḥ samānī́
samānám mánaḥ sahá cittám eṣām
samānám mántram abhí mantraye vaḥ
samānéna vo havíṣā juhomi (3)

samānī́ va ā́kutiḥ
samānā́ hṛ́dayāni vaḥ
samānám astu vo máno
yáthā vaḥ súsahā́sati (4)

(1) "Thou gatherest together, O bull, / O *Agni*, all the (gifts) of the pious one. / They kindle thee on the site of libation. / Bring treasures to us!"

(2) "Come together! Negotiate together! / Make up your minds to-

gether, / Just as the gods of ancient times, agreed (among themselves) and / Sat by (their) portion in the sacrifice."

(3) "A single counsel, a single assembly, / A single thought and mind have they. A single advice to I advise you; / With a single libation do I sacrifice to you."

(4) "Let your intention (be) single, / (And) united (be) your hearts! / Let your thought be single. / So that you (arrive) at a good agreement!"

The main semantic and sound theme of this hymn is connected with the word *sám* "together," "with," which is used both as an independent adverb that introduces the hymn (1a), a *pāda* (2*a*, *b*) or a rhythmic word-group (1c, 2a), and also as a prefix morpheme of a nominal form likewise at the beginning of a *pāda* (2*d*–*saṃjānānā́*) or of a rhythmic group (3a–*sámitiḥ*). Finally, the word *sám* is echoed throughout the hymn by numerous similar words, thus creating a powerful expressive phonic background for this theme. In stanzas 3 and 4 the function of the key word is assumed by *samāná-* "similar," "common," "united," which also begins with *sam-*. Since these stanzas are built around anaphoric repetitions that contain the word, it introduces seven out of eight *pādas* in these stanzas. The high point of intensity of the *sam*-repetitions is reached in the first *pāda* of stanza 3, where the feminine *samānī́* concludes the *pāda*. In addition, there are shadow-like glimpses of *sam* in *vṛṣann* (1*a*), *sá no* (1*d*), *sahá* and *eṣām* (3*b*), *havíṣā* (3*d*), *súsahā́sati* (4*d*).

On the semantic and the phonetic levels the theme of *sám* is directly linked to the theme of *man-* "to think:" a call for the harmony of minds and intentions is the real "message" of the hymn. As an independent theme of the expressive level it achieves its full development in stanza 3, where we see a vigorous play upon various nominal and verbal derivatives of this root: *mántraḥ* (3*a*), *mánaḥ* (3*b*), *mántram*, *mantraye* (3*c*), and it is also present, although in a more restrained manner, in other stanzas: *mánāṃsi* (2*b*), *máno* (4*c*).

A synthesis of these two sound themes is represented by the word *samāná-*, which contains both *sam* and *man* (though etymologically this word is derived from *sam-*) and is basic to the magic *Sprachmalerei* in stanzas 3 and 4. The expressive level can also yield some additional important data. In stanza 1 *Agni* is called upon to bring treasures (*vásūni*) to his worshippers, while the last stanza 4 in the final *pāda* ("so that you (arrive) at a good agreement/harmony") conceals the angram of the word *vásu-*: . . . *vaḥ súsaha* . . . . Thus the answer is rendered by expressive means: the treasure sought is the harmony that unites worshippers. Moreover, the word *vásu* means "good," "kind" (as an adjective) and "goods," "property" (as a substantive).

Summing up, we should say that this programmatic hymn that closes the *Ṛg Veda* collection is distinguished by all the necessary formal marks of a magic spell, and the transmission of the message of the hymn is accomplished with the help of the "poetry of grammar," which plays as important a role as "pure grammar" itself.

The *Sprachmalerei* on the expressive level sometimes symbolizes the name of an addresser of a particular message, i.e., the name of the *Ṛṣi* who has created the hymn. While the situation with the name of the deity-addressee is not very complicated, the case of the *Ṛṣi*-addresser seems to be more complex, and the use of extralinguistic data–though limited–could be helpful. In a purely linguistic discussion there seems no need for a detailed investigation of the problem of individual authorship of the poets. The source of traditional information on the names of the author-*Ṛṣis* is acknowledged to be the *Anukramaṇī*, but its evidence should be treated with reserve. For, along with the names of actual *Ṛṣis* with their patronymics or family names, the list of the authors also contains many theonyms and names of semi-divine beings. There are some other handicaps involved that will be discussed later.

Sometimes the poet openly declares his name or the name of his clan in the body of the hymn, usually in the first or the last stanza. For instance, hymn 5.22 opens with the poet's self-address: *prá viśvasāmann atrivád* / *árca pāvakáśociṣe* / . . . "Proclaim, O Viśvasāman, just as *Atri* (did), / (A hymn) for the pure-flamed (god) . . . !" And he says in the last–fourth–stanza: . . . / *táṃ tvā suśipra dampate* / *stómair vardhanty átrayo* / *gīrbhíḥ śumbhanty átrayaḥ* / "O (god) with shapely jaws, O Housemaster, / Members of the *Atri* clan invigorate thee with praises, / Members of the *Atri* clan decorate (thee) with songs." The *Anukramaṇī* also tells us that *Viśvasāman*, the author of the hymn, comes from the *Atri* clan (the family to whom the whole of Book 5 belongs).

But there are cases when the *Anukramaṇi* contradicts the evidence of the text. Thus in hymn 8.8 (to the *Aśvins*) the *Ṛṣi Vatsa* three times calls himself its author, for example, in stanza 8:

kím anyé páry āsate
'smát stómebhir aśvínā
putráḥ káṇvasya vām ṛ́ṣir
gīrbhír vatsó avīvṛdhat

"Do others than ourselves / Honor the *Aśvins* with praises? / *Kaṇva*'s son, the *Ṛṣi Vatsa* / Has invigorated you with songs."

Equally indicative are the references to *Vatsa* in stanzas 15 and 19. However, the *Anukramaṇī* names *Sadhvaṃsa* as its author. The following hymn 8.9 (also addressed to the *Aśvins*) contains *Vatsa*'s name in the traditional locus (stanza 1): *ā́ nūnám aśvinā yuvám̐ / vatsásya gantam ávase /*. . . "Come right now, O you two *Aśvins, /* To *Vatsa*'s aid! . . . . " Yet, in this case too, the *Anukramaṇī* attributes it to another author–*Śaśakarṇa.* It would be best to rely on the evidence of the text alone (as was Geldner's practice), but in most cases the author's name is not mentioned in the hymns and the *Anukramaṇī* remains our only source.

In the texts the author's name can be symbolized–on the expressive level–by means of sound-hints. On the other hand, in order to realize the communicative nature of such *Sprachmalerei*, the author's name has to be known in advance. Sometimes the name is expressed quite straightforwardly only once, and then the name's sound theme is continued by sound-hints. We can observe this in, for example, 10.24 (to *Indra* and the *Aśvins*), where in stanza 4 the author names himself: *vimadéna yád īḷitā́ / nā́satyā* ". . . you two, O *Nāsatyas*, invoked by *Vimada* . . . . " And so the formula in the three preceding stanzas must be understood as a sound-hint indicating the author's name: *ví vo máde . . . vívakṣase* "I will declare to you in (my) intoxication." The same formula is similarly used in 10.21 and 25 as a refrain whose members are noncontiguous: the verb *vívakṣase* at the end of the verse is always separated by some other words from *ví vo máde*–the latter perceived as a single unit. Here it should be interpreted as an anagram of the author's name as well, for it is already known from 10.24.4, and even earlier, it occurs at 10.20.10, in the final stanza, i.e., in a marked position (note that there is no refrain in this hymn): *evā́ te agne vimadó manīṣā́m / ū́rjo napād amŕ̥tebhiḥ sajóṣāḥ / gíra ā́ vakṣat sumatī́r iyāná /* . . . "Thus to thee, O *Agni*, O son of strength, united with the immortals, *Vimada* has offered (this) prayer and praise-songs, asking for bounties . . . . " This hint of the name is supported by the *Anukramaṇī* ascription of hymns 10.20-26 to *Vimada*. Geldner, in his commentary to 10.21.1, suggested that the two parts of the refrain (*ví vo máde* and *vívakṣase*) could be hints at the author's double name, considering that in 10.20.10 the noun *vimadáḥ* is also followed by the verb *vakṣat.*

Another undoubted example can be seen in the group of hymns 8.39-42, which the *Anukramaṇī* ascribed to the poet *Nābhāka*; the last hymn might also belong to another poet, *Arcanānas*. Every stanza in these hymns (except for 8.42, in which it is true of only the last three out of its six stanzas) ends with a refrain that apparently lacks any connection with the content of the hymns: *nábhantām anyaké same* "May any others burst!" The presence of the verb *nábhantām*, a sound-hint at the *Ṛṣi*'s name, *Nābhāka*, seems to give a clue. And once, at 8.41.2, the author openly names himself: *tám ū ṣú samanā́ girā́ / pitr̥̄ṇā́m̐ ca mánmabhiḥ / nābhākásya práśastibhir /* . . . "It is him (that I praise) beautifully, both with a praise-song and the works of the fathers, (and) *Nābhāka*'s laudations, ... " Twice the text mentions the forefather of *Nābhāka*'s family, whose example is to be followed in the composition of the gods' praises: *nabhākavád* "like *Nabhāka*, the ancestor" at 8.40.4 and 5.

But the situation changes radically when the text of a hymn gives no unequivocal evidence as to the author's name, neither in the guise of a self-address, nor in a third person discourse. The main problem lies in the ambiguity of usage: a number of proper names also occur in the *Ṛg Veda* as appellative nouns, and in some contexts they can be interpreted in both ways, so that the poet's intent remains unclear. Of course, superposition cannot be ruled out, at least in some cases. An example can be seen in 5.74 (to the *Aśvins*) whose author, according to the *Anukramaṇī*, was *Paura* of the *Atri* clan. The noun *paurá-* (root *pur-* "to fill") has the meaning of "filler," "he who satiates," "he who strengthens;" "fullness." The word is played upon in stanza 4: *paurám̐ cid dhy ùdaprútam / paúra paurā́ya jínvathaḥ / . . .* "And even *Paura*, floating on the water, / You (two) revive for fullness (of favors), O (you) fillers (of riches), ... "[86] The intense *Sprachmalerei* of the stanza is quite remarkable and stresses the semantic marking of the passage. Further on, there are two occurrences of the primary *purú-* "numerous," "plentiful:" . . . *purūṇā́m / . . .* in stanza 7, and / *purū́ . . .* in stanza 8, that echo the name *Paurá*. Lastly, the foregoing hymn 5.73, also attributed to *Paura* in the *Anukramaṇī*, contains in its opening verses sound-hints at this name, although the name is never explicitly spelled out:

yád adyá stháḥ parāváti
yád arvāváty aśvinā
yád vā purū́ purubhujā
yád antárikṣa ā́ gatam (1)

ihá tyā́ purubhū́tamā
purū́ dáṃsāṃsi bíbhratā . . . (2)

(1) "If today you are far away, / If (you are) near, O *Aśvins*, / Or if (you are) in many places, O most-helpful (ones), / If (you are) in the aerial space–come (hither)!"

(2) "Hither (may) these two (come), appearing best in many worlds, / Bringing many miraculous powers! . . . . "

Pādas a and *b* in stanza 1 both contain sound-hints at the name of *paurá-*; then the adjective *purú-* is played upon (the immediate basis of *paurá-*), and the remaining verses afford glimpses of syllables and consonances recreating a shadowy image of the name: *vápuṣe vápuś /, / páry . . .*

(3), etc. And this sound play upon the name, absent from this hymn but appearing in the following one, can serve as an argument for the trustworthiness of the *Anukramaṇī* evidence. But there is another aspect to this problem. The compilers of the *Anukramaṇī* had a clear idea of the poets' use of the devices for indicating their names on the expressive level. And so, if those comparatively late exegetes of the *Ṛg Veda* had no traditional knowledge of the authors' names they could make use of this level, look for the key-word and then claim it as the needed *Ṛṣi*'s name. This is the origin of the vicious circle that could not escape the notice of Western interpreters of the *Ṛg Veda*.[87] For example, the *Agni* hymn 5.19 begins in the following way:

abhy àvasthā́ḥ prá jāyante
prá vavrér vavríś ciketa
upásthe mātúr ví caṣṭe (1)

"(Various) states (of *Agni*) are being born in (our) direction. / (One) membrane is becoming manifest out of the (other) membrane. / He is appearing in the mother's womb." A play upon various forms of the word *vavrí-* "membrane, envelope" in *pāda b* was quite sufficient grounds to declare that *Vavri* was the author's name.

The first and the last verses of a hymn being the most marked were the usual sources for such ghost-names. There were also cases when unmarked verses from the middle of a hymn served as such sources, especially if the exegete was mistaken in his interpretation of the context. For instance, the *Anukramaṇī* cites *Avasyu* (*avasyú-* literally "he who seeks help") as the author of 5.31 on the grounds of the word's appearance in stanza 10a-b, in *Uśanas*' direct speech: *vātásya yuktā́n suyújaś cid áśvān / kavíś cid eṣó ajagann avasyúḥ* "(Drive) *Vāta*'s (horse) teams, the most easily harnessed horses! / Even this poet has left, looking for help."

Such examples could be multiplied. Are there any objective criteria that would permit a modern interpreter of the *Ṛg Veda* to establish clearly the character of information conveyed by expressive means? It seems that the answer should be negative, and each concrete case calls for the painstaking collection of all available linguistic, metrical, and extralinguistical data in order to reach a well-founded solution. Thus, for instance, the last stanza 24 of hymn 4.30 is built around the anaphoric repetitions of a magic word:

vāmáṃ-vāmaṃ ta ādure
devó dadātv aryamā́
vāmám pūṣā́ vāmám bhágo
vāmáṃ deváḥ kárūḷatī

"Everything good to thee, may the god *Aryaman* give, O attentive (one), / Good (may) *Pūṣan* (give), (and) good–*Bhaga*, / Good–the gap-toothed god!"

The repetitions of a word in the first or last stanza of a hymn are often associated with the additional semantization of the form. Now, the word *devá-* "god" occurs twice in this stanza. The *Anukramaṇī* names the author of the hymn as *Vāmadeva-* whose family produced the whole of Book 4. Taking into account *Vāmadeva*'s explicit statement of authorship at 4.16.18, our passage must be seen as containing a sound-hint at the *Ṛṣi*'s name (as Geldner correctly noted).

There are examples of another kind. In the *Agni* hymn 5.15 the magic word is *dharúṇa-* "a supporter," "basis." The phonetic shape of the word has influenced the sound-play in the hymn. The word *dharúṇa-* occurs a number of times accompanied by other nominal derivatives of the root *dhar-* "to hold" or governed by finite forms of this verb: stanza 1–*dhartā́ dharúṇo*, stanza 2–*dharúṇaṃ dhārayanta* and *dhárman dharúṇe*. And then the sound theme is kept up by echoes contained in etymologically unrelated words: stanza 3–*kruddhám*, stanza 4–*dhā́yase*, *dádhānaḥ*, stanza 5–*dógham dharúṇaṃ*, *dádhāno*. This semantization of the text is clearly not accidental, and yet it remains unclear what kind of information the poet intended to convey by means of this *Sprachmalerei*. The *Anukramaṇī* takes *dharúṇa-* to be the *Ṛṣi*'s name, which is rather improbable. This name does not appear in the *Anukramaṇī* in other places, nor does it occur as a proper name in the hymns. In this case no clear solution seems to be at hand.

4
Morphology

The data discussed under this heading should be properly regarded as belonging to the liminal area between morphology and syntax. On the one hand, they can be described in terms of a syntax of forms, but on the other, by a semantics of grammatical categories and individual grammemes. Here, the facts will be discussed from a particular view-point: how and in what way do the peculiarities of usage reflect the aims of the communication act as it is represented in the hymns of the *Ṛg Veda*? Later, we will treat the problem with abroader perspective, asking, whether this usage can adequately reflect the model of the Vedic Aryan's universe.

THE NOUN

First, we should discuss the "expressive use" of theonyms occuring in the *Ṛg Veda*. The first scholar to raise this problem was de Saussure, who showed in his "Anagrammes" [135] that in the *Agni* hymn 1.1 which opens the whole *Ṛg Veda* collection, the poet's task was a purely formal one: to use *Agni*'s name in different case-forms in a sequence of stanzas. Thus, in the first five stanzas *Agni*'s name stands at the head of the first *pāda*, that is, in a particularly marked position (1—*agním*; 2—*agníḥ*; 3—*agnínā*; 4—*ágne*; 5—*agnír*); however, in the remaining four stanzas it never occurs in this position, but three times as a vocative at the beginning or in the middle of noninitial *pādas*. Instead—as de Saussure noted—one can observe the intensification of sound-hints at *Agni*'s name resulting in a series of puns (*aṅgá, aṅgiraḥ*).[88]

De Saussure's observations have been fundamental to the further study of the figurative level of the Vedic hymn. Both the very first hymn of the *Ṛg Veda* and the last one (10.191) have a programmatic character. In the last hymn, the "message" theme (harmony, concord) is played upon on the main plane of contect as well as on the expressive plane. This seems to justify our assumption that the use of this hypersemantization of the text is of exceptional importance for the whole hymnic collection.

Solving such formal tasks was a familiar activity to the Vedic *Ṛṣis*, for in the *Ṛg Veda* we come across the genre of *āprī* hymns (*āprī* "propitiation"); liturgical hymns connected with animal sacrifice and remarkable for their formal structure, though not for their rather banal content—the gods are invited to take part in the sacrifice. All the *āprī*-hymns follow a single pre-set scheme. The classic *āprī*-hymn consists of eleven stanzas with a set of key words and phrases. The use of the key word is obligatory in a given stanza, and the rest depends on the author's personal preferences. The first three stanzas of such a hymn must relate to *Agni*: in stanza 1 he must be called "beautifully kindled" (*súsamiddha-*), in stanza 2 *-Nárāśaṃsa-* "the heroes" praise" or, less often, *Tánūnápāt-* "his own offspring" (these words are that god's descriptive names); in stanza 3 he must be called "the invoked one" (*īḷitá-*). The rest of the hymn contains key words that denote other deities or elements of ritual. The formal refinement reaches a stage in which the key word may be omitted from the verse although the context leaves no grounds for doubt as in, for example, *ū́rṇamradā ví prathasva . . . bhávā naḥ śubhra sātáye* (5.5.4) "O soft like wool, be spread! . . . Be of use to us, O well-garbed (sacrificial straw)!" The omitted word *barhís-* "sacrificial straw" plays a key role in stanza 4.

It was not by accident that de Saussure was able to illustrate the magic play upon a theonym with a hymn to *Agni*. Such play is a most characteristic trait of the *Agni* hymns and is most fully reflected there. Agni was probably felt to be the god closest to the Vedic Aryan—the cheerful god of the family hearth, the master in the worshipper's house who is sometimes portrayed as the worshipper's father and sometimes as his son, the god of sacrificial fire who is the examplary mediator between gods and mortals. About a dozen *Agni* hymns are wholly based on that play, like variant solutions of a definite formal problem. These hymns can be found in chronologically different layers: in the family *maṇḍalas*, in Book 1, and in the most recent Book 10. Their structure displays the following distinctive features: 1) the use of the theonym at the beginning of the stanza (or the *pāda*) in the metrical scheme, or not at the beginning; 2) the same case (usually vocative, sometimes nominative) or different cases, in different stanzas, of the name of the god being praised; 3) the presence of the theonym, or of its sound-hints in a stanza. Different sense configuartions of the members of these formal oppositions result indifferent scheme variants of this type of hymn. Here are a few examples from the Agni hymns.

3.20; five stanzas: stanza 1a—*agním* . . . ; 2a—*ágne* . . . ; 3a—*ágne* . . . ; 4a—*agnír* . . . ; 5a— . . . *agním* . . . . Cases: accusative, vocative, nominative. Each stanza (except the last one) begins with the god's name.

3.24; five stanzas: stanza 1a—*ágne* . . . ; 2a—*ágna* (*iḷā́*) . . . ; 3a—*ágne* . . . ; 4a—*ágne* . . . ; 5a—*ágne* . . . . Each stanza begins with the theonym in the vocative.

3.25; five stanzas: stanza 1a—*ágne* . . . ; 2a—*agníḥ* . . . ; 3a—*agnír* . . . ; 4a—*ágna* (*índraś ca*) . . . ; 5a—*ágne* . . . . Cases: vocative, nominative,—all begin the stanza.

5.14; 6 stanzas: stanza 1a—*agním* . . . ; 2a—*táṃ* . . . , 3a—*agním* . . . ; 4a—*agnír* . . . ; 5a—*agním* . . . ; 6a—*agním* . . . . Cases: accusative, nominative. Four stanzas begin with the theonym and two (stanzas 2 and 3)—with a pronoun referring to the god—*tám*; accusative singular "him."[89]

6.14; six stanzas: stanza 1a—*agnā́* . . . ; 2a—*agnír* . . . , 2b—*agnír* . . . , 2c—*agním* . . . ; 3a—*nā́nā hy àgne* . . .; 4a—*agnír* . . . , 4d—*rayír* . . . ; 5a—*áchā* . . . , 5b—*ágne* . . . , 5c—*áṃhāṃsi* . . . . Cases: locative, nominative, accusative, vocative. Along with the theonym are sound-hints that echo it at the beginning of astanza: *nā́nā* and *áchā*—compare *agnā́*, also *áṃhāṃsi* in the middle of the *pāda; rayír*—compare *agnír*.

10.80; seven stanzas: stanza 1a—*agníḥ* . . . , 1b—*agnír* . . . , 1c—*agnī́* (*rọ́dasī*) . . . , 1d—*agnír*; 2a—*agnér* . . . , 2b—*agnír* . . . , 2c—*agnír* . . . , 2d—*agnír* . . . ; 3a—*agnír* . . . , 3b—*agnír* . . . , 3c—*agnír* . . . , 3d—*agnír* . . . ; 4a—*agnír* . . . , 4b—*agnír* . . . , 4c—*agnír* . . . , 4d—*agnír* . . . ; 5a—*agním* . . . , 5b—*agním* . . . , 5c—*agním* . . . , 5d—*agníḥ* . . . ; 6a—*agním* . . . , 6b—*agním* . . . , 6c—*agnír* . . . , 6d—*agnér* . . . ; 7a—*agnáye* . . . , 7b—*agním* . . . , 7c—*ágne* . . . , 7d—*ágne* . . . . Cases: nominative, genitive, accusative, dative, vocative. Each *pāda* of a stanza begins with some case-form of the theonym, and that represents the maximum variant of filling in the scheme. Thus it may be said that this hymn contains a development of the theonym's expressive paradigm which is manifest in the metrically strong positions of each *pāda*.

The number of examples with *Agni*'s name can be easily multiplied with quotations of fragments of other hymns; the examples adduced above have been taken from hymns wholly based on the expressive paradigm. Other theonyms are also used on the expressive plane but on a much smaller scale than *Agni*. This device is most frequent in hymns to Indra, although his name's expressive paradigm is less distinctive than that of *Agni*. The paradigm can be skewed, so that the cases of the theonym are in mutually asymmetrical positions in the *pāda*; sometimes *Indra*'s name is replaced by an anaphoric pronoun. And the style of *Indra*'s hymns makes a most peculiar use of the following syntactic construction: an attributive clause with the relative *yá-* "who, which" + a main clause with the corresponding demonstrative *sá-* "that, he." Most frequently the attributive clause precedes the main one, but the reverse order is not rare. The semantic content of this construction can be roughly expressed by: "he who has performed such-and-such a feat, he is *Indra*," or "he is to be honored." The *Indra*-hymn 2.12

on the whole follows this scheme. Let us quote one of the stanzas:

yáḥ pṛthivī́ṃ vyáthamānām ádṛṃhad
yáḥ párvatān prákupitā̃n áramṇāt
yó antárikṣaṃ vimamé várīyo
yó dyā́m ástabhnāt sá janāsa índraḥ (2)

"He who made fast the tottering earth, / Who made still the quaking mountains, / Who measured out the aerial space farther, / Who propped up the sky,—he, O (my) people, (is) *Indra*!"

Stanzas constructed according to this scheme are quite frequent in the *Indra* hymns and this may be the reason for the deficiencies of the theonym's expressive paradigm as compared to that of *Agni* hymns. Nevertheless, quite a few examples can be quoted from the *Indra* hymns.

2.21; six stanzas: stanza 1d—*índrāya* . . . ; 2d—*índrāya* . . . ; 3d—*índrasya* . . . ; 4d—*índraḥ* . . . ; 5d—*índre* . . . ; 6a—*índra* . . . . Cases: dative, genitive, nominative, locative, vocative.

3.34; eleven stanzas: stanza 1a—*índraḥ* . . . ; 2c—*índra* . . . ; 3a—*índro* . . . ; 4a—*índraḥ* . . . ; 5a—*índras* . . . ; 6b—*índrasya* . . . ; 7a— . . . *índro* . . . ; 8d—*índram* . . . ; 9b—*índraḥ* . . . ; 10a—*índra* . . . ; 11a—*índram*. Cases: nominative, vocative, genitive, accusative. Seven stanzas begin with the theonym.

3.40; nine stanzas: stanza 1a—*índra* . . . ; 2a—*índra kratuvídam* . . . ; 3a—*índra prá* . . . , 3d—*tirá* . . . ; 4a—*índra* . . . , 4b— . . . *prá* . . . , *4c*— . . . *candrāsa índavaḥ*; 5b— . . . *indra* . . . , 5c—*índavaḥ*; 6c—*índra* . . . ; 7a-b— . . . *vanínal índraṃ* . . . ; 8b—*parā́vátaś ca vṛtrahan*, 8c—*giráḥ*; 9a . . . *antarā́ parā́vátam*, 9c—*índra* . . . . Cases: vocative, locative accusative. Four stanzas begin with the theonym. There are glimpses of sound-hints at the syllables of *Indra*'s name. The sound-combination *ra* is played upon in various phonetic contexts: *kra, pra, tra, tira*, and *arā*. The same principle lies at the basis of separate stanzas and of some of their sequences in *Indra* hymns.

The name of the third of the Rig Vedic principal gods, *Soma*, is not used on the expressive level, unlike the names of *Agni* and *Indra*. The whole of Book 9 (114 hymns) is devoted to *Soma-Pavamāna* ("The purified"), but not a single hymn is constructed according to the basic scheme of 1.1. The *Soma*-hymns do not have sequences of several stanzas built around anaphoric repetitions containing the word *sóma*-. In that regard stanza 35 of hymn 9.97 (the longest in the *Ṛg Veda*) is a unique exception:

sómaṃ gā́vo dhenávo vāvaśānā́ḥ
sómaṃ víprā matíbhiḥ pṛchámānāḥ
sómaḥ sutáḥ pūyate ajyámānaḥ
sóme arkā́s triṣṭúbhaḥ sáṃ navante

"Lowing milch-cows come to *Soma*, / The inspired (poets) come to *Soma* with prayers, asking (about him). The pressed *Soma* is purified when he is anointed. / The melodies (and verses) of the *Triṣṭubh* in *Soma* sound together."[90]

It was noted earlier, in the analysis of sound-hints in hymns and stanzas about *Soma*, that the formal play therein is based on various derivatives from the roots *su-* "to press" (whence also *sóma-*) and *pū-* "to purify" (whence the deity's name *pávamāna-* "being purified"[91] of Book 9. In that Book the principal starting point of the *Sprachmalerei* is represented by the root *pū-*. This hypersemantization of the text, resting upon these two verbal roots, once again stresses the specifically ritual character of this deity. The numerous divine epithest, including the constant epithets, function as substitutes for theonyms but do not normally form expressive paradigms in the hymns.

The evidence collected here seems to lead to the conclusion that the word *sóma-* still was not perceived in the oldest parts of the *Ṛg Veda* (including Book 9) as the proper name of a deity, in contrast with theonyms such as *Agni, Indra*, and *Varuṇa*. Apparently *Soma* was not a proper name but a ritual designation of the substance out of which the juice (*sóma-*, or *sutá-*) was pressed (*su-*). The deified ritual substance *sóma-* should therefore be distinguished from the anthropomorphic mythological figure of the marriage hymn 10.85—the *Soma* who was the bridegroom of *Savitar*'s daughter *Sūryā* and whose wedding was the mythic prototype for the Vedic Aryans.

This hypothesis, based on the study of the expressive paradignis of the theonyms in the *Ṛg Veda,* inspires us to reconsider the extralinguistic evidence, in particular, R. Gordon Wasson's hypothesis that *Soma* (the source of *amṛta*) in the *Ṛg Veda* was not an ephedra-like plant but a mushroom, the fly-agaric (*Amanita muscaria*) [150]. However, here the problem of the original source of the juice—the ephedra plant or the fly-agaric—is of secondary importance. We are more interested in the fact that during the long period when the *Ṛg Veda* collection was being compiled and the conquest of India by the Aryans was progressing, the original ritual substance—whatever it had been—had to be replaced by something new which could be procured along their new routes [150].[92] The *Ṛṣis* apparently knew that the word *sóma-* was not the genuine name, that is, it was not the proper name of the original substance but a ritual label for the substitute already in use by the times of the *Ṛg Veda.* This could explain why *sóma-* was not equivalent—on the expressive level—with the names of *Agní-* and *Índra-*.

The development of the expressive paradigm of a theonym is also present in the *Ṛg Veda* in a number of hymns that deal with some other, less important Vedic gods, as well as in hymns to certain deified abstract notions. Here are some examples: Hymn to *Mitra* 3.59;[93] nine stanzas: stanza 1a—*mitró*. . . , 1c—*mitráḥ* . . . , 1d—*mitrā́ya* . . . ; 2a— . . . *mitra márto* . . . ; 3b—*mitájñavo* . . . , 3d— . . . *mitrásya sumataú* . . . ; 4a—*mitró* . . . ; 5d— . . . *mitrā́ya* . . . ; 6a—*mitrásya* . . . ; 7b—*mitró* . . . ; 8a—*mitrā́ya* . . . ; 9a—*mitró* . . . . Cases: nominative, dative, vocative, genitive. Sound-hints at the theonym are quite numerous. Only those words that reflect the *mitrá-* sound image as a whole are cited here. Besides that, in a number of words we find the syllable *-tra: kṣatrá-, citrá-*; different consonant combinations with *ra: pra, vra, śra*, and the syllable *mī́: vratá–prá anamīvā́sa, yemire*, etc. The first verse is programmatic for the expressive paradigm, for anaphoric repetitions of the god's name that occur in each *pāda*:

mitró jánān yātayati bruvāṇó
mitró dādhāra pṛthivī́m utá dyā́m
mitráḥ kṛṣṭī́r ánimiṣābhí caṣṭe
mitrā́ya havyáṃ ghṛtávaj juhota (1)

"*Mitra*, called (the friend), unites people. / *Mitra* keeps fast the earth and the sky. / *Mitra*, without closing (his) eyes, gazes round (his) people. / To *Mitra* offer a libation rich in ghee."

In verses 2-5 the god's name is mentioned only in the middle of the *pāda* of the hymn, but in verses 6-9 it begins three stanzas and one *pāda*, continually backed up by sound echoes.

Hymn to *Uṣas* 3.61; seven stanzas: stanza 1a—*úṣo* . . . ; 1b— . . . *juṣasva* . . . ; 2a—*úṣo* . . . ; 3a—*úṣaḥ* . . . ; 4b—*uṣā́* . . . ; 5a—*áchā* . . . *uṣásaṃ* . . . ; 6c— . . . *uṣásaṃ* . . . ; 6d— . . . *bhíkṣamāṇaḥ*; 7a— . . . *uṣásām iṣanyán*; 7b—*vṛ́ṣā* . . . . Cases: vocative, nominative, accusative, singular, genitive plural. The first three stanzas begin with *Uṣas*'s name in the vocative. The name is also modulated through sound-echoes, and twice such echo words stand at the beginning of the *pāda*: *áchā* and *vṛ́ṣā* (compare the nominative singular sandhi-form *uṣā́*).

Hymn to *Pūṣan* 6.54; ten stanzas: stanza 1a— . . . *pūṣan vidúṣā naya*; 2a— . . . *pūṣṇā́* . . . ; 3a—*pūṣṇáś* . . . ; 4b— . . . *pūṣā́* . . . ; 5a—*pūṣā́* . . . ; 5b—*pūṣā́ rakṣatu* . . . ; 5c—*pūṣā́* . . . ; 5d—*pūṣā́* . . . ; 6a—*pū́ṣann* . . . ; 7a— . . . *neṣan* . . . *riṣan*; 8a— . . . *pūṣáṇam* . . . ; 8c—*ī́śānaṃ* . . . ; 9a—*pū́ṣan* . . . ; 10a— . . . *pūṣā́* . . . ; 10c—*púnar no naṣṭám* . . . . Cases: vocative, instrumental, genitive, nominative, accusative. The main sound key of the hymn is that of the cerebral fricative *ṣ*—compare the various forms of the verb *riṣ-* : *riṣyati, riṣan, riṣyema*, participle *áriṣṭābhir*, compare also *mṛṣyate, rakṣatu, neṣan, vidúṣā, havíṣā, ánaṣṭá; naṣṭám, dákṣiṇam*. The sound-key seems to be even more inclusive, with fricatives and palatal affricates in general, for instance, 3a-b: *pūṣṇáś cakrámṇá riṣyati / ná kóśol' va padyate* "In *Pūṣan*'s (care) a wheel cannot break, a (chariot's) body cannot fall (to the ground)." In stanza 7 the theonym does not appear at all, yet it is symbolized by sound and rhythmic hints: *neṣan, riṣan* (compare *pūṣan*).

Hymn to *Bṛhaspati* 10.68; twelve stanzas: stanza 1d—*bṛ́haspátim* . . . ; 2d—*bṛ́haspate* . . . ; 3c—*bṛ́haspátiḥ* . . . ; 4c—*bṛ́haspátir* . . . ; 5c—*bṛ́haspátir* . . . ; 6b—*bṛ́haspátir* . . . ; 7a—*bṛ́haspátir* . . . ; 8d—*bṛ́haspátir* . . . ; 9c—*bṛ́haspátir* . . . ; 10b—*bṛ́haspátinā* . . . ; 11d—*bṛ́haspátir* . . . ; 12c—*bṛ́haspátiḥ* . . . . Cases: Accusative, vocative, nominative, instrumental.

Bṛhaspati is the god of prayer, and the hymns to this deity are distinguished by their extreme refinement of form.[94] This hymn is notable for the marked position of the theonym in the metrical scheme. Throughout the hymn the name *bṛhaspáti* begins a *páda*, but it begins only one stanza, in the middle of the text, in stanza 7. Throughout stanzas 1-7 the god's name moves from the beginning of the last *páda* to the beginning of the first one: stanzas 1-2—*páda d*, stanzas 305—*pāda c*, stanza 6—*páda b*, stanza 7—*páda a*. Then there are two new and incomplete cycles of the theonym's progression: stanza 8—*páda d*, stanza 9—*páda d*, stanza 9—*páda c*, stanza 10—*páda b* (one cycle, and stanza 11—*páda d*, stanza 12—*páda c* (the other cycle).

The *Ṛg Veda* abounds in examples of magic play upon a theonym in its various forms, relating it in a definite manner to the general metrical scheme of the stanza. Taking into consideration the widespread personification of abstract notions so characteristic of the Vedic vision of the world, any common noun that becomes a proper name denoting the addressee of a message is treated as an ordinary theonym on the expressive plane. An example of this can be seen in a short hymn to *Śraddhā́* "Faith" (10.151). As Geldner pointed out, this notion embraces the worshipper's faith in the gods, the faith of the patron of sacrifice in the abilities of the officiating priests, and the priests' faith in the patron's generosity. Moreover, the personification of *Śraddhā* goes so far that the *Anukramaṇī* lists it as the author of this particular hymn, adding that it/she comes from the *Kāma* family (*kāma-* "love"). Here is the text:

śraddháyāgníḥ sám idhyate
śraddháyā hūyate havíḥ
śraddhā́m bhágasya mūrdháni
vácasā́ vedayāmasi (1)

priyáṃ śraddhe dádataḥ
priyáṃ śraddhe dídāsataḥ
priyáṃ bhojéṣu yájvasv
idám ma uditáṃ kṛdhi (2)

yáthā devā́ ásureṣu
śraddhā́m ugréṣu cakriré
evám bhojéṣu yájvasv
asmā́kam uditáṃ kṛdhi (3)

śraddhā́ṃ devā́ yájamānā
vāyúgopā úpāsate
śraddhā́ṃ hṛdayyàyā́kūtyā
śraddháyā vindate vásu (4)

śraddhā́m prātár havāmahe
śraddhā́m madhyáṃdinam pári
śraddhā́ṃ sū́ryasya nimrúci
śráddhe śrád dhāpayehá naḥ (5)

"(1) With Faith (*Agni*) is kindled, / With Faith the offering is libated. / (This) faith, which is upon the head of happiness, / We proclaim in (our) speech.

(2) O Faith, (make this) pleasant to (the man) who gives, / Pleasant, O faith, to (the man) who wishes to give, / Pleasant to lavish sacrificers, / Make (all) this that I have said.

(3) As the gods created / Faith among the formidable *Asuras*, / So among lavish sacrificers / Make what we have said (to be trusted).

(4) The gods honor Faith, / (They who) offer sacrifices guarded by *Vāyu*, / (They honor) Faith with heartfelt intent. / With Faith they find wealth.

(5) We call to Faith at early morning, / To Faith near midday. / To Faith—at sundown. / Faith, make us trusted here!"

The text is composed in the best tradition of praise-hymns wherein everything pivots upon the magic play with the god's name. The theonym in various case-forms (instrumental, accusative, vocative) appears in each stanza. Some artificial traits of this late composition may perhaps be seen: the theonym does not occur in the nominative, the case-form that is obligatory in classic expressive paradigms. As we have observed in another paper [25.73], this is significant, since such a case paradigm represents a set of real or mythic situation involving a given deity: *Agni* the hotar (nominative), we kindle *Agni* (accusative), together with *Agni* (instrumental), we obtain wealth, etc. The most reduced variety of the paradigm contains only the nominative and/or the vocative. Strictly speaking, the vocative is not a proper case: its function is that of an appeal, a calling attention to, while the nominative has the basic meaning of the subject of the action. The latter is one of the distinctive features of naming the gods: one of them slays with the *vajra*, another one is a messenger, and so forth. But the author of the hymn reproduced all the other details with remarkable fidelity to canonical standards. Three stanzas (out of five) are built around anaphoric repetitions of the theonym. And the very last *páda* (of the last stanza) contains an etymological play upon the name of *śraddhā́*, composed of the noun *śrád-* and the verbal root *dhā-* "to set, to place."

The same type of text is represented by hymn 10.107 in praise of the goddess *Dakṣiṇā*, who is really the personified gift to the priests for performing a sacrifice (*dákṣiṇā-*). Here the name of the goddess occurs a number of times in the nominative. The same expressive tendencies are basic to praise-hymns to dual deities; however, a new parameter on the expressive level is added in this case, *viz.*, the joint or separate appearance of theonyms or, putting it differently, the opposition between a composite of two names and two separate names, usually in the same case.

Here a few additional comments are called for. In the Ṛg Vedic mythological system, dual deities are quite well represented but do not share a single content. Representatives of this type of deity can range between two limits: on the one side, there is a complete identity between both figures as, for example, the *Aśvins*, who share a common name and a common function and whose name is always in the dual (a single exception: the isolated case at 4.3.6 where their second name, the *Nāsatyas*, occurs in the singular). The other limit is reached when the names of two quite dissimilar gods are mechanically combined in a single word. When two mythological figures merge to a certain degree, the most typical features of the one may appear as the property of the other. Thus, for instance, at 1.10.3 the dual deity *Indra-Agni* acquires the epithet "*Vṛtra*'s slayer" (*vṛtrahaṇā*), which can properly define only *Indra*, not *Agni*.

For our purposes it seems to be immaterial whether such a joining results from ritual considerations which are otherwise quite important, especially for such dual deities as *Indra-Agni*, *Indra-Varuṇa*, and *Indra-Vāyu*) or represents a dichotomic unity (compare *Mitra-Varuṇa*), i.e. a combination of two members of an opposition (the two in one).[95] Expressive grammar makes use of the peculiarities of dual theonyms in the hymns widely and in diverse ways.

The names of the dual deities are usually represented in the *Ṛg Veda* by compounds of the *dvandva* type, classified as an archaic subtype (the so-called "Götterdvandva"). This rather loosely established pattern is peculiar in a number of respects. As a rule, in the *Ṛg Veda* both members are accented separately and have their own dual endings, e.g.: *mitrā́váruṇā*—"*Mitra-Varuṇa*" (literally "two *Mitras*-(and)-two *Varuṇas*"), *agnī́-ṣómā*—"*Agni*-(and)-*Soma*," *índrāpuṣáṇā*—"*Indra*-(and)-*Pūṣan*," *dyā́vāpṛthivī́*—

"Sky-(and)-Earth," etc. If such a compound is in an oblique case its ending is joined to the second member while the first retains the fossilized inflexion of the direct form (nominative, accusative, vocative) of the dual, for example: instrumental dual *mitrā́varuṇābhyam*; genitive dual *índrā-váruṇayoḥ*, although in some cases the first member can also have oblique endings (singualar only), as in genitive *divásp̣rthivyós*. The first member tends to lose its independent accent, as in: accusative dual *indrāgnī́*, instrumental dual *somāpūṣábhyām*. There are still quite clear traces of the source of this *dvandva* subtype; the original mere collocation of two separate theonyms [120.124ff.] is reflected in the so-called "syntactical" or "decomposed" *dvandvas*, for example: *índrā nú pūṣáṇā vayáṃ . . . huvéma* (6.57.1) "Now we wish to invoke *Indra* (accusative dual) and *Pūṣan* (accusative dual); *ádhārayatam pṛthivī́m utá dyā́m / mítrarājānā varuṇā máhobhiḥ* (5.62.3) "You have established the earth and the sky, O (you) two kings, *Mitra* and *Varuṇa* (literally "O two kings *Mitras*, two *Varuṇas*), with (your own) energies." The *Ṛg Veda* also contains cases of the so-called elliptical dual, for example: *uṣā́sāv éhá sīdatām* (1.188.6) "*Uṣas* and the Night (literally "two *Uṣases*") may (they) sit (third dual) down here!;" *yuvám mitremáṃ jánaṃ / yátathaḥ sáṃ ca nayathaḥ* (5.65.6) "You two, O *Mitra* (and *Varuṇa*) (literally "O two *Mitras*") arrange (dual) and lead together (dual) these tribes."

Variants in language system make it possible to diversify the *Sprachmalerei* with the help of theonyms. One may start with hymns to the most established and widely attested dual deity in the *Ṛg Veda*, that is, to *Mitra-Varuṇa*. In some hymns, the *dvanda* compound (mostly in the vocative *mitrāvaruṇā / mitrāvaruṇau*) is sure to appear—at least once—in each stanza; thus, for example, in each of the seven stanzas of hymn 5.63, it appears in various positions of the metrical scheme. But some hymns have no incidence of the *dvanda* dual theonym while the god's names appear separately, thus setting up, in a way, two parallel expressive paradigms; in that case, the same stanza usually contains both theonyms in the same-forms. This is the case, for instance, of hymn 1.136, in which six of the seven stanzas (all but the first one) follow this principle—while in stanza 1 *Mitra* and *Varuṇa* are alluded to by their common epithets in the dual: *tā́ samrā́ja ghṛtā́sutī* "these two omnipotent ones whose drink is ghee." The expressive paradigm in the next stanzas presents this picture: stanza 2—*mitrásya* . . . váruṇasya ca; stanza 3—*mitrás* . . . *váruṇo*; stanza 4—*mitrā́ya váruṇāya*; stanza 5—*mitrā́ya váruṇāya*; stanza 6—*mitrā́ya* . . . *váruṇāya*; stanza 7—*mitró váruṇaḥ*. Lastly, there is a third group, in which the two expressive principles are combined: sometimes the theonyms are represented by *dvandas*, and sometimes they are separated into independent paradigms, but usually they parallel. The superiority of one or the other deity in the hymn is frequently marked by sound-hints only. An example of this procedure may be seen in the *Mitra-Varuṇa* hymn 5.62, remarkable for its theonym variants and numerous sound-hints: stanza 1—*rténa rtám . . . dhruvám̐ vām / . . . yátra . . . / . . . / . . . vápuṣām . . . /* ; stanza 2— . . . *mitrāvaruṇā . . .* ; stanza 3— . . . */ mítrarājānā varuṇā . . .* ; stanza 4— . . . *vám áśvāsaḥ . . . vahantu / . . . arvā́k / . . . vartate vām / . . .* ; stanza 5— . . . *śrutā́m / mítrā . . . varuṇā . . .* ; stanza 6—*ákravihastā . . . / . . . trā́sāthe varuṇā . . . / . . . kṣatrám / sahásrasthūṇam . . .* ; stanza 7— . . . *sthū́ṇā / . . . / . . . kṣétre nímitā . . . vā / . . .* ; stanza 8— . . . */ áyasthūṇam . . . / . . . varuṇa mitra . . .* ; stanza 9—*mitrāvaruṇāv . . . .*

This play upon the names of the two gods, which here constitute a special unit, has reached a high degree of complexity. The *dvanda* theonym appears to encircle the hymn: it stands at its beginning (stanza 2) and at its end (stanza 8). In the middle the play consists of bringing them together and taking them apart: the "decomposed" compound whose both members have the dual inflexion (stanza 3 and 5), the elliptical dual in which *Varuṇa*'s dual denotes the pair *Mitra-Varuṇa* (stanza 7), and immediately after that the names are cited separately (stanza 8). Sound-hints, in their turn, keep up the balance between the two theonyms.

The *Mitra-Varuṇa* hymns exhibit the most typical schemes of expressive paradigms of the dual theonyms. Other variants occur in hymns to other dual deities. A rather complex play upon the names of *Indra-Varuṇa* occurs in hymn 4.41. The initial five stanzas of this hymn of eleven stanza begin with the vocative of the theonym in its syntactical *dvandva* form, in which the names in the dual are separated by two or three words: stanza 1—*índrā kó vām̐ varuṇā . . .* ; stanza 2—*índrā ha yó varuṇā . . .* ; stanza 3—*índrā ha rátnam̐ varuṇā . . .* ; stanzas 4-5—*índrā yuvám̐ varunā . . .* ; this creates a certain rhythmic pattern which attracts the hearer's attention. In stanza 6 this construction with the theonyms is carried over to the beginning of *pāda c: índrā no átra varuṇā . . .* , but *páda a* starts with a rhythmic hint: *toké hité tānaya . . .* (compare *índrā ha yó varuṇā*). In stanza 7 the theonyms are not mentioned, but sound-hints at *índra* seem to be present: *prábhūtī, śū́rā*. Further in the text the two gods' names appear in two parallel independent paradigms: stanza 8—*índram̐ . . . váruṇa*; stanza 9— . . . *índram̐ váruṇam . . .* ; stanza 11— */ índra . . . varuṇa*, while stanza 10 yet again contains sound-hints at the name of *índra-* alone: *ráthyasya, rāyáḥ, cakrāṇā́, asmatrā́, rā́yo.* Only once are the gods named together, in stanza 1 (and this is no accident)—yet not at the beginning, where the program is triggered by the rhythmic group *índrā kó vām varuṇā*, but in the concealed compound in the middle of the last *pāda*: . . . *índrāvaruṇā . . . .*

All of this play upon the names of *Indra* and *Varuṇa* seems to be intentional. The *Ṛṣi* at first seems to be trying to symbolize a somewhat fragile union of the two great gods and then displays their separateness, at the same time, by his use of sound-hints, stressing the superiority of *Indra*. And the following hymn (4.42) is, as Kuiper has shown [100.42ff.], a verbal contest between *Varuṇa* and *Indra*, at the end of which *Varuṇa* acknowledges his defeat. The magic play upon the theonyms in the preceding hymn could therefore be the expression of the author's attitude to the protagonists.

An easy transition from hymns to the wind-god *Vāyu* to hymns to the dual deity *Indra-Vāyu* is quite common, as both deities have close connections to the ritual. In hymn 4.47 (to *Vāyu* and *Indra-Vāyu*) the play on theonyms is based on a syntactic structure, typical for the *Ṛg Veda*: when two gods are invoked, one of the names is in the vocative and the other in the nominative followed by the connective *ca* "and;" the two parts may be transposed.[96] The play upon theonyms is backed up here by numerous sound-hints. The text and translation of this short hymn follow below.

vā́yo śukró ayāmi te
mádhvo ágraṃ díviṣṭiṣu
ā́ yāhi sómapītaye
spārhó deva niyútvatā (1)

índraś ca vāyav eṣām
sómānām pītím arhathaḥ
yuvā́ṃ hí yantī́ndavo
nimnám ā́po ná sadhryàk (2)

vā́yav índraś ca śuṣmíṇā
saráthaṃ ṣavasas patī
niyutvantā na ūtáya
ā́ yātaṃ sómapītaye (3)

yā́ vām sánti puruspṛ́ho
niyúto dāśúṣe narā
asmé tā́ yajñavāhasā
índrāvayū ní yachatam (4)

(1) "O *Vāyu*, the pure juice is offered thee, / The best sweet (juice) at sacrifices that seek heaven. / Arrive to drink *Soma*, / O desirable god, yoking gifts!"

(2) "O *Indra* and *Vāyu*, you are entitled / To drink these *Soma*-juices. / It is to you that the (*Soma*) drops are running, / Like waters to a marsh—in one direction!"

(3) "O *Vāyu* and *Indra*, two raving (ones) / Upon a single chariot, O Lords of strength, / Yoking (-gifts), arrive / To help us to drink *Soma*!"

(4) "Those much-desired yokes (-gifts), / That you (two) have gotten for (your) worshipper, O heroes, / Keep them for us, O *Indra* and *Vāyu*, / O (you) whom the sacrifices bring (here)!"

The hymn is introduced by *Vāyu*'s name in the vocative, at which the next words of verse 1 contain sound-hints. The second stanza begins with the above noted construction of the invocation of the two gods, headed by *Indra*; while in stanza 3, in the same position, it is headed by *Vāyu*. Finally, in stanza 4 *pāda d* begins with a *dvandva* compound of both names while the whole stanza begins with an anagram of *Vāyu*'s name. Sound-hints at *Vāyu*'s name clearly dominate over hints at *Indra*'s name. Thus, in spite of the final synthesis of both names, the expressive level throughout the hymn is keyed to *Vāyu*.

The *Indra-Agni* hymn 8.40 has several remarkable aspects from the expressive standpoint. Throughout each stanza it develops two parallel paradigms: the paradigm of each of the theonyms, and the expressive paradigm of the *dvandva* theonym *indrāgnī́-*, with a single accent on the second member but with the dual inflexion of both members. The principal and predominant paradigmis that of the compound: stanza 1— / *índrāgnī* and *agnír*; 2—*índram*; 3—*indrāgnī*; 4—*indrāgnī*; 5—*indrāgníbhyām* and *índraḥ*; 6—*índreṇa*; 7—*indrāgnī́*; 8—*indrāgnyór*: 9—*indra*; 12—*indrāgníbhyām*. Cases of the compound: vocative, accusative, dative, genitive; cases of *índra-*: accusative, nominative, instrumental, vocative; of *agní-*: nominative. In stanzas 10-11 there are no theonyms, but both stanzas begin with a demonstrative that refers to a deity. Interpreters of the *Ṛg Veda* differ as to the deity who is the referent of those demonstratives. There is another pecuoiarity: stanza 11 is a variant of stanza 10—which is quite rare in the *Ṛg Veda* text. Here are the two verses:

táṃ ṣiṣītā suvṛktíbhis
tveṣáṃ sátvānam ṛgmíyam
utó nú cid yá ójasā
śúṣṇasyāṇḍā́ni bhédati
jéṣat svàrvatīr apó
nábhantām anyaké same (10)

táṃ śiśītā svadhvaráṃ
satyáṃ sátvānam ṝtvíyam
utó nú cid yá óhata
āṇḍā́ śúṣṇasya bhédaty
ájaiḥ svàrvatīr apó
nábhantām anyaké same (11)

(10) "Sharpen him with beautiful hymns, / The formidable warrior, worthy of the hymns, / Who at once with (his) might / Shall crush *Śuṣṇa*'s eggs, / Shall conquer the waters and the sun— / May all the others burst!"

(11) "Sharpen him, the excellent institutor of ritual, / The true warrior, the expert on offering times, / Who will dare at once to / Crush *Śuṣṇa*'s eggs— / he has conquered the waters and the sun— / May all the others burst!"

Those scholars who postulate different referents of the demonstrative *tám* in these two stanzas seem to be justified in their interpretation. Oldenberg [114.108], Geldner [74] and Renou [118.14.129] believe that stanza 10 refers to *Indra* (compare stanza 9 containing the call "O *Indra*"), while stanza 11 refers to *Agni*, whose ritual virtues are described in *pādas a-b* (compare the epithets *svadhvará-*, *ṛtvíya-*). Sāyaṇa was of a different opinion: in his view, both stanzas are addressed to *Indra*.

The former hypothesis can be backed up by a purely formal analysis of the stanzas. *Indra-Agni* are perceived as a "bi-unity," two in one, and so they are the addressees of the two stanzas, variants of a single prototype. The transfer of the properties of one god onto the other is not rare in a "bi-unity;" thus *Agni* is described here as *sátvan-* "warrior," the standard epithet of *Indra*.

This exposition of the expressive grammar of theonyms in the hymns of the *Ṛg Veda* would be incomple without mentioning the special role of the vocative in this text. The narrative in the hymns is constantly interrupted by invocations to gods, appeals to them by name, which create a highly emotional tension. The sheer number of vocatives—theonyms or their epithets—that repeatedly break up the Vedic sentence raises the problem of their functional value in this text.

The play upon vocatives in the *Ṛg Veda* should be treated as part of the general Vedic conception of the magic role of the word. Since the knowledge of the deity's name was identified with the knowledge of his true nature, in the worshipper's mind, power could be acquired over the lauded deity. To say the god's name aloud was a kind of declaration of truth, a sacral act. This seems to explain the special role of the vocatives in the *Ṛg Veda*, the peculiarities of which function cannot be defined only in terms of dependence of some hymns upon the ritual (i.e., the need to invoke gods to sacrifice at certain stages of the rite), but rather in terms of the hymns' communicative aims. Such a communicative approach seems to provide a clearer perception of the function of the vocatives.

Certainly, some appeals to the gods by name are presented as a "roll-call" of a ritual and formulaic nature and do not contain any implicit additional information. Such are the appeals in the hymns to the All-Gods, for example, in 5.46.2:

ágna índra váruṇa mítra dévāḥ
śárdhaḥ prá yanta mā́rutotá viṣṇo
ubhā́ nā́satyā rudró ádha gnā́ḥ
pūṣā́ bhágaḥ sárasvatī juṣanta

"O *Agni, Indra, Varuṇa, Mitra* , the gods, / O *Maruts*' band, and *Viṣṇu* grant (us protection!) / Both *Nāsatyas, Rudra*, and the divine wives, / *Pūṣan, Bhaga, Sarasvatī* (—may they) rejoice!" In this stanza one cannot distinguish any specific functions of the vocative in the communication act, and there is no fundamental difference between a series of vocatives and a series of nominatives. All that matters is a certain traditionally fixed sequence of theonyms in the list.

The communicative function of vocatives is much more evident when the god is appealed to by means of epithets, mostly standard epithets functioning as theonyms, as for instance in 8.46.19-20:

prabhaṅgáṃ durmatīnā́m
índra śaviṣṭhā́ bhara
rayím asmábhyaṃ yújyaṃ codayanmate
jyéṣṭhaṃ codayanmate

sánitaḥ súsanitar úgra
cítra cétiṣṭha sū́nṛta
prāsáhā samrāṭ sáhuriṃ sáhantam
bhujyúṃ vā́veṣu pū́rvyam

"Bring us, O mightiest *Indra*, deserved wealth that destroys evil designs, O inspirer of thoughts, the best (wealth), O inspirer of thoughts. O subjugator, O mighty subjugator, terrible, bright, the brightest, magnanimous, autocrator—(wealth) victorious because of (its) power, overcoming (and yet) obedient, first in contests for the prize!"

Using the model of the standard hymn that implies a switch between its descriptive and appellative parts [69.255-68], one could say that *Indra*'s epithets in the vocative contain implicit information about those gifts and deeds which the worshipper might expect of him. Paraphrasing the text: O mightiest one, O inspirer of thoughts grant us such a mighty power of thought that it could destroy the evil designs (of the enemies)!; O powerful subjugator give us the ability to subjugate and be in the forefront!, etc. From this standpoint, *Indra*'s epithets in the vocative and the epithets of wealth demanded of him are related by transformation (in the broad sense of the term).

Such code-switching becomes even more obvious when the same lexemes are used in appeals to a deity, in the description of his attributes or his actions, for example: *índrāvaruṇā sutapāv imáṃ sutáṃ / sómam pibatam mádyam dhṛtavratā* (6.68.19) "O *Indra* and *Varuṇa*, drinking *Soma*, drink this pressed inebriating *Soma*, O (you) whose behest is firm;" or the invocation of *Agni*: *úrukṛt urú ṇas kṛdhi* (8.75.11) "O creator of space, create space for us!;" of *Indra*: *bhū́ridā bhū́ridā bhū́ri dehi no* (4.32.20) "O giver of plenty, give us plenty!"

But this switching is usually actualized in the broad mythological context of the whole of the *Ṛg Veda*. When, for instance, *Uṣas* is called upon: *úṣo vā́jena vājini prácetā / stómaṃ juṣasva gṛṇató maghoni* (3.61.1) "O *Uṣas*, O rewarding with a reward, O understanding one, / Rejoice in the praise-hymn of the praise-hymn of the singer, O liberal one!"—the verse actually seems to mean: Rejoice in the praise-hymn of the singer because you understand the perfection of this hymn; since you are liberal and used to giving rewards, may you liberally reward the reciter of this hymn! This is the foundation upon which the great majority of praise-hymns is built.

The nominative case and the vocative form stand at the point of intersection of two functions of language—descriptive and appellative—and this is reflected in their possible confusion. In the first instance, there is a sufficient number of cases in the *Ṛg Veda* in which the vocative is used predicatively [120.342; 115: 16.1]. The predicate is usually expressed by the copula, sometimes in the imperative, for example: *bodhí prayantar-janitar vásūnām* (1.76.4) "Be a deliverer (of sacrifices), a genitor of goods!" (literally "Be, O deliverer (of sacrifices), O genitor of goods!"); *vásāno átkaṃ surabhím dṛśé káṃ / svàr ṇá nṛtav iṣiró babhūtha* (6.29.3) "Putting on an attractive attire in order to look like the sun, thou hast become an impetuous dancer" (literally " . . . thou hast become impetuous, O dancer)." Sometimes the predicative vocative appears in similes, for example:

vayáṃ hí te ámanmahy
ā́ntād ā́ parākā́t
áśve ná citre aruṣi (1.30.21)

"We did indeed think about thee / From near and from afar, / O bright one, like a fiery mare!" (literally " . . . O bright one like afiery mare!"). Secondly, since the nominative in the *Ṛg Veda* has the functions of the vocative in certain syntactic structures, in those *dvandva* compounds whose members are noncontiguous (in the *Ṛg Veda*, they are usually theonyms) one member may appear as a vocative and the other as a nominative followed by the conjunction *ca* "and," for example: *vā́yav índraś ca cetathaḥ / sutā́nāṃ vājinīvasū* (1.2.5) "O *Vāyu* (vocative) and *Indra* (nominative), you comprehend (second dual) the pressed (*Soma* juices), O (you two) rich in reward (vocative dual);" *yuvám etā́ni diví rocanā́ny / agníś ca soma sákratū adhattam* (1.93.5) "You two, O Agni (nominative) and Soma (vocative), equal in spiritual strength, / Have placed these bright spaces in heaven" (in all the other stanzas the vocative of the compound *ágnīṣomāv* is used instead) [83].

Theonyms in the vocative take part in this expressive play to the same extent as do the other cases: they are symmetrically placed in definite slots of the metrical scheme, creating a certain pattern. They can stand at the beginning of stanzas, as in, for example, the *Soma*-and-*Rudra* hymn 6.74, where three (out of four) stanzas begin with the vocative *sómārudrā "O* Soma and *Rudra*," while *pāda a* of stanza 4 begins with a sound-hint *tigmā́yudhau* "the two sharp-weaponed ones" and the name itself introduces the following *páda b*: *sómarudrāv*. Or, for instance, each of the five stanzas of hymn 3.24 begins with the vocative *ágne*. Frequently there is play upon the combination of the pronoun *tvám* "thou" with the vocative of a theonym, for example, *tvám agne* in hymn 2.1 discussed above.

Generally speaking, this whole play upon vocative forms is possible only when the narrative is told in the second person. Although in the praise-hymns the third person narrative is easily switched to the second person, the play on the vocatives shows noticeable particularities in connection with different deities. And again,[97] the hymns of Book 9 to *Soma Pavamāna* display some differences from the *Agni* or *Indra* hymns. No hymn of that Book is built around the play upon the vocatives of *sóma-* or *pávamāna-*, nor is there any play upon the combination **tváṃ soma* as there is for *Agni* or *Indra*. This is due to the preference for the expressive paradigm of demonstrative, rather than personal, pronouns in the third person.

The names of *Soma* used in the vocative are not very numerous, either. The most common seem to be: *soma* "O *Soma*," *pavamāna* "O being purified," *indo* "O drop," "O juice of *Soma*," *deva* "O god," *rājan* "O king," and their combinations: *soma pavamāna, soma deva* or *deva soma, soma rājan*. Series of vocative-epithets are not typical for that book, but are only rarely attested, for example: *índo samudramiṅkhaya / pávasva viṣvamejaya* (9.35.2) "O *Soma* juice, stirring the ocean, / Purify (thyself), O (thou), starter of everything!" as well as variants of a single formular attested in two adjoining stanzas: *madānām pata / índo* (9.104.5) "O Lord of inebrating drinks,O *Soma* juice!" and *harīṇám pata / índo* "O Lord of bay (-horses), O *soma* juice!"[98] As a matter of fact, multiple vocatives that break up the narrative flow are not characteristic of the hymns in Book 9.

In some hymns, the poet addresses himself or the priests officiating at the sacrifice. One hymn (2.14) is wholly constructed around the play upon the vocative *ádhvaryavo* "O *adhvaryu* (-priests)" that introduces eleven of its stanzas (stanza 12 is a refrain common to a whole group of hymns).

Although the vocative here assumes the marked position usually reserved for the name of the god being praised, this instance of the form does not bear the communicative load typical for the vocative. In only three stanzas (out of eleven) is the vocative immediately followed by a verbal imperative, which means that the address to the priests is functional but not stylistic, for example, instanza 1: *ádhvaryavo bharaténdrāya sómam* "O (you) *adhvaryu* (-priests), bring *Soma* for *Indra*" (the same in stanzas 9 and 10). In all other instances the address to the priests is merely a stylistic device intended to create an atmosphere of spontaneity and to enhance the emotional charge of the narrative. The grammatical framework of the hymn follows the usual scheme: an attributive dependent clause headed by *yá-* refers to the deity, while the main clause has a demonstrative that corresponds to the relative pronoun and serves as the (direct or indirect) object of the verb. The subject of the verb is identical with the denotate of the vocative. In this way, the main scheme appears to be placed within a closed-in construction, with the vocative at the beginning of *pāda a*, and the imperative verb at the end of *pāda d*:

ádhvaryavo yá úraṇaṃ jaghā́na
náva cakhvā́ṃ navatíṃ ca bāhū́n
yó árbudam áva nīcā́ babādhé
tám índraṃsómasya bhṛthé hinota (2.14.4)

"O (you) *Adhvaryus*! (The one) who killed *Uraṇa*, who spread wide ninety-nine arms, / Who pushed down *Arbuda*— / Tha *Indra*—excite (him) to bring *Soma*!" The position of the imperative verb is not rigorously fixed in this hymn. The usual position is in *pāda d*, and, more rarely, in *pāda c*.

THE PRONOUN

Generally speaking, pronouns have an important role in the play upon various designations of deities on the expressive level. The pronoun whose referent is the deity being praised functions in the expressive grammar in the same way as the proper name of that deity; in other words, it can appear as the key-word introducing a hymn that is repeated at the beginning of each stanza or *pāda*. The expressive paradigm of a pronoun can be developed throughout the stanzas. Besides that, general pronominal semantics as well as the existence of various categories of pronouns give a strong impetus to symbolic play upon pronouns. These factors sometimes lead to a certain vagueness of reference.

Since the praise-hymns of the *Rig Veda* are usually a poet's address to a deity, the addressee of this act of communication is denoted by the personal pronoun of the second person (generally singular). The addresser's pronoun of the first person singular is not so essential, and its use is quite restricted. But the use of a subject personal pronoun with the finite verb is optional in the *Rig Veda*, since the inflected finite form contains all the necessary grammatical information about the person and number of the subject. Therefore, the use of action-subject pronouns in the hymn can be regarded to some extent as marked, and this characteristic is widely exploited on the expressive level. In such contexts the personal pronoun of the second person singular *tvám* "thou" is often accompanied by the vocative of the corresponding theonym. Naturally, the vocative may appear with other case-forms of the pronoun referring to the deity, most frequently the accusative.

This principle of construction is basic to many entire hymns in the *Ṛg Veda*, or at least to sufficiently large fragments of them. It is most prominent in the *Agni* and *Indra* hymns, but others follow it, too. Some examples:

The *Agni* hymn 5.8 consists of seven stanzas, each of which begins with the second person singular pronoun followed by the vocative of the theonym: in stanza 4 *tvám agne* (nominative plus vocative) "thou, O *Agni*;" in all the rest: *tvā́m agne* (accusative plus vocative) "thee, O *Agni*."

The *Indra* hymn 1.63 has nine stanzas, seven of which begin with the second person singular pronoun *tvā́m* followed—after a space of two syllables—by the vocative *indra*. Thus, the beginning of each stanza represents the same rhythmic pattern: stanza 1—*tvám (mahā́n̐) indra* "thou (art great). O *Indra*;" 4—*tváṃ (ha tyád) indra* "thou (indeed), O *Indra*;" 5—*tváṃ (ha tyád) indra* "id.;" 6—*tvā́ṃ (ha tyád) indra*—accusative; 7—*tváṃ (ha tyád) indra*—nominative; 8—*tváṃ (tyā́ṃ na) indra* "thou (that one for us), O *Indra*!" The persistent repetition of this rhythmic group at the beginning of many stanzas draws attention to the theonym and to the pronoun referring to the god, to stress and declare them, obviously a magic procedure.

Stanza 2 starts otherwise, for only the vocative *indra* appears in *pāda a*, but in stanza 3 the play upon the pronoun has been intensified to the limit, both initially and internally:

tváṃ satyá indra dhṛṣṇúr etā́n
tváṃ ṛbhukṣā́ náryas tváṃ ṣā́ṭ
tváṃ śúṣṇaṃ vṛjáne pṛkṣá āṇaú
yū́ne kútsāya dyumáte sácāhan

"Thou art true, O *Indra*, (and) brave, / Thou art *Ṛbhukṣan*, virile, the conqueror of those . . . / Thou hast slain *Śuṣṇa* in the contest of strength, in the fight for the chariot's linchpin / For the splendid young *Kutsa* (with whom thou hast been) together."

But the final stanza has another beginning: *ákāri ta indra* "(It) is made for thee, O *Indra* . . . ," and this departure is the rule: the final stanza is not infrequently opposed to the rest of the hymn, a refrain common to a whole group of hymns or a stanza in a metre different from the other stanzas.

The *Agni* hymn 2.1, with sixteen stanzas, is structured as a whole around the pronoun *tvám* "thou" in its various case-forms in definite positions of the metrical scheme. Fifteen stanzas begin with a case-form of *tvám*, which is followed by the vocative *agne* "O *Agni*! in fourteen stanzas, all of which (except for *páda b* in stanza 14) also begin with a case-form of *tvám*. The first two stanzas of the hymn are "oversaturated" with this pronoun, which is used in anaphoric repetitions in balanced syntactic structures as well as in the middle of the *pāda*:

tvám agne dyúbhis tvám aśuśukṣáṇis
tvám adbhyás tvám áśmanas pári
tvám vánebhyas tvám óṣadhībhyas
tvám nṛṇā́ṃ nṛpate jāyase śúciḥ (1)

távāgne hotrám táva potrám ṛtvíyam
táva neṣṭrám tvám agníd ṛtayatáḥ
táva praśāstrám tvám adhvarīyasi
brahmā́ cā́si gṛhápatiś ca no dáme (2)

(1) "Thou, O *Agni*, (art born) with the commencement of days, thou, the joyfully gleaming one, / Thou—from the waters, thou—from stone, / Thou—from the trees, thou—from the plants, / Thou, O Lord of men, art born pure."

(2) "Thine, O *Agni*, (is the) position of the *Hotar*, thine—the regular position of the *Potar*, / Thine—the position of the *Neṣṭar*, thou art the *Agnidh* of the pious (one) / Thine (is) the position of the *Praśāstar*, thou actest as the *Adhvaryu*, / (Thou) art also the *Brahman* and the housemaster in our home."

After this preliminary charge, the *pāda*—initial forms of *tvám* present the following picture in the subsequent stanzas: stanza 3, *pāda a—tvám* . . . , *pāda b—tvám* . . . , *pāda c—tvám* . . . , *pāda d—tváṃ* . . . ; 4, *pāda a—tvám* . . . , *pāda b—tvám* . . . , *pāda c—tvám* . . . , *pāda d—tvám* . . . ; 5, *pāda a—tvám* . . . , *pāda b—táva* . . . , *pāda c—tvám* . . . , *pāda d—tváṃ* . . . ; 6, *pāda a—tvám* . . . , *pāda b—tváṃ* . . . , *pāda c—tváṃ* . . . , *pāda d—tvám* . . . ; 7, *pāda a—tvám* . . . , *pāda b—tváṃ* . . . , *pāda c—tvám* . . . , *pāda d—tváṃ*; 8, *pāda a—tvā́m* . . . , *pāda b—tvā́ṃ* . . . , *pāda c—tváṃ* . . . , *pāda d—tvám* . . . ; 9, *pāda a—tvā́m* . . . , *pāda b—tvā́m* . . . , *pāda c—tvám* . . . , *pāda d—tváṃ* . . . ; 10, *pāda a—tvám* . . . , *pāda b—tváṃ* . . . , *pāda c—tváṃ* . . . , *pāda d—tváṃ* . . . ; 11, *pāda a—tvám* . . . , *pāda b—tváṃ* . . . , *pāda c—tvám . . . , pāda d—tváṃ . . .* ; 12, *pāda a—tvám . . . , pāda b—táva . . . , pāda c—tváṃ . . . , pāda d—tvám . . .* ; 13, *pāda a—tvā́m . . . , pāda b—tvā́ṃ, pāda c—tvā́ṃ . . . , pāda d—tvé . . .* ; 14, *pāda a—tvé . . . , pāda c—tváyā . . . , pāda d—tváṃ . . .* ; 15, *pāda a—tváṃ . . . .*

In the last stanza no pronoun replaces the theonym. Its fourth *pāda d* is a refrain common to a whole group of hymns and so does not count here. But, in return, the words with which all the other *pādas* begin are highly meaningful from the standpoint of expressive grammar: *pāda a—yé* "which" (a relative pronoun referring to worshippers), *pāda b—ágne* "O Agni," *pāda c—asmā́n* "us" (referring to worshippers). The position in the metrical scheme that is filled in all the stanzas by the pronoun referring to the god (and in *pāda b* of this stanza by the theonym) is here taken over by pronouns referring to the worshippers. This device brings the worshipper closer to his deity or, in terms of magic, grants the worshipper power over his deity.

As to the play upon pronouns, this hymn is programmatic. The strong positions in the metrical scheme, at the beginning of the stanza and the *pāda*, are here filled to the maximum by the pronoun *tvám* referring to the deity. The expressive paradigm is fully developed in all cases: nominative (most common), accusative, genitive, locative, instrumental. The worshipper's pronoun takes up the position of the deity's pronoun. Expressive tendencies that regulate pronominal usage in this way are apparent in may other hymns, but are not carried out so thoroughly.

When various mythic events are described or just alluded to, the praised deity is referred to by the third person pronoun, which is also prone to be played upon on the expressive level. The transition from the second person to the third person (and vice versa) is carried out with extreme ease. Compare the use of pronouns in the following stanzas:

próthad áśvo ná yávase' viṣyán
yadā́ maháḥ saṃváraṇād vy ásthāt
ā́d asya vā́to ánu vāti śocír
ádha sma te vrájanaṃ kṛṣṇám asti (7.3.2)

"He snorts in anticipation (of food) like a horse on the meadow, / When it (he) has broken out of a big enclosure. / The wind blows here following after his flame, / And now thy path turns black" (here "he," "his" and "thy" refer to *Agni*);

ádha śrutáṃ kaváṣaṃ vṛddhám apsv
ánu druhyúm ní vṛṇag vájrabāhuḥ
vṛṇānā́ átra sakhyā́ya sakhyáṃ
tvāyánto yé ámadann ánu tvā (7.18.12)

"And the famous old *Kavaṣa* here— / The cudgel-bearer threw (him) into the water, after *Druhyu*, / While (those) who are thy supporters, choosing / Friendship for friendship, greeted thee with joyful shouts" (transition from third to second person);

yó 'vare vṛjáne viśváthā vibhúr
mahā́m u raṇváḥ śávasā vavákṣitha
sá devó devā́n práti paprathe pṛthú
víśvéd u tā́ paribhū́r bráhmaṇas pátiḥ (2.24.11)

"(He) who, distinguishing himself in everything, in the nearest sacrificial community / Has grown (second person singular perfect) in strength,— / This god has spread far (and wide) beyond (the other) gods: / *Brahmaṇaspati* has embraced all these (worlds)."

The relative pronoun *yá-* "who," "which" as the subject is often linked in the *Ṛg Veda* to the second person verb as the predicate. Another construction seems to be more common with the third person than with the second person pronoun: a demonstrative pronoun of the third person in the nominative (subject) plus a verb in the second person singular imperative (predicate). Compare two fragments of the same hymn: *sá no . . . / ū́rjo napād bhádroṣoce / rayíṃ dehi . . .* (8.71.3) "Give thou (literally "he") wealth to us, O offspring of vigor, of the beneficient flame . . . !" and *tvám̐ no agne . . . pāhi . . .* (8.71.1) "Do thou protect us, O *Agni* . . . !"

The existence of various kinds of deities complicates the play on demonstrative pronouns on the expressive plane. It should be noted that the choice of a particular pronoun is not always dependent upon semantic grounds: sometimes the criterion seems to be its phonetic similarity to the deity's name. Thus, for instance, the *Uṣas* hymns tend to use the emphatic demonstrative of the close range *eṣā́* "this," "she" much more often than usual, apparently because its nominative singular is an obvious sound and rhythmic hint at the nominative singular (*sandhi*) form of the theonym. And so, in hymn 5.80 (six stanzas) all the stanzas except the first one begin with this pronoun, while the goddess's name is "hidden" in the middle of *pāda c* (accusative) *uṣásam*. In each stanza, starting with stanza 2, the pronoun *eṣā́* introduced *Uṣas*'s theme, whose name may appear at the beginning of some *pāda*, or else the shadowy presence of the theonym may be alluded to but its sound-hints: stanza 2, *pāda a—eṣā́ . . . , pāda d—uṣā́ . . .* ; 3, *pāda a—eṣā́ . . . , pāda d—puruṣṭutā́ . . .* ; 4, *pāda a—eṣā́ . . .* ; 5, *pāda a—eṣā́ . . . , pāda c— . . . dvéṣo . . . , pāda d—uṣā́ . . . jyotiṣā́ . . .* ; 6, *pāda a—eṣā́ . . . , pāda b—yóṣā . . . , pāda c—dāśúṣe . . . .*

The situation in the *Soma* hymns of Book 9 is rather different. On the expressive level, various classes of demonstratives are obviously preferred to the personal *tvám*, which does occur but is clearly peripheral to other expressive devices. A substantial number of hymns are structured—wholly or to a great extent—around the play upon demonstratives that refer to *Soma*. Most frequent is the close-range demonstrative *eṣá* "this" (masculine). For example, each of the ten stanzas that make up hymn 9.3 begins with *eṣa* in the nominative singular. The first few stanzas (1, 2, 3 and 5) begin with the phrase *eṣá devó* "this god," but further on, the play on this phrase acquires other forms. In stanza 6 its elements are separated: *devó* appears in the middle of *páda b* constituting, however, a single syntagm with *eṣá*. Stanza 9 plays upon the word:

> *eṣá pratnéna jánmanā*
> *devó devébhyaḥ sutáḥ*
> *hárih pavítre arṣate*

"This god, pressed, is flowing into the strainer, in accordance with the ancient custom." Stanzas 7 and 8 are introduced by the phrase *eṣá dívaṃ* "This onto the sky . . . ," which echoes *eṣá devó*. And stanza 10 *pāda b* ends with the word *íṣaḥ* "sacrificial refreshments, which echoes *eṣá*. in hymn 9.15 each of the eight stanzas also beings with a close-range demonstrative: stanzas 1-6—*eṣá* (nominative singular), stanzas 7-8—*etám* (accusative singular). Echo-forms appear here, too: *páruṣā śā́deṣu* (6), *drṓṇeṣu, íṣaḥ* (7). The numerous sound-hints at this pronoun suggest its special semantic marking. At the same time the name of *sóma* is never used in these two hymns. Neither is it mentioned in hymn 9.38: each of the six stanzas (except stanza 2) begins with a combination of two demonstratives *eṣá syá* "this here," but stanza 2 contains a sound-hint at the second member of this phrase. The pattern of the distribution of the pronouns in this hymn is: stanza 1—*eṣa u syá* . . . , 2—*etāṃ tritásya* . . . , 3—*etáṃ tyáṃ* . . . ; 4—*eṣá syá* . . . , 5—*eṣá syá* . . . , 6—*eṣá syá* . . . .

In hymns 9.27 and 28 (both consist of six stanzas) each stanza begins with *eṣá,* yet the name of *sóma* appears in one of the stanzas, and in both hymns it begins the *pāda*: 9.27.3c and 9.28.6b. In hymn 9.22 five (out of seven) stanzas begin with the pronoun *eté* "these," "they" referring to the pressed *Soma* juices, twice an an attribute to the noun *sómāsaḥ* "*Soma* juices" (literally "the *Somas*" plural). And the final stanza begins with the address *tváṃ soma* . . . "thou, O *Soma*, ... " The denotation of *Soma* by means of the demonstrative *eṣá*, with word-play on *eṣa* as the key-word, is peculiarity of the *Soma* hymns.

Other demonstrative pronouns referring to *Soma* can also play the part of the key-word, but they function in the same way in hymns to other gods. For instance, each of the six stanzas of the *Soma* hymn 9.37 begins with the pronoun *sá* "he," and *pāda c* of stanza 5 begins with the name of *sóma*. But the *Indra* hymn 6.32 has almost the same structure: four (out of five) stanzas (all but the first) begin with the pronoun *sá*, and the name of *índra-* is never mentioned. This expressive device is quite in keeping with the suggestive style of many hymns of the *Ṛg Veda*.

Soma can also be denoted by the demonstrative *ayám* "this," which is also played upon in the hymns: for example, in hymn 9.54 three stanzas (out of four) begin with various case-forms of *ayám*: stanza 1—*ásya* . . . , 2—*ayáṃ* . . . , 3—*ayáṃ* . . . . When stanzas about *soma* / *Soma* (either the plant or the god) occur in hymns to other gods, *Soma* can be denoted by the demonstrative *ayám*, while the name *sóma-* is either absent or appears only once. This pronoun is involved in a complex play, creating whimsical patterns, filling in various positions in the metrical scheme, and forming the basis for repetitions of various syntactic structure. Such is the situation, for instance, in hymn 6.47 (to various gods), in which the first stanzas are addressed to *Soma*. Stanza 1:

svādúṣ kílāyám mádhumān̐ utā́yaṃ
tīvráḥ kílāyáṃ rásavān̐ utā́yám
utó nv àsyá papivā́ṃsam índraṃ
ná káś caná sahata āhavéṣu

"Tasty, certainly, it is; sweet it is, too; / Sharp, certainly, it is; strong it is, too. / And *Indra* who has just drunk it— / None will overcome (him) in single combats."

The next four stanzas begin with *ayám: pāda a*—in every case, but sometimes other *pādas* as well. Stanza 2 *pāda a—ayáṃ . . . , páda b—yásya . . . , pāda c— . . . yáś* . . . (relatives correlating with *ayám*); stanza 3, *pāda a—ayám . . . , pāda b—ayám . . . , páda c—ayám* . . . . In stanza 4 the nature of the repeitions has changed: the anaphoric repetition is replaced by chiasmic repetition (to be replaced, in its turn, by the anaphoric). And the last *pāda* begins with the name of *sóma-* itself:

ayáṃ sá yó varimā́ṇam pṛthivyā́
varṣmā́ṇaṃ divó ákṛṇod ayáṃ sáḥ
ayám pīyū́ṣaṃ tisṛ́ṣu pravátsu
sómo dādhārorv àntárikṣam

"He is that one who (created) the breadth of the earth, / The height of the sky he created, this one. / He (created) the cream in three streams. / *Soma* fixed the wide aerial space." In the first two *pādas* the play upon *ayám* is extended to the pronoun *sá*. In stanza 5 the anaphoric repetitions appear again: *pāda a—ayám . . . , pāda —ayám . . . , pāda d*—the sound-hint *úd dyā́m* . . . .

Anaphoric repetitions with *ayám* (for *Soma*) are also attested in several other hymns: 6.39.3-4: 6.44.22-24, etc. Evidently, a certain poetic tradition made regular use of *ayám* as a substitute for *Soma*. Nevertheless, there are other *Soma* hymns in which the name is replaced by a variety of pronouns in the marked initial position in the stanza. Such is the expressive pronominal pattern, for example, in hymn 9.77 where only the fifth (and last) stanza lacks an intial pronoun: stanza 1, *pada a—eṣá* . . . ; 2—, *pāda a—sá* . . . , *pāda c—sá* . . . ; stanza 3, *pāda a—té* (the drops of *Soma*) . . . ; stanza 4, *pāda a—ayáṃ* . . . ; the fragment 9.62.7-11 is identical in structure.

We have been discussing the peculiarities of expressive pronominal patterns in hymns to *Soma*, but the general principle of creating a sequence of stanzas or a whole hymn, in which each stanza begins with a pronoun referring to the lauded deity, is quite frequently attested in the *Ṛg Veda*. Compare, for example, the *Indra* hymn 8.15 in which ten stanzas (out of thirteen) begin with various pronouns, all of them referring to *Indra*: stanza 1—*tám* . . . ; 2—*yásya* . . . ; 3—*sá* . . . ; 4—*tám* . . . ; 5—*yéna* . . . ; 6—*tád* . . . (refers to a feat of *Indra*'s); 7—*táva* . . . ; 8—*táva* . . . ; 9, *páda a—tvā́m* . . . , *pāda c—tvā́ṃ* . . . ; 10—*tvám* . . . .

In one of the variants of this expressive pronominal pattern, a relative *yá-* "who," "which" at the beginning of a stanza is correlated with a demonstrative. In this case, the stanza appears as a balanced syntactic structure, with a subordinate relative clause and a main clause. The hymn to *Indra* 2.12 follows this principle throughout. Take, for example, stanza 9:

yásmān ná ṛté vijáyante jánāso
yáṃ yúdhyamānā ávase hávante
yó víśvasya pratimā́nam babhū́va
yó acyutacyút sá janāsa índraḥ

"(He) without whom people do not conquer, / Whom the fighting (warriors) call on for help, / Who has become the model for everything, / Who shakes the unshakeable—he, O people, is *Indra*!" In this hymn the relative *yá-* is represented by a variety of case-forms, for we are dealing with an expressive paradigm; but, by contrast, the demonstrative *sá-* in the main clause (the refrain) is invariably in the nominative singular.

The distribution of the correlated relatives and demonstratives in the short hymn to The Waters (7.49) is more ambiguous. The demonstrative (nominative plural) is invariably at the beginning of the main clause (the refrain), while the inflected relative pronoun weaves a more complex pattern. In stanzas 2-4 (of the total four) each verse begins with the relative *yá-*; moreover in each of the four stanzas this pronoun occurs in the middle of a *pāda: páda c* in the odd stanzas, *pādas b-c*—in the even ones. Text and translation follow:

samudrájyeṣṭhāḥ salilásya mádhyāt
punānā́ yanty ániviśamānāḥ
índro yā́ vajrī́ vṛṣabhó rarā́da
tā́ ā́po devī́r ihá mā́m avantu (1)

yā́ ā́po divyā́ utá vā srávanti
khanítrimā utá vā yā́ḥ svayaṃjā́ḥ
samudrā́rthā yā́ḥ śúcayaḥ pāvakā́s
tā́ ā́po devī́r ihá mā́m avantu (2)

yā́sām rā́jā váruṇo yā́ti mádhye
satyānṛté avapáśyañ jánānām
madhuścútaḥ śúcayo yā́ḥ pāvakā́s
tā́ ā́po devī́r ihá mā́m avantu (3)

yā́su rā́jā váruṇo yā́su sómo
víśve devā́ yā́sū́rjam mádanti
vaiśvāharó yā́sv agníḥ práviṣṭas
tā́ ā́po devī́r ihá mā́m avantu (4)

(1) "Obeying the (heavenly) ocean, out of the streams's depth / They move without resting, purifying themselves. / (They) for whom *Indra* with the thunderbolt, the bull, bored through (the water-way), May these divine waters help me here!"

(2) "(Those) waters (which are) of the sky, or that flow (on earth), / (Those that) are dug out or (those that) have arisen by themselves, / That have the sea (as their) goal, pure (and) clear, / May these divine waters help me here!"

(3) "Those in whose midst King *Varuṇa* moves, / Looking down upon the truth and falsehood among people, / Those that drip honey, pure (and) clear, / May these divine waters help me here!"

(4) "Those among whom King *Varuṇa*, among whom *Soma*, / (And) the All-Gods inebriate themselves with the nourishing force, (Those) into whom *Agni Vaiśvānara* has entered, / May these divine waters help me here!"

This text shows how the correlated relative and demonstrative pronouns distributed and placed in accordance with a set pattern appear as the framework upon which the whole hymn has been constructed.

The conception of a magic force, bound up—in the poets' mind—with pronouns referring to the deity that is being praised, manifests itself, on the one hand, by placing the pronoun that refers to the worshipper in the marked position of the metrical scheme which is usually reserved, in a given hymn, for the deity's pronoun. On the other hand, magic play can be seen in the tendency to juxtapose the worshipper and the deity pronouns. Cases in which this tendency is in opposition to the regular Vedic word-order are certainly diagnostic. We encounter certain difficulties because the word-order in the Vedic hymns is so free, but even this poetic text displays certain regularities that can be traced and described [8:401ff., 409ff.], and so the problem of singling out diagnostic positions should not be considered purely metaphysical. The type of metrical scheme (i.e., the long or the short *pāda*) in which this pronominal play takes place is of great importance. If, for instance, in a short *Gāyatrī pāda* we come across a sentence like *táṃ tvā vayáṃ havāmahe* (8.43.23) "We invoke such a one (as) thee," there is virtually no possibility for modifications, and it is preferable to choose a *pāda* (or a sequence of *pādas*) of some length with conditions favorable for observations of possible word-order violations.

The following examples seem to be more conclusive in this regard: *tásya vayáṃ sumataú yajñíyasya / -ápi bhadré saumanasé syāma* (6.47.13) "Let us enjoy his favor, (of him) worthy of sacrifices, and in (his) good graces that bring (us) luck!" (literally "in his we favor . . . "); *tváyā vayám pávamānena soma / bháre kṛtáṃ ví cinuyāma śáśvat* (9.97.58) "With thee, (with) *Pavamāna*, O *Soma*, / We wish to make the lucky throw (of the dice) in the context—always! (literally "with thee we (with) *Pavamāna* . . . "); *mā́ tvā vayáṃ sahasāvann avī́rā / mā́psavaḥ pári ṣadāma mā́duvaḥ* (7.4.6) "We do not want to sit around thee, O mighty one, having no sons, nor cattle, nor (thy) attention!" When juxtaposed, pronouns can sometimes be separated by an emphatic particle, for example: *vayám u tvā gṛhapate janānām / agne ákarma samídhā bṛhántam* (6.15.19) "It is thee, O Housemaster among people, O *Agni*, (that) we made big by means of firewood!"

The most important pronoun in the pronominal play of a praise hymn is the one that refers to a deity. Usually it is a second person pronoun, while the first person pronoun refers to the worshipper. But there are a few hymns in the *Ṛg Veda* in which the first person pronoun refers to the deity, not to the worshipper: these are the so-called self-praise hymns (*ātmastuti*). Here the first person singular pronoun usually occupies the marked position at the beginning of the stanza or sometimes the *pāda*-initial, and so can be taken as a formal feature of this genre. Such is the structure—in whole hymns in some cases—for instance, in 10.49 (*Indra*'s self-praise) where ten (out of eleven) stanzas begin with *ahám* ("I"), or with a case-form of it (accusative *mām* in stanza 2), while in stanzas 1-5 and 8-9 *ahám* stands at the beginning of other *pādas*. We use stanza 1 of this hymn as an illustration:

ahám dāṃ gṛṇaté pū́rvyaṃ vásv-
ahám bráhma kṛṇavam máhyaṃ várdhanam
ahám bhuvaṃ yájamānasya coditā́-
áyajvanaḥ sākṣi víśvasmin bháre

"I gave the singer the best wealth: / I wish to make the prayer a support for myself. / I was the inciter of the sacrificer. / In every battle I was victorious over those who do not offer sacrifices."

A similar scheme can be observed in the hymn to *Vāc*, the goddess of Sacred Speech (10.125). All eight stanzas of the hymn begin with the pronoun *ahám* or some of its case-forms (instrumental *máyā* in stanza 4); in stanzas 1-2 and 6-7 the pronoun also occurs at the beginning of other *pādas* or rhythmical groups within a *pāda* (including (genitive case) *máma, pāda*-initial in stanza 7). The highest concentration of this pronoun and the maximum of expressive information is seen in stanza 1 of the hymn:

ahám rudrébhir vásubhiś carāmy
ahám ādityaír utá viśvádevaiḥ
ahám mitrā́váruṇobhā́ bibharmy
ahám indrāgnī́ ahám aśvínobhā́

"I move with the *Rudras*, with the *Vasus*, I (move) with the *Ādityas* and with the All-Gods. / I carry both: *Mitra* and *Varuṇa*, / I (carry) *Indra* and *Agni*, I (carry) both of the *Aśvins*."

Sometimes anaphoric repetitions with *ahám* become the basis for fragments of hymns, such as in 4.26.1-3 or 4.42, the latter of great interest as far as the distribution of personal pronouns is concerned. As Kuiper has shows [98.22ff.], the content of the hymn presents a mythological reflection of actual verbal contests, in which the participants this time are *Varuṇa and* Indra. In the first three stanzas *Varuṇa* is glorifying himself to spite Indra, ascribing to himself all the main cosmogonic feats and even claiming to be *Indra: ahám índro váruṇas* . . . (stanza 3) "I, *Varuṇa* am *Indra* . . . ." As Kuiper notes, each stanza of *Varuṇa*'s self-glorification begins with a form of *ahám*: stanza 1—*máma* (genitive); 2—*ahám* . . . *máhyam* . . . (dative); 3—*ahám*. The next stanzas 4-6 are spoken by *Indra*[99] who, showing his opponent place, decisively demarcates their spheres of influence while claiming superiority. His speech is of self-praise too, and each of the stanzas also begins with a form of *ahám*: stanza 4—*ahám*; 5—*mā́m*; 6—*ahám*. Stanza 7 is spoken by *Varuṇa*, who virtually acknowledge his defeat; this fact is manifest formally in the corresponding distribution of personal pronouns. The last stanzas does not begin with *ahám* but *pādas c-d* begin with the second person *tvám* in place of *ahám*.

THE VERB

In order to clarify the role played by the verb in the poetic grammar of the language of the Vedic hymns—and this role is extremely important—one should take note of two kinds of facts: on the one hand, purely linguistic facts that relate to the Vedic verb structure, and, on the other, extralinguistic facts that include a wide range of problems, beginning with a semantic model of the priase-hymn and ending with the most general conception of time as perceived by the Vedic Aryans. Without reckoning with these numerous factors it would be impossible to understand clearly the functioning of the verb in such an archaic cultic text.

In the language of the *Ṛg Veda* the grammatical category of mood to a large extent dominates the category of tense [8.283]. This can be explained, in the first instance, by the semantics of the text. The appellative part of the praise-hymn, containing petitions to gods, supplications, execrations, and wishes, quite often pushes the descriptive part into the background. But in narrating mythological events, the description is quite often concerned with timeless events presented in a static, rather than dynamic, form: this is expressed linguistically in a particular archaic verbal mood, the so-called injunctive that plays—in Renou's opinion [119.63-80]—not a systemic, but rather a stylistic role. An extreme manifestation of this tendency can be seen in those hymns in which verbs in the indicative are wholly or almost absent. An example of this phenomenon is the *Indra* hymn 1.174:

tvám̐ rā́jendra yé ca devā́
rákṣā nṝ́n pāhy àsura tvám asmā́n
tvám̐ sátpatir maghávā nas tárutras
tvám satyó vásavānaḥ sahodā́ḥ (1)

dáno víśa indra mṛghrávācaḥ
saptá yát púraḥ śárma śā́radīr dárt
ṛṇór apó anavadyā́rṇā
yū́ne vṛtrám purukútsāya randhīḥ (2)

ájā vṛ́ta indra śū́rapatnīr
dyā́m̐ ca yébhiḥ puruhūta nūnám
rákṣo agním aśúṣam̐ tū́rvayāṇam̐
sim̐hó ná dáme ápām̐si vástoḥ (3)

śéṣan nú tá indra sásmin yónau
práśastaye pávīravasya mahnā́
sṛjád árṇām̐sy áva yád yudhā́ gā́s
tíṣṭhad dhárī dhṛṣatā́ mṛṣṭa vā́jān (4)

váha kútsam indra yásmiñ cākán
syūmanyā́ ṛjrā́ vā́tasyā́śvā
prá sū́raś cakráṃ vṛhatād abhī́ke
'bhí spṛ́dho yāsiṣad vájrabāhuḥ (5)

jaghanvā́ñ indra mitrérūñ
codápravṛddho harivo ádāśūn
prá yé páśyann aryamáṇaṃ sácāyós
tváyā śūrtā́ váhamānā ápatyam (6)

rápat kavír indrārkásātau
kṣā́ṃ dāsā́yopabárhaṇīṃ kaḥ
kárat tisró maghávā dā́nucitrā
ní duryoṇé kúyavācam mṛdhí śret (7)

sánā tā́ ta indra návyā ā́guḥ
sáho nábhó 'viraṇāya pūrvī́ḥ
bhinát púro ná bhído ádevīr
nanámo vádhar ádevasya pīyóḥ (8)

tváṃ dhúnir indra dhúnimatīr
ṛṇór apáḥ sīrā́ ná srávantīḥ
prá yát samudrám áti śūra párṣi
pāráyā turváśaṃ yáduṃ svastí (9)

tvám asmā́kam indra viśvádha sya
avṛkátamo narā́ṃ nṛpātā́
sá no víśvāsāṃ spṛdhā́ṃ sahodā́
vidyā́meṣáṃ vṛjánaṃ jīrádānum (10)

(1) "Thou, O *Indra*, art the king (of men) and of (those) who are gods. / Protect (imperative) the heroes! Defend (imperative) us, O *Asura*! / Thou art the lord of (all) being, the liberal one, our savior. / Thou art the owner of goods, the giver of superior strength."

(2) "Thou repressedest (injunctive), O *Indra*, the evil-tongued tribes, / When thou crushedest (injunctive) seven autumnal fortresses, (their) refuge. / Thou lettest flow (injuctive) the water in streams, O Irreproachable one. / Thou handedst over (injunctive). *Vṛtra* into *Purukutsa*'s power."

(3) "O Indra, drive (imperative) (into attack) the hosts for whom (thou art) a hero-lord, / Also (drive those) with whom, O much-invoked, thou (wilt) now (conquer) the sky! / Protect (imperative) *Agni, Aśuṣa, Tūrvayāṇa*! (Threatening) like a forest, (protect) the rites (performed) in the house at dawn!"

(4) "May (all) these (enemies) now fall down (injunctive) into a com-

mon womb O *Indra*, / For the glory of the thunder-cudgel, thanks to (its) greatness! When he let out (injunctive) streams (and) cows for the price of battle, / He sat (injunctive) upon (his) two bay horses (and) daringly seized (injunctive) the prizes."

(5) "Carry (imperative) *Kutsa*, O *Indra*, whom thou lovest (injunctive), / Driving *Vāta*'s ruddy horses with obedient reins! / Tear off (imperative) the sun's wheel at the decisive moment! / Let him (i.e., *Indra*) come out (optative aorist) against (his) adversaries with *vajra* in hand."

(6) "After thou hadst slain (participle perfect active voice) the *Mitrerūs*, who did not worship (the gods), / (And you were) reinforced by *Coda* (?), O master of bay horses, / (Thine enemies), who saw (injunctive) *Aryaman* together with *Āyu*, before (them) / (were) smashed by thee when they were carrying (participle present medial voice) their offspring . . . "

(7) "The poet, O *Indra*, began his whispering (injunctive) during (the) battle for winning the sun: / "Thou hast made (injunctive) the earth a cushion for the *Dāsas*!" / The generous one has made (injunctive) three (rivers) glisten with water! / He has precipitated (injunctive) *Kuyavāc* into an evil womb, into scorn."

(8) "These, O *Indra*, are thy ancient (feats). New (generations) have arrived (aorist indicative). / Overcome (injunctive) the numerous inimical forces so that no dissatisifaction should arise! Split (injunctive) the godless crevices like fortresses! / Bend (injunctive) the deathly weapon of the reviling godless one!"

(9) "Thou, O *Indra*, the exciter, / Hast let the excited waters flow (injunctive) like rushing rivers. / If thou crossest (non-indicative) the ocean, O hero, / Put (imperative) *Turvaśa* and *Yadu* across safely!"

(10) "Mayest thou, o *Indra*, always be (optative) our / Most reliable defender of men! / (May) he (become) for us a giver of superior power over any foe! We want to find (optative) a generous community, one that gives liberally!"

This hymn uses verbal forms in significant ways. The only form of the indicative that occurs here is the third plural aorist *ā́guḥ* "they came" (from *ā́* + *gā-*), which is not quite transparent in its morphology because of the *sandhi* on the juncture between the adverb-prefix and the verb-stem itself. In this case we must rely upon the *Padapāṭha* analysis in *ā́* + *aguḥ*, although Vedic roots of identical structure have been quite well attested: *dá-* "to give"—*duḥ, dhā-* "to put"—*dhuḥ, sthā-* "to stand"—*sthuḥ*, and thus the combination *ā́* + *guḥ* cannot be excluded, theoretically speaking.

None of the other finite verbal forms belongs to the indicative mood. The hymn is interesting from the point of view of the wide range of oblique modal forms, and it is not easy to determine the exact modal grammeme in each case. Direct calls on the deity like "Protect!" "Defend!" "Drive!" etc. are expressed by the imperative; various wishes are expressed by the optative (usually from the present stem, or the precative from the aorist stem). Some of the injunctive forms have various oblique modal meanings which can be defined from the context. Some of the others—also depending on the context—can be treated as forms of the preterite and generally occur in enumerations of *Indra*'s deeds performed in ancient times (stanzas 2 and 7).

Lastly, there are forms with semantics of oblique modality that are rather obscure in their structure. Thus, in stanza 9 the second person singular *parṣi* (from the verb *par-* "to cross over," "to bring over," "to save") is marked in the translation as of the non-indicative mood. The verb *par-* has no present root, although William Whitney lists this unique form as the present [156.100][81]. Such structurally isolated forms of the second person singular usually have the value of imperatives in the *Ṛg Veda* [120.261], and the imperative is not normally used in subordinate clauses, which typically employ the subjunctive. Geldner there notes the unusual syntactic context and grammatical value of the verbal form *parṣi* [74].

Another noteworthy finite form is the verb *kárat* "(The generous one) made . . . ," with which *pāda 7c* begins, while *pāda 7b* ends with the second singular injunctive *kaḥ* "thou madest," from the same verb. In our translation, *kárat* is marked as injunctive, because such an interpretation is quite possible injunctive: Whitney lists a Vedic third plural *karanti* (from *kar-* "to do, make") as a form of the present [74.21]. In addition, in this stanza the grammatical value of *kárat* is identical with that of *kaḥ*. Nevertheless, the interpretation of *kara-* as a present stem remains somewhat doubtful, especially when we take into account the correlation between forms with primary and secondary endings,[100] as well as the grammatical semantics of a number of them. As far as we can see, Arthur Macdonell had sufficient reasons for treating this form as a subjunctive (with the *-a-* marker) of the root aorist although he did voice some doubts [105.171]. However, in this particular context one can not find any subjunctive meaning in the form *kárat*.

The hymn which we have been discussing suggests a number of conclusions that might be applied to the whole of the *Ṛg Veda*. Verbal forms of identical structure could have quite different grammatical meanings and, vice versa, forms of different structure could possess the same grammatical value. Moreover, when one is faced with structually obscure verbal forms, the context can sometimes become a decisive criterion in defining their semantics.

Lastly, there is another curious feature of a general kind worthy of our attention in this hymn. If one asks, "When did the events described there take place?" one is in a quandary. The mythological narrative—if it may be so called—is told in the injunctive: but this modal grammeme does not usually express categories of time as a matter of principle. One may infer—as far as the context permits—that stanzas 2, 6 and 7 tell of events preceding the instant of the discourse. True, there are no overtly marked preterital grammemes here (of the imperfect, aorist or perfect) that usually indicate a past tense, yet in stanza 8 all of those acts are called *Indra*'s ancient deeds, and the only form in the indicative shows that new generations have already come in the recent past after those ancient feats. Nevertheless, in stanzas 3 and 4 *Indra* is addressed in the imperative, with appeals to perform those deeds right now. Other hymns of the *Ṛg Veda* treat *Indra*'s drive with *Kutsa* as a tale of the past similar to the tale that tells how Indra tore the sun's wheel when he won the race against *Etaśa*. In this hymn, 1.17.4, the most important point seems to be not the use of various moods and tenses but rather the general idea of time that was inherent in the Vedic model of the universe.

Some hymns of considerable length have no verbal forms in the indicative. For instance, hymn 7.35 to the All-Gods (fifteen stanzas) has only attested imperative forms. It has a rather monotonous structure based on anaphoric repetitions with the word *śám* "for luck" and the predicative verb in the imperative, usually at the end of a *pāda* or a stanza. For instance, in stanza 5:

śáṃ no dyā́vāpṛthivī pūrváhūtau
śám antárikṣaṃ dṛśáye no astu
śáṃ na óṣadhīr vaníno bhavantu
śáṃ no rájasas pátir astu jiṣṇúḥ

"(Let) the Earth and the Sky (be) lucky for us at the early invocation, / Let the air be lucky for us so that we can see, / Let (the) plants and trees be lucky for us, / Let (the) lord of the aerial space be lucky for us!"

The language of the *Ṛg Veda* has many tenses in which the tense grammemes are opposed to one another in various distinctive features of tense and aspect [8."verb"]. There are more tense grammemes in the language of the *Ṛg Veda* than in Sanskrit: there is a pluperfect grammeme, though it is not sufficiently distinct from other grammemes from the formal point of view on the one hand, and is not semantically opposed to any of them, on the other. There are also even more modal grammemes, such as the rather frequent subjunctive as well as the injunctive, whose semantics has been considerably diluted. But the point is not the number of extra grammemes of tense and mood in Vedic language as compared to Sanskrit;

the essential feature is the basic difference in the very structure of the paradigm in these two languages and in their syntagmatic functioning. As we have shown elsewhere [7.22-35], grammatical markers in Vedic are not generated with the same degree of automatism as in Sanskrit, the combinatorial capabilities of morphemes are much greater, and its grammar in general can be called less "compulsory" and regulated. These features have been exemplified in our discussion of the structure and use of verbal forms in hymn 1.174; but they are generally manifest in different ways in every section of the hypetrophied Vedic verbal system.

The forms of the oblique moods are derived in Vedic not exclusively from the present stem of the verb—as in Sanskrit—but from any temporal stem, though the present stem is the most frequent basis of such derivatives. However, there is no difference in meaning between forms of any mood based on different stems: they convey the same modality without temporal differentiation, for example, the verb *gam-* "to go:" third singular optative *gamyās* (aorist-stem) and *jagamyāt* (perfect stem) both mean "may he go;" *sthā-* "to stand" first plural optative *tiṣṭhema* (present stem) and *stheyāma* (aorist stem)—"may we stand;" *muc-* "to free:" second singular imperative *muñca* (present stem), *muca* (aorist stem), *mumugdhi* perfect stem—"free!"

Among the tense grammemes there is also one for the future. Its invariant meaning is the expression of action following the instant of speech, and its usual variants are modal one, such as the desire to perform an act. In the *Ṛg Veda* a very limited group of verbs has attested forms of the future, but the most usual means of expressing the future tense is the subjunctive, that is, the grammeme of one of the oblique moods. Moreover, the subjunctive mood covers wide range of modality shades: possibility, probability, etc., as well as any implicit dependence of the action upon external circumstances in general. For instance, second singular subjunctive *karasi* and second singular future *kariṣyasi* (from *kar-* "to do, make") can have—in certain contexts—the same meaning "thou wilt make" (compare 6.35.1 and 1.1.6).

And finally, the *Ṛg Veda* is the only document of the Old Indian linguistic tradition that gives us the opportunity and the data to draw conclusions concerning the role of the injunctive, an archaic mood whose semantics were already obscured by the time of the hymns and whose formal features were rather indistinct. Overtly, they may be defined as augmentless forms derived from present or aorist stems with secondary endings.

The injunctive, whose structure and semantics are in an evident opposition to the whole tense-and-aspect system of the *Ṛg Veda*, has been a subject of discussion for a long time. Renou was the first to establish the unsystematic nature of this grammeme for the Vedic period [119.63-80]: in different contexts these forms could have the meaning of the present, past, and future of the indicative (as well as all sorts of modal meanings). Renou maintained that the use of the injunctive in this text was chiefly a stylistic device typical of mythological fragments.

The next important stage in the study of this mood was begun by Karl Hoffmann [96], who argued that the invariant semantics of the injunctive were "memorative." All other verbal grammemes describe the verbal action from different standpoints, while the injunctive merely mentions it and lacks any temporal or modal differentiation. That is why the injunctive—under the influence of different contexts—can be tuned to the meanings of various structurally transparent and clearly marked modal and temporal forms. Context subordinates this archaic grammeme and adapts it to the richly differentiated temporal and aspectual as well as modal systems that colors it with secondary semantics.

This thesis can be illustrated by hymn 7.18, in which recollections of the Battle of the Ten Kings (i.e., of actions in the past), when *Indra* supported king *Sudās*, alternate with demands and requests addressed to *Indra* in the present; but in both cases the verbs are in the injunctive:

ádha śrutáṃ kaváṣaṃ vṛddhám apsv
ánu druhyúṃ ní vṛṇag vájrabāhuḥ
vṛṇānā́ átra sakhyā́ya sakhyáṃ
tvāyánto yé ámadan ánu tvā (12)

ví sadyó viśvā dṛṃhitā́ny eṣām
índraḥ púraḥ sáhasā saptá dardaḥ
vy ā́navasya tṛ́tsave gáyam bhāg
jéṣma pūrúṃ vidáthe mṛdhrávācam (13)

(12) "And there the cudgel-bearer threw the famous old *Kavaṣa* down (injunctive) into the water after *Druhya* / While—choosing friendship for friendship—(Those) who are thy supporters greeted (imperfect) thee joyfully."

(13) "In a single day *Indra* destroyed (infinitive) by force all their fortresses, seven fortresses. / He endowed (injunctive) *Tṛtsu* with the wealth of the *Ānus*' leader. / May we overcome (injunctive) *Pūru* (who) speaks insults at the sharing of the goods!" *Indra*'s actions are here referred to the past, because among the injunctives there is one formally marked imperfect (*ánu ámadan* "they greeted joyfully"). However, the same injunctive form in *pāda 13d* expresses a wish (a meaning synonymous with the optative).

Another example: the *Indra* hymn 6.20 lists various feats performed by the god, his victories over enemies and demons. The verbs rendering these acts are sometimes in the injunctive: *vṛtrám . . . hán* (2) "Thou killedest *Vṛtra*," *vájrasya yát pátane pā́di śúṣṇaḥ* (5) "When *Śuṣṇa* collapsed at the fall of the vajra," *pṛṇág rāyā́ sám . . .* (6) "He overfilled (it) with wealth," etc. The injunctive forms can be interpreted here as actions in the past because the same stanzas contain several forms with the augment: *ā́vat* (3,6) "he helped," *apadran paṇáyaḥ* (4) "the *Paṇis* fell down," etc. But in stanza 9 the injunctive has assumed the semantics of the present as there are some formally clear present forms:

sá īṃ spṛ́dho vanate ápratīto
bíbhrad vájraṃ vṛtrahā́ṇam gábhastau
tíṣṭhad dhárī ádhy ásteva gárte
vacoyújā vahata índram ṛṣvám

"He, who has no equal, conquers (present) (his) foes, / Holding the *vajra* in (his) hand, slaying the enemies. He mounts (injunctive) the horses like a bowman upon the chariot's seat. / The two horses, yoked (only) to the word, carry (present) the huge *Indra*."

How could this category of the injunctive co-exist with the extensive and complex system of Vedic tense-and-aspect and modal oppositions, which are in obvious contrast with it? To clarify the problem we should examine some extralinguistic data more precisely, particularly the peculiar notions of time as perceived by Vedic Aryans.

Many ancient cultures saw time as a cyclial process, which is represented in mythology through the concept of a periodic death of the universe and its subsequent rebirth, though the duration of such a cycle can vary greatly according to different traditions. And the ritual attests to a repetitiveness of certain acts isomorphic with the cosmic cycle; these acts reproduce a certain archetype and thus support the established order in the universe. Mircea Eliade has defined the substance of that conception: "At every instant everything begins with the beginning. The past is nothing else but anticipation of the future. There are no irreversible events, nor definitive transformations. In a sense, it would be possible to say that nothing new can appear in the world since everything is merely a repetition of the same primary archetypes; this repetition after actualizing the mythic instant at which the archetypal act was manifested, endlessly holds the world at the same auroral instant of the origin. Time merely makes possible the appearance and further existence of things. But it does not exert any influence upon this existence, since time itself is ceaselessly being reborn" [49.91].

These general typological considerations provide a framework which accommodates the facts of the hymns quite easily. The conception of time as a cyclic process also provides the basis for Kuiper's view of Vedic mythology as hypothesis only [24], since it is not explicitly stated in Vedic literature [24.49]. Nevertheless, in his elaboration of Hillebrandt's theory (that the *Ṛg Veda* hymns to *Uṣas* are addressed not to the dawn in general, but to the first dawn of the New Year when cosmic forces overcome chaos and re-establish order, Kuiper's investigations have made this hypothesis much more probable. This hypothesis provides a unified interpretation for various rituals and social institutions that are reflected also in the *Ṛg Veda*. Kuiper makes the following statement about rituals connected with the New Year festival and the period of the winter solstice: "The ceremonial contests of poets, who act as the representatives of their patrons (or their parties in general), and whose strife is obviously the counterpart of chariot races and warfare, were at the same time a ritual that aimed at a renewal of life and the winning of the sun" [24.99].

These general considerations can facilitate a better understanding of the matter of the timing of events described in hymn 1.174 (discussed above), a hymn in which *Indra*'s heroic feats are enumerated, while almost simultaneously, he is appealed to perform these feats. The real time of these mythological actions appears to be repeating itself: *Indra* performs his feats, which are invariably of cosmogonic significance, each time that cosmos must overcome chaos after the completion of a cycle. The linguistic expression of such timeless actions is to be found in the injunctive mood, which had already lost its original position in the verbal system of oppositions by the time that a new system of oppositions based on differentiated tenses and moods was established. This new system in itself was hardly adequate to render the concept of cyclical time. The modern interpreter of the *Ṛg Veda* finds even more numerous internal contradictions in such a situation: modern Western (as well as Modern Indo-Aryan) languages have no formal means to render an action merely as a reference lacking any descriptive characteristics, and modern man is accustomed to perceiving time as lineal.

Many contexts in the *Ṛg Veda* reveal the cyclical repetition of acts, which identifies an action taking place in the present or going to happen in the future, but identical with some archetypal action which took place in ancient times. As an example we may adduce the beginning of the *Uṣas* hymn 4.51 where the poet tells—in the first two stanzas—of the appearance of the dawns in the east, using a verb in the aorist (i.e., the action has just taken place, and the speaker sees it with his own eyes), and then the author, in the fourth stanza, asks the following question:

kuvít sá devīḥ sanáyo návo vā
yā́mo babhūyā́d uṣaso vo adyá
yéna návagve áñgire dáśagve
saptā́sye revatī revád ūṣá

"O divine Dawns, will there be (optative) no old or new raid of yours today, thanks to which, O rich ones, you have kindled (perfect) wealth for *Navagva, Añgira, Daśagva* the seven-mouthed one?"

This question presupposes the possibility of realizing a past action in the future, since it is known that the archetypal action—obtaining wealth with the help of *Uṣas*'s light—took place in a mythic past. Moreover, questions introduced by *kuvít* can also denote certainty about the future [71]: "of course, there will be today. . . ."

Finally, the *Ṛg Veda* contains numerous appeals to gods to perform the same famous acts—usually heroic feats of cosmogonic significance—which they had performed long ago. This appeal to *Indra* in 1.80.3 is a good example:

préhy abhī́hi dhṛṣṇuhí
ná te vájro ní yaṃsate
índra nṛmṇáṃ hí te śávo
háno vṛtráṃ jáyā apó
'rcann ánu svarā́jyam

"Come forward! Attack! Be daring! / Thy *vajra* will not be restrained: / Indeed, O *Indra*, thine are virility and strength; / Thou shalt slay (subjunctive) *Vṛtra*, thou shalt conquer (subjunctive) the waters. / May they praise in song (thine) own kingdom!"

The subjunctives "thou shalt slay" (*hánas*), "thou shalt conquer" (*jáyās*) have a future meaning here. The first verse of the same hymn states: *śáviṣṭha vajrinn ójasā / pṛthivyā́ níḥ śaśā áhim* "O mightiest thunderer, thou hast rubbed (injunctive) the serpent off the earth," where Sāyaṇa glossed the injunctive *śaśās* "thou hast rubbed" by an aorist *aśās*. In the second verse the same event is rendered by the perfect: *sá . . . sómaḥ . . . yénā vṛtráṃ nír adbhyó jaghantha* . . . "that . . . *Soma* . . . thanks to whom thou hast knocked (perfect) *Vṛtra* out of the waters." There is no contradiction between these tenses if *Indra*'s cosmogonic act—the killing of *Vṛtra*—is periodically repeated both in the present and in the future. That Act does not reproduce the archetype but, rather, *is* the archetype itself; in other words, it is beyond time.

The character of Sacred Knowledge as seen by the Vedic Aryans was such that theVedic *Ṛṣis* were visionaries for whom knowledge was an illumination, a sudden inner blaze which showed them the view of the whole universe. Since the poet could become a sage, a *Ṛṣi*, only through this force of vision, the knowledge that appeared in his inner sight was static. One picture followed another, and their rapid sequence created an illusion of motion, with no strict and obligatory logical connection between the separate pictures in that kaleidoscope.

These few words could describe the Vedic *Ṛṣis'* process of cognition of the world—but actually there is no process involved here, and we should rather speak of an instant, and of instants, replacing each other. This vision of the world influenced the style of the Vedic hymns in at least one regard: a consecutive, lineal narration of events is rare in this text. No many mythological plots are attested in the *Ṛg Veda*. But those that we have are not, as a rule, "elaborated" in the sense we are accustomed to, i.e., the plots are not set forth as a lineal sequence in which each separate link presents a logical motivation for the following one. Rather, they are simply mentioned or named, quite often in the same stereotyped phrases: the lexical fixation of a myth. Much remains obscure in the causal relationships between events, and we can reconstruct their sequence only when the plots are also attested in later text, such as the *Brāhmaṇas*, the *Upaniṣads*, and the *Mahābhārata*. But when such plots do not appear in later sources, the bare references to them in the *Ṛg Veda* makes them hardly intelligible to a modern reader, though in the time of the *Ṛg Veda* both *Ṛṣis* and their audiences were thoroughly familiar with these traditional plots.

In those few cases when these plots are actually narrated, the tale seems to be illogical and abrupt from a modern point of view, since the logical lineal sequence of episodes that is necessary for us is lacking. For example, the whole hymnic collection harps on *Indra's* principal feat: the slaughter of the serpent *Vṛtra*, who blocked up the rivers until *Indra* killed *Vṛtra* with his *vajra* and let the rivers flow freely. That feat has a cosmogonic interpretation in which *Indra* plays the part of a demiurge who overcomes the resistance of chaos and thus establishes order in the universe [24.29f.]. This principal feat is described more or less coherently in the *Ṛg Veda* only once, in hymn 1.32, and even here there is no lineal narration of events, strictly speaking. The description suggests a periodic return to the same situation, while the sequenc and their logical interrelationship seem to be irrelevant. Here is the beginning of the hymn:

índrasya nú vīryā̀ṇi prá vocaṃ
yā́ni cakā́ra prathamā́ni vajrī́
áhann áhim ánv apás tatarda
prá vakṣáṇā abhinat párvatānām (1)

áhann áhim párvate śiśriyāṇáṃ
tváṣṭāsmai vájraṃ svaryàṃ tatakṣa
vāśrā́ iva dhenávaḥ syándamānā
áñjaḥ samudrám áva jagmur ā́paḥ (2)

vṛṣāyámāṇo 'vṛṇīta sómaṃ
tríkadrukeṣv apibat sutásya
ā́ sā́yakam maghávādatta vájram
áhann enam prathamajā́m áhīnām (3)

(1) "Now I wish to declare the heroic deeds of *Indra,* / The first that the thunderbolt-wielder performed: / He slew the serpent and bored (a path) for the waters; / He split open the bellies of mountains."

(2) "He slew the serpent who lay upon the mountain. / *Tvaṣṭar* chiselled the sonorous cudgel. / Like lowing cows rushing (to their calves), / The waters flowed straight down to the sea."

(3)"Raging like a bull, he chose *Soma* for himself; / He drank (it), pressed in the three vessels. / The generous one seized his hurling *vajra.* / He killed him, the first-born of serpents."

The first verse seizes upon the subject of *Indra*'s deeds at once, and in a synoptic style: the deeds are just enumerated without any details. This style, of short simple sentences that follow one another without any conjunctions, is used to narrate this topic in numerous hymns; it is its stereotyped manifestation. Inverse two the author again returns to the killing of the serpent. The sequence of events in *pādas a-b* is chosen at random, as *Tvaṣṭar* had to fashion a cudgel for *Indra* before *Indra* could kill the serpent with it. The subject-theme of *pādas c-d* is not directly connected with that of *pāda b*, but is rather a consequence of the theme of *pāda a* in the first verse: the waters flow down straight to the sea because *Indra*, after killing the serpent, bored a path for them. The third verse presents an independent approach to the theme of the serpent-slaughter (the formula *áhann áhim* "he killed the serpent" is replaced by its variant *áhann enam* "he killed him"). The content of the stanza does not continue or develop that of the preceding one, since *Indra* had to drink his fill of *Soma* in the first place, and he could kill *Vṛtra* only in his inebriated state.

Another example: the *Ṛg Veda* contains numerous references to the motif of *Agni*'s flight into the waters where he hid himself when afraid of his duties as *hotar*. In the later part of the collection, in hymns 10.51-52 this plot is described in a dialogue between gods, while in the family books the most detailed narrative occurs in 3.9. Here are the first six stanzas (out of the total nine stanzas):

sákhāyas tvā vavṛmahe
devám mártāsa ūtáye
apā́ṃ nápātaṃ subhágaṃ sudī́ditiṃ
suprátūrtim anehásam (1)

kā́yamāno vanā́ tvám
yán mātṝ́r ájagann apáḥ
ná tát te agne pramṛ́ṣe nivártanaṃ
yád dūré sánn ihā́bhavaḥ (2)

áti tṛṣṭáṃ vavakṣitha
-áthaivá sumánā asi
prá-prānyé yánti páry anyá āsate
yéṣāṃ sakhyé asi śritáḥ (3)

īyivā́ṃsam áti srídhaḥ
śáśvatīr áti saścátaḥ
ánv īm avindan nicirā́so adrúho
'psú siṃhám iva śritám (4)

sasṛvā́ṃsam iva tmánā
-agním itthā́ tiróhitam
áinaṃ nayan mātaríśvā parāváto
devébhyo mathitám pári (5)

táṃ tvā mártā agṛ́bhṇata
devébhyo havyavāhana
víśvān yád yajñā́ñ abhipā́si mānuṣa
táva krátvā yaviṣṭhya (6)

(1) We, (thy) friends, have chosen thee, / The god, to help (us), the mortals, / (Thee), the offspring of the waters, the happy, charmingly brilliant (one), / (Thee), who easily overcomes (obstacles), the gentle (one)."

(2) "(Thou), the wood-loving one, when thou went to (thy) mothers, the waters, / Thou shalt not forget about (thy) return; / (Even) being far away, thou shalt not forget that thou hast been here."

(3) "(Now) thou hast outgrown what is coarse (in thee), / And so thou art benevolent now. / Some (people) are coming forward, (and) others are sitting around, / (Those) whose friendship is thy support."

(4) (When he was) coming through defeats, / Through constant mishaps, / the attentive ones found (him), bearing no deception, / Concealing himself in the waters, like a lion (in an ambush)."

(5) "(When) he had run away, as it were, by himself, / *Agni*, hidden in such away,— / *Mātariṣvan* brought him from afar, / Stolen for the gods."[101]

(6) "(And) the mortals seized thee as such, / O driver of offerings to gods, / So that thou shouldst oversee all sacrifices, O (thou) near to man, / Thanks to thy strength, O most youthful one."

Stanza 1 deals with a concrete ritual fire that is kindled by priests to receive libations that are to be transported to the gods by *Agni* the *hotar.* Then, in stanza 2 the poet suddenly takes up the myth of *Agni*'s flight into the waters, and he identifies myth with reality. As Geldner observes,[102] fire obtained by friction cannot flare up for a long time, and its absence is related—in the *Ṛṣi*'s mind—to the time when *Agni* was hidden in the waters. Stanza 3 brings the poet back to reality: the fire is blazing and the smoke is going up (a-b); the priests perform their ritual operations by the fire(c-d). In stanza 4 his thought again makes a leap from reality to myth and recalls how *Agni* disappeared in the waters, where the gods find him. Stanza 5 touches in passing upon the myth of *Mātariśvan*'s theft of *Agni* (where *nayan* "brought" is the only injunctive form in this episode); stanza 6 tells us that, at last, *Agni* is at the disposal of the mortals for use in their rites. And the last three stanzas of the hymn are devoted to *Agni*'s praises.

This manner of narration is typical of the Vedic poets. The injunctive, with its invariant meaning, is extremely suitable for expressing actions that take place (practically) beyond time. However, in Vedic times the injunctive was already an archaic relic, not a living phenomenon, though a ramified system of tense-and-aspect and modal oppositions in the verb was well established. Some echo of the injunctive might be seen in the "injunctivization" of the context when forms of the present and the past clearly marked as such are used in constructions in different to the moment of speech. This usually happens in mythological passages which enumerate (or mention) a deity's actions that took place in ancient times, while some of the verbs are formally in the past tense, and some in the present. Such cases sometimes occur in hymns to the *Aśvins* wherein their acts of supernatural aid to various people are mentioned. Some examples:

yā́bhiḥ śácībhir vṛṣaṇā parāvṛ́jam
prā́ndháṃ śroṇáṃ cákṣasa étave kṛtháḥ
yā́bhir vártikāṃ grasitā́m ámuñcataṃ
tā́bhir ū sú ūtíbhir aśvinā́ gatam (1.112.8)

"With the forces (that you), the two bulls, (bring to) the outcast, / And with which you enable the blind and the lame one to see and walk, / With the (forces with which) you freed the swallowed quail,— / With the same aids come hither, O Aśvins!;"

úd vándanam airataṃ daṃsánābhir
úd rebháṃ dasrā vṛṣanā śácībhiḥ
níṣ ṭaugryám pārayathaḥ samudrā́t
púnaś cyávānaṃ cakrathur yúvānam (1.118.6)

"You (two) have rescued *Vandana* with (your) supernatural forces, /

Re(scued) *Rebha*, O you two miraculous bulls, with (your) manifestations of might. / (Now) you are saving *Tugra*'s son out of the sea. / You have made *Cyavāna* young again."

Sometimes tenses are quite indiscriminately used in hymns to the *Ṛbhus* that list their feats of craftsmanship, for example:

śroṇā́m éka udakám gā́m ávājati
māṃsám ékaḥ piṃśati sūnáyā́bhṛtam
ā́ nimrúcaḥ śákṛd éko ápābharat
kíṃ svit putrébhyaḥ pitárā úpāvatuḥ (1.161.10)

"One (of them) drives the lame cow down to the water. / The other carves up the meat brought in a basket. / The third one carried the dung off until sunset. / But did the parents help (their) sons?"

tád vo vājā ṛbhavaḥ supravācanáṃ
devéṣu vibhvo abhavan mahitvanám
jívrī yát sántā pitárā sanājúrā
púnar yúvānā caráthāya takṣatha (4.36.3)

"This greatness of yours, O *Vājas, Ṛbhus*, / Was excellently proclaimed among the gods, O *Vibhus*: / That when parents have been decrepit, feeble from old age, / You make (them) young again, (capable) to move."

Such examples—and their number can be considerably increased—illustrate the situation that has arisen when an archaic conception of time has come into conflict with a much more evolved and differentiated grammatical system.

The verb in the *Ṛg Veda*, extremely rich in various forms, is characterized by a great number of morphologically obscure forms, or by those that have an ambiguous structure which does not make it possible to classify them as belonging to a system already attested for a given verbal root [6.43f.]. This can be explained by a number of factors that give rise to systematic oppositions often insufficient to identify a given verbal form. This applies to both temporal and modal oppositions.

Tense-and-aspect oppositions in the *Ṛg Veda* constitute three principal systems: 1) of the present, where the stem can be combined both with primary endings (the present) and with secondary endings (the imperfect); 2) of the aorist, where the stem is used only with secondary endings (the aorist); and 3) of the perfect, where the stem has a particular structure (a special type of root reduplication) and an independent (at any rate, in the active voice) series of endings (the perfect). There is also an augmented form of the perfect stem with secondary endings like those of the imperfect and the aorist (the pluperfect). A fourth system, consisting of a stem with a distinctive suffix and primary endings (the future), is not yet fully developed in the *Ṛg Veda*, since the future tense is regularly rendered by one of the grammemes of the oblique moods, such as the subjunctive. A corresponding augmented form of the future stem with secondary endings (the conditional) is represented by a single verb and has the purely modal meaning of an unreal condition.

In principle, formal oppositions should correspond to semantic oppositions of tense and aspect. This brief exposition makes it apparent that the plane of the future does not quite fit the general system of tense oppositions because of its close links with modality. On the planes of the present and the past, semantic differences are, on the whole, more clearly seen in stems with specific unequivocal marks. There is a total often classes of present stems and seven classes of aoristic stems,[103] out of which two classes—radical and thematic—are structurally identical in both systems. Bartold Delbrück, the founder of studies of theVedic verb and its syntax, observed that the root aorist of the *ápāt* type can sometimes have the value of the imperfect, while by contrast, thematic imperfects of the *ákṣarat* type can have an aorist meaning [66.66f.]. The so-called sixth present class in the *Ṛg Veda*—as Renou has shown [127]—is largely fictitious: the number of forms with primary endings is considerably less than that of injunctives, while forms with the augment often have the meaning of the aorist, not of the imperfect. As Paul Thieme has established in a special monograph, the pluperfect was not semantically opposed to other preterital grammemes [142], and its modal forms were sometimes indistinguishable from corresponding forms of the reduplicated imperfect and the aorist.

The opposition between present and aorist stems, based upon their ability to be combined with two (or with one) series of endings, respectively, is disturbed by individual forms peculiar to a group of verbs; such forms do not fit the system, for example, *dhā-* "to put"—present *dádhāti*, imperfect *ádadhāt*, aorist *ádhāt*, and isolated forms of the present type—third person singular *dhāti* (along with securely attested forms of the injunctive: *dhās*, *dhāt*, etc.).

Temporal differences can be detected only in the system of the indicative. Numerically, forms of oblique moods are clearly prevalent in our text, as compared with the indicative. But many modal forms of the verb do not have absolutely clear distinctive structural marks; thus, the subjunctive is marked by the affix *-a-* while the endings can be either primary or secondary, with a special series for this modal grammeme in the middle. If the text contains, for instance, a thematic augmentless form with a secondary ending, it remains unclear whether we are dealing with a root-stem subjunctive or a thematic injunctive, especially since no less than a third of verbal roots in the *Ṛg Veda* possesses several parallel present stems that can sometimes differ in their semantics [10.91-165; 98].

Temporal meanings in the *Ṛg Veda* are expressed not only by tense grammemes but also—and quite regularly—by grammemes of the oblique moods. The present, the preterite, and the future are expressed by the injunctive, and the future is also expressed by the subjunctive.

This brief sketch of the verbal system of the *Ṛg Veda* suggests that quite often the only criterion for establishing the meaning of a concrete verbal form appears to be the context, since its morphological structure as well as its place in the system of morphological opositions may be quite uninformative. But since some of the contexts of the *Ṛg Veda* are notoriously vague, grammar itself provides ample opportunities for the "injunctivization" of the context, for making the tense indeterminate and subordinating it to modality.

5
Syntax

It would be much simpler to discuss specific features of the poetic syntax of the Vedic hymns if we knew the syntactic norm of the Old Indian language of the time, which is usually established by means of prosaic texts. However, since the *ṚgVeda* is the very first document of Old Indian, and no other texts have survived, there is no standard by which comparison can be made. On the other hand, comparison with much later Vedic prose would appear to be an inadmissible breach of the principle of synchronic description. Therefore, in describing syntax one must use only the data of the hymns themselves, even though in some cases this may lead to a confusion between features of the system and its stylistic functions in an ancient cultic text. The only reasonable approach to this troublesome situation should be sought in the selection of a fitting criterion for description.

The focal points in the present description are represented by facts that are specific to this text and that occur only rarely, or not at all, in other literary documents. We shall try, wherever possible, to trace the connections between the syntactic and stylistic features and the communicative aims of the Vedic hymns.

Admittedly, the nucleus of the Vedic sentence is represented by the verb. Its inflexion contains information about the person and number of the word that expresses the subject of an action. The finite form of the verb[104] is the element that is necessary and sufficient to constitute a sentence in the *Ṛg Veda*. A pronoun in the nominative representing the subject of the sentence is not obligatory, and the use of personal pronouns in that function is more or less optional. Renou, for instance, held that this use was basically expressive and emphatic [120.339]. Sentences of the type *tvā́m iye bhágam* (2.17.7) "(I) ask happiness of thee," as well as *bhójaṃ tvā́m indra vayáṃ huvema* (2.17.8) "We want to invoke thee, the generous one, O Indra," are typical.

Later Old Indian grammarians believed that the number of sentences in a text is equal to the number of finite forms of the verb; hence the conclusion that sentences with homogeneous predicates cannot exist. From that point of view, for instance, the following *pādas* consist of two sentences: *ví vṛkṣā́n hanty utá hanti rakṣáso* (5.83.2) "He shatters the trees and kills the rakṣases;" *jáhāti vavrím pitúr eti niṣkṛtám* (9.71.2) "He abandons (his) envelope (and) goes to the tryst with (his) father." In this example two finite verbs are within a single *pāda*, and so we are confronted with the problem of homogeneous sentence parts. If the finite verbs relating to a single subject are found in different *pādas* of a single stanza, it would be expedient–and this is often done–to treat them as predicates of different sentences, as for example:

prá sumedhā́ gātuvíd viśvádevaḥ
sómaḥ punānáḥ sádā eti nítyam
bhúvad víśveṣu kā́vyeṣu rántā-
ánu jánān yatate páñca dhī́raḥ (9.92.3)

"The very wise one who belongs to all the gods, creating the (fortunate) way out, / *Soma*, purifying himself, moves forward to his own place. / He finds pleasure in all poetic gifts. / The insightful one brings order among the five peoples."

Generally speaking, sentences with homogeneous predicates are rather infrequent in the *Ṛg Veda*. In the much more typical way of expressing several actions performed by a single subject, the principal action is expressed by the finite verb and the rest of the actions, perceived as accompanying or preceding the principal action, are expressed by participles in agreement with the explicit or implicit subject. In the *Ṛg Veda*, absolutives are used much more rarely than participles in concord.[105] Some examples:

juṣṭvī́ na indo supáthā sugā́ny
uraú pavasva várivāṃsi kṛṇván
ghanéva víṣvag duritā́ni vighnánn
ádhi ṣṇúnā dhanva sā́no ávye (9.97.16)

"Pleased (absolutive literally "being pleased") by us, O juice, (create for us) an excellent, easily-walked path. / Purify thyself in spacious surroundings, creating (participle, present, literally "the creating one") wide spaces! / Like a hammer, smashing (participle present "the smashing one") calamities in every direction, / rush forth along the surface onto the back of the sheep (strainer)!"; *apā́m bílam ápihitaṃ yád ā́sīd / vṛtráṃ jaghanvā́ñ ápa tád vavāra* (1.32.11) "When he had killed (participle perfect active voice) *Vṛtra* he opened the outlet of the waters that had been closed.;" *pītvī́ sómasya vāvṛdhe* (3.40.7) "He has grown strong, having drunk (absolutive) *Soma*."

But when the subject of an action is expressed by personal pronouns of the second and third person (the functions of the latter being fulfilled by demonstratives), the situation can become complicated. In the *Ṛg Veda*, the verbal predicate in the second person can have as its subject a third person pronoun (though not vice versa). This construction is more or less regularly used with the verb in the second person imperative. Normally, the pronoun is absent in this case while the addressee of the action is in the vocative, for example: *ágne sáhasva pŕ̥tanā / abhímātīr ápāsya* (3.24.1) "O *Agni*, win battles! / Drive off inimical thoughts!"; *vā́jeṣu sāsahír bhava* (3.37.6) "Be a victor in battles for the prize!" Much rarer is the use of the second person personal pronoun with a verb in the second person singular imperative, for example: *ágne tvám̐ no ántama / utá trātā́ śivó bhava varūthyàḥ* (5.24.1) "O *Agni*, be for us a most close and dear rescuer, granting protection." More often we can see the third person singular combined with the second person singular imperative, for example: *sá no bodhi śrudhī́ hávam* (5.24.3) "Take notice of us, hear (our) call!" (literally "he note . . . hear . . . "); *sá no bhaga puraetā́ bhavehá* (7.41.5) "Be here for us, O *Bhaga*, the one who goes in front!" (literally "he be . . . "). Lastly, there is a variant in which the verb in the second person is combined with pronouns of the third and second person, for example: *sá tvám̐ na ūrjām pate rayím̐ rāsva suvī́ryam* (8.23.12) "Grant us (literally "let him/thou"), O lord of powers, wealth (and) virility!"

In contexts of the latter type *sá* appears as a demonstrative pronoun whose referent has been mentioned previously and is known [120.340]. This use of *sá* is attested with pronouns of all three persons, including the third person, for example: *tám mā sám̐ sṛjā várcasā* (1.23.23) "Join me (literally "such me") with brilliance!"; *tā́n va enā́ bráhmaṇā vedayāmasi* (4.36.7) "With this prayer we invite you" (literally "such you"); *yám aíchāma mánasā sò 'yam ā́gād / yajñásya vidvā́n páruṣaś cikitvā́n* (10.53.1) "That one (literally "such he") came, whom we had sought with (our) mind, the expert in sacrifice, understanding (its) articulation." The combination of *sá* with the second person pronoun is most frequent.

Returning to the problem of the form of the personal pronoun that expresses the subject of an imperative verb, everything said about the pronouns in the singular also applies to those in the plural, except that plurals are less frequent, since the grammeme of the plural is marked in contrast to that of the singular, for example: *tá ādityā ā́ gatā sarvátātaye* (1.106.2) "You, O *Ādityas*, come hither so that (we may be) hale" (literally "they . . . come (you)!"); *tā́ no devīḥ suhavāḥ śárma yachata* (5.46.7) "You, O easily invoked goddesses, grant us refuge" (literally "they (feminine) . . . grant (you)!"), where the third person pronoun is used with a second person plural imperative verb.

A similar breach of concord also occurs in phrases with the relative pronoun *yá-* "who," "which," whose paradigm has been adapted to that of *sá-*. In the *yá-* clauses such a breach can be found only in those cases in which the main clause contains the construction–third person pronoun plus second person imperative verb. Apparently, we have to deal here with a syntactic attraction of the subordinate clause to the main clause. The verbal predicate in the subordinate clause does not have to be in the imperative, but may be in the tense and mood required by the context. Some examples: *sá śrudhi yáḥ smā pŕ̥tanāsu kā́su cid / dakṣā́yya indra bhárahūtaye nŕ̥bhir / ási práturtaye nŕ̥bhiḥ* / . . . (1.129.2) "Hear (literally "he hear"), O *Indra*, (thou) who in any battles / Art sought by heroes for a call to combat, / By heroes for a breakthrough forward / . . . . "

> *yé devāso divy ékādaśa sthá*
> *pr̥thivyā́m ádhy ékādaśa sthá*
> *apsukṣíto mahinaíkādaśa sthá*
> *té devāso yajñám imáṃ juṣadhvam* (1.139.11)

"O gods, (you) who are eleven in the sky / (You) are eleven upon the earth, / (You) who are eleven,–inhabiting the waters with (your) might / O gods, accept (literally "they (you) accept") this sacrifice!"

We have been discussing subordinate clauses, but independent clauses in the *Ṛg Veda* sometimes–though very seldomly–contain predicative constructions in which the subject is a third person pronoun, and the predicate is a finite verb in the second person of the indicative (not the imperative), for example: *śā́sy ukthyàḥ* (2.13.2-12) (refrain) "Thou art worthy of a hymn" (literally "He art hymn-worthy"). The refrain in this hymn is variable, and the fullest variant is in stanzas 2-4: *yás tā́kr̥ṇoḥ prathamáṃ śā́sy ukthyàḥ* "Thou, who were the first to perform these (deeds), art worthy of a hymn" (literally "who (thou) performedest . . . "). Another example: *sá vāvr̥dhānā́ óṣadhībhir ukṣitò / 'bhí jráyāṃsi pā́rthivā ví tiṣṭhase* (5.8.7) "(literally "He") Having grown strong, having become big thanks to the plants, / Thou hast spread (thyself) around in the earthen spaces."

These examples suggest that in the act of communication between the worshipper and his deity the more important function was the opposition between the addresser and the nonaddresser, to which the other oppositions, between the addresser and the addressee and between the participant in the speech act and the nonparticipant in the speech act, were subordinate. The fact that in the narrative portions of the hymns, the transition from the third person to the second person takes place smoothly and imperceptibly,[106] also seems to confirm our hypothesis.

In addition to those sentences in which the predicate (expressed by a finite verb) has a pronominal subject, explicit or implied in verbal inflexion, there is another category of subject expressed by a noun in the nominative case. In this case the verbal predicate, in agreement with the subject, is always in the third person in the appropriate number, but the opposite is not necessarily true: the nominative with a third person verb is not necessarily the subject of this verbal predicate, and only the context, either broad or narrow, can aid us in determining the status of such a nominative form.

One peculiarity of Vedic syntax was noted by Renou [126.230-4]. Since a word in the *Ṛg Veda* is quite autonomous and contains all the grammatical information, the word-order in the sentence is altogether free, with a few exceptions concerning the position of some categories of short enclitics or proclitics. As Renou put it, "The Vedic *mantra* is characterized rather by juxtaposition than by syntactic organization" [126.232].

In the system of noun-cases this juxtapositional tendency is governed by the principle of apposition, according to which the nominative of a noun with a third person verb need not be the subject itself but may be an apposition of this subject, which is actually not expressed in the sentence. The subject can be omitted, and ellipsis is a regular feature of Vedic style; yet the subject, though absent, can have its appositions, with which the subject's epithets agree. And, finally, the nominative with the verb can be predicative. Thus, syntactical links in the sentence are not strictly fixed; the word-order permits numerous variants, and the only criterion of the correctness of the actual and syntactic division of the sentence happens to be the context. But the context, in its turn, cannot always be interpreted with absolute certainty. Some examples follow:

The cosmogonic hymn 10.121 is introduced by the following phrase: *hiraṇyagarbháḥ sám avartatā́gre*–and the most natural translation seems to be: "The Golden Embryo arose in the beginning." However, this sentence is understood quite differently by the bulk of the interpreters of the *Ṛg Veda*, who take into consideration the general context of the hymn. Compare, for example, Geldner's version: "Am Anfang wurde er zum goldnen Keim [74.3.347], or Renou's: "Il a évolué en Embryon d'or, aux origines" [122.119]. When we follow the first verse through to its end, the context becomes a little clearer: *bhūtásya jātáḥ pátir éka āsīt / sá dādhāra pṛthivī́ṃ dyā́m utémā́ṃ / kásmai devā́ya havíṣā vidhema* "Once he was born, he became the only lord of creation. / He supported the earth and this sky. / Which god shall we worship with the sacrificial libation?" These *pādas* show clearly that some cosmogonic subject, evolving through various stages, remains unknown to us. Each stanza of the hymn describes various manifestations and acts of the unknown god, and each stanza closes with the same interrogative refrain. Only the final stanza 10 identifies that god with *Prajāpati*, although most scholars believe that this stanza, differing in structure from the rest of the hymn, was appended to the text only at a later stage.

And so the overall context makes it clear that the first *pāda* of the first verse permits only the following interpretation: "In the beginning he arose as the Golden Embryo."

An abstract, purely formal analysis of the preceding sentence, that is, based exclusively on the syntactic relations of words, without consideration of the semantic features of a broader context, does appear to justify taking the nominative singular *hiraṇyagarbháḥ* as the theme while the rest of the sentence belongs to the rheme. A similar actual division occurs in other verses (also from a cosmogonic hymn): *táma āsīt támasā gūḷhám ágre* (10.129.3) "Darkness was hidden by darkness in the beginning;" *kā́mas tád ágre sám avartatā́dhi* (10.129.4) "Amorous desire arose in him in the beginning." In these two instances the nominative of the noun expresses the subject of the third person verb and belongs to the theme of the utterance. We may conclude that sometimes only the data furnished by the broad morphological context make it possible to distinguish between different actual divisions of syntactically analogous sentences.

For instance, *Agni* is a ritually important mediator between men and gods: at the beginning of a rite he is the divine hotar-priest: in his fire the sacrifice is performed, and with his smoke he transports the sacrifice to the gods in his role of the poet's messenger to the divine world. Taking such mythological ideas as the basis for our analysis, phrases of the kind: *sáṃ dūtó adyaud uṣáso viroké* (3.5.2) should be more correctly translated as "He blazed up like a messenger in *Uṣas*' light" (and not as "The messenger blazed up in *Uṣas*' light"). A similar example: the sentence *antár dūtó ródasī dasmá īyate / hótā níṣatto mánuṣaḥ puróhitaḥ* (3.3.2) is to be interpreted as "The amazing one is moving like a messenger between the two worlds, / Set down as the hotar (who is) put before man" (and not: "The amazing messenger is moving . . . "). Incidentally, there are a number of contexts in which these functions of *Agni*'s are explicit and the syntactic parsing presents no difficulties, for example:

sá hí yó mā́nuṣā yugā́
sī́dad dhótā kavíkratuḥ
dūtáś ca havyavā́hanaḥ (6.16.23)

"Indeed, he (is the one) who (during the time of all) human generations / Sits as the hotar (imbued with) spiritual poetic power, / And (acts) as the messenger transporting sacrifices."

This, however, does not mean that in contexts relating to *Agni* the nouns *dūtá-* "messenger" or *hótar-* "hotar-priest" in the nominative can never function as the subject with a verbal predicate in the third person. Since they express *Agni*'s permanent functions these nouns may even acquire the status of almost full-fledged theonyms and as such they may appear as subjects, naming *Agni*, for example: *devā́nā́ṃ dūtáḥ purudhá prásūtó / 'nāgān no vocatu sarvátātā* (3.54.19) "The gods' messenger, many times incited (to it), / May he declare us (to be) sinless–completely!" This example is from a hymn to various deities, and a number of stanzas begin with the name of the god being invoked, *devā́nāṃ dūtáḥ* occupies here the position of a theonym.[107]

When the verbal predicate is in the second person, the nominative of a noun (in contrast with that of a third person pronoun) cannot express the subject: it may be its apposition or it may be related to the predicate, as in, for example: *dūtó devā́nāṃ rájasī sám īyase* (6.15.9) "The gods' messenger, thou reachest the two worlds" (i.e.: "in the capacity of the gods' messenger . . . "); *kavíḥ sīda ní barhíṣi* (9.59.3) "A poet, sit (thou) down upon the sacrificial straw!" (i.e.: "possessing a poetic nature . . . ").

Since syntactic connections are rather weak in the Vedic sentence, which are frequently constructed with the help of a string of adjective-epithets or substantive-appositions in the same case, it is not easy to separate the theme from the rheme in a chain of nouns in the nominative. Some examples: *śū́raḥ sárgam akṛṇod índra eṣām* (7.18.11) literally "The hero arranged a race–*Indra*–among them" which means "*Indra* the hero arranged for them (scilicet for the enemies) (running-) races" (scilicet for making them run from him as though in a race). Geldner's too straightforward version "Der Held *Indra* machte ein Rennen unter ihnen" [74.2.196] obscures the originality of the actual division of the Vedic phrase, in which the final part–*índra eṣām* "*Indra*–among them" is a kind of a replica of the first part, an incomplete phrasal apposition.

gojín naḥ sómo rathajíd dhiraṇyajít
svarjíd abjít pavate sahasrajít
yáṃ devā́saś cakriré pītáye mádaṃ
svā́diṣṭhaṃ drapsám aruṇám mayobhúvam (9.78.4)

"*Soma* purifies himself for our sake, winning cows, winning chariots, winning gold, / Winning the sun, winning the waters, winning thousands; / (He is the one) whom the gods created (as) an inebriating beverage for drinking, / (As) the sweetest drop, the golden one, bringing joy."

From the formal point of view, in *pādas a-b* of this stanza all the epithets that end in *-jit* "winning, conquering" are adjectives in agreement with *sómo*, that is, they make up a chain of the subject's attributes and thus apparently belong to the theme of the utterance. However, from the point of view of the actual division of the sentence, they must belong to the predicate: according to the mythological conceptions of the *Ṛg Veda*, only when purifying himself is *Soma* able to transfer to the worshipper all those qualities that help him in obtaining the desired goods. Thus, the semantic link here should be construed as *pavate gojít, rathajít,* etc.: "He purifies himself as winning cows, winning chariots, etc."

Pādas c-d of the same stanza contain a series of accusatives, of which *yám* is the direct object and all the rest function as accusatives with the same verb (of incomplete predication) *cakriré*. In this case the semantic division of a chain of predicative accusatives presents no difficulties, and the limits between syntagms can be determined with certainty. But the text itself contains no formal criteria that can warrant the correctness of a particular syntactic analysis of a chain of identical case-forms.

A fine example of the ambiguous analysis of a chain of predicative accusatives appears in stanza 1 of the very first hymn (to *Agni*) with which the *Ṛg Veda* begins:

agním īḷe puróhitaṃ
yajñásya devám ṛtvíjam
hótāraṃ ratnadhā́tamam

"(I) invoke *Agni*–(him who is) placed in front, / The god of sacrifice (and) the priest, / The *hotar* with abundant wealth."

This is Renou's version, which reflects his analysis of the chain of predicative accusatives. But in his commentary, he raises a question about the probable adjectival meaning of *devá-* in this passage [118.12.71], since, in form, the stems of the substantive and the adjective are in this case identical. Geldner's proposed division is different: "*Agni* berufe ich als Bevollmächtigten, als Gott-Priester des Opfers, als *Hotṛ*, der am meisten Lohn einbringt," while in the commentary he discusses some difficulties of interpretation related to the uncertainty in deciding whether the predicative accusatives *puróhitam–ṛtvíjam–hótāram* represent a single notion or three independent notions [74.1.1].

The place of the verb that breaks up such a chain of homogenous case-forms cannot usually serve as a criterion of the meaning of this or that case-form. Thus Renou's observation that the verb is quite often the means of balancing the accusatives both preceding and following it seems to be fully justified. One may adduce another example:

tvā́m agne átithim pūrvyáṃ víśaḥ
śocíṣkeśaṃ gṛhápatiṃ ní ṣedire
bṛhátketum purusū́paṃ dhanaspṛ́taṃ
suśármāṇaṃ svávasaṃ jaradvíṣam (5.8.2)

"Thee, O *Agni*, (as) the prime guest of the tribe, / The flame-haired one, they seated (as) the housemaster, / (Thee), with a lofty banner, the multiform, the prize-seizing one, / Granting excellent protection, excellent aid, the eater of old (trees)."

In this stanza, the verb seems to play the part of something like a "balance-wheel" keeping together the accusatives both to the left and to the right of it. The word-order here is determined by formal and stylistic, rather than syntactic, factors. Nor is this example unique: it is quite typical of the language of the hymns. But a chain of homogeneous nominatives or accusatives containing a third person pronoun (in the same case) is not easier to interpret than a purely nominal one. Here the main difficulty lies in the fact that third person pronouns are actually demonstratives, and thus, depending on the syntactic analysis of a sentence, they may function as subjects or their attributes, i.e., "he" or "this," "that." Both syntactic and mythological contexts are frequently quite ambiguous as to the actual division of the sentence.

A fitting illustration can be found in the *Soma* hymns, since it is there that we observe the play upon a demonstrative whose referent is *Soma*.[108] For instance, each of the six stanzas in hymn 9.26 begins with the accusative *tám*. In stanza 3 the demonstrative stands immediately before the noun that here denotes *Soma*:

táṃ vedhā́m medháyāhyan
pávamānam ádhi dyávi
dharṇasím bhū́ridhāyasam

"Him, the establisher (of the rite), they hastened with (their) poetic inspiration, / (Him), *Pavamāna*, in the sky, / The firmly fixed one, the nourisher of the many."

The juxtaposed *táṃ vedhā́ṃ* may be interpreted–from a formal point of view–as a construction in concord where *táṃ* is an attribute of *vedhā́ṃ*; this is Geldner's version ("Diesen Meister") [74.3.27]. But, with equally well-founded reasons, one may treat *vedhā́ṃ* as an apposition to *táṃ*–as is suggested here, and as Renou has done previously: "Lui l'ordonnateur (du culte . . .)" [118.8.17].

There are no formal criteria for the syntactic interpretation of this and similar phrases. The contiguous disposition of its parts seems, at first sight, to argue for its analysis as a construction in concord. But first, the principle of apposition in sentence construction in the *Ṛg Veda* is quite wide-spread, and second, non-contiguous disposition is a non-argument in itself. Moreover, one can always imagine an elliptical phrase, as Geldner did in translating two analogous constructions in different stanzas of the same hymn:

tám amṛkṣanta vājínam
upásthe áditer ádhi
víprāso áṇvyā dhiyā́ (1)

(1) "(Him), this running (-horse), the inspired (poets) cleansed (in Aditi's womb by means of a fine (straining-) prayer."

Geldner renders this non-contiguous collocation as "Diesen Meister," while Renou offers: "Ils l'ont nettoyé, (ce soma) gagnant-du-prix, . . . "

táṃ sā́nāv ádhi jāmáyo
háriṃ hinvanty ádribhiḥ
haryatám bhū́ricakṣasam (5)

(5) "(Him), this bay horse, the sisters / Hurry with stones upon the back (of the strainer), / (Him), the desired one, looking at many (men)." This time Geldner translates "Ihn, den Falben," but Renou finds an ellipsis here: "C'est ce (dieu) alezan."

The number of examples can be easily multiplied. This is one manifestation of what has been called the "non-apparent syntax" of the *Ṛg Veda*. A purely formal analysis of the phrase cannot help in its correct interpretation, since the ambiguity is system-bound. In a number of cases–yet not all!–the key to the correct actual division can be found in the mythological context.

In one particular case–the correlation between a noun and a demonstrative pronoun in a given phrase–the ambiguity persists even when this pronoun is emphatic in form, for example: *etā́ u tyā́ḥ práty adṛśran purástāj / jyóter yáchantīr uṣáso vibhātī́ḥ* (7.78.3) "Now in the east these / Bright (and) brilliant *Uṣasas* appeared, granting light." Although the parts of the phrase are non-contiguous here: *etā́ u tyā́ḥ . . . uṣáso*, neither Geldner nor Renou treats *uṣáso* as an apposition to *etā́* and *tyā́ḥ*.[109] And so, if neither the emphatic character of the pronoun nor the noncontiguous disposition of the members of the construction can be used as criteria for its semantic interpretation, one may reasonably conclude that there is probably no formal criterion.

Among the examples of this stylistic peculiarity of the *Ṛg Veda* (that is, strings of accusatives) there are cases when two accusatives are required by grammar, not by style; that is, the cases of constructions with a double accusative. Such phrases normally occur with verbal stems of a certain grammatical meaning, namely, with causatives as well as with verbal roots of a certain lexical meaning; but the area of lexical meanings is very difficult to define with certainty. Examples include the verb of incomplete predication *kar-* "to make (someone [accusative case] somebody [accusative case]);" verbs of discourse, such as *ah-* "to say" something [accusative case] (to someone [accusative case] or something [accusative case] about someone [accusative case]); *brū-* id., *vac-* id., *prach-* "to ask" (someone [accusative case] about something [accusative case]); and a few verbs of different semantics.

In some cases the interpretation of the double accusative remains ambiguous. Thus, when construed with the verb *kar-* (of incomplete predication), one of the accusatives denotes the object of action, while the other is a predicative substantive or adjective. The predicative character of the second accusative is confirmed by the possible transformation of such a simple sentence into a compound sentence with a final clause in which the predicate is expressed by the copula in the subjunctive and a predicate adjective of the primary sentence in the nominative, while the subject in the nominative is the word that has been in the accusative of the direct object in the primary sentence, for example: *yaśásam bhāgám kṛṇutam no aśvinā / sómam ná cā́ram maghávatsu nas kṛtam* (10.39.2) "O *Aśvins*, make a glorious portion for us! / Make us pleasing to liberal patrons like *Soma*!" In the second sentence one can observe the attraction by number of the predicative accusative, literally "(you) make us–like *Soma*–pleasing;" compare Geldner's translation: "macht uns den Gönnern angenehm wie *Soma*" [74.3.191]. In both sentences the transformation noted above is permissible: **kṛṇutám yáthā* (or *yád*) *no bhāgó yaśā́ ásat* "Act so that our portion will be glorious!" and **kṛtám yáthā* (or *yád*) *vayám sómo ná cā́ravó 'san* "Act so that we become pleasing like *Soma*!"

If the predicate is expressed by verbs of complete predication–and not by *kar-* –there may be homonymy between attributive and predicative constructions with the accusative. Compare, for example, the following examples: *ūrdhvám bhānúm savitévāśret* (4.6.2) "He directed his straight ray like *Savitar*," where *ūrdhvám bhānúm* is an attributive construction; *kṛdhī́ na ūrdhvā́n caráthāya jīváse* (1.36.14) "Stand us upright[110]–for travels (and) for life!" (literally "Make us straight . . . "). A transformation is possible in the latter case where the accusative *ūrdhvā́n* is predicative and governed by the verb *kṛdhí*, but impossible in the former example.

A few verbs with different semantics follow the syntactic pattern of the double accusative with *kar-*. Some examples:

The verb *duh-* "to milk:"

divó nā́ke mádhujihvā asaścáto
venā́ duhanty ukṣáṇam giriṣṭhā́m

apsú drapsáṃ vāvṛdhānám samudrá ā́
síndhor ūrmā́ mádhumantam pavítra ā́ (9.85.10)

"On the heavenly vault the sweet-tongued sagacious (ones) milk inexhaustible (accusative case) (spurts) of the bull (accusative case) who stands upon a mountain; / (They milk out) the drop (accusative case) which has grown in the waters, in the sea, in the wave of the river, full of honey upon the strainer."

A similar construction is attested in Russian: the verb *duh-* combines the government of the two Russian verbs: доить (корову) "to milk (a cow)" and надоить (молоко) "to milk out (the milk)."

The verb *puṣ-* "to make prosper, thrive:"

samídhā yás ta ā́hutiṃ
níśitim mártyo nácat
vayā́vantaṃ sá puṣyati
kṣáyam agne śatā́yuṣam (6.2.5)

"The mortal who successfully libates to thee and sets (thee) on fire with firewood,– / He strives for the prosperity of (his) home (accusative case), O *Agni*, so that he branches out[111] and lives a hundred years" (literally " . . . strives for the prosperity of [his] home, the branching one, living a hundred years." This example illustrates the "nonapparent" character of Vedic syntax, in which the surface syntactic connections can represent ambiguous deep interrelations.

Basically, verbs of discourse in the *Ṛg Veda* typically employ double accusative constructions. The difficulty consists in the fact that the referent of one of the accusatives may be both the addressee of the message and the person about whom the message is sent.[112] The referent of the addressee is represented by a noun or pronoun. The other accusative is always predicative in meaning, and can be represented by a substantive, an adjective, or a participle.

This construction has a variant: verbs of discourse / accusative object / accusative predicate, for example: *yé . . . pṛ́śniṃ vocanta mātáram* (5.52.16) "(Those) who called *Pṛśni* (accusative case) (their) mother (accusative case);" *ánāgān no vocatu sarvátātā* (3.54.19) "May he declare us (accusative case) completely innocent (accusative case)!;" *śvā́nam bastó bodhayitā́ram abravīt* (1.161.13) "The ram said that the dog had awakened (him)" (literally "The ram called the dog (his) awakener (accusative case)").

There is also another variant: verbs of discourse / accusative personae / accusative predicate, for example: *pṛchā́mi tvā páram ántam pṛthivyā́ḥ* / . . .

/ *pṛchā́mi tvā vŕ̥ṣṇo áśvasya rétaḥ* . . . (1.164.34) "I ask thee (accusative case) (what is) the farthest limit (accusative case) of the earth . . . I ask thee (accusative case) the semen (accusative case) of the stud-horse;"

yád adyá tvā puruṣṭuta
brávāma dasra mantumaḥ
tát sú no mánma sādhaya (6.56.4)

"What (accusative case) we will today tell thee (accusative case), O many-famed one, / O marvelous (and) sage (one), / Implement properly that thought (accusative case) of ours!"

Quite frequently the syntactic construction with a verb of discourse is incomplete or mixed: a piece of direct oration is inserted instead of the accusative predicate, and it remains unclear whether one is to take the accusative as a direct object accusative or an accusative of the addressee, for instance: *yáṃ smā pṛchánti kúha séti ghorám / utém āhur naíṣó astī́ty enam* . . . (2.12.5) "(He) about whom (accusative case) they ask, 'Where is he?'–about the terrible one (accusative case), / And they say of him (accusative case), 'He does not exist'." The broader context of the hymn indicates that in this stanza the accusatives refer to the direct object of the verb and not to the addressee of the message: the hymn describes *Indra*'s feats and asserts the existence of the god.

In another context the accusative in such a mixed construction with a verb of discourse should be interpreted as the case of the addressee: *yó mā́yātuṃ yā́tudhānéty ā́ha / yó vā rakṣā́ḥ śúcir asmī́ty ā́ha / índras táṃ hantu* . . . (7.104.16) "(The one) who calls me, (who am) not a sorcerer (accusative case), 'O sorcerer!'–or (the one) who is a rakṣas and says, 'I am innocent,'–let *Indra* kill him . . . !"

However, in the following context the meaning of the accusative with the verb of discourse is rather vague: . . . *yó jāgā́ra tám ayáṃ sóma āha / távāhám asmi sakhyé nyòkāḥ* (5.44.14) "(He) who is awake–to him (accusative case) that *Soma* said: "In friendship with thee I am (as though) at home." The accusative *tám*, in this case, most probably refers to the addressee of the message (this opinion is shared both by Geldner [74.2.49] and Renou [118.5.27]), but one should not exclude its interpretation as the direct object: "this *Soma* said about that." The double accusative construction also occurs with a number of verbs semantically close to verbs of discourse or to verbs of incomplete predication, such as *man-* "to consider (someone to be somebody)," *yāc-* "to ask (someone about something)," for example:

mánye tvā yajñíyaṃ yajñíyānām
mánye tvā cyávanam ácyutānām

mánye tvā sátvānām indra ketúm
mánye tvā vṛṣabhám carṣaṇīnā́m (8.96.4)

"I consider thee (accusative case) sacrifice-worthy (accusative case) among those who are sacrifice-worthy, / I consider thee (accusative case) the shaker (accusative case) of the unshakeable ones, / I consider thee (accusative case), O *Indra*, (to be) the banner (accusative case) of warriors, / I consider thee (accusative case) the bull (accusative case) among peoples;" *apó yācāmi bheṣajám* (10.9.5) "I ask the waters (accusative case) for a cure (accusative case)." These constructions can be used with other verbs too (for example *īḍ-* "to ask, call on," *ní-dhā-* "to establish," etc.), taking their place in the chains of accusative appositions with unclear criteria of actual division.

We have considered various types of predicative constructions and their stylistic interpretation in the *Ṛg Veda*. One of the principal stylistic peculiarities of this text is related to predicativity. This peculiarity lies, on the one hand, in the self-sufficiency of the finite verb, which can appear as an independent clause, and on the other hand, in the optionality of the personal pronoun when it is the subject of the finite verb predicate. Along with other syntactic, morphological, and lexical means, this peculiarity is used to create an obscure suggestive style, casting intentional obscurities over the real subject of an action in a number of contexts.

The importance of this task for the authors of the hymns is confirmed, for instance, by the presence of hymns to the All-Gods (*Viśve Devāḥ*) in which a particular deity has to be guessed by his specific features while he is not directly called by name; the names of those mythological referents are reported only in the late medieval commentary. The riddling principle lies at the basis of, for example, hymn 8.29. Its first stanza runs as follows:

babhrúr éko víṣuṇaḥ sūnáro
yúvāñjy àñkte hiraṇyáyam

"One (of them), brown, changing, noble, young–anoints (himself) with a golden ointment." The solution is *Soma*. The natural color of the pressed juice seems to have been dark brown, but during the ritual process its color lightened as it was mixed with various additives–water, milk, etc.

Verbal sentences without a subject, but with a verbal inflexion that indicated only a few of its grammatical features–number, person–were a promising starting point for intentional vagueness as well as a favorable condition for ambiguity in interpretation. As a yard-stick for plausible interpretations one may employ either a broad mythological context or words and phrases typical of the given deity or myth. Some examples:

ási hí víra sényó
'si bhū́ri purādadíḥ
ási dabhrásya cid vṛdhó
yájamānāya śikṣasi
sunvaté bhū́ri te vásu (1.81.2)

"Since thou, O hero, (art) a warlike (god), / Thou art that one who gives over a large (booty) into (one's) power. / Thou art that one who increasest even (something) small. / Thou wishest to help the sacrificer,– / Thou hast a lot of goods for the *Soma* presser." (The construction in *pādas a-c*, literally: "(Thou) art warlike . . . , / (Thou) art giving into power . . . , / (Thou) art increasing . . . ").

This is a stanza from a hymn to *Indra*, but the identity of the god being addressed would be quite apparent even if the verse were taken in isolation, for the words *vīrá-* "hero" and *sénya-* "warlike" belong to the vocabulary typical of *Indra* hymns: "hero" is usually, and "warlike" is exclusively, applied to *Indra*, as are the praises to the god's marvelous generosity towards the sacrificer.

Often, in sentences in which the subject of an action is expressed only in the verbal inflexion, not every attribute or apposition to the missing subject (that is, chains of nominatives) nor every address to a deity (names in the vocative) belongs to a vocabulary that is specific for a particular deity. The means to identify the subject of an action should therefore be sought in a wider context, for example:

mahā́m̐ asi mahiṣa vṛ́ṣṇyebhir
dhanaspṛ́d ugra sáhamāno anyā́n
éko víśvasya bhúvanasya rā́jā
sá yodháyā ca kṣayáyā ca jánān (3.46.2)

"Thou art great, O buffalo, (in thy) bull's powers, / Seizing the prizes, O terrible one, overcoming the others. / He (is) the only king of the whole world; / Lead the tribes into battle and settle (them) in peace!"

This is also a stanza from a hymn to *Indra*. But in this stanza there is not a single substantive or adjective applied to this god here that could be called specific for him, since each of them (*mahā́n, mahiṣa, dhanaspṛ́d, ugra, sáhamāno, rā́jā*) is often applied to other gods. The verbs *yodháyā* and *kṣayáyā* in *pāda d* are differential: of all the gods only *Indra* leads the tribes into battle and then settles them in peace, i.e., in the Aryan's power.

The unambiguous character of reference of nominative chains–attributes and appositions to the missing subject–can be sometimes established by a direct address to this deity, including his name in the vocative or his characteristic standing epithet, for example:

> *utá sákhāsy aśvínor*
> *utá mātā́ gávām asi*
> *utóṣo vásva íśiṣe* (4.52.3)

"And (thou) art the *Aśvins*' girlfriend, / And (thou) art the cows' mother, / And (thou), O *Uṣas*, possessest the goods."

The name occurs a few more times in other stanzas of the goddess *Uṣas* in this hymn in various cases. But different situations are also possible. Book 9, wholly devoted to the god *Soma-Pavamāna*, contains hymn 112, which seems to have nothing to do with the rest of the monotonous ritual hymns in this book. It was included here only thanks to its refrain, which also occurs in some other hymns of the Book and which contains, in a context typical of *Soma*, the vocative *indo* "O drop!" addressed to its clarified juice: *índrāyendo pári srava* "O drop, flow for Indra!"

The function of the vocative as a means of reference is not limited to a single type of sentences with a finite verbal predicate. Vocatives in semi-nominal sentences with participle predicates, as well as purely nominal clauses, function in the same way.

The problem of identifying the subject when it is expressed exclusively by the predicate finite-verb inflexion, or when it is explicit but expressed by nouns that refer to various deities, becomes quite acute in hymns to the All-Gods or in hymns about abstract topics (cosmogony, knowledge, mysteries of the universe, etc.), where the context is of little help in ascertaining the subject of an action. Here is, for instance, the beginning of the hymn to the All-Gods (5.42):

> *prá śáṃtamā váruṇaṃ dī́dhitī gī́r*
> *mitrám bhágam áditiṃ nūnám aśyāḥ*
> *pṛ́ṣadyoniḥ páñcahotā śṛṇotv*
> *átūrtapanthā ásuro mayobhúḥ* (1)

(1) "May the most beneficent prayer (and) song / now reach *Varuṇa, Mitra, Bhaga, Aditi*! / May (the god) hear (it), (the one) who dwells in speckled (fat), with the five *hotars*, / The encouraging *Asura* whose path is inaccessible!"

It is rather difficult to identify the god who should "hear" (*pādas c-d*). None of the epithets describing him could be termed specific. Sāyaṇa believed that it should be *Vāyu*, but the majority of Western interpreters suppose him to be *Aryaman*, since the rare epithet *átūrtapanthāḥ* is attested in the *Rig Veda* only once more, at 10.64.5, where it is applied to *Aryaman*.[113]

Still, Geldner suggests that here it is *Agni* who is identified with *Aryaman* because the epithet *pŕ̥ṣadyoni-* is synonymous with *Agni*'s standing epithet *ghr̥táyoni-* [74.2.42]. Moreover, *Aryaman* belongs to the *Ādityas*, who include the gods mentioned in *pādas a-b*.[114]

In the following context (from the hymn to the All-Gods 7.34), the subject of the action is not named, and his epithets are few and nonspecific:

utá na eṣú nŕ̥ṣu śrávo dhuḥ
prá rāyé yantu śárdhanto aryáḥ (18)
tápanti śátrum̥ svàr ná bhū́mā
mahā́senāso ámebhir eṣām (19)

(18) "And may they endow with fame these men of ours, / May (they) move forward towards wealth, without reckoning with the alien."

(19) "May they incinerate the enemy as the sun (incinerates) the earth, with a huge host, with their fits of fury."

According to Sāyaṇa, the subjects here are the gods or the *Maruts*. Geldner prefers the *Maruts* [74.2.215], Renou–the gods [118.5.39]. There is also disagreement concerning *pāda* 18*b*. Geldner believes that *pādas a* and *b* have different subjects: in the first *pāda* they are the *Maruts*, and in the second, the patrons of sacrifice, i.e., *nŕ̥-* from *pāda a*. He offers the following translation: "Und sie mögen diesen unseren Herren Ruhm bringen. Zu Reichtum sollen sie ausziehen, über den hohen Herrn triumphierend," and in his commentary he remarks that "über den hohen Herrn" should be understood "Als den Nebenbuhler." But Renou believes that the subject is the same in the two *pādas* and so translates stanza 18 quite differently: "Et encore: qu'auprès de ces seigneurs (les dieux) nous confèrent une distinction, qu'ils avancent pour (nous donner) la richesse, en faisant fi de l'Étranger."

In hymns on abstract themes the problem of the identity of the subject of cosmogonic and various other actions acquires an "ideological" character, if one may put it so. The purpose of such a hymn is to find out who was the subject of the cosmogonic feats, who was the demiurge (10.121). Usually this problem is acknowledged to be insoluble (10.121; 129). Quite often a whole series of rhetorical questions is asked, or a number of mutually incompatible solutions is offered (10.72). If the subject is actually expressed, it is rendered by means of the neuter pronoun *tád* or *tád ékam* "That One," whose reference is unclear. The subject of the action may be hinted at by the grammatical information contained in verbal endings, or else it may be denoted by the relative pronoun *yá-* "who," "which" as, for instance, in some stanzas of hymn 10.121.[115] The uncertainty as to the referent is here reflected on the linguistic level by correlated pairs of relative and interrogative pronouns, for example:

yáś cid ā́po mahinā́ paryápaśyad
dákṣaṃ dádhānā janáyantīr yajñám
yó devéṣv ádhi devá éka ā́sīt
kásmai devā́ya havíṣā vidhema (10.121.8)

"(He) who in (his) greatness looked over the waters, / Which are pregnant with *Dakṣa*, bringing forth the sacrifice, / (He) who was the one god over the gods,– / Who (is the) god whom we shall worship with the libation?"

The hymn to "Knowledge" (10.71–*jñāna*, as it is called in the *Anukramaṇī)* opens with the following stanza:

bṛ́haspate prathamáṃ vācó ágraṃ
yát praírata nāmadhéyaṃ dádhānāḥ
yád eṣāṃ śréṣṭhaṃ yád aripráṃ ā́sīt
preṇā́ tád eṣāṃ níhitaṃ gúhāvíḥ (1)

(1) "O Bṛhaspati, the first beginning of Speech (appeared), / When (they) began to act, giving names (to things). / What they had of the best (and) immaculate, / What was hidden in them, was revealed through love." Presumably, the subjects of the actions here are the ancient *Ṛṣis* who established the cult some time in the past: in stanza 2 they are called "wise in thought" (*dhī́rā mánasā*). The identification of the subject of action expressed only by verbal inflexion is a particular case of a much wider problem: the use of references to create an obscure esoteric style that quite often presupposes a multivalent interpretation.

As Renou has stressed [126.230-1], the mutual disposition of cases in the Vedic phrase is not conditioned exclusively by rules of syntax. Indeed, this question is to be seen as part and parcel of a much wider range of general problems concerning the word-order in the sentence as it is found in the hymns. And here various formal and semantic factors come into play. For instance, the principle of repetitions is fundamental to any text transmitted orally, in syntax it is expressed in symmetrically balanced structures of various types, which have been described in detail by Gonda [87]. We will touch upon this particular topic here only in passing, and moreover, from a somewhat differing point of view, examining the degree of influence of the principle of repetition upon the word-order in the sentence.

Any versified text is based on regular repetition of certain metrical schemes. The syllabic versification of the *Ṛg Veda* employs repetitions of certain combinations of verse-lines characterized by a definite structure, with a pre-set number of syllables and a certain regularity in the sequence of long and short syllables which is most strictly observed in the cadence. In general, when a rhythm based on the correlation of durations is established, the role of the speech rhythm conditioned by syntactic structures is usually diminished [48.67]. Metrical limitations certainly influence the word-order in a phrase, at least in a phrase of a cadence wherein the choice and sequence of words conforms to the prescribed quantitative specification of the verse-line ending, for example:

> *dvā́ suparṇā́ sayújā sákhayā*
> *samānáṃ vṛkṣám pári ṣasvajāte*
> *táyor anyáḥ píppalaṃ svādv átty*
> *ánaśnann anyó abhí cākaśīti* (1.164.20)

"Two eagles, two friends joined together, / Embraced the same tree. / One of them eats the sweet fig-fruit. / Without eating the other looks on."

In this stanza, the attribute in each attributive construction–except one–precedes the determined member in concord (*dvā́ suparṇā́, sayújā sákhayā, samānáṃ vṛkṣám, ánaśnann anyó*); only in *pāda c* are the members in a reversed order: *píppalaṃ svādú*. A prepositive adjectival attribute in attributive constructions is appropriate for the language of the *Rig Veda*, for two reasons: first, the preposed position is assumed for the early PIE stage [99.89], and second, it is attested in Sanskrit.[116] The place of *svādu* in the attributive construction is determined exclusively by metrical considerations. In the *Triṣṭubh* verse the *pāda* cadence is ¯˘¯˘̄, and is represented by *svādú atti* (¯ ˘ ¯ ˘), but it would be impossible for **píppalam atti*. Similar examples abound in the hymns, and it would serve no purpose to cite them here.

In order to define briefly the tendencies that regulate the word-order in the simple sentence with a finite verbal predicate in the Vedic language (mostly, in prose texts), one should single out the closed-in construction of the sentence, in which the predicate takes the final position–which is the most strictly fixed one–and the subject takes up the beginning, while the rest of the sentence occupies the remaining space. In various elementary syntactic constructions one can observe the tendency to prepose the dependent (agreeing, or governed) member to the independent member [8.26f.]. The direct object in the accusative usually stands immediately before the verb.

Sentences with finite verbal predicates are quite noticeably preponderant in the language of the *Ṛg Veda*. But there are also purely nominal sentences consisting of two nouns (a variant: pronoun plus substantive) or of a substantive with a predicate adjective. There are also semi-nominal sentences in which the predicative function is fulfilled by participles, and their number increases in the later Books. The predicative element in such sentences should have occupied the final position, which is the usual place of the finite verb according to the norms of the later language. Nominal sentences in Vedic prose tend to have their predicative element in the initial position, yet in many cases the problem seems to have no clear-cut solution and often needs the help of a wider context.

In addition to sentences with a finite verbal predicate, there are also purely nominal and semi-nominal sentences. Here is the beginning of the marriage hymn 10.85, in which such a nominal construction is predominant:

satyénóttabhitā bhū́miḥ
sū́ryeṇóttabhitā dyaúḥ
ṛténādityā́s tiṣṭhanti
diví sómo ádhi śritáḥ (1)

sómenādityā́ balínaḥ
sómena pṛthivī́ mahī́
átho nákṣatrāṇām eṣā́m
upásthe sóma ā́hitaḥ (2)

(1) "The earth is propped up by truth. / The sky is propped up by the sun. / Through the law the *Ādityas* exist, / (And) *Soma* is placed in the sky."

(2) "Through *Soma* the *Ādityas* are mighty. / Through *Soma* the earth is great. / And in the lap of these constellations *Soma* has been set."

The translation is as literal as possible in attempting to convey the nature of the predicative element and its position in the sentence. This position is determined not by syntactic norms but by isomorphism of parallel balanced constructions. In stanza 1 the structure of *pāda a* (instrumental–participle–nominative case) is repeated in full in *pāda b*. In *pāda c* the construction changes, but its beginning echoes the two preceding *pādas* (compare the instrumentals *satyéna–sū́ryeṇa–ṛténa*). The predicative construction of *pāda c* is of the S-V type (with V=finite verb). The same order of elements is seen in the predicative construction in *pāda d*, where V is expressed by the participle. In stanza 2 *pādas a-b* are parallel balanced constructions linked by the anaphoric repetition of the instrumental *sómena* (compare *pādas a-c* in stanza 1). These predicative constructions are purely nominal: the predicative adjectives end the phrases, and the predicative construction in *pāda d*, with its predicative participle, takes its orientation from them.

One may conclude that in hymns with elementary syntactic constructions, or at least in a considerable number of them, the constituent elements and the types of their interrelations are morphologically predetermined, but their sequence is not, in fact, predetermined. The sequence becomes ordered only in context and is determined by various stylistic factors, among which the principle of repetition is most important. See, for example, how the members of the same nominal predicative construction change their places depending upon the particular scheme of repetition in which they occur:

ayám me hásto bhágavān
ayám me bhágavattaraḥ
ayám me viśvábheṣajo
'yáṃ śivā́bhimarśanaḥ (10.60.12)

"This hand of mine is beneficent; / This (hand) of mine is (even) more beneficent. / This of mine is all-healing, / (And) this (one) touches with comfort;"

vṛ́ṣaṇas te abhī́śavo
vṛ́ṣā káśā hiraṇyáyī
vṛ́ṣā rátho maghavan vṛ́ṣaṇā hárī
vṛ́ṣā tváṃ śatakrato (8.33.11)

"Brave (are) thy reins, / Brave (is) the golden whip, / Brave (is) the chariot, O generous one, brave (is) thy pair of bays, / Brave (art) thou (thyself), O hundred-witted one!"

The greatest difficulties arise when one tries to identify those predicative constructions whose subject and predicate are both nouns. There is no agreement in gender and number between nouns in such constructions and therefore no formal criterion for determining the direction of the connection between them. Such a criterion could have been found in the order of the elements were it not too loose and too free to be of much use. In later Vedic prose there was a tendency to prepose the substantive predicate, but this was not carried out consistently enough, and quite often the help of a wider mythological context seems indispensable to determine the theme and the predicate.[117]

In the prose of the *Upaniṣads* this is already one of the gravest problems of textual interpretation. Later, this nominal style was widely employed in philosophical and scientific prose. The *Ṛg Veda* attests to the very beginning of this process. An example of this construction from the Riddling hymn can be interpreted with certainty only because its semantics reflects well-known Vedic mythological views:

dyaúr me pitā́ janitā́ nā́bhir átra
bándhur me mātā́ pṛthivī́ mahī́yám
uttānáyoś camvòr yónir antár
átrā pitā́ duhitúr gárbham ā́dhāt (1.164.33)

"The sky (is) my father, (my) progenitor; There (is my) navel. / This great Earth (is) my kin, (my) mother. / Inside (these) two bowls stretched apart (is my) womb. / Here the father placed the embryo in the daughter." *Pāda b* reverses the word-order of *pāda a*: literally "Kin my mother Earth great this." But there are contexts that remain obscure both formally and mythologically. Here is an example:

ahám índro váruṇas te mahitvā́-
urvī́ gabhīré rájasī suméke
tváṣṭeva víśvā bhúvanāni vidvā́n
sám airayaṃ ródasī dhāráyaṃ ca (4.42.3)

"I, *Varuṇa*, (am) *Indra*. These two wide, deep, well-established spaces I set in motion by (my) greatness and supported (these) two halves of the universe, knowing, like *Tvaṣṭar*, all the creatures."[118] The bone of contention is the nominal sentence *ahám índro váruṇas*. This whole hymn has been interpreted by Kuiper as a verbal contest (*vívāc-*) between *Varuṇa* and *Indra*, in which both of them are engaged in self-glorification, ascribing to themselves all the greatest cosmogonic feats [100.23]. The challenger is *Varuṇa*, (stanzas 1-3 are ascribed to him) who declares himself to be *Indra*. *Indra*, in uttering stanzas 4-6 (as Kuiper believes), delimitates their respective spheres of activity and insists on his own supremacy. As a result, *Varuṇa* has to acknowledge his defeat (stanza 7).

Kuiper's interpretation is more convincing than some other proposals and is supported by his general conception of the role of verbal contests in the *Ṛg Veda* [*Ancient Indian Cosmogony*. Essays selected and introduced by John Irwin. Delhi, 1983, 151-215]. The gravity of difficulties that scholars encounter in interpreting such passages is attested to by the endless discussion of this stanza, from the end of the last century.

Hymn 4.42 is a dialogue in form. In the text of the *Ṛg Veda* there are no indications of the speaker of each stanza, and the first stanza of this hymn is most ambiguous. Oldenberg hesitated in its attribution, declaring that if its speaker is *Varuṇa* it should be understood as: "I, *Varuṇa*, being (the true) *Indra*," but if it was spoken by *Indra*, the meaning would be: "I, *Indra*, being (the true) *Varuṇa*" [114.1.302].[119] Geldner attributes the stanza to *Varuṇa* and translates: "Ich *Varuṇa* bin *Indra*" [74.1.474]. Renou believes that the speaker is *Indra*, and understands the phrase in the following way: "C'est moi *Indra* (qui suis celui qui croit être) *Varuṇa*" [118.5.97], but in his commentary he remarks that the phrase can be equally attributed to *Varuṇa* [118.7.78]. In short, the meaning remains obscure, and this obscurity cannot be definitively cleared up by a linguistic analysis of the phrase, by a stylistic analysis of the whole hymn, or by reasoning based on mythological data; the feats that are listed in this stanza can be ascribed both to *Varuṇa* and *Indra*, or, even, to some other great god of the *Ṛg Veda*. The last interpretation of this hymn was published after this manuscript had been completed. According to it, the speaker is King Trasadasyu, who identified himself with the gods *Varuṇa* and *Indra*.–Hans-Peter Schmidt. "The place of Ṛgveda 4.42–Ritual, state and history in South Asia." *Essays in Honour of J. C. Heesterman*. Brill. Leiden-New York-Köln. 1992 (323-349).

Among the peculiarities of predicativity in the *Ṛg Veda* is a type of sentence in which the predicate is expressed by the infinitive. The range of functions of the infinitive was wider in Vedic than in Sanskrit, and its morphological types were much more diversified. The basic function of the infinitive consists in forming special half-independent phrases that complete simple sentences in which the infinitive depends on the finite verb or–more rarely–on the noun; compare for example: *tā́ vām̐ vā́stūny uśmasi gámadhyai / yátra gā́vo bhū́riśṛṅgā ayā́saḥ* (1.154.6) "We wish to go to your (dual) places, / Where (there are) many-horned untiring bulls;" *nahí grábhāyā́raṇaḥ suśévo / 'nyódaryo mánasā mántavā́ u* (7.4.8) "Indeed, another's (son) born of a strange womb is not so dear to hold (him) on, / to think (of) with (one's) mind!" These infinitival phrases are very close in meaning to final clauses in complex sentences.

The infinitive can also function as predicate–most commonly the dative infinitive.[120] Normally such sentences are impersonal, and the infinitive is negated: *ná párvatā nináme tasthivā́ṃsaḥ* (3.56.1) "Not for bending (are the upright) standing mountains;" *nahí te ántaḥ śávasaḥ parīṇáśe* (1.54.1) "Not to reach (i.e., unreachable) (is) the limit of thy power!"; *agnér iva prásitir nā́ha vártave / yáṃ-yaṃ yújaṃ kṛṇuté bráhmaṇas pátiḥ* (2.25.3) "Like a gust of fire, not to be held up (is the one,) / Whom *Brahmaṇaspati* makes his ally."

In these sentences the noun that expresses the logical object of the transitive verb is in the nominative. The natural conclusion is that the infinitive in this particular syntactic context has a passive meaning (although the diathesis finds no morphological expression in the infinitive).[121]

If the sentence with the predicative infinitive also mentions the logical agent, the word expressing it (noun or pronoun) is in the instrumental or genitive case; that is, the construction is identical with that containing a predicative participle with passive meaning, for example: *vā́tasyeva prajavó nā́nyena / stómo vasiṣṭhā ánvetave vaḥ* (7.33.8) "Nobody can catch up with your praise (which is) speedy like the wind, O *Vasiṣṭhas*" (literally "by nobody to catch up . . . ")–compare a similar construction in an infinitival phrase: *etā́ arṣanti hṛ́dyāt samudrā́c / chatávrajā ripúṇā nā́vacákṣe* (4.58.5) "They flow from the heart-ocean, / Enclosed by a hundred fences, so that the enemy cannot see (them)" (literally "not for seeing by the enemy"); *ná tát te agne pramṛ́ṣe nivártanam* (3.9.2) "Thou shouldst not, O *Agni*, forget about this return!" (literally) "For thee it should not be forgotten . . . ").

The most interesting syntactic construction is found in sentences which use the predicative infinitive without a negation. The grammatical meaning of these infinitives is determined exclusively by the construction. Renou believes that the locative infinitives in *-sani* have the meaning of imperatives [120.361]. Among the various types of dative infinitives in this syntactic context most scholars usually find a number of modal meanings: desire, intention, obligation, etc. (although modal oppositions are not morphologically expressed in the infinitive). Some examples of dative infinitives follow:

ubhā́ vām indrāgnī āhuvádhyā
ubhā́ rā́dhasaḥ sahá mādayádhyai
ubhā́ dātā́rāv iṣā́ṃ rayīṇā́m
ubhā́ vā́jasya sātáye huve vām (6.60.13)

"Both of you, O *Indra-Agni* (I wish) to invoke. / May both (of you) enjoy the (sacrificial) gift together. / Both (of you are) donors of sacrificial refreshments (and) riches. / I call on both of you to obtain the reward."

In *pādas a* and *b* of this stanza the predicate is expressed by an infinitive without a negation. Geldner, basing his argument upon the context, translates these infinitives by means of finite active forms with modal meanings: *pāda a*–"will ich herrufen" (compare the finite form *huve* from the same root in *pāda d*); *pāda b*–"beide sollen sich . . . erfreuen" [74.2.162]. Renou offers the following translation of the first two *pādas*: "Que tous deux ô *Indra* et *Agni*, soyez appelés (par moi). Que tous deux vous enivriez ensemble du don (que je vous fais)!" [118.14.54-5]. The first infinitive is translated in the passive, and the second in the active; in the commentary, however, he renders the imperative meaning of *mādayádhyai* in the passive: "laissez vous envirer" [118.14.125]. Nevertheless, the infinitive in *pāda a* is hardly to be translated by the passive voice: even if *ubhā́* is ambiguous (nominative case-accusative case), the enclitic pronoun *vām* cannot be nominative case in any case.

Kás ta uṣaḥ . . . bhujé márto . . . (1.30.20) "What mortal (can) enjoy thee, O *Uṣas*?" This is how it is understood by the majority of scholars (Ludwig, Pischel, Geldner, Renou). The predicative construction of this sentence–nominative case of the subject, infinitive of the predicate–presupposes an active meaning of the infinitive, but on the whole it looks abnormal: the sentence is not an impersonal one, but the *Ṛg Veda* tolerates parataxis between the subject and the verbal predicate. Oldenberg, observing that the subject of an action expressed by an infinitive may or may not coincide with the subject of the sentence, admits that there can be two ways of understanding the passage: "Wer [ist] dir, O *Uṣas*, [dazu da, dafür genehm], dass et [deine Segnungen] geniessen möge" in the first case; the second interpretation: "Wer etc., dass du [sein Opfer, seinen Preis] geniessen mögest" [114.1.26]. Since the infinitive has no morphological means to express a number of verbal categories, and since at the same time, elliptical constructions are wide-spread in the *Rig Veda*, there does not seem to be any objective criterion for choosing between interpretations in this case.

Predicative constructions of the same type sometimes occur with other types of dative infinitives, for example: *utá tyā́ me yaśásā śvetanā́yai / vyántā pā́ntauśijó huvádhyai* (1.122.4) "And more, (I) *Uśij*'s son, want to call unto me / These two resplendent ones that come (and) drink so that dawn should come." Here the subject is nominative case *auśijó*; the predicate, the infinitive *huvádhyai*, and the syntactic link between them can be defined only as paratactic. Both Geldner and Renou translate this construction in the active voice: " . . . will (ich,) der Uśij Sohn, . . . rufen" [74.1.168] and " . . . je veux appeler à moi, . . . –moi, fils d'Uśij . . . " [118.5.6]. Renou notes a certain degree of ambiguity here, caused by the presence of the enclitic pronoun *me* which may be interpreted as the genitive of the subject if the infinitive has a passive meaning. He also points out that there is stylistic play based on the ambiguous use of the infinitive and the additional ambiguity of the syntactic construction: *huvádhyai* is related to the frequent form *huvé*, and is also an "esoteric" substitute for the latter: "I call on them, and at the same time: let them be called by me" [118.4.27]. It is no accident that the predicative infinitive *huvádhyai* in the final marked position in *pāda b* draws into its sphere of influence the rhyming form of dative singular feminine *śvetanā́yai* (from *śvetanā́*–"brightening, clearing up, dawn," root *śvit-* "to be white," "to be bright") which, according to Renou, here acquires a semi-infinitival sense: "pour éclairer" means "pour marquer le blanchissement (de la nuit)."[122]

The predicative infinitives, especially when used without any negation, are part of somewhat unclear syntactic constructions containing various possibilities of interpretation, as has been illustrated by the predicative dative infinitives. The same applies to other infinitival structures. Clear cases of the predicative infinitive are rare, for example: *ījānám íd dyaúr gūrtā́vasur / ījānám bhū́mir abhí prabhūṣáṇi* (10.132.1) "Now the Sky of famed wealth (should help) the sacrificer, / The Earth should help the sacrificer!" The infinitive in *-(s)ani* functions here as the predicate, whose imperative sense is determined by the context. Logical subjects of action are represented by nominatives. Another example: *agním-agniṃ vaḥ samídhā duvasyata / priyám-priyaṃ vo átithiṃ gṛṇīṣáṇi / úpa vo gīrbhír amṛ́taṃ vivāsata / . . .* (6.15.6) "Honor your *Agni* with firewood time after time! / Sing (praises) of your dear guest time after time! / With your songs try to attract the immortal one! / . . . . " The infinitive *gṛṇīṣáṇi* is translated here as the second person plural imperative since forms of this grammeme are symmetrically disposed in *pādas a* and *c* (i.e., in the *pāda*-final position).

More often the infinitive does not function as an independent predicate, but constitutes a part of it, which depends on the finite verb, for example: *ahám bhuvaṃ yájamānasya rājáni* (10.49.4) "I was for the reign (infinitive) of the sacrificer" (that is, so that the sacrificer should be able to reign). Since the infinitive has not yet severed all ties with the respective case-forms in the *Ṛg Veda*, its verbal nature is not so evident in all cases. Compare, for instance, the different interpretations of 3.11.3:

agnír dhiyā́ sá cetati
ketúr yajñásya pūrvyáḥ
árthaṃ hy àsya taráṇi

"*Agni* appears through the strength of the (priests') prayer (Like) the ancient banner of sacrifice: / Indeed, his aim (lies in) overcoming (obstacles)." In this translation the infinitive *taráṇi* is rendered by a case-form of the noun. Renou's syntactical division of the stanza is practically identical, but he translates *taráṇi* by means of an infinitive: " . . . car son but est de traverser (les obstacles)" [118.12.58]. However, Geldner sees here only one sentence containing the complex predicate *cetati . . . taráṇi*: "Denn *Agni*, das erste Banner des Opfers, versteht es mit Kunst, sein Ziel zu erreichen" [74.1.348].

The Vedic *Ṛṣis* used the semantic vagueness and the weakness of syntactic links in phrases with predicative infinitives as one of the means for creating an obscure and enigmatic style.

We have been discussing problems of word-order in the Vedic sentence only in direct–or indirect–connection with our analysis of predicative constructions. Now they should be considered in a broader framework. We have already mentioned in passing[123] the basic rules determining the word-order in the verbal sentence of late Vedic prose; which is the only yard-stick at the scholars' disposal, since there are no texts closer to the *Ṛg Veda* in time. These rules belong, so to speak, to the language system, and if one tries to transfer them to the hymns they prove to be inapplicable in most cases. The reason lies not only in the chronological gap but, rather, in the peculiarities of the genre and in the purpose of the text. As Renou has observed, "The Vedic sentence reflects the facts of language (langue) only in the light of stylistic habits" [126.234]. This assertion is quite true, though it needs some expansion and supplementation.

It is impossible to define a set of rules describing the *Ṛg Veda* word-order since the sequence of words in the sentence is the result, as far as one can judge, of interaction among a number of tendencies–many of them non-linguistic. It is better to speak of sequence and juxtaposition, because it is not really word-order in the accepted sense of the word. Among the factors that influence the sequence of words in the *Ṛg Veda* the following features seem to deserve special attention:

1) The poetic character of the text presupposes a dynamic state of language, the coexistence of extreme archaisms–the heritage of the *indogermanische Dichtersprache*–with various tentative and occasional formations. The poetic function of language in this text is appreciably more important than the other functions, such as the descriptive, the appellative, etc.
2) The text has a clearly expressed, cultic communicative function: the hymn serves as a means of communication between the deity and the worshipper, who has a magical attitude towards the word;
3) The oral transmission of the text directly influenced the presence of clichés and repetitions on every level of the language;
4) The extremely elaborated flective structure of the language of this text secured the autonomous status of the word, which, in its turn, presupposes a relatively free word-order in the sentence.

First among the stylistic trends that are manifest in Vedic sentence structure is the principle of repetitions.[124] This principle, although inherent in any orally transmitted text, was widely used in the *Ṛg Veda* for stylistic purposes, as Gonda has shown. The principle of repetitions is evident on every linguistic level in this text.

The repetition of lexical units in the *Ṛg Veda* concerns a nominal stem in different case-forms, or its presence is part of a compound in the same context with its appearance as an independent case-form. The juxtaposition of various derivatives from the same root (i.e., *figura etymologica*) is quite widespread.

The hymns tend to juxtapose within a single phrase different case-forms of the same stem; those case-forms usually belong to different elementary syntactic constructions, and the contiguity of two case-forms of the same stem is not always due to rules of syntax. For example: *devó devébhir ā́ gamat* (1.1.5) "May the god come with the gods!"; *mahā́n mahī́bhir ūtíbhiḥ saraṇyán* (3.1.19) "The great one hastening with great supports;" *prá te agnáyo 'gníbhyo váraṃ níḥ . . . śośucanta . . .* (7.1.4)

"These bonfires (are) better than (other) bonfires . . . (they) glare brightly;" *séd agnír agnī́ṁr áty astv anyā́n* (7.1.14) "Let this one bonfire surpass the other bonfires!" The adjective *anyā́n*, an attribute of *agnī́n*, here ends the phrase, regardless of every rule of syntax, just so that two case-forms of *agní* should be juxtaposed; *yád indra rā́dho ásti te / mā́ghonam maghavattama* (8.54.5) "When, O *Indra*, thou hast a gift, / A generous one, O (thou), the most generous one . . . " (where *mā́ghona-* is a stem derived from *maghávan-/maghávant-*), etc. And sometimes word repetitions follow one another as in, for example: *kárhi svit tád indra yán nṛ́bhir nṝ́n / vīraír vīrā́n nīḷáyāse jáyājī́n* (6.35.2) "When does this really happen, O *Indra*, that thou bringest together (?) men with men, heroes with heroes? Win the contests!" Repetitions of nouns placed around the juncture of two *pādas* thus make up a chiasmic figure. Upon that background the final short phrase *jáya* plus *ājī́n* in the *sandhi* sounds like a repetition, too.

According to the rules of traditional Old Indian grammar, the repetition of a nominal stem in the same case joined by the common accent upon the first word is regarded as a special type of compound–the *āmreḍita*. Such repetitions are regularly played upon in the hymns and are placed in marked positions of the metrical scheme, for example:

yajñā́-yajñā vo agnáye
girā́-girā ca dákṣase
prá-pra vayám amṛ́taṃ jātávedasam
priyám mitráṃ ná śaṃsiṣam (6.48.1)

"With each sacrifice of yours to *Agni*, / And with each praise-song to the skillful one / We want to glorify immortal *Jātavedas* like a dear friend:"[125]

samít-samit sumánā bodhy asmé
śucā́-śucā sumatíṃ rāsi vásvaḥ
ā́ deva devā́n yajáthāya vakṣi
sákhā sákhīn sumánā yakṣy agne (3.4.1)

"With each log (of the fire) be (more) favorable to us! / With each blaze of flame transmit *Vasu*'s favor (to us)! / O god, bring the gods to the sacrifice! / Honor the friends like a friend, being favorable (thyself), O *Agni*!"

Composites of the *tatpuruṣa* type that have *-pati* as their second element ("lord, master of something") are quite often juxtaposed with the genitive case plural (sometimes singular) of the stem which constitutes the first element of that *tatpuruṣa*. For example: *rayipátī rayīṇā́ṃ* (2.9.4) "the lord-of-riches (nominative case singular) of the riches (genitive case plural);" *vásupate vásūnām* (3.30.19) "O lord-of-goods (vocative) of the goods (genitive case plural);" or *vásor índraṃ vásupatiṃ* (1.9.9) "*Indra*, the master-of-goods (accusative case singular) of the goods (genitive case singular);" *viśpátiṃ viśā́ṃ* (10.92.1) "The lord-of-tribes (accusative case singular) of the tribes (genitive case plural)." The same construction, though quite rare, is also attested for *tatpuruṣas* with other second elements, for example: *ṛtupā́ ṛtūnā́m* (5.12.3) "the keeper-of-sacrificial-times (nominative case singular) of the sacrificial-times (genitive case plural)." Such a tautological phrase, typical of poetic speech with its tendency to use redundant forms of expression, should also be regarded as a kind of lexical repetition.

Sometimes a whole stanza is built around the repetition of a single lexeme, for example:

> *úlūkayātuṃ śuśulū́kayātuṃ*
> *jahí śváyātum utá kókayātum*
> *suparṇáyātum utá gŕ̥dhrayātuṃ*
> *dr̥ṣádeva prá mr̥ṇa rákṣa indra* (7.104.22)

"(Him), the owl-sorcerer, the screech-owl-sorcerer, / Kill (him), the dog-sorcerer and the duck-sorcerer! / (Him), the eagle-sorcerer and the hawk-sorcerer / –Grind, O *Indra*, the *rakṣas*, as a millstone (grinds grains)!" This stanza from the magic spell that concludes Book 7 is wholly built upon repetitions of lexemes, grammatical forms and isomorphic word-groups. But the most frequent type of repetition is the *figura etymologica* attested in the *Rig Veda* in every possible variety of form. The hymns present the fullest possible set of nominal case-forms in combinations with verbs or other nouns derived from the same root. For instance, the most common combinations with verb-forms are the following: verb[126] plus nominative case: *dviṣó yuyotu yū́yuviḥ* (5.50.3) "Let the remover remove the enemies;" *agníṃ vr̥ṇānā́ vr̥ṇate kavíkratum* (5.11.4) "Choosing *Agni*, they choose him who has the gift of poetry" (literally) "Those choosing *Agni* choose . . . "); verb plus accusative case: *sunvanti sómaṃ* (3.30.1) "They press *Soma*;" verb plus instrumental case: *átyā hiyānā́ ná hetŕ̥bhir* . . . (9.13.5) "Like horses driven by the drivers;" verb plus dative case: *yáthā prásūtā savitúḥ savā́ya* (1.113.1) "As (she herself) is incited to life through *Savitar*'s incentive . . . " (literally " . . . incited through the incitement of the Inciter . . . "); verb plus locative case: *śáye śayā́su* (3.55.4) "He rests in the resting (mothers)."

Most typical of noun combinations are constructions which govern those cases that are not used (or very seldomly used) in verbal combinations, namely: ablative case plus noun:[127] *yá ugrébhyaś cin ójīyāñ / chū́rebhyaś cic chū́ratarah* (9.66.17) "Who is even stronger than the strong ones, / Even braver than the brave ones;" genitive case plus noun: *ugrā́ṇām ójiṣṭhaḥ* (9.66.16) "the strongest of the strong ones;" *uṣáso vyùṣṭiśu* (2.34.12) "at the dawnings of the dawn." There are also constructions of agreement between adjectives and substantives derived from the same root, for example: *śáviṣṭhaṃ na ā́ bhara śūra śáva / ójiṣṭham ójo abhibhūta ugrám* (6.19.6) "Bring us, O hero, the strongest strength, / The mightiest mighty might, O (thou) surpassing (everyone)!" Each *pāda* here contains three words from the same root: *śáviṣṭham–śūra–śávas* and *ójiṣṭham–ójo–ugrám*. The same construction can be used predicatively, for example: *ninditā́ro níndyāso bhavantu* (5.2.6) "Let the despisers be despised!"

Various types of *figura etymologica* as well as repetitions in general were obviously regarded as distinguished marks of artful style, judging by their frequency and lexical density in some stanzas, for example: *mádhvā mādhvī mádhu vām pruṣāyan* (4.43.5) "They sprinkle your mead with mead, O (you), mead-lovers, . . . ;" *ayáṃ rocayad arúco rucānó* (6.39.4) "Giving light, he lit up the lightless (worlds);" *śrudhī́ hávam ā́ huvató huvānó* (6.21.10) "Having been called, hear the call of the one calling (thee)!"

Derivational affixes–prefixes, suffixes–can also be played upon in such repetitions, and words that contain them can take up marked symmetrical positions in the respective *pādas* as, for example, the suffix *-tar-*: *nicetā́ro hí marúto gṛṇántam / praṇetā́ro yájamānasya mánma* (7.57.2) "Indeed, the *Maruts* notice the eulogizer; / They lead forward the sacrificer's thought" (literally "The noticers . . . the leaders"); the suffix *-enya-*: *ābhūṣéṇyaṃ vo maruto mahitvanáṃ / didṛkṣéṇyaṃ sū́ryasyeva cákṣaṇam* (5.55.4) "Worthy of honor (is) your greatness, O *Maruts*, / Worthy of gazes like the sun's appearance;" the suffix *-ka-*: *nahí vo ásty arbhakó / dévāso ná kumārakáḥ* (8.30.1) "Not one of you is small, / O gods, not one a little child;" the suffix *-tama-*:

tvám agne sáhasā sáhantamaḥ
śuṣmíntamo jāyase devátātaye
rayír ná devátātaye
śuṣmíntamo hí te mádo
dyumíntama utá krátuḥ
ádha smā te pári caranty ajara
śruṣṭīvā́no nā́jara (1.127.9)

"Thou (art), O *Agni*, the strongest in strength, / The most violent; thou art born for serving the gods, / Like wealth, for serving the gods, / Indeed, thy intoxication (is) the most violent, / And (thy) spiritual power (is) the most brilliant. / That is why they serve thee, O unaging one, / Like servants, O unaging one."

Sometimes, too, there are repetitions of adverbial suffixes, for example, *-vat*: *eté vadanti śatávat sahásravad* . . . (10.94.2) "They speak in a hundred ways, a thousand ways;" *-āt*: *prā́ktād ápāktād adharā́d údaktād / abhí jahi rakṣásaḥ párvatena* (7.104.19) "From in front, from behind, from below, from above– / Strike the *rakṣases* with the mountain!"

Repetitions of derivational prefixes are played upon in a similar manner; most frequent are the adjectival prefix *su-* "good, beautiful" and the negative *a-*, for example: *sváśvo agne suráthaḥ surā́dhā / éd u vaha suhavíṣe jánāya* (4.2.4) "O *Agni*, (thou) with beautiful horses, with a beautiful chariot, with beautiful gifts– / Bring (them), then, to the man with beautiful libations!";

> *átr̥pṇuvantaṃ víyatam abudhyám*
> *ábudhyamānaṃ suṣupāṇám indra*
> *saptá práti praváta āśáyānam*
> *áhiṃ vájreṇa ví riṇā aparván* (4.19.3)

"(Him) the insatiable stretched out serpent, / Who is not to be awakened, the wakelessly sleeping (one), O *Indra*, / (The one) sprawled over seven streams,– / (Him) thou hast smitten with the *vajra* upon (his) jointless (mass)." Here the repetition of the negative prefix *a-* is a means of organizing the stanza from both the semantic and the formal points of view. Since they mark both the beginning and the end of the stanza as well as the boundary between *pādas a* and *b*, the words around the boundary between *pādas c* and *d*– . . . *āśáyānam / áhiṃ* . . . , which also begin with *ā̆*, though they have quite a different morphemic structure, are perceived as sound-echoes of the words with this negative prefix *a-*.

Repetitions of inflexional elements are manifest in the hymns through the formation of strings of identical case-forms and attributive appositions. The greatest difficulties present themselves in the actual division of the strings of accusatives (see below) because of the frequent absence of any criterion for their classification as theme or rheme. This absence is caused, in turn, by the absence of clear-cut semantic boundaries between direct object accusatives, and predicative and final accusatives. But the cyclization of accusatives is the most frequent case.

All other cases can also be repeated, forming strings, but the relations among members of such strings are usually much simpler than those among accusatives. As a rule, such relations are merely enumerative, with the exception of participial phrases (absolute locative case and absolute genitive case), but these phrases are made up of only two members. Nominal forms in these strings are sometimes arranged according to the flexion-type when a single case-grammeme is expressed differently depending on the nominal stem-class; sometimes they alternate in forming groups, and sometimes they are juxtaposed based on semantic similarity or semantic contrast. Long strings of words in the same case give the impression of rhythmed lists: compare, for example, 10.65:

agnír índro váruṇo mitró aryamā́
vāyúḥ pūṣā́ sárasvatī sajóṣasaḥ
ādityā́ víṣṇur marútaḥ svàr bṛhát
sómo rudró áditir bráhmaṇas pátiḥ (1)

indrāgnī́ vṛtrahátyeṣu sátpatī
mithó hinvānā́ tanvā̀ sámokasā
antárikṣam máhy ā́ paprur ójasā
sómo ghṛtaśrī́r mahimā́nam īráyan (2)

(1) "*Agni, Indra, Varuṇa, Mitra, Aryaman, / Vāyu, Pūṣan,* the unanimous *Sarasvatīs, /* the *Ādityas, Viṣṇu,* the *Maruts,* high Heaven. / *Soma, Rudra, Aditi, Brahmaṇaspati*"

(2) "*Indra* and *Agni*, the true lords in the battles against *Vṛtra*, / mutually encouraging (each other), living together, / They filled the great aerial space with (their) strength, / (And) *Soma* the ghee-ornamented, setting in motion (their) greatness." The momentum of the theonyms enumerated in this hymn is so great that in stanza 9 the first half-stanza continues the run of nominatives. But then the syntactic link is broken off (the anacoluthon), and the construction is wholly changed in the second half-stanza:

parjányāvā́tā vṛṣabhā́ purīṣíṇā-
indravāyū́ váruṇo mitró aryamā́
devā́m̐ ādityā́m̐ áditiṃ havāmahe
yé pā́rthivāso divyā́so apsú yé

"*Parjanya* and *Vāta*, the two fructifying bulls, / *Indra* and *Vāyu, Varuṇa, Mitra, Aryaman,*– / The gods *Ādityas* (and) *Aditi*–(them) we invoke, / (All those) who (are) terrestrial, celestial (and those) who (are) in the waters."

In the following example from hymn 2.21 the repetitions of datives are combined with lexical repetitions and the datives themselves are grouped according to flexion-types, thus forming a certain pattern of repetitions:

viśvajíte dhanajíte svarjíte
satrājíte nṛjíta urvarājíte
aśvajíte gojíte abjíte bhara-
índrāya sómaṃ yajatā́ya haryatám (1)

abhibhúve 'bhibhaṅgā́ya vanvaté
'ṣāḷhāya sáhamānāya vedháse
tuvigráye váhnaye duṣṭárītave
satrāsā́he náma índrāya vocata (2)

(1) "To the one winning everything, winning booty, winning the sky, / To the one winning always, winning men, winning arable land, / To the one winning horses, winning cows, winning waters–bring / To *Indra* the oblation-worthy, the desirable *Soma*!"

(2) "(To him), surpassing (everyone), the breaker-through, the subjugator, / (To him), the never-overpowered yet overpowering (one), the arranger, / (To him), the devourer, the hardly-overpowered charioteer, / To the ever-overcoming *Indra* declare reverence!" In these strings of datives–besides the play on variants of the same flexion and derivations of the same root–the words are combined on the basis of consonance (for example, in 2*a* the play upon *-bh-*, and then upon *-ān-*/*-an-*) or of semantic contrast (*a-*: *áṣāḷhāya sáhamānāya*).

Such case-repetitions are not rare within the limits of repeated isomorphic syntagms (or "balanced structures," as Gonda calls them). Such are, for instance, the repetitions of locatives at 1.114.8: *mā́ nas toké tánaye mā́ na āyaú / mā́ no góṣu mā́ no áśveṣu rīriṣaḥ* "Do not harm our children (or) grandchildren, nor our life-span, / Nor our cows, nor our horses!" Among these repetitions the combination of the stems *toká-* and *tánaya-* is firmly established and can be considered a stereotyped phrase. Such clichés often occur in strings of repeated case forms. Compare, for example, the chain of ablatives in 4.21.3:

ā́ yātv índro divá ā́ pṛthivyā́
makṣū́ samudrā́d utá vā púrīṣāt
svàrṇarād ávase no marútvān
parāváto vā sádanād ṛtásya

"May *Indra* come from the sky, from the earth, / Or speedily–from the ocean, from the (heavenly) source, / From the solar space (may he come) to help us, together with the *Maruts*, / Or from afar, from the seat of the Law." In this sequence of ablatives the combination *divá ā́ pṛthivyā́ḥ* is a variety of stereotyped phrase whose two members may be also used in some other case; moreover, they form a *dvandva* compound *dyā́vāpṛthivī́*, the name of the dual deity Sky-and-Earth.

Repetitions of instrumentals give rise to a great formal and semantic variety of strings and stylistic figures. For instance, there are simple enumerations, like those quoted above: *agníṃ yajadhvaṃ havíṣā tánā girā́*

(2.2.1) "Honor *Agni* with a libation, with a continuous song!" Such repetitions can serve as the foundation for a stanza, and then they appear in metrically marked positions, often as part of balanced syntactic structures, for example:

yajñébhir yajñávāhasaṃ
somébhiḥ somapā́tamam
hótrābhir índraṃ vāvṛdhur vy ā̀naśuḥ (8.12.20)

"With sacrifices–(him), attracted by sacrifices, / With *Soma* juices–(him), the best *Soma* drinker, / With sacrificial gifts they strengthened *Indra*. They succeeded."

Sometimes a whole hymn is built upon the anaphoric repetitions of instrumentals in balanced structures. Thus the hymn to the *Aśvins* (1.112) of 25 stanzas is based upon isomorphic compound sentences with attributive clauses beginning with *yá-*. The stanza scheme of this hymn may be rendered in this way: "With (the supports) with which you call forth the goods for the worshipper, with the same supports come hither, O *Aśvins*!" This scheme is present in *pādas c-d* of stanzas 1-3 and–wholly–in stanzas 4-23; see, for example, stanza 6:

yā́bhir ántakaṃ jásamānam ā́raṇe
bhujyúṃ yā́bhir avyathíbhir jijinváthuḥ
yā́bhiḥ karkándhuṃ vayyàṃ ca jínvathas
tā́bhir ū ṣú ūtíbhir aśvinā́ gatam

"With (the supports with which you revived) *Antaka*, lingering in the precipice, / With the unshakeable (supports) with which you revived *Bhujyu*, / With which you are reviving *Karkandhu* and *Vayya*,– / With these supports come hither, O *Aśvins*!"

The two concluding stanzas of the hymn are built along different lines (compare the tendency to end a hymn with a stanza in a different metre); in the final stanza 25 there is again a play on instrumentals but the principle is quite different. Here are *pādas a-b* of the stanza: *dyúbhir aktúbhiḥ pári pātam asmā́n / áriṣṭebhir aśvinā saúbhagebhiḥ* "By day and by night protect us on all sides, O *Aśvins*, with indestructible luck!" In *pāda a* the instrumentals have a temporal, semi-adverbial meaning, and in *pāda b* they denote the instrument of action. With such a variety of meanings, this case is often ambiguously interpreted in repetitions, for example:

vayáṃ śū́rebhir ástṛbhir
índra tváyā yujā́ vayám
sāsahyā́ma pṛtanyatáḥ (1.8.4)

"Together with brave archers, / O *Indra*, together with thee (as) an ally we / Want to overcome the hostile ones!"

The second instrumental in *pāda b*, which permits a predicative transformation, differs in meaning from the other sociative instrumental forms.

Genitive case-forms have a less important part to play in such repetitions because the genitive is the only case that is chiefly adnominal. Its use with verbs is very limited, and the repetitions of balanced structures are mostly based upon verbal predicates governing various cases. An example of this kind can be seen in the verb *kar-/kir-* "to recollect with praises" which governs the genitive:

dadhikrā́vṇa íd u carkirāma
víśvā ín mā́m uṣásaḥ sūdayantu
apā́m agnér uṣásaḥ sū́ryasya
bṛ́haspáter āṅgirasásya jiṣṇóḥ (4.40.1)

"Now we shall remember *Dadhikrāvan*, praising (him),– / Let all the dawns prepare me (for this)–(We shall also be remembering) the waters, *Agni*, *Uṣas*, *Sūrya*, / *Bṛhaspati*, the victorious *Aṅgiras*." Genitives in repetitions are usual in nominal constructions, for example: *sómasya rā́jño váruṇasya dhármaṇi* / *bṛ́haspáter ánumatyā u śármaṇi* (10.167.3) "According to the prescriptions of king *Soma* (and) *Varuṇa*, / Under the protection of *Bṛhaspati* (and) *Anumatī* . . . . "

One way of juxtaposing forms in the same case is through attraction by case, that is, the acquisition by a noun of the case of the neighboring noun, in defiance of the semantics. This phenomenon is quite widespread in the *Ṛg Veda*, especially for the dative as the most frequent infinitive type, which regularly causes a dative form of the dependent noun (even when the semantics require a genitive or an accusative form), for example: *índraṃ vṛtrā́ya hántave . . . úpa bruve* (3.37.5) "I appeal to *Indra* (accusative case) for killing (dative infinitive) of *Vṛtra* (dative case) (literally "for killing for *Vṛtra*"); *máhi śaviṣṭha nas kṛdhi* / *saṃcákṣe bhujé asyaí* (1.127.11) "Create for us the great one, O mightiest one, / So that (we) should see (dative infinitive) him (dative case) and enjoy (dative infinitive)!" (literally "for seeing for enjoying for him"); *ā́raik pánthāṃ yā́tave sū́ryāya* (1.113.16) "She cleared the way so that the sun should move" (literally "for moving for the sun").

There are examples of case-attraction with other types of infinitives, for instance, with the ablative: *druhó riṣáḥ sampṛ́caḥ pāhi sūrī́n* (2.35.6) "Guard our patrons from contact (ablative infinitive) with deceit (ablative case), with injury (ablative case)" (literally "from contacting from deceit from injury"), although the verb *sam* plus *parc-* requires the instrumental of the indirect object.

The phenomenon of attraction is not due exclusively to the influence of infinitives. It may also be caused by an abstract noun in the dative, with functions close to those of the infinitive, for example:

jihmaśyè cáritave maghony
ābhogáya iṣṭáye rāyá u tvam
dabhrám páśyadbhya urviyā́ vicákṣa
uṣā́ ajīgar bhúvanāni víśvā (1.113.5)

"(Him), lying prone (dative case), (she), the generous one, (incites) to movement (dative infinitive). Another one (accusative case) (she incites) to searching (dative case) for food (dative case) and wealth (dative case), / Those with poor sight (dative case)–to seeing (dative infinitive) far– / *Uṣas* has awakened all creatures."

In *pāda b* of the stanza the form *iṣṭáye* "for searching" (dative case of abstract noun *iṣṭí-*) influences the adjacent nouns in the same way as the actual infinitives in *pādas a* and *c*. Another example: *tujé nas táne párvatāḥ santu* (5.41.9) "May the mountains be (merciful) to us for extending (dative case) the offspring (dative case)." The phrase *tujé . . . táne* "for extending the offspring" Renou describes as an "asyndeton of two elements that complement one another" [115.4.61] and translates *táne* with an infinitive [115.5.20].

The attraction of datives in most cases follows the pattern of dative infinitives. But other cases can also be involved in this process; thus the accusative: *jánmeva nítyaṃ tánayaṃ juṣasva / stómam me agne tanvā̀ sujāta* (3.15.2) "Rejoice–as in the birth (accusative case) of (thine) own child (accusative case)– / With (thy) whole being in my praise (accusative case), O *Agni* the fine-born one!" In his commentary on this passage Geldner points out that the phrase *jánma–nítyaṃ tánayaṃ* is either a hendiadyoin or an asyndeton [72.1.351]. In the following example the attraction involves the instrumental case:

prá mā́trābhī ririce rócamānaḥ
prá devébhir viśváto ápratītaḥ
prá majmánā divá índraḥ pṛthivyā́ḥ
prórór mahó antárikṣād ṛjīṣī́ (3.46.3)

"In (his) dimensions (instrumental case) he, the bright one, / The irresistible in everything, surpasses the gods (instrumental case), / *Indra* (surpasses) in greatness the sky (and) the earth, / Sur(passes) the wide, great aerial space, (he), the drinker of (*Soma*) pressings." The phrase with the double instrumental in *pādas a-b*: *prá mā́trābhī ririce . . . prá devébhir . . .* is not syntactically justifiable; symmetry would lead us to expect the ablative. Here, therefore, the instrumental seems to have been attracted by case, as Geldner has suggested [74.1.387].

The tendency to juxtapose identical grammatical forms is manifest in various types of attraction, among which the most frequent is the attraction by case, and only rarely attraction by number or gender, for example: *tísro dyā́vaḥ savitúr dvā́ upásthām̐ / ékā yamásya bhúvane virāṣā́ṭ / . . .* (1.35.6) "(There are) three skies. Two (of them are) in the lap of *Savitar*. / One (is) in the world of *Yama*, (the one that is) with the heroes-victors." The original is literally "two laps of *Savitar*," the result of a double attraction by number and case. Another example of a combined attraction by case and by number:

> *sá hótā yásya ródasī cid urvī́*
> *yajñám-yajñam abhí vṛdhé gṛṇītáḥ*
> *prā́cī adhvaréva tasthatuḥ suméke*
> *ṛtā́varī ṛtájātasya satyé* (3.6.10)

"He is the hotar-priest whose every sacrifice even the two wide halves of the world rejoicingly greet in order that it should grow. / Both of them are facing east, (they are) well-fixed–as if for a rite, devoted to the law, true, (the two mothers of *Agni*) born by the law." In the original text the nominative case dual masculine "like two rites," appears under the influence of the numerous forms of the nominative case dual feminine, in agreement with *ródasī* "the two halves of the world." Incidentally, Geldner, unlike Renou,[128] sees here only attraction by number (not by case) and translates: "Beide stehen bereit da wie das Opfer" [74.1.343].

An example of attraction by gender can be seen in the following stanzas:

> *puṣṭír ná raṇvā́ kṣitír ná pṛthvī́*
> *girír ná bhújma kṣódo ná śambhú*
> *átyo nā́jman sárgaprataktaḥ*
> *síndhur ná kṣódaḥ ká īṃ varāte* (1.65.5-6)

"Pleasant like blossoming, broad like a settlement, / Satiating like a mountain, charitable like a turbulent stream, / Like a horse on the racing track, jumping like a shot, / Like a turbulent river: Who will stop him?" This is a description of *Agni*. In these stanzas (the metre is *dvipadā virāj*) the god's epithets are enumerated in a series of comparisons, in each of which the adjective agrees in gender with the corresponding substantive, not with the name *agní-*, which is masculine. The literal translation of these *pādas* is: "Pleasant like blossoming (feminine), broad like a settlement (feminine)," etc.

Cases of formal attraction between substantives in juxtaposition are quite numerous and diverse in the *Ṛg Veda*. They testify to the strong tendency to repeat similar elements (in this instance–grammatical elements) as well as to the domination of "contextual attraction" over the grammatical system.

Repetitions of the same finite verb-forms occur far more rarely than repetitions of nominal case-forms, and the "list" of such forms is much shorter, for example:

ádribhiḥ sutáḥ pavate gábhastyor
vṛṣāyáte nábhasā vépate matī́
sá modate násate sā́dhate girā́
nenikté apsú yájate párīmaṇi (9.71.3)

"Pressed by the stones, he is purified in the (priest's) hands; / He reaches manhood thanks to the rain-cloud; he trembles thanks to the prayer. / He rejoices, he caresses, he reaches the target thanks to the song, / He washes himself in the waters–he is fully sacrificed."

From the point of view of Vedic grammar, repetitions of finite verbs are not identical with repetitions of nominal forms. The disposition of accents shows that only the first verb of the series follows the rules of phrasal accentuation, while the rest of the verbal predicates, relating to the same subject, are treated as introducing a new sentence. Old Indian grammar did not tolerate more than one verbal predicate in a single clause.

There are more frequent repetitions of finite verbs as parts of various isomorphic syntactic structures, often second person present imperatives, for example: *hatáṃ ca śátrūn yátataṃ ca mitríṇaḥ / prajā́ṃ ca dhattáṃ dráviṇaṃ ca dhattam* (8.35.12) "And kill (you two) the enemies, and unite the allies, / And give (us) progeny, and give (us) wealth!" Units of the syntactic level may also be repeated, from syntactic phrases up to whole sentences, both simple and complex [87]. In repetitions of all kinds of syntactic structures, the word-order is determined by the particular type of repetition. The word-order in the first of the structures depends upon various syntactic rules, stylistic and metrical tendencies. The following repeated "balanced structures" take their cue from the first one. They may be isomorphic with the first structure as in, for example:

sómaḥ pavate janitā́ matīnā́ṃ
janitā́ divó janitā́ pṛthivyā́ḥ
janitā́gner janitā́ sū́ryasya
janiténdrasya janitóta víṣṇoḥ (9.96.5)

"*Soma* purifies himself, the genitor of prayers. / The genitor of the Sky, the genitor of the Earth, / The genitor of *Agni*, the genitor of *Sūrya*, the genitor of *Viṣṇu* as well." In *pāda a*, *janitā́* is an apposition to the subject *sómaḥ*, and the order of members of the elementary nominal construction with the attributive genitive is determined here by reasons of meter: the reverse order–incidentally, the "normal" one according to rules of syntax–would have violated the necessary sequence of the long and short syllables in the cadence. In the following *pādas* the repeated attributive constructions in apposition are isomorphic with the corresponding construction in *pāda a*.

Sometimes repetitions of isomorphic syntactic constructions when combined with lexical repetitions create a rather capricious pattern which, in its turn, begins to dominate the word-sequence in the stanza, for example:

sád íd dhí te tuvijātásya manye
sáhaḥ sahiṣṭha turatás turásya
ugrám ugrásya tavásas távīyó
'radhrasya radhratúro babhūva (6.18.4)

"True I believe (to be) the strength in thee, O strongest one, in the victorious victor. / Terrible has become (the strength) of the terrible one, stronger than the strong, the disobedient one, helping the obedient ones."

The *Ṛg Veda* contains whole hymns in which every stanza is represented by a sentence syntactically isomorphic with all the others. This, for instance, is the structure of the spell against consumption (10.163), of six stanzas, where each one (except the final stanza, which has slight variants) wholly repeats the syntactic structure of the first stanza. See, for example, the first two stanzas:

akṣī́bhyāṃ te nā́sikābhyāṃ
kárṇābhyāṃ chúbukād ádhi
yákṣmaṃ śīrṣaṇyàṃ mastíṣkāj
jihvā́yā ví vṛhāmi te (1)

grīvā́bhyas ta uṣṇíhābhyaḥ
kī́kasābhyo anūkyā̀t
yákṣmaṃ doṣaṇyàm áṃsābhyām
bāhúbhyāṃ ví vṛhāmi te (2), etc.

(1) "Out of thine eyes (and) nostrils, / Out of the ears (and) the chin, / (This) consumption of the head, out of the brain, / Out of the tongue I tear it."

(2) "Out of thine occiput (and) cervical vertebrae, / Out of the ribs (and) the spinal ridge, / The consumption of the forearm, out of the shoulders, / Out of thine arms I tear it."

The direct-object accusative *yákṣmam* "consumption" and the following adjectival attribute are separated–in violation of the "syntactic norm"–from the verbal predicate by ablatives. Here the accusatives serve as dividers or beams that keep the balance between the ablatives on the right and on the left.

We have already discussed hymns constructed upon repetitions of isomorphic structures, compound sentences with attributive subordinate clauses with the relative pronoun *yá-* "who," "which" [compare 2.12; 1.112, etc.–see pp. 177].

If the *pāda* begins with an anaphoric repetition with a verbal predicate, such an unusual word-order may be kept up in the following *pādas*, for example:

ágachad u vípratamaḥ sakhīyánn
ásūdayat sukṛ́te gárbham ádriḥ
sasā́na máryo yúvabhir makhasyánn
áthābhavad áñgirāḥ sadyó árcan (3.31.7)

"The most inspired one came, assuming a friendly attitude. / The rock made ripe (its) fruit for the one who performs the kind deed. / The young hero attained (his aim) with the youths, assuming a warlike attitude. / And here, right away, the singing *Añgiras* appeared." Three (out of four) *pādas* end in a present participle in the nominative; here the end of the *pāda* is a weaker position than its beginning, which seems conditioned by the fixed character of its quantitative structure. Generally speaking, the anaphora is much more prevalent than the epiphora.

Strings of accusatives that depend on the transitive verb are quite widespread in the *Ṛg Veda*, and we have observed cases in which the place of the verb among these homogeneous nominal forms depends mainly upon rhythmic factors. However, there are also cases in which the verbal predicate appears outside the series of repeated forms or constructions. For example, it can stand at the very end of such a series as in 1.60.1:

váhniṃ yaśásaṃ vidáthasya ketúṃ
suprāvyā̀ṃ dūtáṃ sadyóartham
dvijánmānaṃ rayím iva praśastáṃ
rātím bharad bhṛ́gave mātaríśvā

"The famed charioteer, the banner of sacrificial distributions, / The most useful messenger, who immediately (rushes) to the target, / The twice-born one, famous like wealth,– / (This) gift *Mātariśvan* brought to the *Bhṛgu*." This stylistic figure causes the dative of the indirect object and the nominative of the subject to be "bracketed out" in violation of the normal word-order.

By contrast, in a zeugmatic repetition the verb governing a series of homogeneous case-forms stands at the head of this series as in, for example, 10.63.9:

bháreṣv índraṃ suhávaṃ havāmahe
'ṃhomúcaṃ sukṛ́taṃ daívyaṃ jánam
agním mitráṃ váruṇaṃ sātáye
bhágaṃ dyā́vāpṛthivī́ marútaḥ svastáye

"We invoke *Indra*, the one easily invoked in battles, / (Who) saves (us) from trouble, the beneficent one, (and) the divine kin: / *Agni, Mitra, Varuṇa*–for winning (happiness), / (And) *Bhaga*, the Sky and the Earth, the *Maruts*–for blessing!" Here, the first sentence in *pāda a* presents the usual construction with the final verb-predicate; all the following accusatives depend on this verb, while *pādas c* and *d* contain isomorphic constructions made up of the sequence of three accusatives and a dative of purpose.

The word-order in a sentence can also follow the pattern of chiasmic repetitions, in which the neighboring syntactic structures are made up of members in reverse order, for example: *bráhma jinvatam utá jinvataṃ dhíyo* (8.35.16) "The sacred word strengthen (you two–dual) and strengthen (dual) the prayers!" The sequence of words in two adjacent stanzas can follow the pattern of chiasmic repetitions more or less strictly as in, for example, 3.27:

īḷényo namasyàs
tirás támāṃsi darśatáḥ
sám agnír idhyate vṛ́ṣā (13)

vṛ́ṣo agníḥ sám idhyaté
'śvo ná devavā́hanaḥ
táṃ havíṣmanta īḷate (14)

(13) "Worthy of invocation, worthy of reverence, / Visible through darkness, / *Agni* is kindled, the bull.

(14) "The bull *Agni* is kindled, / Like a horse carrying the gods. / (The people) invoke him with libations."

In the adjacent *pādas* 13*c* and 14*a* the words are arranged in reverse order, though not quite consequently. Stanza 13 begins with a participial form of *īḍ-* "to invoke" while stanza 14 ends with a finite form of the same verb. The examples cited above suffice to show that in repetitions of various kinds the word-order in the sentence is primarily determined by the syntax of these repetitions and not by the syntax of the system, and this should be taken into consideration in conjunction with the dominant role of the principle of repetition in this text, which Gonda's classic work has duly stressed [87].

Phonetic tendencies that influence the word-order have already been discussed in connection with the use of sound-hints at names of the praised deities in marked positions of the metrical scheme. The "magic grammar" that we already dealt with could not help but influence the word-order in the sentence. If, for instance, the author's task was to begin each stanza with the name of the praised deity or with a pronoun correlated with it, then the rest of the words in the sentence should take into account that key-word. In practice, there are many hymns and stanzas in which the key-word is a theonym in the nominative or in the vocative at the *pāda* beginning: this does not violate the word-order which is conventionally taken as the norm. But if this theonym is in some other case, the syntax of the sentence is changed, for example:

agním ukthaír ŕ̥ṣayo ví hvayante
'gnímṃ náro yā́mani bādhitā́saḥ
agnímṃ váyo antárikṣe pátanto
'gníḥ sahásrā pári yāti gónām (10.80.5)

"The *Ṛṣis* invoke *Agni* with hymns from all sides, / Men in trouble during a campaign (invoke) *Agni*–, / birds flying in the air (invoke) *Agni*. / *Agni* makes the rounds (protecting) thousands of cows." The sequence of words in this stanza is determined by the accusative of *Agni* at the beginning of *pādas a-c* and by the zeugmatic repetitions of the construction.

Here is a similar example in which the initial position is taken up by a pronoun in most *pādas* whose referent is the deity being lauded:

tvé agne víśve amŕ̥tāso adrúha
āsā́ devā́ havír adanty ā́hūtam
tváyā mártāsaḥ svadanta āsutímṃ
tvámṃ gárbho vīrúdhāmṃ jajñiṣe śúciḥ (2.1.14)

"In thee, O *Agni*, all the immortal undeceivable / Gods taste the libated libation with (thy) mouth. / With thy help the mortals enjoy the pressed beverage. / Thou art born pure (as) the plants' offspring."

In *pādas a* and *c* the personal pronoun is placed at the beginning of the *pāda* so that the syntax of the phrase acquires an emphatic character and the relationship among the parts of the sentence is wholly changed. In *pāda d*, beginning with the nominative of the pronoun *tvám*, the word-order is preserved, since in theory, the sentence should begin with the subject.

The changes in the word-order which result from a special device of "magic grammar" (the juxtaposition of the deity's pronoun with that of the worshipper) have been treated in the preceding chapter. There is also another tendency of "magic" word-order in the *Ṛg Veda*: epithet strings (or other attributive word-combinations) that relate to the deity and alternate often with epithets relating to the worshipper. In such sequences, the syntactic links are somewhat weakened, and the description is rather static. Some examples:

prá tát te adyá śipiviṣṭa nā́ma-
aryáḥ śaṃsāmi vayúnāni vidvā́n
táṃ tvā gṛṇāmi tavásam átavyān
kṣáyantam asyá rájasaḥ parāké (7.100.5)

"Today I glorify this name of thine, / O *Śipiviṣṭa*, (the name) of the noble lord, I the expert in sacrifice. / I, the weaker one, sing the praises of thee, of the one (who is) so strong, / (of thee) who rulest far beyond the limits of this space;"

áraṃ dāśó ná mīḷhúṣe karāṇy
aháṃ devā́ya bhū́rṇayé 'nāgāḥ
ácetayad acíto devó aryó
gṛ́tsaṃ rāyé kavítaro junāti (7.86.7)

"May I serve as a slave (serves) a generous master, / I, the sinless one, (serving) the furious god! / The noble god made the unreasonable ones listen to reason. / The wiser (god) speeds the clever (man) to wealth;" *híraṇyavarṇān kakuhā́n yatásruco / brahmaṇyántaḥ śáṃsyaṃ rā́dha īmahe* (2.34.11) "Holding out the ladle to (these gods) of golden hue, the prominent ones, we pray with sacred words for the favor of (the one) worthy of glorification." One of the epithets in juxtaposition, namely, the divine epithet, can be represented by a vocative, for example: *mā́ ta énasvanto yakṣin bhujema* (7.88.6) "May we who have committed a sin not taste of thy (punishment), O overtaker!"

Such a juxtaposition of epithets establishes real contacts between the sphere of a deity and the sphere of his worshippers by linguistic means. The words in a Vedic sentence may be arranged according to a semantic feature: in a series of epithets, appositions, or isomorphic syntactic structures they are put together on the basis of semantic similarity or semantic contrast.

As Renou has noted [126.231], the style of the *Ṛg Veda* is characterized by the juxtaposition of two synonyms (or, one may add, of two words belonging to the same sphere) in the same case without a connective conjunction; asyndeton is generally quite prominent in the hymns. Some examples: *śúciḥ pāvaká ucyate sómaḥ* (9.24.7) "Pure, bright–*Soma* is called;"[129] *bṛhád vadanti madiréṇa mandínā-* . . . (10.94.4) "They speak loudly, (intoxicated) by the inebriating, enlivening (*Soma*);" *ā́ no . . . gántā . . . ṛcā́ girā́* . . . (8.27.5) "Come to us at the call of a hymn (and) a praise-song . . . !"; *vidhema . . . gīrbhír ukthaír* . . . (6.1.10) "We want to honor with praise-songs (and) praise-poems." Some of these pairs have become fixed locutions, as for example: *tokā́ya tánayāya* "for children (and) for descendants," *toké tánaye* "in children (and) in offspring," *śáṃ yós* "(for) luck and good," etc. Sometimes whole stanzas are based upon the principle of semantic similarity, for example:

abhrātáro ná yóṣaṇo vyántaḥ
patirípo ná jánayo durévāḥ
pāpā́saḥ sánto anṛtā́ asatyā́
idám padám ajanatā gabhīrám (4.5.5)

"Importunate as brotherless women, / As misbehaving wives who deceive (their) husbands, / Wanton, lawless, untruthful, / They have engendered this secret word." Words and isomorphic constructions are even more frequently juxtaposed in the sentence on the basis of semantic contrast. One may say that these stylistic figures reflect, in different ways, every fundamental opposition of the Vedic model of the universe.

Antonyms that are juxtaposed in the phrase or are played upon in the stanza can have the same stem, with the negative prefix *a-* and without it, for example:

cíttim ácittiṃ cinavad ví vidvā́n
pṛṣṭhéva vītā́ vṛjinā́ ca mártān
rāyé ca naḥ svapatyā́ya deva
dítiṃ ca rā́svā́ditim uruṣya (4.2.11)

"May he distinguish between reason and unreason as an expert / Among people, as (they do between) the straight and curved backs (of horses)! / For wealth, for fine posterity, O god, / Reward us with generosity, deliver us from nongenerosity!" The opposition *cíttim-ácittim* opens *pāda a*; both members of the opposition *dítim-áditim* open both of the rhythmic groups in *pāda d*; the opposition *vītā́-vṛjinā́*, expressed by different lexemes, is in juxtaposition in *pāda b* on the border between two rhythmic groups separated by the caesura. As a result, the whole stanza is built upon the play with semantic contrast in marked positions of the rhythmic scheme.

Ácikitvā́ñ cikitúṣaś cid átra / kavī́n pṛchāmi vidmáne ná vidvā́n

(1.164.6) "(I), the unseeing one, (ask) the seeing visionaries about it; / I, the unknowing one, ask in order to know." Here the half stanza is based upon a chiasmic repetition, yet the semantically contrasted phrases that are repeated are not isomorphic in structure.

Jīvó mṛtásya carati svadhā́bhir / ámartyo mártyenā sáyoniḥ (1.164.30) "The life-spirit of the dead one wanders as it wills. / The immortal (is) of the same womb as the mortal." In this half-stanza the former opposition is expressed by different lexemes, while the latter is expressed by the negative and the negationless forms of the same stem. In their invariant meaning both oppositions are, practically speaking, identical; in this case, the left member of the opposition, with positive semantics, can be formally expressed both by the independent lexeme *jīvá-* "living, alive;" masculine "living creature," "spirit of life," and by a stem with the negative prefix *a-* –*ámartya-* "immortal" (= "living"), and this reflects the general structural and semantical features of antonymic oppositions in the *Ṛg Veda* [8.57].

Devayánn íd ádevayantam abhy àsat / . . . / yájvéd áyajyor ví bhajāti bhójanam (2.26.1b, c) "Only the one devoted to gods shall overcome the one who is not devoted to gods. / . . . / Only the one sacrificing (to gods) shall share the property of the nonsacrificer." The even *pādas* of this stanza contain symmetrically placed oppositions of antonyms, and these oppositions are quite close semantically. In the second opposition the respective stems also have different suffixes: *yájvan-* –*ayajyu-*.

This structural correlation of stems also appears in the semantic opposition of two members. They may be antonyms, as in the example just cited, or they may be contrasted in a single distinctive feature, for example: *índram ajuryáṃ jaráyantam . . . havāmahe* (2.16.1) "We invoke . . . *Indra*, not growing old (himself, but) making (others) old;" *prahetā́ram áprahitam / . . . / iṣkartā́ramániṣkṛtaṃ . . . índram ávase havāmahe* (8.99.7-8) "We call on *Indra* for help . . . on the encouraging one who needs no encouragement, the healing one who needs no healing (himself);" *bahū́ni me ákṛtā kártvāni* (4.18.2) "Many (deeds) yet undone must be done by me;" *antár jātéṣūtá yé jánitvāḥ* (4.18.4) "Among those who are born and (those) who are to be born;" *yád bhūtáṃ yác ca bhávyam* (10.90.2) "Whatever has been and whatever will be."

Some stylistic figures consist in repetitions of forms which are opposed to each other as antonyms; they are made up of a verbal form (finite or participial) and a nominal form, governed by the verbal form and derived from the same root but having the negative prefix *a-*, for example: *tváṃ hí ṣmā cyāváyann ácyutāni* (3.30.4) "Since thou (art the one), shaking the unshakeable, . . ;" *prém ā́yus tārīd átīrṇam* (8.79.6) "Let him prolong the life-span yet unlived!" (literally "May he let cross the (yet) uncrossed . . . ").

The most general and most cardinal opposition in the Vedic model of the universe–*ṛtá-* "just;" "law," "order:" *ánṛta-* "unjust;" "lawlessness," "chaos"–is conveyed by the same formal structure: the stem without *a-* versus the stem with *a-*. Compare the play upon members of this opposition in rhythmic repetitions: *kád va ṛtáṃ kád ánṛtam* (1.105.5) "What is just, what is unjust according to you?"; or: *ṛtám píparty ánṛtaṃ ní tārīt* (1.152.3) "He safeguards law, suppresses lawlessness."

There is also widespread employment of the juxtaposition based on a semantic contrast of words (that is, of different lexemes) or their repetitions within balanced syntactic structures. These repetitions and formulas, some exceptionally archaic in character, most clearly express some of the essential oppositions inherent in the Vedic model of the universe, such as the general opposition between *devá-* "god" and *mártya-* "mortal":

távāhám agna ūtíbhir
nédiṣṭhābhiḥ saceya jóṣam ā́ vaso
sádā devásya mártyaḥ (8.19.28)

"Through thee, O *Agni*, I would like to enjoy (thy) closest supports for (my) pleasure, O *Vasu*, / Always, (I), the mortal–through the god!"

The juxtaposition of these two words–*devásya mártyaḥ*–and their removal outside the sentence into what is actually a separate *pāda*, can be explained by the fact that these words are members of a very important semantic opposition. There is a "magic" juxtaposition of the god's and the worshipper's pronouns at the beginning of the stanza, which also modifies the usual order of words in the sentence. The same formal characteristics can be observed in sentences which express some particular variants of the general opposition, such as: "wise" (god) versus "foolish" (mortal), for example: *sá mā dhī́raḥ pā́kam atrā́ viveśa* (1.164.21) "There he, the wise one, entered me, the foolish one."

Frequently, the members of such semantic oppositions are played upon at the syntactic level so that they form a kind of rhythmic nucleus of the sentence. For instance, terms of spatial orientation seem to play such a role in the following sentences: *ná dakṣiṇā́ ví cikite ná savyā́ / ná prācī́nam ādityā nótá paścā́* (2.27.11) "I cannot see clearly on the right, nor on the left, / Nor from in front, O *Ādityas*, nor from behind;" *yó no dūré aghá́śaṃso yó ánty / ágne mā́kiṣ ṭe vyáthir ā́ dadharṣīt* (4.4.3) "Who(ever) speaks ill of us in the distance, who(ever) (does it) near by, / O *Agni*, may no one dare interfere with thy hurling!"; *kvà svid asyá rájaso mahás páraṃ / kvā́varam maruto yásmin āyayá* (1.168.6) "Now, where (is) in that vast space the distant (thing), / Where (is the thing) near by, O *Maruts*, (in that space) where you have arrived?" These sentences are of quite different types (negative, affirmative, and interrogative), but they share the rhythmic principle of balanced repeated structures in which the semantic centers are represented by oppositions of spatial orientation.

When members of the most multifarious semantic oppositions are somewhat marked, by being juxtaposed at the beginning of a *pāda* or by occupying symmetrical positions in balanced structures, they are able to determine the position of all the other words in the sentence: *yuvám páya usríyāyām adhattam / pakvám āmā́yām áva pū́rvyaṃ góḥ* (1.180.3) "The two of you have placed milk in the cow, / The boiled–in the raw, the ancient (wealth) of the cow; *stávā nú ta indra pūrvyā́ mahā́ny / utá stavāma nū́tanā kṛtā́ni* (2.11.6) "Now I want to extol thy former great (deeds) O *Indra*, / And we also want to extol (thy) present deeds," etc.

In sum, the order and sequence of words in the Vedic sentence depends not so much on the rules of syntax but rather on a complex interplay of various stylistic, rhythmic, communicative, and other tendencies.

In the syntax of the simple sentence in the *Ṛg Veda*, participial attributes of substantives play a special role. Though they do not formally differ in any way from adjectival attributes, they can still imply a meaning which can be discovered by syntactic means, that is, by transformations. A correct interpretation of very complicated instances is possible only when a wider mythological context is involved in the discussion. The decision in such cases requires great caution, as we are dealing with a kind of unmanifest character of the language system, this time on the syntactic level, and there still remain many cases that admit of no unique interpretations.

In describing the semantics of participles that function as attributes in agreement, we will arrange them along a continuum, starting with obvious cases in which the participle is equivalent to a subordinate clause (temporal, conditional, explanatory, and so on) and ending with equally obvious cases in which a participial attribute is functionally identical with an adjectival attribute. The most interesting cases occupy the intermediate part of the range.

Phrases usually termed locativus absolutus are rather easy to classify. They consist of a noun (or a pronoun) and a participle that agrees with it; both are in the locative case and function as a temporal or conditional clause, for example:

yáḥ snī́hitīṣu pūrvyáḥ
saṃjagmānā́su kṛṣṭíṣu
árakṣad dāśúṣe gáyam (1.74.2)

"(*Agni*), who was in the front (ranks) in the battles / When the peoples clashed, / Saved the domestic belongings for him who honors (*Agni*)" (literally " . . . among the clashing peoples . . . "); *uṣā́ uchántī samidhānė́ agnā́ / udyán sū́rya urviyā́ jyótir aśret* (1.124.1) "When the fire is kindled, the blazing *Uṣas* / (And) the rising *Sūrya* spread (their) light into the distance" (literally " . . . at the fire being kindled . . . "). In this half-stanza there are two more participial attributes in the nominative: *uchántī* and *udyán*, both agreeing with their substantives and functioning as adjectival attributes, while their position, preposed or postposed, plays no role.

The absolute character of absolute genitive phrases, consisting of a noun in the genitive with a participle in agreement is less obvious. They seem to have the same functions as the subordinate clauses that correspond to the locative absolute, for example: *mahás te sató ví caranty arcáyo / diví spṛśanti bhānávaḥ* (1.36.3) "When thou growest big the tongues of (thy) flame stretch far out / The rays touch the sky!" (literally "Of thee, growing big . . . "); *bráhmaṇas pátir abhavad yathāvaśáṃ / satyó manyúr máhi kármā kariṣyatáḥ* (2.24.14) "*Brahmaṇaspati*'s ardor found its outlet according to his will / When he was going to perform (his) great feats" (literally " . . . with him going to perform . . . ").

The genitive absolute in the *Ṛg Veda* is often on the borderline between an absolute phrase and a syntagma functioning as part of a simple sentence. Although the locative absolute is more autonomous than the genitive absolute, one can, nevertheless, find a number of contexts wherein the absolute nature of the two juxtaposed locatives (the nominal and the participial) is far from obvious, for example:

sutá ít tváṃ nímiśla indra sóme
stóme bráhmaṇi śasyámāna ukthé
yád vā yuktā́bhyām maghavan háribhyām
bíbhrad vájram bāhvór indra yā́si (6.23.1)

"It is to the pressed *Soma* that thou art bound, O *Indra*, / To the praise, to the prayer, to the uttered hymn, / When, O generous one, on a pair of harnessed horses / Thou art riding, O *Indra*, holding the *vajra* in (thy) hands, ... "

The sequence of locatives, with the attributive participle and the noun –*sutá . . . sóme* and *śasyámāna ukthé*–apparently do not constitute absolute phrases, and the substantive locatives are governed by the adjective *nímiśla-*.

We have discussed the double accusative constructions with verbs of speaking, learning, perceiving, etc. If one of the accusatives is represented by a participle of a verb of thinking or perceiving, the phrase is close in meaning to the absolute accusative and close in function to an explanatory subordinate clause. An example, with the verb *paś-* "to see":

kím aṅgá tvā bráhmaṇaḥ soma gopā́m
kím aṅgá tvāhur abhiśastipā́m naḥ
kím aṅgá naḥ paśyasi nidyámānān
brahmadvíṣe tápuṣiṃ hetím asya (6.52.3)

"Why, then (do they call) thee (accusative case), O *Soma*, the guardian (accusative case) of prayer? / Why, then, do they call thee (accusative case) our guardian (accusative case) from evil speech? / Why, then, dost thou look at our reviling? / Hurl the heated javelin at the hater of prayer!" *Pāda c* may be literally rendered as "Why, then, dost thou look at us (accusative case) (who are) being reviled (accusative case)?" In this stanza the phrase is the third in a row of double accusatives with verbs of particular semantics. It differs from the first two in that the second accusative is a participle, not a substantive, and so it acquires a meaning close to an explanatory subordinate clause.

yátredā́nīm páśyasi jātavedas
tíṣṭhantam agna utá vā cárantam
yád vāntárikṣe pathíbhiḥ pátantaṃ
tám ástā vidhya śárvā śíśānaḥ (10.87.6)

"(And) where now thou seest, O *Jātavedas*, / That he is standing, O *Agni*, or he is wandering, / Or (that) he is flying (along his) ways in the air, / Pierce him as an archer (pierces) with a sharpened arrow!" The literal translation of the phrase under discussion is: "Thou wilt see him standing or wandering or flying."

An example concerning the verb *śru-* "to hear:" *evā́ hí tvā́m ṛtuthā́ yātáyantam / maghā́ víprebhyo dádataṃ śṛṇómi* (5.32.12) "Indeed, I also hear that thou rewardest in time, / That thou givest liberally to the inspired singers." Compare the literal translation of the construction: "I hear thee rewarding, liberally giving," although one would rather expect the accusatives to be predicative, i.e., "I hear about thee, the rewarding one . . . . " The exact meaning of the phrase is reflected in its transformation into an explanatory subordinate clause.

An example of the verb *man-* "to think," "to consider:" *kó maṃsate sántam índraṃ kó ánti* (1.84.17) "Who will think that *Indra* exists? Who (will think), that he is near by?"; and the literal translation: "Who thinks of *Indra* being?" It is significant that although Renou believes that only the locative absolute is attested in the *Ṛg Veda*, and although he sees in the genitive absolute and the accusative absolute parts of the simple sentence, not absolute phrases [120.355], he still translates this *pāda* in the following manner: "Qui se demanderait si Indra existe, (s'il est) près (de nous)?" [118.17.33].

Áśvād iyāyéti yád vádanty / ójaso jātám utá manya enam (10.73.10) "When they say, 'He went out of the horse', I believe that he is born of strenth" (literally "I consider him born of strength"). Judging by the context, *pāda b* is to be understood as oblique speech in contrast to direct speech in *pāda a*; however, oblique speech has not yet been fully developed in the *Ṛg Veda*.

Lastly, the simple sentence employs attributive constructions that consist of a noun and a participle in concord with it (in the nominative), and this noun functions as the subject. Such constructions are quite close in meaning to various subordinate clauses–temporal, conditional, explaṇatory, etc. From the formal point of view they do not differ in any way from attributive constructions with an adjectival attribute; yet they contain an additional shade of meaning that is revealed only by means of a transformation. The pre- or postposed place of such a participial attribute plays no decisive part in semantic interpretations. Some examples: *śíśāno agníḥ krátubhiḥ sámiddhaḥ / sá no dívā sá riṣáḥ pātu náktam* (10.87.1) "Sharpening himself, after he is kindled with (certain) intentions, / May this *Agni* protect us from harm by day and by night!" Compare the literal translation of the first *pāda*: "The sharpening (himself) *Agni* with intentions kindled." This half-stanza describes the usual circulation between the worshipper and his deity when, at first, the worshipper honors the god (here, *Agni*), and the god is strengthened as a result (here, sharpened); in response, the deity presents the worshipper with gifts and defends him (in this case–protects him from harm). Geldner offers the following translation: "*Agni* soll sich scharf machen, nachdem er mit bestimmten Absichten entzündet ist, und uns am Tag und des Nachts vor Schaden bewahren" [74.3.277]. His translation makes explicit the correlation between the theme and the rheme: one of the attributes, the participle *śíśāno*, belongs to the rheme, and the other–*sámiddhaḥ*–to the theme.

Quite often this construction appears in a truncated form in which only the participial attribute is in evidence, while the main noun (or pronoun) is absent; the presence of a subject (especially, a personal pronoun) with a finite verb is optional, for example: *jyótir vṛṇīta támaso vijānánn / āré syāma duritā́d abhī́ke* (3.39.7) "He has chosen light against darkness, knowing the difference. / May we be far from trouble at the decisive moment!" The literal translation of *pāda a* is as follows: "Knowing the difference [he] has chosen light against darkness." Geldner in his translation makes explicit–as is his wont–the deep syntactic connections basic to this construction: "Das Licht zog er dem Dunkel vor, da er den Unterschied kennt"

[74.1.382]; however, Renou keeps to the original, without uncovering the nonapparent syntactic links: "Il choisit la lumiere (par evincement) des ténèbres, lui qui discrimine . . . " [118.17.82].

In the truncated variant of this construction the subject is often expressed by the vocative (not the nominative), and in that case the verbal predicate is in the second person present, for example: *gṛṇānā́ indra stuvaté váyo dhāḥ* (4.17.18) "Praised, O *Indra*, thou givest the life-force to the eulogizer" which can mean: "After being praised, thou . . . " or "If thou art praised . . . . "

Only a wider syntactic context can determine the attributive or predicative nature of the construction in concord: noun (pronoun) in the nominative plus participle. An example of this can be seen in the predicative construction in the next stanza of the same hymn (4.17.19): *stutá índro maghávā yád dha vṛtrā́ / bhū́rīṇy éko apratī́ni hanti* "Glorified (is) the generous *Indra* (for the fact) that he alone / Breaks down numerous obstacles (that are) unequalled."

Such constructions with the nominative are very frequent in the *Ṛg Veda*,[130] in part because the *Ṛg Veda* prefers the participle perfect active voice in concord over absolutives when expressing an accessory action that precedes the main action, for example: *cakṛvā́ṃsa ṛbhavas tád apṛchata* (1.161.4) "Having done (this) you, the *Ṛbhus*, asked this (question) . . . . "

But on the whole, the constructions in concord that have been treated here, with a participle and a noun/pronoun, are part of the syntactic level on which the unmanifest character of the language system can be actualized only within the framework of a wider context.

So much for the simple sentence. The isolation and analysis of the composite sentence is bound up with specific difficulties that reflect the peculiarities of the *Ṛg Veda*, since even the separation of the text into sentences is not always self-evident. There are no punctuation marks in the metrical text, only dividers between stanzas and half-stanzas. As a rule, the end of the sentence coincides with the end of the stanza, although a minority of cases do not adhere to this rule, which complicates the task of syntactic division. The stanza quite often consists of several sentences connected by links of coordination or subordination. The metrical limits of *pādas* and half-stanzas, are sufficient in most cases to determine the correct number of sentences in a stanza; yet they do not make it possible to determine the relationship between those sentences.

This problem of the syntactic division of the text does not arise if the link between sentences is expressed by means of some formal element– a conjunction, either coordinating or subordinating, or the relative pronoun *yá-* "who," "which" coordinated with a demonstrative pronoun in the principal clause. But the problem appears at once when formally expressed connections between sentences are either wholly absent or too vague and unclear.

Asyndeton is a characteristic feature of Vedic syntax; often a sequence of clauses is distributed over several *pādas*, or, when long meters are used, over a short phrase contained within a single *pāda*; and it is often difficult to determine the relations between clauses.

Phrasal accent is an important criterion of syntactic division. The general rule states that the finite verbal form in an independent clause has no accent if this form does not begin a sentence or a *pāda*, but it has an accent in a subordinate clause, for example:

agníṃ vaḥ pūrvyáṃ huve
hótāraṃ carṣaṇīnā́m
tám ayā́ vācā́ gṛṇe tám u va stuṣe (8.23.7)

"*Agni* I invoke (accentless) for you, the ancient / *Hotar*-priest of the peoples; / Him I sing (accentless) with this speech; him, too, I glorify (accentless) for you." None of the finite verbs in these independent clauses (*huva, gṛṇe, stuṣe*) has an accent, since they do not begin a sentence or a *pāda*.

pávante vā́jasātaye
sómāḥ sahásrapājasaḥ
gṛṇānā́ devávītaye (9.13.3)

"For prize-winning they purify (accented) / The *Soma* juices with a thousand forms, / (That are) praised for inviting the gods."

Since it begins both the sentence and the *pāda*, the finite verb *pávante* has an accent. The finite verb in an independent clause can be used with an adverb-prefix, which is formally an independent word but, in terms of semantics, forms a unity with that verb. In that case the finite verb becomes an enclitic of the accent-bearing adverb-prefix, which usually precedes the verb (although it is sometimes postposed) and often appears at the beginning of a clause, for example: *ā́ gā́vo agmann utá bhadrám akran* (6.28.1) "The cows came (*ā́ . . . agman*) and wrought a boon;" *ví me purutrā́ patayanti kā́māḥ* (3.55.3) "In many directions my wishes fly asunder" (*ví . . . patayanti*). Quite often the accented adverb-prefix and the respective enclitic finite verb form a closed-in construction embracing the whole sentence, for example: *úd u jyótir amṛ́taṃ viśvájanyam / viśvā́naraḥ savitā́ devó aśret* (7.76.1) "God *Savitar*, belonging to all men, raised up (*úd . . . aśret*) (to heaven) the immortal light, belonging to all people."

In a dependent clause (mainly in subordinate clauses of compound sentences) the finite verb always has an accent; in a prefixal formation two variants are possible: either the prefix loses its accent and becomes a morpheme of the verbal form (as often happens in later Books) or it keeps the accent with its status of an independent word,[131] for example: *evaívā́pāg ápare santu dūḍhyó / 'śvā yéṣāṃ duryúja āyuyujré* (10.44.7) "Just so may other malefactors be left behind, (those ones) for whom ill-harnessed horses have been harnessed (*ā́yuyujre*)!";

ā́ yád yóniṃ hiraṇyáyaṃ
váruṇa mítra sádathaḥ
dhartā́rā carṣaṇīnā́ṃ
yantáṃ sumnáṃ riśādasā (5.67.2)

"When you two sit down (*ā́ . . . sádathaḥ*) upon (your) golden lap, O *Varuṇa*, O *Mitra*, / (As) supporters of peoples, extend (to us) the well-wishing thought, O foe-chastisers(?)!"

The range of the opposition between the dependent and the independent sentence is wider than that of the more particular opposition between a subordinate and a principal (or: simple independent) clause. The formal marker of the former opposition is the presence or absence of the accent on the finite verb in the clause. The finite verb always bears the accent in subordinate clauses of compound sentences with explicit markers of syntactic subordination, as well as in sentences with no formally marked hypotaxis. But from the semantic standpoint, these finite verbs are dependent on some other sentences in a given wider context, and the utterances contained in them can be treated as conditioned by some other utterance, as opposed to it or in some way connected with it. As can be seen from our discussion, the semantic criterion is too vague, while the general tendency to asyndeton in the language of the hymns results in the situation in which, in a certain number of cases, the criteria for an adequate syntactic division of the texts are to be sought on the prosodic level.

Thus we may use not semantics but phrasal accent as a basis for the analysis of the text. Often, semantic links between sentences seem–from the modern observer's point of view–to belong quite obviously to the domain of hypotaxis while the hymn's author perceived those sentences as independent of each other, with the result that their predicative finite verb had no accent. And, by contrast in some sentences that have an accented finite verb, the grounds for the appearance of the accent remain quite obscure. An example of the former case can be seen in 5.3.11:

tvám aṅgá jaritā́raṃ yaviṣṭha
víśvāny agne duritā́ti parṣi
stenā́ adṛśran ripávo jánāsó
'jñātaketā vṛjinā́ abhūvan

"Carry the singer, O youngest / *Agni*, over all misadventures! / Thieves have appeared, hostile people; / With incomprehensible designs, the wily ones have turned up!" Apparently *Agni* is asked to "carry over," i.e., to save, the singer because his enemies ("thieves"), threatening him, have appeared. However, judging by the phrasal accent the sentences should be treated as independent sentences.

A case of the latter type can be found in 1.152.3, from the *Mitra-Varuṇa* hymn, where various feats of these gods who protect the universal law of *ṛtá-* are described in the guise of riddles with nonunique solutions:132

apā́d eti prathamā́ padvátīnāṃ
kás tád mitrāvaruṇā́ ciketa
gárbho bhārám bharaty ā́ cid asya
ṛtám píparty ánṛtaṃ ní tārīt

"(She), the legless one, goes in advance of those with legs. / Who has understood this (creation of yours), O *Mitra-Varuṇa*? / The embryo bears the burden of this (universe) itself: / He saves (*píparti*) the law, suppresses the un-law." This obscure, esoteric language is used to describe the appearance of the morning dawn, *Uṣas* (= the legless one) and her act of giving birth to *Sūrya* the sun (= the embryo), whose steady and regular movement supports the functioning of the universal cyclic law *ṛtá-*. The first verb in *pāda d*, with its accent and its non-initial position, suggests the need for a colon (or even a full stop) in the translation after *pāda c*, since the sense seems to be: by keeping (= saving) the law, the embryo *Sūrya* bears the burden of the universe.

Sometimes the dependent nature of the sentence that contains the accented finite verb is more or less evident but the exact links remain unclear; that is, it is not clear whether the sentence depends upon the preceding or the following sentence, for example:

víśvā ródhāṃsi pravátaś ca pūrvī́r
dyaúr ṛṣvā́j jániman rejata kṣā́ḥ
ā́ mātárā bhárati śuṣmy ā́ gór
nṛvát párijman nonuvanta vā́tāḥ (4.22.4)

"All dams and numerous streams, / The sky and the earth, shook because of the huge one at (his) birth, / (Since) the furious one carries off the two mothers from the bull. / Like men, the winds make a loud noise all through the neighborhood." The accent-bearing *bhárati* in *pāda c* argues for the dependent character of the sentence. The present translation–following Geldner–reflects its dependence upon the preceding sentence. But in his comments Geldner admits the alternative possibility of its dependence upon *pāda d* (i.e., "because . . . he carries off . . . , the winds make noise").

Of course, there are more or less straightforward cases in which the phrasal accent points unambiguously at a relation of dependence, for example:

kíṃ no asyá dráviṇaṃ kád dha rátnaṃ
ví no voco jātavedaś cikitvā́n
gúhā́dhvanaḥ paramáṃ yán no asyá
réku padáṃ ná nidānā́ áganma (4.5.12)

"What shall we have out of his wealth? What treasure? / Declare (it) to us, O *Jātavedas*, as an expert! / The farthest (end) of this road that (is prepared) for us, hidden / (The place whither) we have gone, as though foredoomed, (following) a false track." Geldner has translated *pāda d* with the accented verb in the following way: "(ob) wir als die Getadelten gleichsam die falsche Fährte gegangen sind" [74.1.426], while Renou observes in his commentary: "qu'Agni dise si 'nous ne sommes pas allés vers un lieu vide" [118.2.58-9]: the syntactic dependence of *pāda d* upon *pāda c* is beyond doubt.

There are also certain particular rules which can influence the phrasal accent in independent sentences. We have mentioned the restriction concerning the accent-bearing finite verb at the beginning of a sentence; and the Old Indian view that only one finite verb-form may be present in a single sentence. But, if several finite verbs seemed to relate to a single subject, each one of them was treated as beginning a sentence and consequently bore an accent, for example:

yás túbhyam agne amṛ́tāya mártyaḥ
samídhā dā́śad utá vā havíṣkṛti
tásya hótā bhavasi yā́si dūtyàm
úpa brūṣe yájasi adhvarīyási (10.91.11)

"The mortal, O *Agni*, who to thee, the immortal one, / Shows respect with firewood or with a sacrificial libation, / For him thou becomest the *hotar*-priest, thou performest (*yā́si*) (for his sake) the duties of a messenger, / Thou invokest (the gods for his sake), performest the sacrifices (*yájasi*) (and) rites (*adhvarīyási*)."

In *pādas c-d*, in the principal clause the verbs *yā́si, yájasi, adhvarīyási* bear the accent although they do not begin a *pāda*. All of them are correlated with a single subject ("thou"), as is evidenced by the verbal inflexion. Since none of them is the first verbal predicate in its *pāda*, they are treated as beginning a new sentence, although the first finite verbs in these *pādas*

(. . . *bhavasi* and *úpa brūṣe*) lack the accent as they do not begin a *pāda* or a sentence.

If the verb is preceded by a vocative at the beginning of a sentence, the finite verb still has an accent because a vocative has an accent when it occupies an initial position and, therefore, is treated as an independent sentence, for example: *ā́ sū́ryo ná bhānumádbhir arkaír / ágne tatántha ródasī ví bhāsā́* (6.4.6) "Like the sun with (its) bright rays / O *Agni*, thou hast filled (*tatántha . . . ví*) both worlds with light."

In this way, in case of asyndeton the choice can sometimes arise between a simple and a composite sentence in the analysis of the hymns; if one chooses the latter, the next step is to make a choice between a complex and a compound sentence. The interpretation hinges upon the phrasal accent manifest in the finite verb. If there is no finite verb, but only half-nominal (participle as predicate) or purely nominal (substantive or adjective as predicate) sentences, there is no opportunity to apply the criterion of phrasal accent of the text to the analysis; compare for instance:

vedhā́ ádṛpto agnír vijānánn
ū́dhar ná gónāṃ svā́dmā pitunā́m
jáne ná śéva āhū́ryaḥ sán
mádhye níṣatto raṇvó duroṇé (1.69.3-4)

"*Agni* (is) the unerring establisher (of the rite), knowing the path, / Similar to the udder of cows, the sweetness of viands . . . / Apparently kindly to people, yet able to harm, / He (is) seated in the middle, the joy in the home."

The authors of the existing translations[133] have differently interpreted these stanzas (in the *Dvipadā virāj* meter according to syntactic analyses that vary greatly. There are no formal criteria in favor of their interpretation of the stanzas as a string of independent sentences (even their number remains unclear), or as a complex sentence. Nor can one discover any kind of dependence of one sentence upon another in this string. Such loosely-connected static descriptions that are based on strings of expanded epithets characterizing the deities, and that admit of both an attributive and a predicative interpretation, are quite typical of *Ṛg Veda* style.

The presence of a finite verb in a sentence does not constitute a necessary and sufficient condition by which to judge the distinctive functions of phrasal accent: the finite verb must also occupy a diagnostic position, that is, it should not begin either a *pāda*- or a sentence, where it always bears the accent. Thus, for example, at 1.157.1a: *ábodhy agnír jmá úd eti sū́ryo* "*Agni* has awakened. The sun rises from the earth:" the initial position of the finite verb *ábodhi* gives no grounds for conclusions concerning the interdependence of these two sentences, although logically speaking, one cannot exclude the possibility of treating the former as a temporal or final clause.

The language of the *Ṛg Veda* displays a tendency to place the accent upon a finite verb followed by an emphatic particle, and this is yet another corroboration of the thesis that a neutral verb in an independent clause never bears the accent but can acquire the accent only when emphasized, i.e., placed in the initial position or reinforced by means of a particle. Such a function can be fulfilled by the particles *íd* "just," "even," "precisely;" *kuvíd* "whether," "certainly," "perhaps;" *caná* "even;" *nahí* "since not;" *hí* "since," "indeed." Some examples:

The particle *íd*: *amarmáṇo vidád íd asya márma* (5.32.5) "He who had no vulnerable spot found at last that one's vulnerable spot;"

> *iyáṃ ta ṛtvíyāvatī*
> *dhītír eti návīyasī*
> *saparyántī purupriyā́ mímīta ít*[134] (8.12.10)

"For thee this timely / Prayer is moving again; / Respectful, very pleasing, it is precisely commensurate" (with the meter). In this independent sentence the particle *íd*, immediately following the finite verbal form, gives it an accent.

The particle *kuvíd*:[135] *imáṃ sv àsmai hṛdá ā́ sútaṣṭam / mántraṃ vocema kuvíd asya védat / . . .* (2.35.2) "This (coming) from the heart, beautifully fashioned / Work we will proclaim to him. Doesn't he know it?" (or: " . . . Surely he does know it"); *íti vā íti me máno / gā́m áśvaṃ sanuyām íti / kuvít sómasyā́pām íti* (10.119.1) "Thus and thus it is on my mind: / I would like to win a bull and a horse:– / Have I not drunk *Soma*?" (or: " . . . Certainly, I have drunk *Soma*").[136]

The emphatic interrogative particle *kuvíd*, occupying the initial position in an interrogative sentence, causes the finite verb to bear the accent. However, if the particle *kuvíd* and the finite verb are in different *pādas*, the verb may lack the accent, for example:

> *úpem asṛkṣi vājayúr vacasyā́ṃ*
> *cáno dadhīta nādyó gíro me*
> *apā́ṃ nápād āśuhémā kuvít sá*
> *supéśasas karati jóṣiṣad dhí* (2.35.1)

"Striving for the prize, I have poured out (my) eloquence. / May the river (-god) find pleasure in my songs! / *Apām Napāt*, urging on the horses, surely he / Will adorn (my) songs, for he enjoys (them)." In this stanza the interrogative particle *kuvít* in *pāda c* does not influence the accentuation of the finite verb third singular subjunctive *karati* in *pāda d*: it remains without accent. But the other finite form in the same *pāda*–third singular subjunctive *jóṣiṣad* has acquired the accent because of the following particle *hí*, though the verb's position is not diagnostic here: the verb is treated as if it began the sentence.

The particle *caná*: *joṣavākám̐ vádataḥ . . . ná devā bhasáthaś caná* (6.59.4) "O (you) two gods, indeed you do not devour (those who) pronounce the speech pleasing (to you)!" If the particle immediately follows the finite verb, the latter acquires the accent; as a matter of principle, this particle marks out a separate word and is used mostly after pronouns and nouns. When *caná* underscores not the finite verb but some other word in the sentence, the verbal form remains without accent. An exception occurs when the repetition of *caná* implies a kind of markedness (if not a degree of contrast); thus in the following example: *mámac caná tvā yuvatíḥ parā́sa / mámac caná tvā kuṣávā jagā́ra* (4.18.8) "It is because of me that the young wife did not throw thee away, (and) because of me that *Kuṣavā* did not swallow thee up." Both of the verbal predicates in these clauses bear the accent (the form *parā́sa* is analysed in the *Padapāṭha* as *parā-ā́sa*) just as in repetitions of other types (conjunctions, pronominal adjectives). An example of the particle *nahí*:

nahí vām ásti dūraké
yátrā ráthena gáchathaḥ
áśvinā somíno gṛhám (1.22.4)

"Indeed, it is not far away for you– / When you two are riding in the chariot, / O *Aśvins*,–the house of (him who) offers *Soma* (in sacrifice);" *nahí me ásty ághnyā / ná svádhitir vánanvati* (8.102.19) "I do not have a cow, / Nor is there an axe for the tree-lord." This particle of emphatic negation originated from the coalescence of the negation *ná* and the particle *hí*; it begins the sentence (like *ná*) and makes the finite verb accented (i.e., the function of *hí*).

The particle *hí*: *krátvā hí dróṇe ajyásé / 'gne vājī́ ná kṛ́tvyaḥ* (6.2.8) "Indeed, they anoint thee with circumspection in a wooden (vat), / O *Agni*, like a runner (horse) able to get the reward;"

índravāyū imé sutā́
úpa práyobhir ā́ gatam
índavo vām uśánti hí (1.2.4)

"O *Indra-Vāyu*, here (are) these pressed out (*Soma*) juices. / Come with joyful feelings: / Indeed, the (*Soma*) drops are speeding to you!" The particle *hí* tends to stand near the beginning of the *pāda*, right after the first or second word, but it can also stand after words in non-initial positions. The presence of the particle causes the finite verb to bear the accent, while the sentence containing this particle is virtually identified with a final or conditional clause, or with an indication of the general motivation of an action that cannot be confined to a rigid framework of a subordinate clause but should be understood from a wider context. The particle may follow the independent clause but more often precedes it, for example: *śúnaś cid chépaṃ níditaṃ sahásrād / yū́pād amuñco áśamiṣṭha hí ṣáḥ* (5.2.7) "Even the bound *Śunaḥśepa* thou settest free from a thousand sacrificial stakes: indeed, he toiled (at the sacrifice)" (= "for he toiled"); *śáśvanto hí śátravo rāradhúṣ ṭe / bhedásya cic chárdhato vinda rándhim* (7.18.18) "Indeed, all enemies obey thee. Find a way (to make) obedient even the arrogant *Bheda*!"

The ability of some emphatic particles in the *Ṛg Veda* to make finite verbal forms bear the accent has far-reaching consequences, since several particles can function as conjunctions in composite sentences. In the Vedic language there is no clear-cut distinction between emphatic particles, conjunctions and a group of pronominal and adverbial forms.[137] These subclasses of uninflected forms are distinct in part, yet a certain number of them combine the functions of different subclasses. At the same time, their relations to phrasal accent as manifest in the finite verb are rather variable and cannot always be established with certainty. One may speak here only about more or less clearly manifest tendencies.

Thus the particle *ā́t* (originally ablative case singular from the pronominal root *a-*) "then," "thereafter," "here;" "and," "further;" "that," "indeed,"– can sometimes induce the appearance of accent in the finite verb, for example: *ā́n ménāṃ kṛṇvánn ácyuto bhúvad góḥ / pátir diváḥ sanajā́ ápratītaḥ* (10.111.3) "Here, creating a female for the bull, the unshakeable lord of heaven, the age-born one, has become unequalled." The accent on *bhúvad* can be explained only by the presence of *ā́t*. The same effect is attested for *ā́t* in combination with the emphatic particle *áha* (incidentally, combinations of particles with various short syntactic words always drift to the beginning of the sentence):

> *ā́d áha svadhā́m ánu*
> *púnar garbhatvám eriré*
> *dádhānā nā́ma yajñíyam* (1.6.4)

"And then they arranged that of his own free will / He started to be born again (and again), / And they made a name for themselves, worthy of sacrifice" (literally "they set in motion the rebirth again").

If one sentence follows another with repeated conjunctions (the so-called paired conjunctions), particles, or pronominal forms, the verb of the first sentence usually bears the accent. In meaning, the two sentences are usually in contraposition, or if the copulative conjunction *ca . . . ca* "and" is involved, they are simply combined; originally, too, this conjunction was an emphatic particle (–this function can be still detected in *ca* within the *Ṛg Veda*). Some examples: *ádha . . . ádha* "What if . . . what if," "both . . . and:" *ádhā śáyīta nírṛter upásthé / 'dhainaṃ vṛ́kā rabhasā́so adyúḥ* (10.95.14) "What if he should find peace in the lap of nonexistence? / What if the ferocious wolves should devour him?" Here both finite verbs have accents. But compare: *ádhā náro ny òhaté / 'dhā niyúta ohate* (5.52.11) "Both the men favor (it) / And (their) (horse-) teams favor (it–scilicet the sacrifice)." In this case both finite verbs lack the accent; *ca . . . ca* "both . . . and;" "if . . . then" (rare): *sáṃ ca tvé jagmúr gíra indra pūrvī́r / ví ca tvád yanti vibhvò manīṣā́ḥ* (6.34.1) "O *Indra*, many praise-songs have come together in thee, / And out of thee come powerful thoughts;" *ayám asmā́n vánaspátir / mā́ ca hā́ mā́ ca rīriṣat* (3. 53.20) "This forest tree, may it not leave us and may it not harm (us)!"; *ā́ ca huvé ní ca satsīhá devaíḥ* (1.76.4) "If I call upon thee–then sit down here with the gods!" This conjunction is used as a postpositional enclitic (compare the atonic emphatic particles). When the finite verb is used with an adverb-prefix the conjunction follows the prefix and thus begins the sentence, a position characteristic of particles. The coupled conjunction *ca . . . ca* attracts the accent to the first of the finite verbal forms.

The single copulative conjunction *ca* takes its place after the second verb, thus giving it an accent, for example: *sá dhārayat pṛthivī́m papráthac ca* (1.103.2) "He fixed the earth and broadened (it)." But this position is not diagnostic, since here there are two verbs relating to a single noun-subject: in this case the second verb is treated as introducing a new sentence.

The paired atonic disjunctive conjunction *vā . . . vā* "either . . . or" that connects two independent sentences quite often causes the finite verb in the former sentence to bear the accent. This conjunction occupies the syntactic position of an enclitic particle, that is, immediately after its basic-word. If the latter is a verb with the adverb-prefix normally gravitating to the beginning of the sentence, the conjunction follows the adverb, for example: *úd vā siñcádhvam úpa vā pṛṇadhvam / ā́d íd vo devá ohate* (7.16.11) "Pour (it) out completely or fill (it): only then will the god favor you!"; . . . *áhaye vā tā́n pradádātu sóma / ā́ vā dadhātu nírṛter upásthe* (7.104.9) " . . . let *Soma* deliver them over to the serpent, or let (him) set (them) in the lap of Destruction!" Compare, however, a counter-example where this conjunction, in an identical syntactic context, does not influence the accent of the finite verb: *kó vā yajñaíḥ pári dákṣaṃ ta āpa / kéna vā te mánasā dāśema* (1.76.1) "Or, (perhaps), someone has seized thy force of action by means of sacrifices? Or with what mind shall we honor thee?"

These examples show that conjunctions (mostly paired) in complex sentences are closely related syntactically to emphatic particles, with all the resulting consequences. If the speaker perceives even a slight degree of contraposition between the simple sentences that make up a complex one, that feeling entails the appearance of the accent in the verb of the first sentence. The semantic criterion seems to be quite subjective in this case.

The same semantic criterion is in operation when two independent sentences employ the pronominal adjectives *anyá- . . . anyá-* "one . . . (the) other" (literally "other . . . other") and the sentences are in semantic contrast: the verb in the former sentence bears the accent, for example: *vṛtrā́ṇy anyáḥ samithéṣu jíghnate / vratā́ny anyó abhí rakṣate sádā* (7.83.9) "The one kills the enemies in battles, / the other always protects the vows." Even if the latter sentence should lack a verb, the verb in the former still has the accent, for example: *aruṣásya duhitárā vírūpe / stṛ́bhir anyā́ pipiśé sū́ro anyā́* (6.49.3) "The two daughters of the purple one are of different appearance: / One is adorned with stars, the other–with the sun's (rays)."

It should be noted that when another word is used in the same function–*éka . . . éka* "one . . . another" (literally "one . . . one"), which is a less frequent means for expressing the same meaning, the phrasal accent remains uninfluenced by it, for example:

tráyaḥ keśína ṛtuthā́ ví cakṣate
saṃvatsaré vapata éka eṣām
víśvam éko abhí caṣṭe śácībhir
dhrā́jir ékasya dadṛśe ná rūpám (1.164.44)

"The three hairy ones appear at the appointed time. / Throughout the year one of them cuts his hair. / The other gazes round everything through (his) powers. / The onrush not the form of the third one is visible," (literally "one . . . one . . . one"). In those isolated instances when this meaning is conveyed by the opposition of different lexical units: *éka- . . . anyá-* "one . . . another"–this circumstance does not influence the verbal accent in the *Ṛg Veda*, either; compare, for example: *ā́po bhū́yiṣṭhā íty éko abravīt / agnír bhū́yiṣṭha íty anyó abravīt* (1.161.9) "'Water is the most prominent,' thus said the one; / 'Fire is the most prominent,' thus said the other." These facts indicate that neither phrasal accent nor semantics can be accepted as an indisputable criterion for the syntactic division of a text. Since such criteria appear to be sometimes purely formal and sometimes semantic, neither can be consistently applied.

The most frequent type of compound sentences is the one with the relative clause with *yá-* "who," "which." This type is remarkable for the loose relationship between the main and the subordinate clauses. As a rule, *yá-* in the relative clause is correlated with a demonstrative pronoun (or sometimes with an adverb) in the main clause. More often than not, the subordinate clause precedes the main one, but the reverse occurs rather frequently as well. In keeping with this rule, the relative and demonstrative pronouns may stand in the same or in different cases, for example:

yā́s phalínīr yā́ aphalā́
apuṣpā́ yā́ś ca puṣpíṇīḥ
bṛ́haspátiprasutā̄s
tā́ no muñcantv áṃhasaḥ (10.97.15)

"(Those) which (are) with fruit, which (are) fruitless, / Which (are) flowerless and with flowers, / Incited by *Bṛhaspati*, / Let them free us from anguish!" Another variant: *yó na indrābhíto jáno / vṛkāyúr ādídeśati / adhaspadáṃ tám īṃ kṛdhi . . .* (10.133.4) "(Those) people, O *Indra*, who aim at us on all sides, the hostile ones, / Hurl them under our feet!"

The hymns contain repeated and varying deviations from the norm of a complete and correctly constructed compound sentence, and such deviations represent one of the distinguishing features of Vedic language. The principal sentence may lack the demonstrative correlated with the relative pronoun of the subordinate clause, with a resulting anacoluthon, for example:

śúciḥ ṣma yásmā atrivát
prá svádhitīva rī́yate
suṣū́r asūta mātā́
krāṇā́ yád ānaśé bhágam (5.7.8)

"(Him), for whom we, like the *Atris*, (make), very clear (fat, which) / Flows down, like a (gliding) axe,– / (Him, his) mother bore quite easily / After she had willingly tasted amorous joy."

Quite often *yá-* in the subordinate clause is correlated with a substantive in the main one; the noun can be omitted and in that case the pronoun's referent has to be guessed, as in, for example:

prā́smai gāyatrám arcata
vāvā́tur yáḥ puraṃdaráḥ
yā́bhiḥ kāṇvásyópa barhír āsádaṃ
yā́sad vajrī́ bhinát púraḥ (8.1.8)

"Sing for him the canticle (masculine) which (masculine) smashes the fortress for the worshipper's sake, / (the songs) because of which (instrumental case plural feminine) the thunderer would come to sit upon the

Kāṇvas' sacrificial straw (and) would crush the fortresses!"

In the first two *pādas* one can observe a coordination between the main and the subordinate clauses (*gāyatrám–yáḥ*), while in the last two *pādas* the main clause lacks the required feminine noun agreeing in gender with *yā́bhiḥ*, which has to be supplied. But the referent of the pronoun that has been omitted in the main clause quite often cannot be restored with confidence, for example: *prá sadyó agne áty eṣy anyā́n / āvír yásmai cā́rutamo babhū́tha* (5.1.9) "At once, O *Agni*, thou passest by the others / (Making for the one) for whom thou appearest as the dearest one . . . . "

Our translation follows Renou's interpretation, according to whom both *anyā́n* and *yásmai* have referents that belong to the same class, mortals in this context, those worshippers who try to entice *Agni* to the detriment of rival worshippers. Renou's version: "D'emblée, ô *Agni*, tu vas outre les autres (gens, vers celui) auquel tu t'es-toujours manifesté (comme étant) le plus cher (à ses yeux) . . . " [118.13.18]. But Geldner sees quite a different meaning in that half-stanza: "Du, *Agni*, hast alsbald den Vorrang vor den anderen (Göttern), bei jedem, dem du sehr willkommen erschienen bist, . . . " [74.2.2]. For him, *anyā́n* refers to the gods, and *yásmai*–to the mortals.

Sometimes the referent of the relative pronoun in the subordinate clause may be ascertained only from a wider mythological context, for example:

ékasya cin me vibhv àstv ójo
yā́ nú dadhṛṣvā́n kṛṇávai manīṣā́
ahám hy ùgró maruto vídāno
yā́ni cyávam índra íd īśa eṣām (1.165.10)

"Even when I am alone, may my power be formidable! / Whatever (accusative case plural neuter) (feats) I shall dare (to perform), I shall do (them) deliberately! / For I am known, O *Maruts*, as terrible. / Whatever (accusative case plural neuter) (feats) I set in motion, / only *Indra* is master of them!"

In the mythological context of the *Ṛg Veda*, the figure of *Indra* is inseparable from his heroic deeds, or feats–his *vīryà*–(neuter). Frequently the main clause omits the demonstrative in the nominative case, which serves as the focus for the relative pronoun in the subordinate clause, so that the latter is left "hanging loose;" this occurs particularly in enumerations, for example:

nahí te kṣatrám ná sáho ná manyúm
váyaś canā́mī́ patáyanta āpúḥ
némā́ ā́po animiṣám cárantīr
ná yé vā́tasya praminánty ábhvam (1.24.6)

"Neither thy power, nor force, nor fury,– / Ever reached (them), either those fluttering birds, / Or these ever-moving waters, / Or (those) which surpass the wind's rage." The members that are enumerated can be joined by the conjunction *ca* "and," for example: *mā́ vo riṣat khanitā́ / yásmai cāhám̐ khánāmi vaḥ* (10.97.20) "May the (man) digging (you) up not be harmed by you, / And (he) for whom I dig you up!" (concerning the healing plants).

This loose syntactic connection between the subordinate and the principal clauses from time to time causes the attraction-by-case of the relative in the subordinate clause or of the demonstrative (resp. of the noun) in the principal clause (an interpretation that may be suggested for 1.24.6–above). Some examples: *nā́smai vidyún ná tanyatúḥ siṣedha / ná yā́m míham ákirad dhrādúnim̐ ca* (1.32.13) "Neither the lightning nor thunder helped him, / Nor (that) fog that he had scattered about, nor hail" (literally " . . . nor which fog (accusative case singular) he had scattered about . . . "). In this classic example, habitually adduced in the handbooks, the noun *míham* "fog" is brought over from the main clause into the subordinate one in the case required by the verb of the latter clause.[138]

Another example is remarkable in several respects:

sató nūnám̐ kavayaḥ sám̐ śiśīta
vā́śībhir yā́bhir amŕ̥tāya tákṣatha
vidvā́m̐saḥ padā́ gúhyāni kartana
yéna devā́so amr̥tatvám ānaśúḥ (10.54.10)

"Now sharpen evenly the axes, O poets, / With which you hew (them) out for the immortal one! / As experts you make secret words / Through which the gods achieved immortality." The first half-stanza is to be translated literally as follows: " . . . sharpen (you) with which axes you hew out . . . ," that is, here a noun from the main clause is attracted by case and included in the subordinate clause. In the second half-stanza the instrumental case singular *yéna* is correlated *ad sensum* with a whole sentence (not a separate word, noun or pronoun) and functions almost as a conjunction. This was the way some of the forms of the relative pronoun evolved in the history of the language.

The violations of formal relations between the main clause and the subordinate relative clause with *yá-* are sometimes so considerable that they have to be established on the basis of general contextual semantics. One example:

gā́vo bhágo gā́va índro me achān
gā́vaḥ sómasya prathamásya bhakṣáḥ

imā́ yā́ gā́vaḥ sá janāsa índra
ichā́mī́d dhṛdhā́ mánasā cid índram (6.28.5)

"The cows (are) *Bhaga*, the cows seemed to me to be *Indra*, / The cows (are) the taste of fresh *Soma*. / These cows–they (are) *Indra*, O people. / For I am striving for *Indra* with (my) heart and mind." The literal translation of *pāda c* is: "These, which cows, he, O people, *Indra*." In the principal clause one can note the attraction of the demonstrative pronoun by gender and number.

As a result of all these violations and breaches in syntactic connections, the use of the relative *yá-* becomes very loose in extreme cases: a case-form of this pronoun in the subordinate clause may have no formal correlates in the following main clause. Such cases can be interpreted in two senses: either *yá-* possesses an adverbial or conjunctional function, or the two clauses are unrelated. But the second alternative implies that the first clause is a subordinate without a principal. For example:

prá yā́bhir yā́si dāśvā́ṃsam áchā
niyúdbhir vāyav iṣṭáye duroṇé
ní no rayíṃ subhójasaṃ yuvasva
ní vīráṃ gávyam áśvyaṃ ca rā́dhaḥ (7.92.3)

"When thou goest to the worshipper / On (thy horse) teams, O *Vāyu*, to seek (for him) at (his) home, / Grant us wealth consisting in beautiful delight, / (Give us) a virile hero and an honorary gift of cows and horses!" The literal translation of this construction is: "On which teams thou goest . . . –grant us wealth . . . !" Geldner sees here a case of the loose use of the relative in a compound sentence [74.2.263]. Renou, however, analyses the text as consisting of two independent sentences of which the former is incomplete [118.15.109]. Another example of this kind:

yé vāṃ dáṃsāṃsy aśvinā
víprāsaḥ parimāmṛśúḥ
evét kāṇvásya bodhatam (8.9.3)

"O *Aśvins*, however the inspired poets consider your miracles, / Take notice only of (the poet from) the *Kāṇva* family!" Literally: "Which . . . inspired-poets consider . . . , so notice only . . . ! This case, which Renou called a banal anacoluthon with an ellipsis [118.16.56], should rather be seen as a whole compound sentence, since the formal link between the clauses finds its expression: the second clause is introduced by the particle *eva* "thus, so."

These numerous variants of anacoluthon that occur in compound sentences with the *yá-* relative subordinate clause testify to a certain degree of indeterminacy and ambiguity due to the laxity of syntactic links between parts of this most frequent (in the *Ṛg Veda*) type of composite sentences. In order to clear up such uncertainty one must have recourse to the context, which sometimes has to be very wide indeed.

Yád "what," the neuter singular of *yá-* is frequently used in the *Ṛg Veda* as a subordinating conjunction with a very wide range of meanings, extremely divergent as compared with its original semantics. This type of compound sentence is second in frequency only to the *yá-* relative.

Because of the semantic range of the conjunction, which has not yet wholly separated itself from the original relative pronoun by the time of the *Ṛg Veda*, one has to look for various syntactic criteria in order to determine the exact meaning of compound sentences introduced by *yád*. None of the particular features of these sentences can serve as absolute criteria for determining the exact semantics of *yád* and, accordingly, of this type of compound sentence. Among such features can be mentioned the place of the subordinate clause (before or after the principal clause)–the presence or absence in the main clause of a demonstrative pronoun, adverb, or particle, that correlates with *yád* in the subordinate clause, or the mood of the verbs in both types of clauses.

There is a whole series of cases in which *yád* appears as a neuter pronoun in a relative subordinate clause, and serves as an attribute to a neuter substantive noun. But in the main clause its correlative is a demonstrative pronoun, for example: *tvám agna uruśáṃsāya vāgháte / spārháṃ yád rékṇaḥ paramáṃ vanóṣi tát* (1.31.14) "Thou, O *Agni*, obtainest that which (is) the highest desirable wealth for the priest with far-resounding words" (literally " . . . which desirable highest wealth that thou obtainest"). Here *yád* determines the neuter noun *rékṇas-* "wealth" with a corresponding *tát* in the main clause. Another instance: *jyótiṣ kartā yád uśmási* (1.86.10) "Create the light which we want!" In this case *yád* correlates with the neuter noun *jyótis* in the main clause: there is no corresponding demonstrative pronoun and the subordinate clause follows the main one, but it clearly represents the type of relative sentences with *yá-*.

At the same time, in other contexts but under identical syntactic conditions *yád* can function as a conditional or temporal conjunction; some contexts admit of a double interpretation, for example:

etát tyán ná yójanam aceti
sasvár ha yán maruto gótamo vaḥ
páśyan híraṇyacakrān
áyodaṃṣṭrān vidhā́vato varā́hūn (1.88.5)

"This span was not visible, / When in full secret, O *Maruts*, *Gotama* (managed to see) you, / Seeing the golden-wheeled / (And) iron-tusked boars running away."

This context has the same formal characteristics as those treated above, that is, the principal clause contains a neuter substantive noun (*yójanam*) with the pronominal attributes *etát tyát* agreeing with it. Nevertheless, *yád* of the subordinate clause can hardly be considered to be coordinated with these pronouns. Judging by the overall sense of the passage, *yád* here is the conjunction "when," and this is the opinion of Geldner, Renou and other interpreters of the text. The following stanza admits of a two-fold interpretation:

> *yád aṅgá dāśúṣe tvám*
> *ágne bhadráṃ kariṣyási*
> *távét tát satyám aṅgiraḥ* (1.1.6)

"When thou really wishest, / O *Agni*, to do good for (the one) who worships (thee), / Then that is true through thee, O *Aṅgiras*." One may also see *yád* as an attribute of *bhadrám*, a neuter substantive in coordination with the demonstrative *tád* in the main clause, thus giving the sense: "Whatever real good thou wishest to do . . . , then this is true through thee."

When *yád* has the function of an expounding conjunction ("then"), the subordinate clause usually–but not necessarily–follows the principal one, for example: *mahát tát sómo mahiṣáś cakāra- / apā́ṃ yád gárbhó 'vṛṇīta devā́n* (9.97.41) "That (was) the great deed the buffalo *Soma* performed / That (he), the waters' offspring, chose the gods." The verb in this type of subordinate clauses is usually in one of the tenses of the indicative, yet neither the verbal mood nor the subordinate clause in postposition can be seen as reliable criteria for determining the functions of *yád*. Compare this stanza, for instance:

> *idám āpaḥ prá vahata*
> *yát kíṃ ca duritám máyi*
> *yád vāhám abhidudróha*
> *yád vā śepá utā́nṛtam* (10.9.8)

"O waters, carry away (all of) this / That (is) somehow wrong in me: / Whether I have betrayed something, / Or I have sworn something falsely!" This stanza, whose syntactic framework follows the scheme of the preceding example, is a compound sentence with several relative clauses in which *yád* is a pronoun.

If *yád* has the meaning of "so that," "in order to" the verb in the subordinate clause is usually in one of the oblique moods, for example: *prá vāṃ sá mitrāvaruṇāv ṛtā́vā / vípro mánmāni dīrghaśrúd iyarti / . . . / ā́ yát krátvā ná śarádaḥ pṛṇaíthe* (7.61.2) "To you, O *Mitra-Varuṇa*, this pious / Inspired (singer), far-audible, sends up (his) canticles, / . . . / So that you will make full (his) years according to his will!"

The conjunction *yád* in its expounding and consecutive meanings is comparatively rare in the *Ṛg Veda*. Much more frequently it expresses various shades of temporal ("when," "after") or conditional ("if"–real condition) meanings. In these cases the subordinate clauses with *yád* generally precede the principal clauses, and the verbal predicates in the subordinate clauses have no special limitations as to mood or tense. The conjunction *yád* can have various correlates in the principal clause: the adverbial-pronominal forms *tád*, *téna*, adverbs, or particles. Thus it can be said that the syntactic distinctive features of such compound sentences are not specific for them. Some examples:

yát kíṃ cedáṃ varuṇa daívye jáne
'bhidrohám manuṣyā̀ś cárāmasi
ácittī yát táva dhármā yuyopimá
mā́ nas tásmād énaso deva rīriṣaḥ (7.89.5)

"If somehow, O *Varuṇa*, in regard to the divine race / We humans commit some offence, / When through unreason we have violated thy prescriptions,– / Do not punish us for that sin, O god!"; *sáṃ yád ā́naḷ ádhvana ā́d íd áśvair / vimócanaṃ kṛṇute tát tv àsya* (3.30.12) "Only after (the sun) has reached the end of (its) roads, does it unyoke the horses: such is its (work)."

When a conditional sentence contains an unreal condition the usual meaning of *yád* is "if it were," and the verbal predicates in both the main and the subordinate clauses are usually in the optative, for example:

yád indra yā́vatas tvám
etā́vad ahám ī́śīya
stotā́ram íd didhiṣeya radāvaso
ná pāpatvā́ya rāsīya (7.32.18)

"If I, O *Indra*, possessed as much as thou, / I should try to win over the eulogizer, O opener of goods! / I would not deliver him up to indigence!" This type of composite sentences with a marked mood in the verbal form is relatively rare. Nor is the causal *yád* very frequent, for example: *kím ā́ga āsa varuṇa jyéṣṭhaṃ / yát stotā́raṃ jíghāṃsasi sákhāyam* (7.86.4) "What has been that greatest sin, O *Varuṇa*, / That (or: "because of which") thou desirest to slay the praiser, (thy) friend?"

In conclusion, it should be remarked that *yád* in the language of the *Ṛg Veda* is used in all types of compound sentences and covers the whole range of meanings of a subordinating conjunction par excellence. Moreover, the conjunction *yád* in many cases cannot be separated from the neuter relative pronoun *yád* and, accordingly, various types of clauses with the subordinating *yád* possess no clear distinguishing structural features when compared with relative clauses containing the pronoun *yád*. The conjunction *yád* in its manifold functions is synonymous with various formally differentiated conjunctions: *yadā́* "when," *yádi* "if," *yáthā* "so that," etc., but it is much more common than any of them. Under these circumstances, as reliable semantic and syntactic criteria are generally absent, the interpretation of a sentence often remains doubtful, and one should look for leads in the wider context.

We have summarized the complete variants of structural schemes basic to simple and composite sentences. But the actual text of the hymns frequently shows ellipsis, that is, the omission of one or several words whose presumable meaning can be inferred from the context with a greater or lesser degree of probability. Ellipsis is generally considered to be one of the most conspicuous features of Vedic style. Its basic types are quite well known but the causes for the extremely wide currency of this phenomenon in the language of this cultic text still remain unclear.

Gonda, the author of a monograph on ellipsis in the *Ṛg Veda*, has given the following definition: "By ellipsis is here intended the phenomenon that part of an expression which is current in normal usage or part of a construction which is, in a given milieu, usual, is omitted, because at the moment of speaking (or writing) it may be dispensed with and inevitably and as a matter of course supplied by the audience or understood by them in the construction of the sentence" [78.6]. This definition and description contains an outline of the general range of this phenomenon. First, a part of a verbal cliché that was of a routine character for the authors of the time and their audience may be omitted. Secondly, although this part cannot be restored from the context at present, by falling back upon the overall cultural milieu to fill in the contents, it is possible that a part of the sentence whose lexical meaning can be restored may be omitted, to a certain degree, on the basis of the syntactic construction. These two groups, as a whole, cover the full range of ellipsis in the *Ṛg Veda*. Moreover, the definition quoted above also mentions the fact that at the moment of uttering the text the omitted parts can be dispensed with. Yet the whole problem converges on this particular fact: why should one manage without those parts and what is the cause for such a need? For all of this cannot be due to accident if we consider the scale of this phenomenon in the *Ṛg Veda*. These questions are not answered in Gonda's book, and presumably, there can be no cut-and-dried solution, although some thoughts on the problem–however self-contradictory–can be found, here and there, in his monograph. Yet it seems highly desirable that an attempt–however hypothetical–at an interpretation of the multifarious manifestations of ellipsis should be made within the framework of a general unified theory. The value of Gonda's book, which lays the groundwork for the study of Vedic stylistics, lies in its full presentation of Vedic data as well as in its argued and careful classification.

Renou also dealt with ellipsis in the *Ṛg Veda*, concluding that this stylistic phenomenon must be based on purely linguistic processes [124. 29-43].

Here we shall cite some examples in order to illustrate Gonda's two types of ellipsis.[139] For instance, one of the hymns presents the *Vala* myth in the following terms:

asmā́ ukthā́ya párvatasya gárbho
mahī́nāṃ janúṣe pūrvyā́ya
ví párvato jíhīta sā́dhata dyaúr
āvívāsanto dasyanta bhū́ma (5.45.3)

"Before this hymn the mountain's entrails (gaped) / For the first birth of the great (dawns). / The mountain opened up, the sky attained (its) goal. / (The *Aṅgirases*), striving to lure, made the earth yield." To supply the gaps in the text and to identify its content correctly, one must be aware of the general mythological context: the *Aṅgirases*, by means of their singing, broke into the core of the *Vala* rock where the dawns had been hidden together with light, etc.; all of them then emerged to serve the *Aryans*.

Another mythological example taken from *Indra*'s hymn of self-praise:

ahám átkaṃ kaváye śiśnathaṃ háthair
ahámṃ kútsam āvam ābhír ūtíbhiḥ
ahámṃ śúṣṇasya śnáthitā vádhar yamaṃ
ná yó rará ā́ryaṃ nā́ma dásyave (10.49.3)

"I (gave him my) garment. For *Kavi*'s sake I pierced (*Śuśṇa*) with thrusts. / I aided *Kutsa* with these acts of support. / I, the piercer of *Śuṣṇa*, delivered a mortal weapon (to *Kutsa*), / (I), who did not give up the *Aryan* name to the *Dasyu*." In order to understand this stanza more clearly, one must resort to various mythological details gleaned from the whole of the *Ṛg Veda*: *Kutsa*, *Indra*'s charioteer, was both aided and persecuted by *Indra*, and *Śuṣṇa*, a demon, was slain by the god. Moreover, during the stuggle with *Śuṣṇa* *Indra* used to assume the outward appearance (or at least the attire) of *Kutsa*; *Kavi* (*kaví-* "poet") is the same person as *Kutsa*, who takes *Kavi*'s name in some *Ṛg Veda* passages. And lastly, the phrase "to give up a name" meant "to ruin the name-bearer."

In the following extracts the omitted word can be guessed from the sentence structure itself, for example: *ácha ṛṣe mā́rutaṃ gaṇáṃ / dānā́ mitráṃ ná yoṣáṇā* (5.52.14) "O *Ṛṣi*, in(vite) the troop of the *Maruts* / By means of a gift, as a woman (invites her) friend." The adverb-prefix *ácha* points the action towards the speaker, and the presence of the vocative "O *Ṛṣi*" makes it probable that the missing verb was meant to be in the imperative.

Another example: *ṛ́ṣistutā jaráyantī maghóny / uṣā́ uchati váhnibhir gṛṇānā́* (7.75.5) "Praised by the *Ṛṣis*, awakening (the whole world), the generous / *Uṣas* sheds light, extolled by the sacrifice-offerers." The causative participle *jaráyantī* "(she), the awakening one"[140] is construed with a direct object that has to be supplied by something like "the whole world," "every living creature," etc.

Gonda and some other scholars have described the most common structural types of ellipsis in the *Ṛg Veda*. The most important type involves the omission of the substantive with its attributive adjective in concord, for example:

etáṃ tyáṃ haríto dáśa
marmṛjyante apasyúvaḥ
yā́bhir mádāya śúmbhate (9.38.3)

"It is him that the ten golden active (fingers) polish diligently, / With whose aid he adorns himself for inebriation."

In the *Soma*-hymns of Book 9, the fingers of the priest who presses the juice are mentioned time and again. They are called "golden" because the *Soma* juice tints them with its distinctive color. So in this instance, the omitted noun is not hard to supply.

In this established combination of an epithet (adjective) and a substantive, the substantive is apt to be omitted. But such a combination can also be subject to ellipsis, for example: *tvám etā́n rudató jákṣataś ca- / áyodhayo rájasa indra pāré* (1.33.7) "These sobbing and cackling (enemies)– / Thou hast overcome (them), O *Indra*, driving them to the end of space." The situation can be complicated by the uncertainty of the line of demarcation between ellipsis as such and the substantivized use of a standing epithet, as both Gonda [78.18] and Renou [120.399] have noted.

The standing epithets of various gods in the *Ṛg Veda* tend to become substantives and thus acquire the functions of theonyms. For example, *Indra*'s conventional epithet *maghávan-* "generous, liberal," though used occasionally as an attribute of the theonym, more often appears as its substitute. Compare the following contexts: *índraḥ suśípro maghávā tárutro / mahā́vrātas tuvikūrmír ṛ́ghāvān . . .* (3.30.3) "*Indra*, fine-lipped, generous, transversing (perils), / Great-hosted, resolute-in-deed (?), furious . . . " and:

índraś ca yád yuyudhā́te áhiś ca- / utā́parī́bhyo maghávā ví jigye (1.32.13) "When *Indra* and the serpent fought, / The generous one became victorious for (all) future times." *Indra*'s generosity in the latter instance lacks any motivation, and so the epithet *maghávan* in *pāda d* acquires the function of the name *índra-* from *pāda c.*

It is not always clear whether there is an ellipsis of the substantive or a substantivization of the adjective, when an epithet is used. Statistics might be of help in deciding such cases: thus, if epithet-adjectives are used without their substantives noticeably more often than with them, the former usage should perhaps be regarded as substantivization. For example, the epithet *hári-* "golden," "bay" for *Indra*'s horses is much more frequently used independently, meaning "a bay horse" (often in the dual) as in 2.11.17: *yāhí háribhyāṃ sutásya pītím* "Come upon a pair of bays to drink the pressed (*Soma*)." The substantivized use of *hári-* is prevalent, but the complete phrase occasionally occurs as well, as for example in 6.44.19:

ā́ tvā hárayo vṛ́ṣaṇo yujānā́
vṛ́ṣarathāso vṛ́ṣaraśmayó 'tyāḥ
asmatrā́ñco vṛ́ṣaṇo vajravā́ho
vṛ́ṣṇe mádāya suyújo vahantu

"May the powerfully-yoked bay horses bring thee (here) on a powerful chariot, with powerful reins, the powerful ones, carrying (thy) *vajra*, well-yoked–to us for (thy) powerful inebriation!"

But the complications with *hári-* do not stop here, since the suggested interpretation is valid only in the context of *Indra*'s horses (the most common meaning). But *hári-* often denotes *Soma* and its juice, and sometimes even *Agni*, *Savitar* and certain other deities. There are hymns that intentionally play upon the vagueness of the epithet. Compare the following stanza from such a hymn:

áraṃ kā́māya hárayo dadhanvire
sthirā́ya hinvan hárayo hárī turā́
árvadbhir yó háribhir jóṣam ī́yate
só asya kā́maṃ hárivantam ānaśe (10.96.7)

"Fittingly, the golden ones (i.e., *Soma*'s drops and the horses) sped along at (thy) will. / The golden (drops of *Soma*) urge on the golden victorious pair (of horses) for the firmly standing (*Indra*). / (He) who rides the golden runners (-horses) with pleasure, / He satisfied his desire for the golden (*Soma*)." This whole hymn is built around puns on *hári-*, as is hymn 3.44.

Another typical example can be seen in another epithet of *Soma* already discussed–*sutá-*,[141] literally "pressed (out)" (past participle from the verb *su-*

"to press, squeeze"), which occurs very frequently and denotes the *Soma* juice even without its substantive (compare above at 2.11.17). In both Grassmann's and the Böhtlingk-Roth's dictionaries, the word *sutá-* is cited only under the lemma *su-* (verb). Grassmann takes its substantival use as an ellipsis.[142] But Geldner, in his translation, regularly renders the substantival *sutá-* as "der *Soma*" without regarding it as a case of ellipsis.

In nominal constructions that contain a genitival attribute, the noun which governs the genitive can be omitted; sometimes the narrow syntactic context suggests the omitted noun, as in the following instance: *índrasya tvám̐ táva vayám̐ sákhāyaḥ* (9.97.43) "Thou (art) *Indra*'s (friend), we (are) thy friends." And sometimes the pointer is to be found in a wider mythological context, especially when the standing epithets of deities are concerned, for example, *duhitár- diváḥ* "the sky's daughter" (= *Uṣas*), *sáhasaḥ sūnú-* "the son of strength" (= *Agni*), where the noun governing the genitive can be omitted [76.13].

In constructions of subordination where the case of the noun depends upon the verb, the noun is regularly omitted. Any case-form can be omitted, but the most common is the ellipsis of the direct-object accusative, for example: *índrāya sunávāma* (4.25.4) "We shall press (*Soma*) for *Indra*;" *híraṇyajihvaḥ suvitā́ya návyase rákṣā* (6.71.3) "(O) golden-tongued (one), save (us) for a new lucky chance!" The other oblique case-forms may also be elided: *dhattám̐ sūríbhya utá vā sváśvyam̐* (1.180.9) "Give excellent horses to liberal patrons (dative case) as well as (to singers)!" (a frequent Vedic formula); *sámiddho agna āhuta / devā́n yakṣi svadhvara* (5.28.5) "O *Agni*, kindled, poured upon (with ghee), / (O thou), honor the gods, who makest the rite successful!" (the instrumental case dropped here can be supplied on the basis of the well-known ritual); *yuvám̐ bhujyúm bhurámāṇam̐ víbhir gatám̐ / sváyuktibhir niváhantā pitŕ̥bhya ā́* (1.119.4) "To *Bhujyu*, floundering (in the sea), you two went upon self-yoking birds (and) carried him home from the fathers" (the more complete versions of the *Bhujyu* legend attested in other passages suggest the restoration of a locative here).

Quite often a hint at the omitted substantive is contained in an attribute–adjective, numeral, or pronoun–that agrees with it in gender, number, and case, for example:

> *tvám etád adhārayaḥ*
> *kr̥ṣṇā́su róhiṇīṣu ca*
> *páruṣṇīṣu rúśat páyaḥ* (8.93.13)

"Thou hast placed this white milk in the black (locative case plural feminine) and red (locative case plural feminine), speckled (locative case plural feminine) (cows):" a well-known Vedic riddle; *ā́bhir hí māyā́ úpa dásyum ā́gān / míhaḥ prá tamrā́ avapat támāṃsi* (10.73.5) "Since he struck the (evil) charms (and) the *Dasyu* by means of these (instrumental case plural feminine) (magic forces), he dispersed the stifling mists (and) darkness;" as Geldner has shown [72.3.253], *ā́bhiḥ* implies *māyā́bhiḥ*, i.e., *Indra*'s ability to cause magic transformations. Here is another example:

duhánti saptaíkām
úpa dvā́ páñca sṛjataḥ
tīrthé síndhor ádhi svaré (8.72.7)

"Seven (nominative case plural) (priests) milk one (accusative case singular feminine) (cow), / Two (nominative case dual masculine) (hands) activate five (accusative case plural) (fingers each), / accompanied by a roar on the river bank." This numerical riddle is a description of priests pressing the *Soma* juices.

The nominative of the subject of the action (i.e., the subject of the sentence) may undergo the process of ellipsis as well, and the explanation of this fact should be sought on various levels of linguistic description. The essential and sufficient core of the Vedic sentence is represented by the finite verb, while the subject-pronoun is optional and its function is mostly emphatic.[143] In other words, there are purely linguistic grounds to extend the ellipsis of the subject.

This phenomenon seems to have roots in the Vedic model of the universe. In the words of Renou, "On many occasions it is of little consequence for the poet that the subject's nature remains uncertain and it remains unknown whether the agent of a particular action was the poet himself, the performer of the rite, the patron of the sacrifice, or the deity . . . " [120.36]. The subject-nominative seems most frequently to have been omitted in mythological passages. Compare, for instance, the following stanza from a hymn to *Indra* and *Agni* which resembles a riddle because of the ellipsis of three different subjects:

índrāgnī apā́d iyám
pū́rvā́gāt padvátībhyaḥ
hitvī́ śíro jihváyā vā́vadac cárat
triṃśát padā́ ny àkramīt (6.59.6)

"O *Indra*-and-*Agni*, she, the legless one, / Came before (those) with legs (ablative case plural feminine) (viz., cows). / Having left (his) head, (*Agni*) wanders, loudly wagging (his) tongue, / (And *Sūrya*) took thirty steps." Our version follows that of Geldner, who determined the subjects by comparing various Vedic contexts. Geldner–following Sāyaṇa–sees *Uṣas* as the subject of *pādas a-b*; other authorities think it is *Vāc*, the goddess of Sacred Speech.

Sometimes the omitted subject can be inferred quite unequivocally by means of general mythological data or details of ritual, for example:

tvā́ṃ víśve sajóṣaso
devā́so dūtám akrata
saparyántas tvā kave
yajñéṣu devám īḷate (5.21.3)

"All the unanimous gods have made thee a messenger for themselves. / Honoring thee, O poet, (people) call to (thee), the god, at sacrifices." One of the basic oppositions of the Vedic model of the universe–gods *vs.* people–leaves no room for doubt when *Agni* is the subject of the action:

pávamānā divás páry
antárikṣād asṛkṣata
pṛthivyā́ ádhi sā́navi (9.63.27)

"The purified (*Soma* juices) poured down from the sky, out of the air / Upon the elevated surface of the earth."

Both the usual phraseology of Book 9 and the details of the ritual suggest that the subject is the *Soma* juices, especially since two stanzas earlier, the same predicative phrase appears in a fuller form: *pávamānā asṛkṣata sómāḥ* (9.63.25) "The clarifying *Soma* juices poured forth."

No less common is the ellipsis of finite verbal forms. The *Ṛg Veda* most typically omits the verbal form in the presence of adverbs-prefixes that express the direction of the action. The ellipsis of verbs of motion is most common, especially those denoting various ritual actions, but generally speaking, this phenomenon is not limited to certain lexical groups. Although the adverb-prefix forms a single whole with the verbal stem semantically, it is quite autonomous formally: it is an independent word in the sentence and bears the accent. There are usually sufficient indications of the direction of the action to determine the approximate sense of the finite verb in a given context, for example: *sá sukrátur yó ví dúraḥ paṇīnā́m* (7.9.2) "He (is) of mighty spirit who un(closes) the misers' doors:" we may supply the verb *ví + var-*, which often has *dúraḥ* as the direct object; *ā́ no mitrāvaruṇā havyájuṣṭiṃ / ghṛtaír gávyūtim ukṣatam íḷābhiḥ / práti vām átra váram ā́ jánāya / . . .* (7.65.4) "(Come) hither, O *Mitra-Varuṇa*, to taste our oblation! / Sprinkle the pasture with ghee (and) with supplies! / I in(voke) you here for the good of the people! . . . ," where the *ā́* + accusative case of the goal is the regular phrase for invitation, and the combination *práti . . . huve* "I invoke" occurs in the first stanza of the hymn;

pári yád indra ródasī ubhé
ábubhojīr mahinā́ viśvátaḥ sīm
ámanyamānāñ̐ *abhí* *mányamānair*
nír brahmábhir adhamo dásyum indra (1.33.9)

"When thou, O *Indra*, embracedst both worlds with (thy) greatness on all sides, / Thou con(queredst) the imprudent with the help of the prudent: / By means of incantations thou blewest the *Dasyu* away, O *Indra*."

Since the set of "distinctive" contexts, typical for the *Ṛg Veda*, is not very large, one can observe a natural process in the course of which each of these adverbs-prefixes in absolute use tends to be assigned a definite semantic sphere. As Renou has noted, *abhí* has the connotation of attack, *práti*–of defence, *áti*–the flow of juice through the strainer (of *Soma* in Book 9), *ví* induces the image of opening doors or gates, etc. [120.32].

But finite verbs may also be omitted when they are not combined with adverbs-prefixes. This happens most often with forms of the imperative, since the directionality of its grammemes obviously compensates for the absence of these adverbs, but other modal forms are sometimes omitted as well. Compare for the ellipses of the imperative: *prathamáṃ no ráthaṃ kṛdhi / upamáṃ vājayú śrávaḥ* (8.80.5) "Make foremost our chariot! / (Give us) the highest glory, the prize-bringing!"; *śunáṃ naḥ phā́lā ví kṛṣantu bhū́miṃ / śunáṃ kīnā́śā abhí yantu vāhaíḥ / śunám parjányo mádhunā páyobhiḥ / . . .* (4.57.8) "For luck let our ploughshares carve the soil! / For luck let the tillers come out with (their) draft animals! / For luck (let) *Parjanya* (rain) with honey and milk! . . . " Other modal forms also undergo ellipsis:

ácyutā cid vo ájmann ā́
nā́nadati párvatāso vánaspátiḥ
bhū́mir yā́meṣu rejate (8.20.5)

"Even (what is) unshakeable (trembles) upon your path; / Loudly the mountains (and) the forest-tree resound; / The ground trembles at (your) journeys (hymn to the *Maruts*);" *agnír gā́ndharvīm pathyā̀m ṛtásya* (10.80.6) "*Agni* (knows) the law-path of the *Gandharvas*."

Sometimes doubts can arise as to the tense of the omitted verb, even when its lexical meaning is established with a degree of certainty from the available context, for example:

idáṃ vām āsyè havíḥ
priyám indrābṛhaspatī
ukthám mádaś ca śasyate (4.49.1)

"This pleasing libation (has been poured) into your mouth, O *Indra-Bṛhaspati.* / Praise and the inebriating drink (are) proclaimed." This interpretation follows that of Renou, who translated *pāda a* as "Cette oblation-ci (a été mise) dans votre bouche . . . " [118.15.62]; this is quite convincing, since first the oblation has to be offered, and only then should its qualities be praised. But Geldner differs: "Diese leibe Spende (opfere ich) in euren Mund" [74.1.480].

We have discussed the omission of only one member of an elementary syntactic construction, but syntactic constructions can be omitted as a whole, even predicative constructions and various parts of simple and composite sentences. We have already mentioned the ellipsis of a demonstrative pronoun coordinated with a relative in the subordinate clause.[144] Now we should touch upon the problems concerning such a "hard" ellipsis in a simple extended sentence.

When several words are omitted in a given sentence, the key to the text should often be sought in an adjoining sentence–sometimes even in adjacent stanzas that may contain the missing words, for example: *dádhāti putráḥ pitrór apīcyàṃ / nā́ma tṛtī́yam ádhi rocané diváḥ* (9.75.2) "The son gives the secret (name) to the two parents. / The third name (he gives) to the bright space of the sky."

Another example:

yásmin devā́ vidáthe mādáyante
vivásvataḥ sádane dhāráyante
sū́rye jyótir ádadhur māsy àktū́n
pári dyotaníṃ carato ájasrā (10.12.7)

"The sacrificial distribution at which the gods rejoice, / The place of *Vivasvat*'s that they have, (we do not know that). / They have put light into the sun, nights into the moon. / Fireless, (these) two are moving in a circle (and) spreading light." Geldner has commented on the basic idea of this stanza: we do not know the gods' abode nor their intentions. We are able to see only their creations–the sun and the moon. It is possible to penetrate the sense of the stanza and to supply the main clause in *pādas a-b*–"we do not know"–only because it is explicitly stated in the next stanza: *yásmin devā́ mánmani saṃcáranty / apīcyè ná vayám asya vidma* (10.12.8) "The secret thought at which the gods come together,–we do not know that."

There are certain stereotypes of ellipsis, as for instance, the absolute use of the adverb *antár* "between" in contexts concerned with *Agni*, the messenger god, who travels between sky and earth, and in other contexts, as for example:

ṛjipyá īm índrāvato ná bhujyúṃ
śyenó jabhāra bṛható ádhi ṣṇóḥ
antáḥ patat patatry àsya parṇám
ádha yā́mani prásitasya tád véḥ (4.27.4)

". . . (Then) the straight-flying eagle bore him, / Like *Bhujyu*, from the high summit down to *Indra*'s adherents. / Between (sky and earth) this wing-feather fell away from this / Bird as it swooped on its path." In other contexts the complete *antár*-formula is attested, for example: *híraṇyapāṇiḥ savitā́ vícarṣaṇir / ubhé dyā́vāpṛthivī́ antár īyate* (1.35.9) "Golden-handed *Savitar*, the master of human-kind, / Travels between the two, between sky and earth." Naturally, such a "hard" ellipsis makes the very presence of a sentence as such rather questionable, and the border-line between ellipsis and anacoluthon can be rather indistinct. In particular, this problem arises when an ellipsis breaks up a predicative construction, for example:

āśásanaṃ viśásanam
átho adhivikártanam
sūryā́yāḥ paśya rūpā́ṇi
tā́ni brahmā́ tú śundhati (10.85.35)

"Cutting up, cutting out / And slitting through– / Look at the colors of *Sūrya*! / Indeed, the brahman will cleanse them." The stanza belongs to the marriage hymn and is recited when the bride's robe is handed over to the brahman. Our translation on the whole follows that of Geldner who, moreover, sees an implicit comparison in *pādas a-b*: "(Es ist wie) das Schlachten, Zerlegen und Zerschneiden" [74.3.272]. Renou renders the passage as containing a breach in the syntactic bond, but without any ellipsis: "Coupage, découpage et mise en pièces . . . " [122.88].

Another example of a predicative construction undergoing ellipsis:

utá smainám̐ vastramáthiṃ ná tāyúm
ánu krośanti kṣitáyo bháreṣu
nīcā́yamānaṃ jásuriṃ ná śyenám̐
śrávaś cā́chā paśumác ca yūthám (4.38.5)

"And more: peoples shout after him in battles, / As after a thief (who has) stolen a garment, / When, like a weakened kite, falling down, / (*Dadhikrā* rushes forth) to fame and to a cattle-herd!." This translation follows the interpretation suggested by Renou [118.15.162-3]. Geldner does not find any ellipsis in this stanza and treats the accusatives of *pāda d* as governed by the participle *áyamānaṃ* in *pāda c*. Geldner's translation raises grave doubts as to the stanza's exact meaning; compare " . . . wenn er wie ein niederstossender hungriger Adler auf den Ruhmespreis und auf die Viehherde losstürmt" [74.1.470].

Ellipsis is most commonly encountered in subordinate comparative clauses, and comparisons in general are extremely common in the *Ṛg Veda*. But this kind of proper comparative clause is rather rare; incomplete comparative phrases are much more frequent. The degree of ellipticity varies: on the one hand, it can be limited to the omission of a single word, usually the predicate, since as a rule the predicates are identical in the main clause and in the comparative phrase. On the other hand, even quite essential parts of the sentence can be omitted so that the comparison becomes logically flawed and its correct understanding becomes well-nigh impossible; this is brachylogy.

Occasionally a comparison appears in the text in both an elliptic and a full version, for example: *abhí táṣṭeva dīdhayā manīṣā́m* (3.38.1) "Like a carpenter, I conceived of a poetic work:" the comparison would have remained unclear if it had not occurred in a complete form elsewhere: *asmā́ íd u stómaṃ sáṃ hinomi / ráthaṃ ná táṣṭeva tátsināya / gíraś ca gírvāhase suvṛktī́ndrāya / . . .* (1.61.4) "It is for him that I compose (this) praise, / For him who rewards, like a carpenter (working on) a chariot, / And praise-songs with successful orations for *Indra*, captivated by praise-songs, . . . "

Another example of the same kind: *anūpé gómān góbhir akṣāḥ / sómo dugdhā́bhir akṣāḥ / samudráṃ ná saṃváraṇāny agman / . . .* (9.107.9) "(Like) a cow-owner with (his) cows upon a riverside, / *Soma* flowed, with the milked-out (streams of milk) he flowed. / They went to (their) (cow-) sheds as though to the sea." This is a description of mixing the expressed *Soma* juice with water and milk. The comparison with the sea makes sense when its complete version appears in the very next hymn: *índrasya hā́rdi somadhā́nam ā́ viśa / samudrám iva síndhavaḥ* (9.108.16) "Do enter *Indra*'s heart, the *Soma* container, / As rivers (enter) the ocean."

Thus it appears that a noun in a certain case-form, combined with a particle of comparison, serves as a word-sign for the full comparison: "as a carpenter" implies "constructs a chariot," "as into the sea" implies "the rivers fall," "as cow(s)" or "as mothers" implies "lick(s) a calf," "like rivalling wives" implies "torment their husband," etc.

Sometimes the elliptic comparison is structured inexactly, for example: *ṛtásya devā́ ánu vratā́ gur / bhúvat páriṣṭir dyaúr ná bhū́ma* (1.65.3) "The gods followed the stipulations of the universal law. / (*Agni*) was enclosed, as the sky (encloses) the earth," where the verb omitted in the comparative phrase should not have differed in voice from that in the main clause. Another instance of the same kind: *nábho ná rūpáṃ jarimā́ mināti* (1.71.10) "As a cloud (changes its appearance), old age changes beauty."

The distinction between ellipsis in comparison and brachylogy can be a very delicate one indeed. What seems a violation of logical reasoning to a modern scholar could very possibly give rise to quite definite and established associations in the minds of the *Ṛṣi* and his audience. Compare, for example, this verse addressed to the *Maruts*: *kvà vo gā́vo ná raṇyanti* (1.38.2) literally "Where do (they) rejoice in you like cows?"–scilicet "as cows rejoice in a pasture," which is an integral image of extreme importance in the perception of the Vedic world [135.1-12].

Brachylogy can appear rather unnatural, as in the following example: *prá va éko mimaya bhū́ry ā́go / yán mā pitéva kitaváṃ śaśāsá* (2.29.5) "I alone have committed many sinful acts against you / So that you could punish me as a father (punishes his son), a gambler." In order to supply the missing part of the ellipsis it must be remembered that the oppositions "father–son," "mother–child" are often expressed in the *Ṛg Veda* in an elliptic form. Compare, for example, the words of the rivers addressed to the *Ṛṣi Viśvāmitra* who is asking for their help: *ā́ te kāro śṛṇavāmā vácāṃsi / yayā́tha dūrā́d ánasā ráthena / ní te naṃsai pīpyānéva yóṣā / . . .* (3.33.10) "We shall listen, O eulogizer, to thy words. / Thou hast arrived from afar with a cart(-train) and a chariot. / I wish to bend over thee, like a woman swollen (with milk over her child)." Another example:

yásyekṣvākúr úpa vraté
revā́n marāyy édhate
divī̀va páñca kṛṣṭáyaḥ (10.60.4)

" . . . Under his dominion *Ikṣvāku*, the rich *Marāyin* (and) the five tribes thrive, like (the sun) in the sky."

It is impossible to connect the comparative phrase with the predicate of the main clause for semantic reasons, since only human kings are mentioned, whilst the "five tribes" denote the whole Aryan world. At the same time, "the sun in the sky" is an established image in Vedic poetry, and this phrase actually appears in the next stanza of the hymn: *divī̀va sū́ryaṃ dṛśé* (10.60.5) "In order to see the sun in the sky."

Quite often the comparative particle is omitted, in accordance with Vedic usage. Nevertheless, as Renou has pointed out [118.15.40], objective criteria are hard to find, since the stylistic peculiarities of the text do not preclude the treatment of many cases of this kind as simple juxtaposition of nouns within a sentence as, for example, in: *eṣá stómo acikradad vṛ́ṣā te* (7.20.9) "This praise-tune roared up for thee (like) a bull" (but one cannot exclude: "This bull, being a praise-tune, roared up for thee").

Western interpreters have disagreed about the following example: *īḷényaḥ pávamāno / rayír ví rājati dyumā́n / . . .* (9.5.3) "Worthy of appeals, purifying himself, (*Agni*) / Shines brightly, (like) brilliant wealth." This translation follows that of Geldner, who sees the ellipsis of the comparative particle here [74.3.13]–a well-founded view. But Renou believes that *rayír . . . dyumā́n* is an epithet of *Agni*; he appeals to analogous instances in other contexts, and suggests: " . . . (*Agni* qui est) *Pavamāna*, richesse éclatante brille au loin . . . " [118.8.5, 52]. Because there are contexts where *Agni* is compared to wealth, while the comparative phrases contain the comparative particle *ná* (1.127.9, 1.128.1), the whole problem remains unresolved.

The examples adduced above seem to be sufficient to demonstrate the extremely widespread character of ellipsis in the *Ṛg Veda*, an essential constituent of Vedic poetics that helps to achieve vagueness, suggestiveness, various double-entendres, in short, all the distinguishing features of esoteric poetry.

There are word-classes that cannot undergo ellipsis in the *Ṛg Veda*: emphatic particles and adverbs-prefixes. Emphatic particles determine the emotional level of the discourse and underscore the words which are most important on the communicative level. An act of communication is not possible without emotional scaling, and a Vedic hymn always represents such an act. Adverb-prefixes serve primarily as pointers at the directionality of an action, and their basic semantic component determines all the rest. In the hymn as a communication act the direction of the action (towards the worshipper from the deity, from the worshipper towards the deity, together or separately, etc.) is functionally more important than its lexical meaning, whose approximate value can be usually extracted from the context. The original nature of ellipsis is inextricably tied to the existence of two classes of words with similar semantics that may not be omitted from the text.[145]

It should, however, be mentioned here that Renou has discussed the possibility that adverbs-prefixes may undergo ellipsis. Notwithstanding the fact that in some contexts a simple verb may have a meaning usually seen in combination with such adverbs, Renou still concludes that it would be hazardous to speak of prefix-ellipsis both because of the vagueness of verbal semantics and because many verbal-roots are attested by very few forms in the text [124.35].

In his monograph on ellipsis in the *Ṛg Veda*, Gonda provides a series of explanations for the high frequency of this phenomenon. First, he stresses that ellipsis is a hallmark of colloquial speech [78.7], and believes that the ellipsis of the verb should be linked with the relationship between the literary and the colloquial language of a given culture at a given time [78.46]. He states that ellipsis in the *Ṛg Veda* can hardly be attributed to a special priestly language [78.9], and that the ellipsis of nouns can be called one of the marks of the esoteric nature of poetry [78.24]. In the first instance, ellipsis is due to a linguistic taboo [78.23], and in the second it is caused by the desire of the Vedic poet to match syntactic and metric units [78.71]. Although these observations are quite justified, they apply to details and not to general norms.

By the time of the constitution of the text, ellipsis had become an extremely widespread phenomenon. It would be interesting to delineate the general sphere of contexts that might have been the original source of ellipsis. Although this phenomenon occurs much more frequently in modern colloquial languages than in literary languages, the situation in the *Ṛg Veda* appears to be quite different. Thus there is much less ellipsis in the dialogue hymns than in hymns of other genres. It therefore appears that in this cultic text ellipsis had no original links with prophanic dialogues, whose basis lay in the *ākhyāna* genre, but that rather, its sources should be sought in quite different areas.

Because of their various elliptic constructions, Vedic stanzas, whose content reflects mythological plots and ritual actions, often resemble riddles in form. Their solution presupposes a thorough acquaintance with the religious and mythological traditions of that period. One can therefore hypothesize that the original function of ellipsis might be explained in the light of this usage.

According to Hillebrandt's hypothesis–further developed by Kuiper– the nucleus of the hymns had to do with the transition from the Old Year to the New Year, which was seen as the transition from the undifferentiated state of Chaos to the Cosmos that was being organized anew. By the end of each yearly cycle the Cosmos returned to its original chaotic state and was restored by the priests, who used every ritual means: verbal contests, chariot races, etc. [22.47-100, 151-215]. The hymns of the ancient nucleus were directly linked to the ritual; Kuiper has investigated the ritual connection of the *Uṣas* hymns and of some of the hymns to *Indra*. The cosmogonic riddles of the *brahmodya* (literally "talking about the brahman") were part of the ritual aimed at the restoration of the Cosmos [43.31f]. As Renou demonstrated [128.22-46 (Le brahmodya védique)], the *brahmodya* appeared in the form of a dialogue between two priests with alternating questions and answers about the structure of the cosmos. The dialogic construction of the *brahmodya* corresponds to an archaic ritual built upon binary oppositions and ultimately reflecting a social structure of the dual type which is controlled by the institution of universal exchange [15.14-46]. The *brahmodya*, or verbal exchange, conveys information about the integrity of the world and its identity with the model that was "in the beginning." Thus, the *brahmodya* is not a riddle in function, but it is very similar to a riddle in appearance.

The close links between the ritual and the peculiar form of its verbal component are of great help in understanding the function of elliptic phrases. While the ritual consists of a sequence of acts, its verbal accompaniment needs only some indication of the direction of these acts without naming them, as they take place right before the participants: compare the use of adverbs-prefixes without the finite verb. In this way the adverbs-prefixes could serve as verbal signs for the priests' gestures. Since the *brahmodyas* were verbal contests between priests, all sorts of understatement and omission of words and phrases could serve as proofs that the rival-participant of this verbal contest was fully initiated in the knowledge of hidden senses and was able to give a correct reply using the vaguest hints. With the spread of ellipsis in the hymns of the *Ṛg Veda*, its original functional charge was gradually diluted, and the phenomenon became a characteristic of the Vedic poetic style.

Haplology is also quite frequently associated with ellipsis in the *Ṛg Veda*. Haplology can be viewed as ellipsis on the phonetical level, operating within a word or a word-combination. A syllable is subject to haplology when it is omitted under the influence of the following, phonetically similar syllable. Examples of the process within a word: the infinitive *irádhyai* "to strive to obtain" instead of the expected **iradhadhyai*; dative case singular feminine *svapatyaí* from *svapatyā́-* "having beautiful offspring," instead of **svapatyā́yai*. Examples of word- or syllabic haplology on the boundary of two words: *sá vípraś carṣaṇīnā́m . . . áti vidhyati* (4.8.8) "This inspired one pierces (the inspiration of all) tribes . . . " where *vípraḥ* results from the haplology of **vípo vípraḥ*; *vánde dārúṃ vándamāno vivakmi* (7.6.1) "I proclaim while praising . . . , I praise (in that) the eulogizer," where *vánde dārúṃ* is a haplology from **vánde vandārúm* in a string of words derived from the root *vand-*.[146] Renou regarded haplology in the *Ṛg Veda* as an artificial feature, a kind of pun [120.400].

The last point to be mentioned in connection with ellipsis is a variety of anacoluthon. In this case the breach in syntactic links is such that the sentence is actually destroyed. In simple sentences this occurs when the predicative elementary syntactic construction is broken up, and in composite sentences when only the subordinate clause is left. At the same time one cannot always confirm violations of predicativity, since the relevant passages can be interpreted as predicative nominal sentences, as cases with ellipsis of a verbal predicate or, finally, as parts of a sentence syntactically linked to the following stanza. Some examples:

haṃsáḥ śuciṣád vásur antarikṣasád
dhótā vediṣád átithir duroṇasát
nṛṣád varasád ṛtasád vyomasád
abjā́ gojā́ ṛtajā́ adrijā́ ṛtám (4.40.5)

"The swan in the clear (sky), *Vasu* in the air, / The *hotar*-priest at the altar, the guest in house, / (The god) among people, in the best (place), upon the lap of the law, upon the sky-vault, / Born of the waters, born of the cows, born of the law, born of the rock–the Law!"

This stanza concludes the hymn to the divine horse *Dadhikrāvan*, here apparently identified with the Sun. It is cited in the *Upaniṣads* in connection with the doctrine of identifications; actually, it is an enumeration of divine epithets, made up of compounds with similar structure (*pādas a-c* of one type, *pāda d* of another) that are in contrast with the final word *ṛtám* "the Law." This unusual structure may point to a special syntactic role of *ṛtám* in this string of epithets. Renou treats this word as a predicative nominative distinct from all the other nominal attributes of the omitted subject: " . . . né de la montagne, (il est) l'Ordre (même)" [118.15.166]. Geldner does not dissociate *ṛtám* from the rest of the nominatives, and so his version of the stanza looks like a list of nouns without a predicate: "Der Schwan, . . . der . . . felsgeborene, die Wahrheit (selbst)" [74.1.472].

Such lists of epithets can fill only half a stanza, not a whole one, and this case may be treated as an independent "sentence," or it may be joined to the second half-stanza, with an anacoluthon in the middle of this single "sentence," for example:

rāyó budhnáḥ saṃgámano vásūnāṃ
yajñásya ketúr manmasā́dhano véḥ
amṛtatvā́ṃ rákṣamāṇāsa enaṃ
devā́ agníṃ dhārayan draviṇodā́m (1.96.6)

"Foundation of wealth, confluence of goods, / Banner of sacrifice, reciter of prayers, bird . . . / Protecting their immortality / The gods supported this *Agni*, the wealth-giver." Geldner understands the stanza as a single sentence; he marks the anacoluthon between the two half-stanzas with a dash [74.2.65].

There are some contexts in which nominal predicativity is hard to perceive. These are static descriptions of a deity, an enumeration of his specific features and attributes that are expressed by adjectives, compounds of the *bahuvrīhi* type, nominal constructions in alternation with comparative phrases, for example:

vā́tatviṣo marúto varṣánirṇijo
yamā́ iva súsadṛśaḥ supéśasaḥ
piśáñgāśvā aruṇā́śvā arepásaḥ
prátvakṣaso mahinā́ dyaúr ivorávaḥ (5.57.4)

"The *Maruts*, strong in the wind, rain-robed, / Completely identical, like twins, wonderfully adorned, / With golden horses, with purple horses, irreproachable, / of remarkable strength, broad in greatness, like the sky . . . . "

But Geldner who avoids such "unpredicative stanzas" in his translation as a matter of principle, joined this stanza to the next one [74.2.65]. The same kind of syntactic relationship in composite sentences is rendered by one or a series of subordinate clauses without the principal clause. As a rule, these are relative clauses in *yá-*, which enumerate the deity's feats or characteristics. This can be seen, for instance, in this stanza from a hymn to *Agni*:

ā́ yáṃ háste ná khādínaṃ
śíśuṃ jātáṃ ná bíbhrati
viśā́m agníṃ svadhvarám (6.16.40)

"(He) whom they wear as a bracelet on the arm, / (Which they carry) like a newborn child, / (Him), *Agni*, (the maker) of fine rituals among the tribes . . . . " In this case, too, Geldner joins the stanza to the next one [74.2.18]. One more example from a hymn to the same god:

asyá vā́sā́ u arcíṣā
yá ā́yukta tujā́ girā́
divó ná yásya rétasā
bṛhác chócanty arcáyaḥ (5.17.3)

"He has yoked in with his mouth (and) flame, / Thanks to the (priest's) zeal (and) the praise-song, / And his flaming tongues glare on high / Like (lightnings), thanks to heaven's semen . . . . "

These examples demonstrate how static the descriptions of mythic figures of the *Ṛg Veda* could be, appearing in the hymns as lists of features or enumerations of epithets, whose "suspended nature," that is, whose implicit or potential predicativity, blurs the distinctions between nominal and predicative constructions.[147] This kind of style may have represented most adequately the visual nature of the Vedic *Ṛṣis'* creative activity.

6
Conclusion

This investigation has been concerned with the ways in which the language and style of the *Ṛg Veda* reflect essential features of the mythological, cultural and historical views characteristic of the time and milieu that produced this particular text. The following results seem to be most important.

An essential characteristic of the vocabulary of this text is polysemy; the most multivalent words denote the basic concepts of the Vedic model of the universe. The peculiarity of this polysemy consists in the word's semantics being correlated with denotates of different levels, usually with the myth and the ritual; this becomes the basis for stylistic play. Such intentional double reference creates serious obstacles for our comprehension of the text, and in order to identify correctly the meaning of individual words one must determine the reference type of a large segment of the text in which the particular word occurs.

In a large group of Vedic words this polysemy acquires a symbolic character. There is a closed subgroup of lexemes denoting human body-parts that symbolize parts of the cosmos: this reflects an archaic idea of creating elements of the cosmos out of the human body.

Extreme cases of polysemy may give a word antonymic meanings. The ambivalent semantics of such words is used for stylistic purposes: the opposed meanings are distributed between a "favorable zone" (gods and their worshippers) and a "hostile zone" (demons and the impious enemies of the Aryans). But semantic bifurcation can also occur within the "favorable zone:" part of the latter's vocabulary is characterized by conversive semantics, that is, the logical point of gravity of the meaning changes when a word applies to a deity or to a worshipper. This semantic difference is quite well-established and cuts through various word-classes, derivation types, primary and compound words.

A well-developed synonymy is also typical of Vedic vocabulary, as it is of any literary language as compared to colloquial speech. But the *Ṛg Veda* has a specific functional synonymy that allows words with quite different meanings to appear as synonyms in certain contexts: this can be explained by the cultic nature of the text and the *Ṛṣi*'s view of the world.

The *Ṛg Veda* has no opposition of synonyms between the "language of gods" and the "language of men." The *Ṛṣis* believed that the language of the *Ṛg Veda* was wholly sacred, that it was the actual "language of gods." The real "language of men," that is, the vernacular of the time, might have been represented by some archaic variety of Middle Indian.

The mythological problem of the relations between "gods" and "powers" is linguistically reflected in the semantics of a number of nominal stems with their peculiar expression of the category of gender. In such stems there is a contradiction between the gender grammeme and the grammatical meaning of the stem, or (in nondiagnostic contexts) the degree of personification of an abstract notion is obscured; this is true not only for root stems but also for stems with the suffixes *-ti, -as, -man* and the word *vṛtrá-*.

The process of transformation of appellative nouns into proper names is crucial for Vedic vocabulary. The status of a proper name was considered. According to the magic world-view, the name reflected the nature of the name-bearer, and the enunciation of the name actually meant the acquisition of power over its bearer. The hymns continually play upon proper names. The degree of personification of an abstract notion is constantly shifted while the degree of indeterminacy is heightened. The solution of this problem, the distinction between "proper name" or "appellative noun", thus largely depends upon the particular way in which a given passage, or the text as a whole, is understood; in other words, the key should be sought in the reference of the text.

Metrics has several functions in the *Ṛg Veda*: First, metrics employ a purely technical means of organizing a text. Second, metrics serve as an additional channel for conveying certain information from the worshipper to the deity in the communication act. Third, metrics may acquire an independent mythological value. Metrical speech, measured in the *akṣara*-syllables, is also sacred, and it is personified by the goddess *Vāc*, who is one of the cosmogonic powers. Individual verse-meters also appear as mythological figures, frequently perceived as half-personified powers.

The role of the poet-*Ṛṣi* with respect to Sacred Speech was to reveal its hidden nature and to make visible what was nonmanifest. Herein lies one of the fundamental principles of *Ṛg Veda* poetics. The poetic language of the *Ṛg Veda* practices a symbolic use of the *pāda*, or verse-line, when the violation of the traditional syllable-count, the sequence of quantities, and the position of the caesura formally symbolize the events described in the verses (Thieme's "*Sprachmalerei*"). An irregular change in the meter can also be symbolic.

The bulk of expressive information is conveyed within the framework of the metrical scheme of the stanza, at a certain position within the *pāda*.

Words or sound-sequences containing this information occupy marked positions in the stanza: either the strong position at the beginning of the *pāda*, or at some other position(s) in the *pāda*(s), which are often mutually symmetrical. On the prosodic level there are rhythmical hints at the word which is either a theonym or denotes some other key notion.

However, the most common way of conveying expressive information is at the phonetic, or sound level. Basically, it can be described as the semantization of a sound-sequence. As a rule, the information concerns the addressee of the act of communication, that is, the deity that is being praised. It (i.e., the information) can also belong to the sphere of the "message" and somehow reproduce the name of the addressing *Ṛṣi*. Since the act was one-sided—the *Ṛṣi* recited the hymn and the deity hearkened to it—it was extremely important to capture the god's attention by pronouncing his name. The theonym occurred in marked metrical positions, and the name's sound theme was kept up by sound-hints. These sound-hints could have a basis in etymology (in the case of a play upon derivatives from the same root), but they generally represent semantizations of fortuitous sound combinations.

The hymns of Book 9 (to *Soma-Pavamāna*) often play upon various forms derived from the verb *pū-* "to purify" (of which *pávamāna-* is the participle present medial voice form), including nouns, as distinct from those derived from the verb *su-* "to press (out)" (of which *sóma-* is a nominal derivative root). This circumstance argues for the purely liturgical application of hymns of this Book, since the focal point of the *Soma* preparation ritual was the purification of the juice.

Sometimes the vocabulary that is specific for a certain deity seems to be based upon the expressive principle, so that the deity's name (for example, *Indra*) resounds as it were in the respective lexical units. Sometimes the key to the hymn's expressive information is to be found in adverbs-prefixes and particles that tend to begin the sentence and, correspondingly, the *pāda*.

The metrical markedness of an appellative noun that denotes a deity, its strong position at the beginning of a *pāda*, can sometimes serve as the decisive argument for treating this appellative noun as a theonym (compare 10.121). The sound-theme of the "message" can be polyphonic (compare the cosmogonic hymns). In Vedic "spells" it is normally based upon the key magic word. Sometimes the *Sprachmalerei* conveys the information about the addresser of the communication act, that is, the author of the hymn. However, in such a case, in order to become aware of the communicative nature of the *Sprachmalerei* one must have an advance knowledge of the author's name. On the other hand, the later Brahmanical commentatorial tradition (which is based upon the sound-play in a given hymn) quite often takes the key-word of the hymn for the author's name.

Along with grammar proper, which belongs to the system of language, the *Ṛg Veda* employs an expressive grammar, or a grammar of poetry (as Jakobson put it). The aims of the speech act do determine a great deal in the syntax of forms, in the semantics of grammatical categories and grammemes, and in the frequency of their use.

Praise-hymns typically employ the "expressive paradigm" of the name of the deity being praised, in which the various case-forms of the theonym begin the stanza- or *pāda* (de Saussure). The formal use of a proper key-word in every stanza of the *Āprī* hymns was also obligatory. The names of the majority of the grand deities of the *Ṛg Veda*, and some of the deified abstract notions, often form such paradigms in the praise-hymns. The only exception is the name of *Soma*, one of the three principal gods of the *Ṛg Veda*. This obvious breach in the general trend prompts the conclusion that the word *sóma-* was perceived not as the proper name of a god, but only as a name for the ritual substance which was used to obtain the juice necessary for the preparation of the divine drink of immortality.

In hymns to a pair of deities, the range of possibilities for a formal play upon theonyms was noticeably greater. These theonyms were used in marked positions of the metrical scheme either in the form of a *dvandva* compound, or separately, forming as it were, two parallel expressive paradigms. There are hymns in which this complex play (of associating and dissociating the two theonyms) is clearly symbolic, and reflects the author's perception of their interrelationship (compare 4.41).

The Vedic expressive grammar of theonyms plays upon vocatives, which repeatedly break the narrative thread to create a particular emotionally charged tenor. The play upon vocatives should be treated in the general context of the Vedic ideas concerning the magic of the proper name. Calling upon gods by name in the form of lists could be conditioned by the requirements of the ritual. But the communicative function of vocatives comes to the fore when the god is invoked by means of epithets, often of a suggestive, or evocative nature: this situation presupposes a switching of codes: "O Generous one!" ↔ "be generous to us!"

Lastly, the use of vocatives can be conditioned by purely syntactic reasons when, for instance, they cut the conjunctionless string of nouns in the same case, and so function as a kind of balance-wheel. The expressive paradigm of a pronoun whose referent is a deity does not differ in any way from that of a noun. The praise-hymns play most commonly upon the second person singular *tvám* "thou," which occurs in strong positions of the metrical scheme in its different case-forms. The existence of various types of deities complicates the play upon demonstrative pronouns. In the expressive usage of Book 9, the demonstratives whose referent is *Soma* are clearly preferred to the personal pronoun of the second person.

One of the variants of the expressive pronominal scheme is used in subordinate relative clauses in which the initial position in every stanza is occupied by a case-form of the relative pronoun *yá-* that has a demonstrative as its correlate in the main clause. The magic play upon pronouns can be also seen in the fact that the marked position of the metrical scheme, which is occupied in most stanzas by a pronoun referring to the deity, is sometimes filled in—in one of the stanzas—by a pronoun referring to the worshipper. A formal indicator of the genre of self-laudations is the first person singular pronoun *ahám* "I" at the beginning of the stanza.

In the verbal system, the influence of text-semantics can be detected, first of all, in the dominant role of the category of mood as compared with the category of tense: in a praise-hymn, requests and wishes are much more more frequent than descriptions. The notion of time as a cyclical process is expressed in the injunctive used predominantly in mythological fragments of the hymns. This archaic mood is at odds with the whole system of tense-and-aspect and modal differentiation (it only mentions the action—the memorative, in Hoffmann's terms), but it happens to be an extremely convenient device for mentioning events that are not related to the moment of speech, which occurs beyond time and is cyclically repeated.

The absence from the language system of rigid restrictions upon various types of morpheme combinations, as well as the nonobligatory character of a direct correspondence between the system of grammatical meanings and their formal structural oppositions—all of this contributed to the dominance of the category of mood over the category of tense. Thus various modal forms are based on different temporal stems but have identical meaning; and the subjunctive grammeme is used as the main form of the future tense. As a result, the language of the text has at its disposal a vast system of tense-and-aspect oppositions in the verb, yet the temporal meaning has to be elicited from a wider context.

And finally, the use of the tenses in certain mythological contexts (such as the hymns to the *Aśvins*) in enumerations of the deities' deeds, also helped to level out the temporal oppositions—since the relation of the action to the moment of speech is practically of no importance, or, as Renou has put it, its use is "pseudohistorical."

Syntactic peculiarities of the Ṛg Vedic language have been widely used to create the special, suggestive style of the text. The self-sufficient character of the verb, which contains all the necessary grammatical information, along with the optional character of the subject pronoun, created favorable conditions for a deliberate vagueness as to the subject of the action. The fact that pronouns of the second and the third persons are interchangeable in certain syntactic contexts makes it reasonable to suppose that in the speech act between the deity and the worshipper the opposition "addresser: nonaddresser" occupied a higher place in the hierarchy than other oppositions such as "addresser: addressee" and "participant of the speech act: nonparticipant of the speech act."

The free word-order and the absence of rigid syntactic bonds in the sentence make the context—in many cases—the only criterion for a corrrect actual division of the sentence. Basic to the nominal forms is the collocational principle, or the principle of appositions, according to which the nominative of a noun with a verbal predicate quite often appears to function not as the subject but as its apposition, thus creating uncertainty as to identity of the subject of the action.

Strings of adjectives-epithets and substantives-appositions in the same case are characterized by very loose syntactic bonds, and relations between the theme-or-rheme are not easy to determine. Most typical are strings of nominatives and accusatives, parts of which can be predicative. In order to establish the predicative character of those parts—such as the nominative with an intransitive verb, or the double accusative with a transitive one—one has to fall back upon the context or the most general mythological data.

When the nominative is absent, the vocative acquires a special role and becomes the sole means of reference for the whole context (compare the hymns to the All-Gods). In the cosmogonic hymns the absence of the subject nominative becomes the linguistic basis for speculations concerning the incomprehensible and unknowable nature of the demiurge.

The order of the words in a phrase or, more exactly, their combination, results from the interaction between the various functions of the language (the poetic, the communication) and those tendencies which are related to the oral transmission of the text—mainly, the repeated balanced syntactic structures. The extremely developed inflectional structure of the language results in the autonomous character of word-forms and the full realization of those tendencies. These principles are applicable both to verbal and nominal sentences. Only the morphological elements of the nuclear syntactic constructions happen to be obligatory, but not the sequence of the elements, nor the relations between the constructions.

A problem apart is the identification of the subject of nominal sentences. Since a fixed word-order is lacking, very often only the mythological context can be used as a criterion for such an identification.

Forms with identical case-endings or derivational affixes, are often juxtaposed or symmetrically disposed within a stanza of syntagms or clauses with isomorphic structures. This tendency results in numerous instances of attraction by case, number, or gender. The order of the words in such cases is determined by the syntax of repetitions, not by the syntax of the sentence. "Magic grammar" with its play upon key-words also exerts a heavy influence upon the word-order: the key-word is brought forward to the beginning of the *pāda*. The pronoun that refers to the deity and the pronoun that refers to the worshipper are brought into juxtaposition, or the one is substituted for the other. Epithets of the god and the worshipper alternate in the string of epithets.

However, linguistic factors also influenced the word-order. Words can be juxtaposed according to some semantic feature: close synonyms, sometimes almost tautological, or—on the contrary—antonyms, as well as words expressing oppositions that are essential for the Vedic model of the universe. Participles in attributive constructions have an additional shade of meaning which rings them closer to subordinate clauses. This "unmanifest" trait of the syntax often makes the interpretation of a phrase wholly dependent on the context.

Asyndeton is a typical feature of Vedic syntax that explains the difficulties in analysing the text into simple and composite sentences, and further, into complex and compound sentences. Such problems may be solved with the help of prosodic data, although phrasal accent is distinctive only in a certain number of syntactic contexts. The vagueness of boundaries between emphatic particles that function as conjunction and conjunctions proper also contributes to syntactic ambiguities. The most widespread type of compound sentence with the relative pronoun *yá-* is notable for the rather loose coordination of *ya-* with the demonstrative pronoun in the main clause, which can be explained by ellipsis or some kind of attraction. In extreme cases the relative *ya-* is downgraded to the status of a particle, while the neuter of this pronoun (*yád*) is identical with the conjunction. The most common conjunction, *yád* is so polysemantic that the type of the subordinate clause introduced by it can be determined exclusively from the wider context.

Ellipsis can affect any part of the sentence, including the subject and the predicate; in the latter case the finite verb is most commonly omitted, and the independent adverb-prefix remains. Ellipsis is extremely frequent in comparisons, where even the comparative particle may be dropped, blurring the boundary between a comparative phrase and an apposition. The phenomenon of ellipsis is an important means of creating the suggestive style of this text.

Of all the word-classes, only emphatic particles and adverbs-prefixes are not affected by ellipsis. This fact lends probability to the hypothesis that before ellipsis became part of Vedic poetics, it had been a distinctive feature of the text which used to accompany the ritual. The particles furnished the text with the apposite emotional tone, while the adverbs-prefixes served as verbal indicators of the actions performed in the ritual and functioned as their verbal equivalents. Highly elliptical phrases, especially in mythological fragments, are similar in type to the cosmogonic riddles (*brahmodya*) that were a constituent part of the verbal contests that were included in a more comprehensive ritual.The *brahmodya* appears to have been a kind of password or test that warranted the knowledge of the hidden truth. Ellipsis seems to have played a similar role in the language of the *Ṛg Veda*.

The variety of anacoluthon that lacks predicativity and occurs in descriptions of mythological figures should be more conveniently treated as a static portrayal of such figures as a list of features and not as a particular case of ellipsis. This interpretation is more suitable to the static nature of the Vedic *Ṛṣis*' vision.

Generally speaking, the genre of the *Ṛg Veda*, an archaic cultic poetic text, determines the functioning of its grammatical system even in details. This grammatical system cannot be studied as a mere hierarchy of abstract oppositions taken in isolation from the purpose of the text and its cultural milieu. Something that contradicts the system at a certain synchronic stage may happen to be functionally valid (and even more suitable for rendering the text's archaic concepts) than the basic core of its linguistic system. This is true of the injunctive, the contradiction between the grammatical meaning of a nominal stem and the particulars of its gender expression, ellipsis, and anacoluthon with infringements of predicativity. On the other hand, something that is systemic can be levelled out in certain contexts under the influence of their communicative aim or of the peculiarities of the authors' model of the universe. This is true of the blurring of oppositions in tense and the general predominance of the category of mood, indifference to tense-grammeme oppositions in "pseudohistorical" contexts, and words that have different lexical meanings but function as synonyms in certain contexts.

These features of the vocabulary and grammatical system of Vedic language are all used to create a special style that fits the purpose of the text. The development of nominal polysemy is basic to the distribution of meanings in the "favorable" and "unfavorable" semantic sphere, with a further opposition in the "favorable" sphere: "deity"—*versus* "worshipper." The same purpose is served by the use of verbs from different stems, each with their corresponding semantics.

The self-sufficient nature of an individual finite verbal form which contains in its structure (the stem-class and inflexion) all the necessary grammatical information makes superfluous the presence of the personal pronoun as the subject of this predicate, and this fact is played upon in the hymns to create vagueness concerning the subject of an action.

The tendency for asyndeton results in the appearance of strings of substantives-appositions and adjectives-attributes in the same case with very loose syntactic links. These strings represent a kind of static description that is very common in the *Ṛg Veda* and corresponds quite precisely to the visual nature of the *Ṛṣis*'s knowledge.

The cases of "covertness" in the system of oppositions of some of the values include voice and mood in the infinitive, the verbal meaning of the participle in an attributive phrase, fluctuations between emphatic particles and conjunctions, and neutralization of the distinctive functions of the phrasal accent in nondiagnostic positions. All of these provide for stylistic interpretations in an atmosphere of uncertainty, understatement, and double-entendre. This grammatical "covertness" originated with the *Ṛg Veda* and was fully developed during the later stages: when it became transformed into mytho-poetical and philosophical "unmanifestness."

In the poetic language of the *Ṛg Veda* the interrelationship of linguistic functions is very different from that in ordinary speech. The expressive—also known as iconic—function of the language acquires immense importance. The basic "meaningful" text thus obtains an overstructure—an "expressive" text. The form there becomes semanticized and symbolizes certain information. This information is generated not according to the laws of a language system but by the requirements of the communication act. It contains the data concerning the main constituents of the communication act—in the first place about the addressee, i.e., the deity: the expressive paradigm of his name, sound and rhythmic hints at it, and magic play upon the pronoun that refers to the deity. Less "expressive information" is passed about the addresser of the communication act, i.e., the *Ṛṣi*, the author of the hymn: and this information is usually contained in sound-hints at his name. The sound-play upon the "message" of the communication act—either a request to the deity or the basic idea of an abstract hymn—consists in sound and rhythmic hints, or in the correlation between the first and the last words of a hymn, and often displays a polyphonic character.

The language of the Vedic hymns is distinguished by the strengthening of the appellative function, which is formally rendered by the imperative of the verb and the vocative of the noun. The magic treatment of a theonym results in unbridled juggling of divine names and epithets in the vocative, which in its turn creates the tense and emotional style of the hymns. Moreover, other factors determine the use of vocatives: they counterbalance the strings of homogeneous nominal case-forms by breaking them up in certain positions, while the vocative-epithet appears as a transformation of the "message" when the appellative and the descriptive portions of a hymn are switched.

The imperative, as the only verbal mood with inherent directionality, is best suited to render the "message" of the praise-hymns. The frequent indiscriminate use of the second and third person pronouns as subjects with the imperative verb reflects the fluid boundaries between the appellative and the descriptive functions of the language in the text. The same phenomenon is evidenced by the interchangeability of the vocative and the nominative in certain syntactic contexts, such as the predicative vocative, the "vocative-nominative + *ca*" construction.

The main descriptive function of the language is somewhat reduced in the *Ṛg Veda*. The principal means of the discursive narration of events in a linear sequence is represented by the category of tense. But tense is here displaced to a certain degree by the category of mood. Plots in the *Ṛg Veda* are not usually narrated but only mentioned in passing, since they are known both to the *Ṛṣis* and to their audience. The particular vehicle for such references to events in mythological fragments was the injunctive grammeme. A certain class of mythological contexts makes a peculiar use of temporal grammemes that is somewhat indifferent to the logic of events. The same purpose is served by the enumeration of the deity's deeds—or, rather, by a list of the deity's distinctive features—expressed by finite verbs which are not actually related to the moment of speech.

In sum, the *Ṛg Veda*, a collection of hymns, a poetic text with a clear phatic function (directed at contact), is distinguished by the overdevelopment of the expressive and appellative functions of the language accompanied by a slightly reduced descriptive function.

Notes

1. The term "Sanskrit" in Renou's study [121] is used in its broad application, it covers all varieties of the Old Indian language, both Vedic and Sanskrit proper.

2. First published in 1943.

3. See its brief description in Emil Benveniste's paper [55.73-9].

4. See Jean Starobinski's publication of DE Saussure's notes on this subject [138; 139].

5. Compare Vjačeslav V. Ivanov on DE Saussure's interpretation of ancient Indo-European poetic texts [19.263f.; 20.11f].

6. I am grateful to Calvert Watkins for kindly letting me consult his unpublished work.

7. Compare the Old Irish treatise on grammar and poetics in his treatment of the problem "the language of gods"—"the language of men" [154.1-17].

8. I have attempted to use such a procedure in order to give a description of several figures in the *Ṛg Veda* pantheon, such as *Uṣas* [17.66-84; 13.173-188].

9. Another view considers *Pūṣán*'s connection with the sun to be secondary, regarding him originally as a pastoral deity concerned with cattle-breeding [64.91-117]. But on the synchronic level—for the time of the *Ṛg Veda*—*Pūṣán* can be considered a solar deity.

10. See the still-valuable classic study by the Polish scholar Stanislaw Schayer [130].

11. For details see our study of the *Atharva Veda* [2.21ff.].

12. In translating the *Ṛg Veda* verses we tried to maintain the original line-divisions.

13. Mayrhofer, KEWA, I. 1953, p.53. But in the second edition of his dictionary the author voices some doubts; see KEWA², Bd.I, Lief.4. 1988. p.

261. One should also keep in mind the connections between the two roots **ers-* "flow" and **eres-* "be furious, evil-minded." See J. Pokorny, *Indogermanisches etymologisches Wörterbuch.* Bd.I. Bern/München, 1959, pp. 936-7.

14. For etymology see Manfred Mayrhofer [108.340, 343].

15. Geldner's translation of this passage, "in rechter Absicht," remains quite doubtful [74.2.312].

16. This notion has been treated by Gonda in a special article. He is justified in considering "a new song" to be both a means of helping the deity, and at the same time a source of the worshipper's strength at certain critical points of life's cyclical rebirth [77].

17. Or "vision."

18. Compare in this regard the custom prevalent in Old Indian science when an author chose the name of his famous predecessor in the field.

19. See the list of publications compiled by Ram Nath Dandekar [63, 32 (Vedic and Related Personalities)].

20. See Geldner, op. cit. (this passage): "mit Verstand."

21. One cannot exclude the possibility of viewing the polysemy of *manas-* and *hṛd-* as a particular case of the universal polysemy of the type "container" *vs.* "contents" [1], although not everthing can be patterned after this general opposition.

22. The correlation between the active/middle and transitive/intransitive forms of this verb is not invariable in later Sanskrit, in which some active forms can have a transitive meaning.

23. Here we cite only those meanings which are of immediate concern to us, but in the texts the polysemy may be represented much more fully.

24. Compare the overview table presented by Vladimir Toporov [43.46].

25. Taking into consideration all the evidence gathered since the appearance of Renou's study one can assume that this ambivalence is a reflection of the ambiguous relationship between the *devās* and the *asurās* as interpreted, for example, by Kuiper.

26. It should be noted that not all shades of this semantic bifurcation are precisely conveyed by the term "conversive," although this term seems

to be the most adequate one. Compare the definition of "conversives" by Yuriy D. Apresyan [1.257].

27. In the following discussion only the oppositions representing the relationship "deity—worshipper" will be adduced, leaving aside the rest of the semantics of the verb.

28. This example may be assigned to subject (1) as well.

29. Gonda applied these terms to attributive adjectives [79.180].

30. Compare Geldner's "Anerkennung" and Renou's "une recompense-digne du panegyrique" [118.t.10.35].

31. Sāyaṇa's gloss on *sūnṛtāvate* is: "for the sake of the praiser, offerer of laudations."

32. We accept the interpretation of this verse by Sāyaṇa, who correctly noted in his commentary the different meanings of *dāśvā́ṃs-*, dependent upon the subject. Geldner's translation is superficially correct, but does not render the essentially circular nature of the act: " . . . kommet her, als Spender des Spenders."

33. The standing epithet of the *Aśvins*, *dhíṣṇya* is a word that has inspired a multitude of interpretations. Here we agree with Renou's suggestion [118.t.4.19].

34. But Geldner translates, violating the context: "die somawürdigen Freunde;" Renou: "les amis fidèles-au-soma" [118.17.68].

35. Here and in the following, only those meanings are illustrated that are synonymous with verbs denoting mental perception.

36. Renou has: "je constate" [118:9.71].

37. Geldner's translation—"Schau him, schau aus" does not fit contextually, nor is his rendering of the prefixes felicitous.

38. The translation follows Renou, who renders *ví caṣṭe* by "révèle," and *kéta* by "intuition" [118.5.94]; its meaning is interpreted in the commentary as "lumière spirituelle" [118.7.73].

39. Or: "recognizing through mind."

40. Compare Renou: "qui considèrent-avec-égards" [118: t.8.58].

41. Having noted the unusual character of such a construction for the verb *īḍ-*, Renou proposed the translation: "(L'homme) qui t'invoque (pour)

le sacrifice avec hommage, . . . ;" he believed that the verb meant here "t'appelle pour le sacrifice" [118.13.27, 112].

42. As *námasā* is at variance with the meaning of *gā́ye*, Geldner offers the following translation: "ich besinge dich unter Verbeugung mit Lobeswort" [74:2.365].

43. Compare the authorized translation into French by Oguibenine [112].

44. On the close functional ties between the priest and the grammarian see Schlerath [133] and Toporov [41].

45. Here we mention only the most important and fundamental studies; our comments do not claim to be exhaustive.

46. From this standpoint, the previous Russian translations of this passage do not convey the hidden sense of the opposition. In Boris L. Smirnov's version: " . . . both in the world and in the *Veda* am I confirmed as the *Puruṣottama*" [26.153]; Vsevolod S. Sementsov: "And because of that among men and in the *Veda* I am famed as the Supreme *Puruṣa*" [34.208].

47. The intricate and knotty problem of the actual meaning of *bhāṣā* as described by Pāṇini does not concern us here. For us it is sufficient that it was opposed to *chandas*.

48. This quotation was kindly supplied to me by Elena P. Ostrovskaya.

49. I am grateful to Andrey V. Paribok both for this parallel and for the *Jātaka* quotation.

50. The critique of Kuiper's theory presented by Wash Edward Hale needs correction and clarification as his interpretation of some *Ṛg Veda* passages gives rise to serious objections [95].

51. This hypothesis has been discussed in more detail in another paper [68] which is the basis for the present exposition.

52. The mythological system of the *Ṛg Veda* is discussed in greater detail in my Russian edition of this text [31.493-506].

53. The double gender of the agent noun in Böhtlingk-Roth and Grassmann makes possible a semi-personal interpretation of the abstract notion of "harm, damage."

54. More details on this may be found in my "Grammar of the Vedic

Language" (in Russian) [8.141-2].

55. See also 2.19.4, where the passage is even more knotty on the syntactical side.

56. A collection of theVedic *Ṛṣi*'s views concerning the concept of name is to be found in Gonda's book [81].

57. On the PIE origins of the creative function of name-giving see Ivanov's paper [18].

58. Compare Gonda's analysis of this passage [81:87].

59. See the list of suggested explanations in Mayrhofer's Dictionary [108.4.151-3].

60. This has been noted by Renou [118.1.10].

61. Geldner in his comments ad 1.34.4 suggests that originally there had been a difference in the position of stress corresponding to a semantic difference: *ákṣarā* "speech—*akṣárā* "cow;" later this opposition was neutralized.

62. When we call the *pāda* "a foot" its difference from the Greek verse-foot should be kept in mind.

63. Following Oldenberg we do not note the quantitative values of syllables in the first halves of the *pādas* in the *pāda*-diagrams, although there seem to be preferences for syllables of certain quantity in some positions: for instance, at the beginning of the *pāda*, even syllables tend to be long [113]. Other authors describe the prosodic features of the whole syllable sequence in the *pāda*, noting the high number of deviations.

64. E. Vernon Arnold observed that Western criticism of Vedic metrics, confronted with such anomalies, split into two camps. Some scholars, respecting the age of the text, considered them mere metrical irregularities. Others, trusting the consummate skill of the Vedic poets, preferred to emend the written text [53.2-3].

65. For more details, see Gonda [88].

66. The *Upaniṣads* develop this topic and enlarge upon the preeminence of the *Gāyatrī*. The *Chāndogya Upaniṣad* 12.1-2, asserts that the *Gāyatrī* encompasses the whole creation, and this metre is identified with speech. In the *Bṛhadāraṇyaka Upaniṣad* 14.1, the *Gāyatrī* is equated with the three worlds: the Earth, the Atmosphere, and the Sky.

67. Compare Arnold's remarks on the relationship between chronological and individual peculiarities in Vedic metrics [53:176] as well as the table of poetic families and metre correlations [53.48].

68. Here the division into *pādas* is rather hypothetical.

69. Geldner calls the two final *pādas* of the refrain "half-prose."

70. For more details see the "Introduction" to my selected translations from the *Atharva Veda* [2.26].

71. See on this "Introduction," pp. 8, 15ff.

72. Address to the *Ṛṣi* who has to attract *Indra* by means of his hymn.

73. More on this, citing examples, can be found in our paper "Old Indian poetics and its Indo-European origins" [14.36-88].

74. For more details on this device and other "deformations" of poetic speech, see the monograph [21.2].

75. See the complete list in "Grammar of theVedic Language" [8.45].

76. The etymological link between *sóma-* and *savá-* (and in other similar cases) is lost in the translation, though it was obvious for the poet and his audience.

77. The names of the ritual drink are underscored with a straight line, and the sound-hints—with a wavy one.

78. The word is to be pronounced *suādhíaḥ*.

79. Incidentally, this hymn displays a more limited play on the initial of the name *mar-*, compare stanza 15, *pāda* " . . . *mártyaḥ* "a mortal;" stanza 30, *pāda c: / . . . marḍikébhir* . . . "out of compassion . . . ." These devices are much more prominent in, for example, 5.59, with its frequent use of *máryāḥ* "young men" for the *Maruts*.

80. We cannot discuss here the details of the whole set of *Rudra*'s functions which represents an archaic combination of "death-fertility-life."

81. On the diachronic analysis of the text built around the key-word *ká* see Toporov's paper [146:157ff.].

82. The usual dictionary form of the verb is *hary-*.

83. This mode of description becomes widespread in later Old Indian philosophic and religious teaching, such as the Buddhist descriptions of *nirvāṇa*.

84. See the analysis of this particular structure as represented in the *Atharva Veda* in [16:43-73].

85. The previous literature also includes a formal analysis of the hymn [25:70] as well as its interpretation against a Common Indo-European background [20.12].

86. We interpret *paúra* here (following Sāyaṇa and Geldner) as vocative dual instead of *paúrā*, considering that many epithets of the *Aśvins* contain the element *purú-*, from which *paurá-* is derived.

87. Thus Geldner in his commentary quite regularly notes cases of false interpretation of various words as names of the authors.

88. The weakening of the theonym's sound-theme here is accompanied by the strengthening of the semantic theme of the worshipper and his requests addressed to the god.

89. On the expressive use of pronouns, see below.

90. In his brief commentary on this stanza Renou points out: "four times soma (exceptionally)" [118.9.109].

91. See the chapter on "Phonetics" in the present work.

92. The problem of this Indo-Iranian cultic hallucinogen is clarified by the results of the latest archaeological excavations in Soviet Central Asia. In the temple of Togolok 21 in Southern Turkmenia excavated by Victor I. Sarianidi and dated to the early first millennium BC, the bottom-parts of ritual vessels were found to contain tiny residues of ephedra twigs and poppy grain [33.152-69]. However, the discussion carried out by the "Vestnik drevnej istorii" as to this temple's Proto-Zoroastrian attribution has remained inconclusive; see the critique by Vladimir A. Livshits, Ivan M. Steblin-Kamenski, Boris A. Litvinski [32.174-6, 177-9]; see also Victor I. Sarianidi's rejoinder [32.178-81].

On other grounds, of philology and cultural history, Harry Falk has also come to the conclusion that the Vedic *Soma* was ephedra [72.77-90]; compare G. Windfuhr's identification of *Soma* as "root of ginseng" in the *Festschrift* for Mary Boyce.

93. See the more detailed analysis of the expressive structure of this hymn, and several others, in [25.71ff.].

94. Compare our analysis of the hypersemantic features of another hymn to this god (2.23) [25.72].

95. Gonda presents a review of opinions on this problem [76:1 Introduction (General Discussion of the Problems Connected with the Dual Deities)]. Here we may note Schlerath's observation that the pronominal *ubha-* "both" usually marks the unity of two different notions (see Schlerath, "Bemerkungen zum Gebrauch von *ubha-* "beide" im Ṛgveda," In: AINIRMA. Festschrift für Helmut Rahn. Hdlb., 1987, p. 271-9).

96. On the specific features of this construction and its relationship with *dvandva*-compounds, see Stephanie Jamison. *Vāyav Inraś ca* revisited. In: MSS, Hft. 49:1988.

97. Compare the peculiarities of the expressive use of the proper name *soma* in these hymns as a whole.

98. And, as a matter of fact, Renou regards hymn 105 as a variant of 104 [118.9.115].

99. Geldner suggests a different attribution of stanzas: he ascribes stanza 4 to *Varuṇa*, not *Indra*; but he does not take into account the echo correlation between stanza 3 and 4 based on the verb *dhāráyam* "I established;" each of the two gods claims this cosmogonic feat as his own, his assumption upsets the symmetrical construction of the hymn: three stanzas are spoken by one of the contestants, the other three by the second, and finally, the last stanza is a summing up.

100. Whitney also affirms (in a note) that this aorist stem *parṣ-* (from the verb *par-*) has almost become a secondary root.

101. This translation follows Kuiper's interpretation (see his article "An Indian Prometheus?") *Asiatische Studien*, xxv. Bern, 1971 (pp. 85-98).

102. See Geldner's translation [74].

103. Sergej Nikolayev and Sergej Starostin [28] have formulated a fresh formal classification of Vedic verbs in two groups, depending upon the correlation between the types of the present and the aorist, as well as the character of the root.

104. Sentences with finite forms as predicates are the most numerous ones in the *Ṛg Veda*. Nominal and semi-nominal sentences, with the participle as predicate are also attested, but they do not concern us here.

105. During the further evolution of the language, the importance of absolutives grew under the influence of closer contacts with the Dravidian languages. But according to the most recent opinion, the use of absolutives in the *Ṛg Veda* is determined not only by the relative chronology of various

parts of this text, but also by the "type of discourse" [144.83].

106. See above, chapter "Morphology," p. 175f.

107. Renou, however, treats *dūtá-* as an apposition in his translation of the passage: "Qu' (*Agni,*) messager des dieux . . . " [118.5.14].

108. See chapter "Morphology" in this book.

109. See the translations by Geldner [74.2.251] and Renou [118.3.97].

110. The upright, erect position symbolized life in the Vedic model of the universe, and the horizontal recumbent position was death.

111. According to Sāyaṇa, branches signify offspring consisting of sons and grandsons.

112. Verbs of discourse—along with the double accusative construction—employ another frequent construction, with the dative of the person to whom the speech is addressed.

113. Renou, for instance, translates: "(L')entende le Maître (Aryaman) qui séjourne dans (la graisse) diaprée, . . . " [118.5.21-2].

114. For more details see the arguments adduced by Hale [95.46].

115. See above (p. 203f.).

116. Compare the pattern proposed by Speyer: *vṛddhaḥ pitā* "the old father" [137:30].

117. Gunilla Gren-Eklund has suggested interesting methods of analyzing such constructions in the *Upaniṣads* [92].

118. The translation cannot preserve the *pāda* division or the original syntax.

119. See the bibliography on this problem [114.1].

120. Incidentally, infinitives in the *Ṛg Veda* have preserved their close connections with the respective cases, and are not always quite distinguishable from the case-forms of a noun of action; compare the last example, in which the dative singular *grábhāya* and the infinitive *mántavā́ u* are isofunctional.

121. Macdonell observed that dative infinitives in *-tavaí, -tave*, and *-e* when used predicatively are equivalent to the participle future passive [105.335]. Disterheft in her article on Indo-Iranian predicative infinitives presents a differentiated analysis of constructions with these infinitives. In

negative sentences they possess only a passive meaning, but in affirmative sentences the meaning can be both passive and active.—See *Disterheft*. The Indo-Iranian Predicate Infinitive.—KZ, Bd.95, H.1,1981, 110-121.

122. This is Renou's example—grammaire de la védique [120.361].

123. See this chapter p. 217.

124. See this chapter pp. 216f.

125. Geldner proposes a different syntactic division of this stanza, but his proposal does not concern the repetition under discussion [74].

126. The verb includes both finite verbs and participles.

127. Where the noun can be both a substantive and an adjective.

128. Compare Renou's version: "tournées vers l'Est comme pour le rite" [118.12.56].

129. Renou translates: "Pur, purificateur s'appelle le soma" [118: 8.16].

130. See in this chapter pp. 218f. above.

131. For details see Macdonell's grammar [105:466f.].

132. Compare Renou's brief description of the hymn [118:7.37].

133. Compare, for instance, the punctuation in Geldner's translation [74.1.90] and in Renou's [118.12.15].

134. The same emphatic form is repeated in the next two stanzas in a partial refrain.

135. On the peculiarities of questions with the particle *kuvíd* deriving from the pronominal stem **ku-* and the emphatic particle *íd*, see Annemarie Etter's monograph [71].

136. The same refrain is repeated in each of the thirteen stanzas of the hymn.

137. On details see "The Grammar of the Vedic language" [8:264f.].

138. Another interpretation of similar instances cannot be excluded out of hand: it is possible that the main clause omits not only the noun but the corresponding demonstrative pronoun as well.

139. The distinction should be preserved for classificatory purposes, although they can appear in a contaminated form in various contexts.

140. The same can be applied to the homonymous *jaráyantī* "(she), making (somebody) old:" a double-sense pun quite typical of the *Ṛg Veda*.

141. See previous chapter "Phonetics."

142. "*sutá-* masculine (ergänze *soma*), der ausgepresste Somasaft" [91.1522].

143. See this chapter p. 199ff.

144. See this chapter (pp. 262f. above).

145. Incidentally, these two classes are far from equivalent, as their obligatory syntactic connections are very different in nature. Since the absence of an emphatic particle does not destroy the whole syntactic structure of a sentence, ellipsis is used here in a broader sense.

146. Compare the cases of haplology listed by Geldner [74.1.147.(3)].

147. This problem has been discussed in passing in the author's paper "On the art of the Vedic *Ṛṣis*" [12:151f.].

Bibliography

Bibliographical Abbreviations

ВДИ-Вестник древней истории. М.

ВЯ-Вопросы языкознания. М.

ABORI–Annals of the Bhandarkar Oriental Research Institute, Poona.

BSLP–Bulletin de las Société de linguistique de Paris.

BSO(A)S–Bulletin of the School of Oriental (and African) Studies. London Institution (University of London).

ÉVP–Renou L. Études védiques et pāṇinéennes. T. 1-17. Paris, 1955-1969.

HOS–Harvard Oriental Series.

IF–Indogermanische Forschungen.

IIJ–Indo-Iranian Journal. Leiden.

JA–Journal asiatique. Paris.

JOAS–Journal of the American Oriental Society. New York/New Haven.

KZ–Zeitschrift für vergleichende Sprachforschung auf dem Gebiete der indogermanischen Sprachen.

MSS–Münchener Studien zur Sprachwissenschaft.

ZDMG–Zeitschrift der Deutschen Morgenländischen Gesellschaft. Leipzig, Wiesbaden.

WZKM–Wiener Zeitschrift für die Kunde des Morgenlandes.

1. Апресян Ю. Д. Лексическая семантика. М., 1974. Наука.

2. Атхарваведа. Избранное. Перевод, комментарий и вступительная статья Т. Я. Елизаренковой. М., 1976. Наука.

3. Барроу Т. Санскрит. Пер. с английского Н. Лариной. М., 1976. Прогресс.

4. Герценберг Л. Г. Морфологическая структура слова в древних индоиранских языках. Л., 1979. Наука.

5. Гринцер П. А. Древнеиндийский эпос. М., 1974. Наука.

6. Елизаренкова Т. Я. Аорист в "Ригведе". М., 1960. Наука.

7. Елизаренкова Т. Я. Ведийский и санскрит: к проблеме вариации лингвистического типа.-ВЯ. 1980, № 3.

8. Елизаренкова Т. Я. Грамматика ведийского языка. М., 1982. Наука.

9. Елизаренкова Т. Я. Древнейший памятник индийской культуры.-Ригведа. Избранные гимны. М., 1972. Наука.

10. Елизаренкова Т. Я. Значения основ презенса в "Ригведе".-Языки Индии. М., 1961. Наука.

11. Елизаренкова Т. Я. Об Атхарваведе.-Атхарваведа. Избранное. М., 1976. Наука.

12. Елизаренкова Т. Я. Об искусстве ведийских риши.-Переднеазиатский сборник. IУ. М., 1986. Наука.

13. Елизаренкова Т. Я., Сыркин А. Я. К анализу индийского свадебного гимна (Ригведа X.85).-Труды по знаковым системам. П. Тарту, 1965. Тартуский государственный университет.

14. Елизаренкова Т. Я., Топоров В. Н. Древнеиндийская поэтика и ее индоевропейские истоки.-Литература и культура древней и средневековой Индии. М., 1979. Наука.

15. Елизаренкова Т. Я., Топоров В. Н. О ведийской загадке типа brahmodya.-Паремиологические исследования. М., 1984. Наука.

16. Елизаренкова Т. Я., Топоров В. Н. К структуре АВ X,2: опыт толкования в свете ведийской антропологии.-Литература и культура древней и средневековой Индии. М., 1987. Наука.

17. Елизаренкова Т. Я., Топоров В. Н. О древнеиндийской Ушас (Uṣas) и ее балтийском соответствии (Ūsiņš).-Индия в древности. М., 1964. Наука.

18. Иванов Вяч. Вс. Древнеиндийский миф об установлении имени и его параллель в греческой традиции.-Индия в древности. М., 1964. Наука.

19. Иванов Вяч. Вс. Очерки по истории семиотики в СССР. М., 1976. Наука.

20. Иванов Вяч. Вс. Эстетическое наследие древней и средневековой Индии.-Литература и культура древней и средневековой Индии. М., 1979. Наука.

21. Калыгин В. П. Язык древнейшей ирландской поэзии. М., 1986. Наука.

22. Кёйпер Ф. Б. Я. Древний арийский словесный поединок.-Труды по ведийской мифологии. М., 1986. Наука. (= Kuiper F. B. J. Ancient Indian Cosmogony. Delhi, 1983. Vikas Publishing House, pp. 151-215).

23. Кёйпер Ф. Б. Я. Основополагающая концепция ведийской религии.-Труды по ведийской мифологии. М., 1986. Наука. (= Kuiper F. B. J. Ancient Indian Cosmogony. Delhi, 1983. Vikas Publishing House, pp. 9-22).

24. Кёйпер Ф. Б. Я. Труды по ведийской мифологии. М., 1986. Наука.

25. Литература и культура древней и средневековой Индии. М., 1979. Наука.

26. Махабхарата. П. Бхагавадгита. Пер. Б. Л. Смирнова. Ашхабад, 1960. Издательство Академии Наук Туркменской ССР.

27. Мифы народов мира. Т.2. М., 1982. Советская энциклопедия.

28. Николаев С. Л., Старостин С. А. Парадигматические классы индоевропейского глагола.-Балто-славянские исследования. 1981. М., 1982. Наука.

29. Огибенин Б. Л. Вопросы ведийской ономастики (Собственные имена в "Ригведе").-Структурная типология языков. М., 1966. Наука.

30. Огибенин Б. Л. Структура мифологических текстов "Ригведы". М., 1968. Наука.

31. Ригведа-великое начало индийской литературы и культуры.-Ригведа. Мандалы I-IУ. Изд. подготовлено Т. Я. Елизаренковой. М. 1989. Наука.

32. Сарианиди В. И. Зороастрийская проблема в свете новейших археологических открытий.-ВДИ. 1989, № 2.

33. Сарианиди В. И. Протозороастрийский храм в Маргиане и проблема возникновения зороастризма.-ВДИ. 1989, № 2.

34. Семенцов В. С. Бхагавадгита в традиции и в современной научной критике. М., 1985. Наука.

35. Семенцов В. С. Проблемы интерпретации брахманической прозы (ритуальный символизм). М., 1981. Наука.

36. Столнейкер Р. С. Прагматика.-Новое в зарубежной лингвистике. Вып. ХУI. Лингвистическая прагматика. М., 1985. Прогресс.

37. Сыркин А. Я. Некоторые проблемы изучения упанишад. М., 1971. Наука.

38. Топоров В. Н. Мифопоэтический локус санскрита.-Тезисы докладов и сообщений советских ученых к У Международной конференции по санскритологии. М., 1981. Наука.

39. Топоров В. Н. Об одном примере звукового символизма (Ригведа X, 125).-Труды по знаковым системам. П. Тарту, 1965. Тартуский государственный университет.

40. Топоров В. Н. О двух типах древнеиндийских текстов, трактующих отношение целостности-расчлененности и спасения.-Переднеазиатский сборник. Ш. М., 1979. Наука.

41. Топоров В. Н. О метаязыковом аспекте древнеиндийской поэтики.-Санскрит и древнеиндийская культура. П. М., 1979, Наука.

42. Топоров В. Н. О ритуале. Введение в проблематику.-Архаический ритуал в фольклорных и раннелитературных памятниках. М., 1988. Наука.

43. Топоров В. Н. О структуре некоторых архаических текстов, соотносимых с концепцией “мирового дерева”.-Труды по знаковым системам. У. Тарту, 1971. Тартуский государственный университет.

44. Трубачев О. Н. Славянская этимология и праславянская культура.-Славянское языкознание. X Международный съезд славистов. М., 1988. Наука.

45. Тэрнер В. Ритуальный процесс. Структура и антиструктура.-Символ и ритуал. М., 1983. Наука.

46. Тэрнер В. Символ и ритуал. М., 1983. Наука.

47. Фасмер М. Этимологический словарь русского языка. Т.1-4. М., 1967. Прогресс.

48. Харлап М. Г. Ритм и метр в музыке устной традиции. М., 1986. Музыка.

49. Элиаде М. Космос и история. М., 1987. Прогресс.

50. Якобсон Р. О. Лингвистика и поэтика.-Структурализм: "за" и "против". М., 1975. Прогресс. (= Jakobson R. Linguistics and Poetics.–Selected Writings. III. Mouton, 1981, pp. 18-51).

51. Якобсон Р. О. Речевая коммуникация.-Якобсон Р. О. Избранные работы. М., 1985. Прогресс. (= Jakobson R. Verbal Communication.–Selected Writings. VII. Mouton, 1985, pp. 81-92).

52. Якобсон Р. О. Язык в отношении к другим системам коммуникации.-Якобсон Р. О. Избранные работы. М., 1985. Прогресс. (= Jacobson R. Language in Relation to Other Communication Systems.–Selected Writings. II. Mouton. 1971, pp. 697-710).

53. Arnold E. V. Vedic Metre. Delhi, 1967 (Reprint. 1st Edition 1905). Motilal Banarsidass.

54. Benveniste E. Indo-European Language and Society. (Engl. Transl.). London, 1973. Faber & Faber.

55. ——. Noms d'agent et noms d'action en indo-européen. Paris, 1948.

56. ——. Phraséologie poétique de l'indo-iranien. Mélanges d'indianisme á la mémoire de Louis Renou. Paris, 1968. E. de Boccard.

57. ——. Problèmes de linguistique générale. Paris, 1966. Gallimard.

58. ——. Le vocabulaire des institutions indo-europeénnes. T.I-II. Paris, 1969.

59. The Bhagavad-Gītā, with a Commentary Based on the Original Sources by R. C. Zaehner. Oxford, 1969. At the Clarendon Press.

60. Böhtlingk O. Sanskrit Wörterbuch in kürzerer Fassung. 1-7. Theil. St. Petersburg, 1879-1889. Buchdruckerei der Kaiserlichen Akademie der Wissenschaften.

61. Brown N. The Creative Role of the Goddess Vāc in the Rig-Veda. Pratidānam. The Hague-Paris, 1968. Mouton.

62. Campanile E. Ricerche di cultura poetica indoeuropea. Pisa, 1977.

63. Dandekar R. N. Vedic Bibliography. Poona. Vol. 3, 1973; vol. 4, 1975 (32. Vedic and Related Personalities). The Bhandarkar Institute Press.

64. —. Vedic Mythological Tracts. Select Writings. I. Delhi, 1979.

65. Debrunner A. Die Nominalsuffixe (Altindische Grammatik von Jakob Wackernagel. Bd.II, 2). Göttingen, 1954.

66. Delbrück B. Syntaktische Forschungen. II. Altindische Tempuslehre. Halle, 1876.

67. Disterheft D. The Indo-Iranian Predicate Infinitive. KZ. Bd.95, N 1, 1981.

68. Elizarenkova T. Y. About Traces of a Prakrit Dialectal Basis in the Language of the Ṛgveda. Dialectes dans les litteratures indo-aryennes. Paris, 1989. Edition-Diffusion de Boccard.

69. —. An Approach to the Description of the Contents of the Ṛgveda. Mélanges d'indianisme a la mémoire de Louis Renou. Paris, 1968.

70. —. Concerning a Peculiarity of the Ṛgvedic Vocabulary.–ABORI (Diamond Jubilee Volume). Poona, 1977-1978.

71. Etter A. Dei Fragesätze im Ṛgveda. Berlin-New York, 1985.

72. Falk H. Soma I and II. BSO(A)S. Vol.52. pt 1, 1989.

73. Fausböll V. Ed. The Jataka. Vols. 1-7. London, 1877-1897.

74. Geldner K. F. Der Rig-Veda aus dem Sanskrit ins Deutsche übersetzt und mit einem laufenden Kommentar versehen. Teil 1-3. Cambridge, Mass., 1951 (= HOS. Vol. 33-35). Harvard University Press.

75. —. Der Rig-Veda aus dem Sanskrit ins Deutsche übersetzt. 4.T. Namen und Sachregister zur Übersetzung. Hrsg. von J. Nobel. Cambridge, Mass., 1957 (= HOS. Vol. 36). Harvard University Press.

76. Gonda J. The Dual Deities in the religion of the Veda. Amsterdam-London, 1974. North-Holland Publishing Company.

77. —. Ein neues Lied.–WZKM, 48, Berlin, 1941.

78. —. Ellipsis, Brachylogy and Other Forms of Brevity in Speech in the Ṛgveda. Amsterdam, 1960.

79. —. Epithets in the Ṛgveda. The Hague –'s-Gravenhage, 1959.

80. ——. The Meaning of the Sanskrit Term Dhāman. Amsterdam, 1967.

81. ——. Notes on Names and the Name of God in Ancient India. Amsterdam-London, 1970. North-Holland Publishing Company.

82. ——. Old Indian (Handbuch der Orientalistik. II. Indien). Leiden, 1971. J. B. Brill.

83. ——. On Nominatives Joining or "Replacing" Vocatives, Selected Studies. Vol. 1, Leiden, 1975.

84. ——. Die Religionen Indiens. 1. Stuttgart, 1960. (= Die Religionen der Menscheit. Hrsg. von Ch. M. Schröder. Bd.11). W. Kohlhammer Verlag.

85. ——. Remarks on Similes in Sanskrit Literature. Leiden, 1949.

86. ——. Some Observations on the Relations between "Gods" and "Powers" in the Veda, a propos of the Phrase Sūnuḥ sahasaḥ. 's-Gravenhage, 1957.

87. ——. Stylistic Repetition in the Veda. Amsterdam, 1959.

88. ——. Triads in the Veda. Amsterdam–London–New York, 1976. North-Holland Publishing Company.

89. ——. Vedic Literature (Saṃhitās and Brāhmaṇas). Wiesbaden, 1975. Otto Harrassowitz.

90. ——. The Vision of the Vedic Poets. The Hague, 1963.

91. Grassmann H. Wörterbuch zum Rig-Veda. 3. Aufl. Wiesbaden, 1955. (1. Aufl., 1872). Otto Harrassowitz.

92. Gren-Eklund G. A Study of Nominal Sentences in the Oldest Upaniṣads. Uppsala, 1978. Almqvist & Wiksell International.

93. Güntert H. Über die ahurischen und daevischen Ausdrücke im Awesta. Eine semasiologische Studie. Sitzungsberichte der Heidelberger Akademie der Wissenschaften. Philosophisch-historische Klasse. Jahrgang, 1914. 13. Abhandlung.

94. ——. Von der Sprache der Götter und Geister. Halle (Saale), 1921.

95. Hale W. E. Asura- in Early Vedic Religion. Delhi, Varanasi, Patna, Madras, 1986.

96. Hoffmann K. Der Injunktiv im Veda: eine synchronische Funktionsuntersuchung. Heidelberg, 1967. Carl Winter. Universitätsverlag.

97. Jamison S. Vāyav Indraś ca Revisited. MSS. H.49, 1988.

98. Joachim U. Mehrfachpräsentien im Ṛgveda. Frankfurt–Bern–Las Vegas, 1978.

99. Kuhn A. – KZ. Bd.2, 1853.

100. Kuiper F. B. J. Varuṇa and Vidūṣaka. On the Origin of the Sanskrit Drama. Amsterdam–Oxford–New York, 1979. North-Holland Publishing Company.

101. Lehmann W. P. Proto-Indo-European Syntax. Austin and London. 1974.

102. Liebich B. Einführung in die indische einheimische Sprachwissenschaft. – Sitzungsberichte d.Heidelb. Akad. d. Wiss., phil.-hist.-kl. 1919, 15, Abhandl.

103. Lord A. B. The Singer of Tales. Cambridge, Mass., 1964.

104. Lüders H. Varuṇa. II. Göttingen, 1959.

105. Macdonell A. A. A Vedic Grammar for Students. Fourth impression. Oxford–London, 1955. Oxford University Press.

106. ——. Vedic Mythology. Strassburg, 1897. Verlag von Karl J. Trübner.

107. Mauss M. Essai sur le don, forme archaique de l'échange. Paris, 1925. (The Gift. Forms and Function of Exchange in Archaic Societies. Engl. Transl. London, 1954).

108. Mayrhofer M. Kurzgefasstes etymologisches Wörterbuch des Altindischen, Bd. 1-4. Heidelberg, 1956-1980. Carl Winter Universitätsverlag.

109. Meid W. Dichter und Dichtkunst in indogermanischer Zeit. Einige allgemeine Gedanken zum Problem der indogermanischen Dichtersprache und der sprachlichen Tradition überhaupt. Innsbruck, 1978 (= Innsbrucker Beiträge zur Sprachwissenschaft. Vorträge 20).

110. Mélanges d'indianisme a la mémoire de Louis Renou. Paris, 1968. Editions E. de Boccard.

111. Neisser W. Zum Wörterbuch des Ṛgveda. H.1. Leipzig, 1924.

112. Oguibenin B. L. Structure d'un myth védique. The Hague–Paris, 1973 (= Approaches to Semiotics. Ed. by T. A. Sebeok).

113. Oldenberg H. Die Hymnen des Ṛigveda. Metrische und textgeschichtliche Prolegomena. Berlin, 1888 (Die Metrik des Ṛigveda).

114. ——. Ṛgveda. Textkritische und exegetische Noten. Berlin, Bd.1, 1909; Bd.2, 1912. Weidmannsche Buchhandlung.

115. ——. Über die Liederverfasser des Rigveda. ZDMG. Bd. 42, 1888.

116. Parry M. Studies in the Epic Technique of Oral Verse. I. Homer and Homeric Style. Harvard Studies in Classical Philology. Vol. 41, 1930. II. The Homeric Language as the Language of an Oral Poetry. Harvard Studies in Classical Philology. Vol. 43, 1932.

117. Renou L. L'ambiguité du vocabulaire du Ṛgveda. JA. T.231, 4-6. Paris, 1939.

118. ——. Etudes védiques et pāṇinéennes. T.1-17. Paris, 1955-1969. E. de Boccard.

119. ——. Les formes dites d'injonctif dans le Ṛgveda. Étrennes de linguistique E. Benveniste. Paris, 1928.

120. ——. Grammaire de la langue védique. Lyon–Paris, 1952. IAC.

121. ——. Histoire de la langue sanskrite. Lyon, 1956. IAC.

122. ——. Hymnes spéculatifs du Veda. 1956. Gallimard.

123. ——. Les noms pour "don" dans le Ṛgveda. BSO(A)S. Vol. 20, 1957.

124. ——. Le problème de l'ellipse dans le Ṛgveda. EVP. T.1. Paris, 1955.

125. ——. Les pouvoirs de la parole dans le Ṛgveda. EVP. T.1. Paris, 1955.

126. ——. Remarqués générales sur la phrase védique. Symbolae linguisticae in honorem Georgi Kuryłowicz Wrocław–Warszawa–Kraków, 1965. Zaklad narodowy imienia Ossolińskich. Wydawnictwo Polskiej Akademii Nauk.

127. ——. Le type védique tudáti. Mélanges linguistiques offertes à Vendryes. Paris, 1925.

128. ——, (avec Silburn L.). Sur la notion de *bráhman*. JA. T. 237, 1949.

129. ——, Filliozat J. L'Inde classique. Paris, 1947.

130. Schayer S. Die Struktur der magischen Weltanschauung nach dem Atharva-Veda und den Brāhmaṇa-Texten. München–Neubiberg, 1925.

131. Schlerath B. Bemerkungen zum Gebrauch von *ubhá-* "beide" im Rigveda. – AINIΓMA. Festschrift für Helmut Rahn. Hrsg. von F. R. Varwig. Heidelberg, 1987.

132. ——. Bemerkungen zu den vedischen Metaphern und Identifikationen. Sanskrit and World Culture. Berlin, 1986. Akademie-Verlag.

133. ——. Gedanke, Wort und Werk im Veda und im Awesta. Antiquitates Indogermanicae. Güntert Commemoration Volume. Innsbruck, 1974.

134. ——. Das Königtum im Rig- und Atharvaveda. Wiesbaden, 1960. Komissionsverlag Franz Steiner GMBH.

135. Schmid W. P. Die Kuh auf der Weide. IF. 64, 1959.

136. Schmitt R. Dichtung und Dichtersprache in indogermanischen Zeit. Wiesbaden, 1967.

137. Speyer J. S. Vedische und Sanskrit Syntax. Strassburg, 1896. Verlag von Karl J. Trübner.

138. Starobinski J. Les anagrammes de Ferdinand de Saussure. Textes inédits. Mercure de France. 1964, Février.

139. ——. Les mots sous les mots. Les anagrammes de Ferdinand de Saussure. Paris, 1971.

140. Tarkasangraha. Ed. by S. Chandrasekhara Sastrigal. Madras, 1920.

141. Thieme P. Mitra and Aryaman. New Haven, 1957.

142. ——. Das Plusquamperfectum im Veda. Göttingen, 1929.

143. ——. "Sprachmalerei". KZ. Bd.86, H. 1, 1972.

144. Tikkanen B. The Sanskrit Gerund: a Synchronic, Diachronic and Typological Analysis. Helsinki, 1987. Studia Orientalia. Vol. 62.

145. Toporov V. N. Poetica. II. The Hague–Paris, Warszawa, 1966.

146. ——. The Veda and Avesta Sub specie of Reconstruction of the Indo-Iranian Proto-Text. Summaries of Papers Presented by Soviet Scholars to the VIth World Sanskrit Conference. October 13-20, 1984. Philadelphia, Pennsylvania, USA. Moscow, 1984. Nauka.

147. ——. Die Ursprünge der indoeuropäischen Poetik. – Poetica. 13. 1981.

148. Wackernagel J., Renou L. Altindische Grammatik. Introduction générale. Göttingen, 1957.

149. Wackernagel J. Indogermanische Dichtersprache. Kleine Schriften. Bd.1. Göttingen, 1953.

150. Wasson R. G. Soma. Divine Mushroom of Immortality. New York, 1968. Harcourt, Brace & World, Inc.

151. Watkins C. Aspects of Indo-European Poetics. The Indo-Europeans in the Fourth and Third Millennia. E. C. Polomé Ed. Ann Arbor, 1982. Karona Publishers, Inc.

152. ——. The Comparison of Formulaic Sequences. Proceedings of 1986 IREX Conference. Austin. Texas. E. Polomé Ed.

153. ——. How to Kill a Dragon in Indo-European. Studies in Memory of Warren Cowgill. Berlin–New York, 1987.

154. ——. Language of Gods and Language of Men: Remarks on Some Indo-European Metalinguistic Traditions–Myth and Law among the Indo-Europeans. Studies in Indo-European Comparative Mythology. J. Puhvel Ed. Berkeley–Los Angeles–London, 1970.

155. ——. Questions linguistiques de poetique, de mythologie et de prédroit en indo-européen. Lalies. Actes des sessions de linguistique et de littérature. V. Paris, 1987.

156. Whitney W. D. The Roots, Verb-Forms and Primary Derivatives of the Sanskrit Language. Leipzig, 1885. Breitkopf and Härtel.

157. Witzel M. On Magical Thought in the Veda. Leiden, 1979.

Index

Action(s), poetic, 9
 See also Hymn(s), praise
Aditi, Goddess, 46, 105, 108
Ādityas, 55, 63, 78, 105
Agni (God of Fire), 10-11, 104
 and Goddess *Vāc*, 108, 108-109, 109-110
 as mediator of other Gods, 44, 49-50, 64-65, 192, 204, 283, 283-284
 Ṛg Veda hymn to, 13, 23, 33-34, 38, 44, 48, 49-50, 51, 53, 57-58, 68, 72, 87, 146, 152, 156, 172-174, 253
 symbolic references to, 34, 36, 39, 43, 49, 94, 133-134, 146, 160
 See also Sacrifice
Ahuric words, 75-76
Akṣara syllable, 110
 and metrical *pādas*, 111
 See also Pādas (verses)
Amṛta (God(s)), 11
Aṃśa (God of Bestowal), 13
Añgirases family, 21, 22
Anukramaṇī, 21
 and *Agni*, 146
 Brāhmans and, 26
 metrical formulas in, 116, 136, 148
 worshipper/deity and, 135-136
Anuṣṭubh metre, 118-119, 146
Aruṣá (red/fire), 13
Aryaman (the Good Ruler), 13, 63, 104
 prayer and, 56
Aryan poetics, 2
 and cosmology, 10, 11-12
 and names of God, 101, 153-170
 and sacred knowledge, 14, 20, 82, 146, 153
 and space, 11-12
 time and, 7-8, 10-11, 12, 181-182, 188
 universal body and, 39-43
Ásurāḥ (Gods of the primordial world), 11
Asuras (demons), 77, 78
Aśvins, 12, 32
 hymnic references to, 38, 47, 51, 116, 132, 194
 invocation of, 60
Aśvins family, 25
Atharva Veda, 14, 83-84
 message exchange and, 143
 metrical formulae in, 118
Ātmastuti (self-praise hymns), 179-180
Atri, Ṛṣi, 21
Attributes, poetic, 9
 of deity, 9, 12, 51-67, 70-75, 125, 136, 167-168, 170-197, 200-224, 231-266, 271-282
 and myth, 12, 74-75, 83, 98-99, 107, 261-262, 280-282, 283, 285
 and names of God, 100-102, 113-114, 121, 125-128, 136, 153-156, 159-166, 168-170
 See also Hymn(s), praise
Avestan poetics, 2, 75, 78
 synonyms and, 74-75, 79

Bhagavad Gītā
 Vedic language and, 77
Bhṛgus family, 21, 22
Bhúvanasya nā́bhi (navel of the Earth), 12
 symbolic references to, 37
Brachylogy, 278
Brāhmaṇas, 13, 77, 191